NEOLITHIC BRITAIN

NEOLITHIC BRITAIN

THE TRANSFORMATION OF SOCIAL WORLDS

KEITH RAY

AND

JULIAN THOMAS

OXFORD

UNIVERSITY PRESS

UNIVERSITY PRESS

Great Clarendon Street, Oxford, OX2 6DP,
United Kingdom

Oxford University Press is a department of the University of Oxford.
It furthers the University's objective of excellence in research, scholarship,
and education by publishing worldwide. Oxford is a registered trade mark of
Oxford University Press in the UK and in certain other countries

First Edition published in 2018

Impression: 1

Published in the United States of America by Oxford University Press
198 Madison Avenue, New York, NY 10016, United States of America

British Library Cataloguing in Publication Data
Data available

Library of Congress Control Number: 2018935372

ISBN 978–0–19–882389–6

Printed and bound by
CPI Group (UK) Ltd, Croydon, CR0 4YY

This book is dedicated to the memory of
Andrew Sherratt (1946–2006)

Former Assistant Keeper of Antiquities at the Ashmolean Museum, and
Professor of Archaeology at the Universities of Oxford and Sheffield

An original thinker, scholar, and prehistorian

Foreword

This wonderful book is published in 2018, at a time when Britain is convulsed over questions of identity, trying to forge a sustainable future whilst faced with alarming anxieties and insecurities. And here are these two eloquent men, Ray and Thomas, mining our deep history and finding evidence of migrations and climate change, trade routes and new technologies, new patterns of food and farming, clear practices of government and belief. Neolithic Britain suddenly seems thrillingly familiar.

Time is the great theme of the book. We begin to understand not only how we might see our modern world in the context of a society that evolved between six and four thousand years ago, but also, and spectacularly, how those ancestors might have understood and celebrated their own sense of the past. The authors convey brilliantly the ways in which memory and commemoration are captured in the life of household objects, rituals, and architecture.

There's a joy in finding history told here not by 'the victors' but by the scientists and the storytellers. For this lay reader, one of the pleasures of the book is how—at a fingertip level—these archaeologists work, and the sophistication with which modern technology helps them clarify what they find. This pleasure is redoubled by the dialogue that ensues about interpretation. In the dynamic exchange of ideas Ray and Thomas keep the past with us, part of our contemporary reality.

There's a delightful irony in the way this is the written history that itself was a technology unavailable to the people whose story they tell. The book's illustrations and photographs serve as vivid representation of the objects and artefacts and traces of lives that unearth their truths. At best, it gives the reader not the results of Ray and Thomas's archaeology, but the experience of being part of their excavations and discoveries.

There's a nagging sense, though, whether you have dipped into this book over months or wolfed it at one sitting, that it isn't the last word on the subject. Rather, it feels like the starting point for a conversation about who we are. It's a conversation with two exceptional guides who inform our understanding of humanity through their curiosity about the nature of evidence and their reading of stone, and land, and water. It's the story of civilization.

Peter Florence
Director,
Hay Festival

Acknowledgements

This book has arisen from conversations between the co-authors about both archaeology and Neolithic studies over the course of three decades, starting in 1987 when we both found ourselves on the staff of the then St David's University College (University of Wales), Lampeter. These talks have been sustained at intervals, but each of us has also benefited from discussions with many other people who, like us, have become absorbed in the study of the Neolithic of Britain and Europe. We first developed the idea of writing this book as a joint project in 2009, embarking in earnest upon the enterprise in 2014. We would like to acknowledge here with thanks those individual scholars, field archaeologists, and scientific specialists who have had relevant conversations with one or other of us, and who have in many cases provided key insights and have shared information. The list is long, and includes: Mike Allen, Hugo Anderson-Whymark, Martyn Barber, Alistair Barclay, Gordon Barclay, John Barrett, Lara Bishop, Richard Bradley, Bill and Jenny Britnell, Marcus Brittain, Kenny Brophy, Nick Card, Andrew Chamberlain, Chantal Conneller, Gabriel Cooney, Vicki Cummings, Timothy Darvill, Ruth van Dyke, Mark Edmonds, Andrew Fleming, Tony Fleming, Chris Fowler, Irene Garcia Rovira, Julie Gardiner, Duncan Garrow, Paul Garwood, Alex Gibson, Seren Griffiths, Oliver Harris, Frances Healy, Gill Hey, Ian Hodder, Tim Hoverd, Robin Jackson, Mats Larsson, Matt Leivers, Gavin Lucas, Lesley McFadyen, Jackie McKinley, Koji Mizoguchi, Jenny Moore, Jacqui Mulville, Nick Overton, Stuart Palmer, Mike Parker Pearson, Rick Peterson, Josh Pollard, Ffion Reynolds, Colin Richards, John Robb, Chris Scarre, Niall Sharples, the late Ian Shepherd, Alison Sheridan, Adam Stanford, Anne Teather, Christopher Tilley, Kate Welham, Alasdair Whittle, and Ann Woodward.

We are grateful to all those who have provided, or who have helped to source, illustrations for the book. Appropriate credits are given in the captions and/or the illustrations list. However, we would especially like to thank Richard Scott Jones for pre-publication images, and Aaron Watson and

Tim Hoverd for archaeological drawings and reconstructions. The artist Anna Dillon, wood-engraver Hilary Paynter, and photographer Adam Stanford have been outstandingly generous in permitting us to use examples of their work to enliven the book visually. We thank the editorial and production team at Oxford University Press, and especially Charlotte Loveridge, for their painstaking efforts and their support in seeing the book through to print.

We would like to take this opportunity to thank Peter Florence for accomplishing two things for us. First, for his 'test-driving' of the manuscript prior to publication; and secondly for his agreement to write a Foreword with which to 'launch' the book from the perspective of someone who, though not a professional historian or archaeologist, nonetheless has a keen sense of both history and historicity in our own times, and their value to a society that still sometimes struggles with a non-pecuniary sense of the importance of history or literary culture.

We want, of course, to take this opportunity to express our gratitude for the forbearance of Catherine, Morag, Rowan, Anna, Lucie, Sophie, Anna, Robin, and Dylan, in our respective families, during the long haul of production of yet another archaeology book.

And finally, we would also like to express our appreciation to Professor Susan Sherratt, for her kind permission for us to dedicate the book to the memory of her late husband. Andrew was a one-off: someone who with both wit and wisdom, and deep scholarship borne lightly, could convey in a telling phrase the vividness and the wonder of a distant Neolithic world that none of us have, of course, experienced, but which we have, just occasionally, the sense of having glimpsed.

Contents

List of figures

Whilst every effort has been made to secure permission to reproduce the illustrations, we may have failed in a few cases to trace the copyright holders. If contacted, the publisher will be pleased to rectify any omissions at the earliest opportunity.

Frontispiece: Skara Brae, Orkney, at twilight

This photograph captures perfectly the passage of the long summer twilights experienced in the northern latitudes of Britain in the Orkney archipelago. By the same token, the softly lit interior of 'House 1' at Skara Brae as shown here ('Skara Brae' is the modern name of the place traditionally known locally as 'Skerrabra') conjures up the warmth and security of hearth and home once enjoyed by the Neolithic inhabitants. The basic design of these linked houses comprised a large square or oval room with a central slab-defined hearth built to contain the household fire, flanked to right and left by stone-defined beds (which probably would have held in place paillasses stuffed with heather and grasses), and with a large shelved stone 'dresser' facing the door. This often double-decked shelving cabinet would have been the normal storage-place for flat-based bowls and other cooking and working gear. Around and about on the floor other equipment, including grinding-stones for processing and preparing foodstuffs, was placed.

Photograph: August 2014, © Adam Stanford (website: http://www.aerial-cam.co.uk/).

Introduction

Neolithic Britain—encounters and reflections

Introductory frontispiece: 'Wayland's Smithy' (painting, Anna Dillon)

While there are many fine and often atmospheric photographs of Wayland's Smithy chambered long barrow (on the Ridgeway in south Oxfordshire) in existence, the artist is freed up from the recorded moment and can produce an abstraction of place (and in this case ancient monument) that conveys more than the camera can. We know from excavation that the barrow as visible today represents a complete rebuilding of a smaller, dismantled, earlier structure: and it is the imposing south-facing façade of the more monumental-scale edifice shown here that leaves such a strong impression upon the visitor even today. While still referencing the modern condition of the barrow, and the planted beech trees that encircle it, Anna Dillon has here managed to capture the sense of mysterious ceremony that may have attended the rites that took place in the forecourt of the tomb nearly six millennia ago.

Painting: 2016 © Anna Dillon (website: http://www.annadillon.com/).

Is it possible to *experience* the Neolithic period (*c*.4000—*c*.2400 BCE) in Britain today? Of course not, or not in any literal sense. And yet, there are devices that we can create, and places that we can visit, that can to some extent stand in for that experience. These enable us, however fleetingly, to bridge the gulf of time that separates us from the distant world of thousands of years ago. One new way of traversing this chasm became available to us in 2013, when English Heritage opened a new visitor centre at Stonehenge. Inside the airy modern structure the latest audio-visual technology introduces visitors to the site and its surrounding prehistoric landscape. Remarkably, before the year was out, that centre had hosted a visit by the then President of the United States of America. Barack Obama made an unscheduled stop at the World Heritage Site en route from a NATO summit in Wales on 5 September 2014. Apparently, visiting Stonehenge, widely regarded as the most extraordinary of all prehistoric sites in Europe, was on the personal 'bucket list' of that recent incumbent of the White House. Among the things that the US President would have seen at the Stonehenge centre were *reconstructed* Late Neolithic houses from the area, and the visitor can now enter and walk around in these buildings, made using authentic materials (Fig. 0.1).

These newly constructed timber and daub buildings had been created on the basis of evidence recovered from Durrington Walls, a colossal Late Neolithic complex 2 miles (3.2 km) from Stonehenge, where settings of concentric rings of massive posts were contained within an embanked enclosure half a kilometre across. Surprisingly, if the visitor centre had been built when it had originally been planned a decade earlier, it would not have been possible to recreate these 4,500-year-old houses, with their square ground plans and central hearths. This is because the excavations that would reveal these striking vestiges of the Stonehenge people were then only just beginning. This is an indication of the pace of discovery in the study of Neolithic Britain, and the immediacy of this process is one of the things that we would like to convey in this book.

If you are a local Wiltshire school student, it is now possible to take part in a field studies sleepover in one of these houses, of the kind that had been occupied for short periods by the participants in the seasonal gatherings that took place at Durrington many centuries ago. Of course, this does not enable the students to experience life as it was lived on what is now Salisbury Plain in the Late Neolithic, any more than those who attended the Stonehenge Free Festivals in the 1970s and 1980s shared the same feelings as

Fig. 0.1 Reconstructed 'Durrington' buildings at the Stonehenge Visitor Centre, June 2014

This photograph was taken a month after the completion of the huts, built experimentally by volunteers under supervision from English Heritage architects. The location and form of the doorways and hearths were known from excavation, as was something of the nature of the walls (including the formation and use of chalk 'cob' in their construction: a method of construction in use into the twentieth century locally). However, four different designs for the superstructures were explored, to try to find the most likely above-ground configuration. Flint axes were used to cut timbers, and in total 12 tonnes of chalk and 2,500 bundles of hazel and willow rods were needed to complete the reconstructions.
Photograph: Keith Ray

their prehistoric forerunners. But the sensation of standing close to, or even amongst, the settings of sarsens and bluestones at Stonehenge itself is, as President Obama put it, 'really cool . . . there's something elemental about it'.

This experience of being amongst the remains of a Neolithic monument is not exclusive to Stonehenge. It can be encountered in many parts of Britain, and perhaps most profoundly in the remoter uplands of the north and west, where groups of uprights, or even single stones represent the traces of structures built as much as 6,000 years ago. In human terms, this period would extend back as long as 240 generations. Modern DNA studies in Cheddar have indicated that some of the contemporary inhabitants may be descended from people who lived in the Mendips as far back as the end of the Ice Age, and the same may be true of other parts of Britain. However, it is equally likely that people from various parts of continental Europe migrated into Britain, in smaller or larger numbers, at various junctures throughout prehistory. So in a variety of ways it is possible to feel a sense of connectedness through time to past people and ancient places, particularly where structures and monuments have only been superficially altered by natural processes of decay and changes in land use across those immense spans (which nonetheless, of course, in planetary or cosmological terms are but a blink).

These modern-day activities (standing within reconstructed buildings, seeing media visualizations, or visiting ancient monuments) clearly do not expose someone to the visceral experience of a living Neolithic world, not least because the sites concerned do not for the most part, or for long, wholly enclose you. A candlelit stooping walk along the carefully restored slab-lined entrance passage and into the central chamber-space of the Neolithic tomb of Maes Howe on the Orkney Mainland comes close to providing such an immersive experience, given the sheer amount of rock from nearby Neolithic quarries that surrounds you (see Fig. 0.2 for the similar Cuween Hill).

Yet you soon realize that the chamber was re-roofed only 100 years or so ago as an act of restoration after a Viking tomb-raiding expedition had broken through the original corbelled roof a thousand years ago. And of course, you would also have to ignore the modern Historic Scotland safety paraphernalia. In contrast, however, descent some ten metres down the shaft (albeit its top is enclosed by a modern concrete cover) of one of the 'flint mines' in the chalk rock at Grimes Graves in Norfolk (excavated, or more properly 're-excavated', nearly fifty years ago) and onto its floor is a truly inspirational experience (see Figure 4.1). This is especially the case if one does not suffer from claustrophobia and can explore one of the side-galleries that were dug to follow the seams of flint banded horizontally in the chalk. Here in these galleries even the soot from the Neolithic miners' lamps has left its unmistakable traces on the exposed chalk walls, and the strike-marks of the miners' red deer antler-pick tines are evident alongside the seams of flint in the chalk where lumps were prised out.

Otherwise, besides the more engaging among national and local museum displays, the most direct contact that can be made with the world of Neolithic Britain is through the act of archaeological excavation. The raw encounter with a residue that formed 4,400 years ago and more, the feel in your hand of an object that had last been touched by the people who made,

Fig. 0.2 Inside the roofed central chamber of Cuween Hill cairn, Orkney

Cuween chambered cairn nestles into the upper north-east-facing slopes of a hill overlooking the Burn of Grimbister just to the east of Kirkwall on the Orkney Mainland, and looking out beyond that to the northern islands of the archipelago. It has a deeply recessed entrance, the furthest end of which has a low slab-roofed and -walled passage. This photograph features the inner end of this passage with daylight penetrating down it, with three of the four entrances to small side-chambers visible to left and right. Like the considerably larger chamber at Maes Howe nearby, the skilfully corbelled roof had been broken into long ago. When excavated inwards from the entrance passage in 1901, the latter was found to have been carefully blocked during Neolithic times. Inside were found the bones from up to eight human skeletons (mostly skulls) along with the skulls of twenty-four dogs.

Photograph: August 2012, © Adam Stanford (website: http://www.aerial-cam.co.uk/).

or used, or deposited it (or all three) all those centuries distant, are highly personal experiences. This is the lure that draws so many people, whether students or volunteers, to give up their free time to endure hardships, occasional boredom, and frustration, to contribute to the archaeological endeavour. In some places, as at the Ness of Brodgar excavations, again on the mainland of Orkney, this encounter can be a three-dimensional one, working (and walking) in among the stone-slabbed walls of structures that were used 5,000 years ago, with incised wall-decorations and even occasional 'paintwork' in view.

Alternatively, as at the Stonehenge visitor centre, one can observe a visualization created by archaeologists of a landscape or an event featuring both the objects and the scientific evidence that can illuminate that distant Neolithic world. This imagery could take a number of different forms, but is perhaps most often encountered through a digital fly-through model very familiar to a generation brought up on computer games.

And inevitably, visualizations of this kind involve either anachronisms or a level of simplification that strips out much of the texture that would have made the experience of being alive, and living within a social nexus comprising family and acquaintances, meaningful in the Neolithic period.

And finally, there is the written word. A particularly vivid way of rendering the warp and weft of the world of Neolithic Britain, as recorded through the encounters that archaeologists have made with these remains from Britain's earliest farming past, has been evident in the writings of Aubrey Burl. In his book *Rites of the Gods*, for example, Burl describes Neolithic life and practices as he understood them over thirty years ago, based upon the (then) already thirty years or so of his working life spent 'among the stones'. He distilled there his thoughts and impressions concerning Neolithic religion, magic, and the kinds of practices that led to the manufacture of objects that will always remain enigmatic, but that have often been entirely ignored by archaeologists—to the impoverishment of wider understandings.

So, for example, concerning one kind of artefact repeatedly encountered, but difficult to comprehend the purpose of, Burl ventured:

> The stone discs found at Cairnholy, small enough to fit comfortably in the palm of one's hand, are puzzling. Their edges have been roughly flaked but their surfaces have been beautifully smoothed. Yet there is no carving or anything upon them...By themselves the Cairnholy discs might be ignored, but others have been discovered...Made of slate, sandstone, sarsen, quartz, anything from one to five inches in size, [and] found with burials, with cremations, in chambered tombs, stone circles and in the ditches of enclosures such as Windmill Hill and Avebury, even as far north as the circle-henge of Stenness in the Orkneys, their mystery remains...The discs may have been lids [for pots used to store ancestral bones] but it is arguable that they were ancestor-stones, or *talismen* [sic], or representations of the sun or moon.
>
> (1981: 77–8; compare with Fig. 0.3)

Other archaeologists have envisaged the routine practices, and their implications, which characterized the making of Neolithic objects and the fulfilment of seasonal rounds in Britain. Among these works is the book *Ancestral Geographies of the Neolithic*, published in 1999. Written by Mark Edmonds in part as an experiment in re-envisioning Neolithic lives in Britain, this book is discussed further in our review of the development of Neolithic studies in Chapter 1.

Neolithic Britain: The Transformation of Social Worlds invites the reader to experience Neolithic Britain in an entirely different way, however. Our aim

Fig. 0.3 Ty Isaf, Breconshire (Powys): stone discs

Eight of the ten discs recorded as having been found at Ty Isaf chambered tomb are depicted here (these eight are now located in the National Museum collections). Two of them were found among human bones in one of the chambers, and the others are presumed to have come from similar contexts within the structure. Such stone discs are also known from Penywyrlod barrow nearby, and from two other chambered tombs in Wales: one in Anglesey and the other in coastal Glamorgan. The discs shown here are clearly size-graded, as apparently also were the Late Neolithic 'chalk drums' known from sites in Yorkshire and Dorset. The reasons for this 'grading' or 'nesting' of sizes, however, and for their interment with the remains of the dead, are entirely opaque.

Photograph: Jim Wild © Amgueddfa Cymru—National Museum Wales, Cardiff.

is not to evoke the presence of Neolithic people in Britain by visualization (though we hope that the often vivid illustrations do convey something of the complexities of Neolithic life and the impact of their created places today), nor to attempt to see that world through their eyes, nor even to stimulate any depth of thought about the unseen worlds that Aubrey Burl explored in *Rites of the Gods*. Rather, the purpose of this book is to provide the reader with a concise panorama of the history of Neolithic Britain, principally through two narrative approaches. Before setting out how following these approaches has influenced the way that the book is organized by chapter, it may be helpful to explain two things: first, what we mean by 'narrative', and, secondly, how we envisage this book being perceived by its potential readership.

The simplest definition of narrative that we employ here is 'a written account of connected events, comprising a story'. This is what is most often meant by a historical narrative: a dynamic account of the sequential passage of selected events. This is selective because it is always a matter of choice as to which events to give prominence to, especially in terms of causation. However, in line with what has been termed the 'multivocality' of the past, and of the different sources of evidence that we routinely draw upon as archaeologists, we also refer to narratives as arising from the piecing together of stories from the study of a variety of different Neolithic materials and interpretive perspectives. So there is, for instance, a narrative, a story, or a historical account that arises from an awareness of the phenomenon of 'big houses' built (apparently) during a brief period in the early fourth millennium BCE. Equally there is another distinct story that, later on in that millennium, concerns the building and use of 'causewayed camps' (ditched enclosures that are discussed at length in Chapters 3 and 4). We pursue these stories in our accounts of what we understand to be the principal cultural developments in different parts of Britain across those considerable time spans, woven around particular cultural practices or patterns of material remains. This kind of narrative writing is considerably assisted nowadays by the conduct in recent years of studies specifically devoted to the development of fine chronologies for multiple sites belonging to the Neolithic in Britain.

Secondly, as far as our prospective readership is concerned, the book should not be envisaged as a textbook, although it can be read in part as such. Nor do we consider it a contribution to new research, although some of the ideas contained within it are new. Rather, we hope that it will serve to mark a 'pause for reflection' in the process of interpreting and assimilating new research and new data. This is not only to assimilate such new information in broader narrative terms, however, but also to explore the breadth of narrative that can be created by integrating both old and new data in new ways. In particular, our aim on the one hand is to explore the social dimensions of the cultural practices manifest in the artefacts and residues encountered by archaeologists investigating Neolithic material and places; and on the other hand to situate those practices within a dynamic, historical framework where the understanding that Neolithic people may have had of their own past becomes itself a focus for discussion.

For the non-specialist reader we want to illuminate the Neolithic by providing a window into just how fascinating the world of Neolithic Britain can be: not only as a consequence of its unfamiliarity, but also precisely because of the intellectual challenges the complexity (and incompleteness) of its traces presents us with. These traces were created within a world entirely contrasting with the one we occupy today, heavily influenced as ours is by the intellectual frameworks, and habits, bequeathed to us by the European Enlightment. As such, we cannot achieve a workable understanding of the Neolithic world by rendering it in narrative terms as a world 'just like our own'. We anticipate that while the specific arguments rehearsed in the book may be unfamiliar to (many of) our intended readership, they will nonetheless recognize the generality of debates within the social and historical sciences that have played out across numerous subject areas and periods in other disciplines.

The first of the two narrative approaches that we have adopted in this book is, therefore, one that provides a sequential, unfolding story comprising a series of particular accounts of diverse cultural and historical phenomena. It is organized within three chapters, spanning the nearly two millennia concerned. While there are parallel stories within the overall narrative that concern specific kinds of material or practice, the account concerns, both in outline and in detail, developments through time: from the last centuries of the fifth millennium BCE in the first of these chapters, from the long centuries of the fourth millennium in the second, and from the early centuries of the third millennium in the third chronological chapter.

The second narrative approach is one that is deliberately placed, in two intervening chapters, between and after these more obviously sequential accounts. This approach is more thematically focused, and in the first of the two chapters it involves explaining our understanding of some key social and cultural practices (or groups of related practices) such as 'dwelling' and 'dealing with the dead', citing examples drawn from across the whole span of the Neolithic in Britain. In the second thematic chapter we examine particular kinds of evidence, and specific circumstances, to explore a dawning appreciation among archaeologists studying the Neolithic period in Britain, that Neolithic history comprises more than simply its unfolding. We are gradually becoming aware, rather, that not only did those temporally far-distant communities have their own inheritance of places, practices, and resources, but that at least some people among them also had their own consciousness of that inheritance. We suggest that they may have viewed this in their own terms as a legacy from the past, and as a history that they could commemorate by developing their own practices of citation.

These contrasting approaches are employed in this way across a series of five chapters that make up the main body of the book. They follow an opening chapter, however, that describes and explains the different interpretive and research perspectives that have provided the framework for the study of the Neolithic period in Britain over the past sixty years and more. The first of the three historical narrative accounts, Chapter 2, explores contemporary understanding of the crucial transitional period either side of 4000 BCE. The unfolding of this period has become more closely defined chronologically in recent years, and this has led to a restatement of the idea of an invasion of farmers: a process that saw what some archaeologists have termed a 'tsunami' of farming practices and a fully Neolithic lifestyle sweep across Britain from the Thames Estuary northwards and westwards within a century or so. In our view, however, there is little doubt that there were trans-Channel contacts before the advent of the 'British' Neolithic, as much as that there were piecemeal movements of people relocating permanently from the Continent into Britain during the crucial transitional period. The lived situation cannot therefore be reduced exclusively to the past importation of a 'package' of Neolithic practices by a discrete group of vigorous migrants. Several of the characteristic features of Neolithic life in Britain that emerged by 3800 BCE had clear antecedents among the existing late Mesolithic communities. And many places of resort favoured in the centuries before 4000 BCE were precisely the places where many subsequent 'Neolithic' focal activities took place.

A second historical narrative account, Chapter 3, then takes up the story to describe the considerable further transformations that occurred across the succeeding centuries down to around 3000 BCE. Prominent among these were the construction of 'big houses', quite possibly as places of assembly; the growth of exchange networks across considerable distances; the construction of mounds marking ancestral presences and places where remains of the dead might be interred; the digging and filling of pits as markers of place and practices (and not only as rubbish disposal facilities); the creation of reserved spaces defined by the digging of strings of ditch-segments and associated banks; and later, the digging of long and (mostly) narrow parallel-ditched enclosures. There was also a great diversity within practices of broadly similar character across Britain, although some areas such as Cornwall, Wales and the Marches, lowland Scotland, the Hebrides, and the Orkney Islands began developing distinctive features of material culture and practice from early on.

The first of the two more overtly thematic accounts (Chapter 4) then explores aspects of Neolithic life and culture across the whole span of the Neolithic in Britain with specific reference to both the immediate and the cumulative significance of particular kinds of practice. The chapter opens with an exploration of the fascinating detail that has been observed concerning the mining of flint in Sussex and Norfolk, and its implications for actions and cultural exchanges sometimes hundreds of miles away. Prominent among the ostensibly more prosaic aspects of Neolithic life are the practice of collective feasting and the question of what constitutes 'dwelling' in a context where recognizably domestic residences, or houses, are less common than the evidence for middens, pits, and various ephemeral structures. The practices of herding and hunting are then looked at, as a prelude to a discussion of conflict and the evidence for warfare and injury. The working and raising of timber, the forms and uses of pottery, the circulation of stone axes, and the practices of weaving and basketry as indicated obliquely in ceramics are also described. A closing section assesses the relation between death and identity as currently inferred from the study of burials and the deposition of human remains.

The third historical narrative account, Chapter 5, focuses upon the third millennium BCE and the development of Britain-wide networks of sociality and cultural exchange and contact in the Later Neolithic. The extraordinary complexity of activity on the Orkney Mainland is examined, and the apparent implications of Later Neolithic chronology for the transmission of a 'Grooved Ware complex' southwards across Britain culminating in the creation of dense complexes of monuments in many places, and especially in the Stonehenge/ Avebury area. The relation of this profusion of monumental forms and evidence for gathering, feasting, and mortuary activities to the arrival of a pan-European suite of practices bound up with a particular form of pottery, conventionally referred to as Beakers, along with the first use of metals in society, is then reviewed at some length.

The second more thematic essay (Chapter 6) focuses upon the importance of descent among the human communities of Neolithic Britain. Avowedly interpretive, and in some respects overtly speculative, this account nonetheless provides what are, it is hoped, some new insights into a suite of practices that implicate the existence of forms of historical consciousness on the part of Neolithic people themselves. The book is concluded by a brief essay that explores whether there was a way of 'being Neolithic' that (despite the historical artificiality of the continuing use of a label first coined more than 150 years ago based on a particular classification of stone tool use) still lends coherence to the study of the fourth and third millennia BCE in Britain.

Moving beyond this, the Conclusion also evaluates the usefulness of the study and 'experiencing' of Neolithic Britain more widely. It contests the view that the primary subject of the Neolithic is the advent of farming and the inexorable process that it set in train regarding a reliance upon food production. Such a perspective is rooted in a materialistic conception of history, and one that imparts motives to people in the past that accord with modern conceptions of the inevitability of social evolution determined by advances in technology. In contrast, we restate our argument that the Neolithic concerned a move to a different conception of sociality made possible through, but not determined by, the arrival and adoption of domesticates in these islands.

By *these islands*, of course, we mean the whole of the north-west European archipelago. However, in this book we will restrict ourselves primarily to England, Scotland, and Wales. There are several reasons for this. First, Irish archaeology has had a tradition of research quite as rich and complicated as that of Britain, and we do not have space to do it justice here. More importantly, the Irish Neolithic may have run parallel with, and been linked to, that of the British mainland, but it cannot be reduced to it. At times developments in the two regions were comparable, but at others they diverged appreciably. Equally, the degree of contact and influence between Britain and Ireland fluctuated throughout prehistory. Necessarily, we will make reference to sites and happenings in Ireland where they have direct bearing on our narrative of Neolithic Britain, but to cover the island properly would require another book, and there are others better placed than ourselves to write such a volume.

ONE

Writing Neolithic Britain:
an interpretive journey

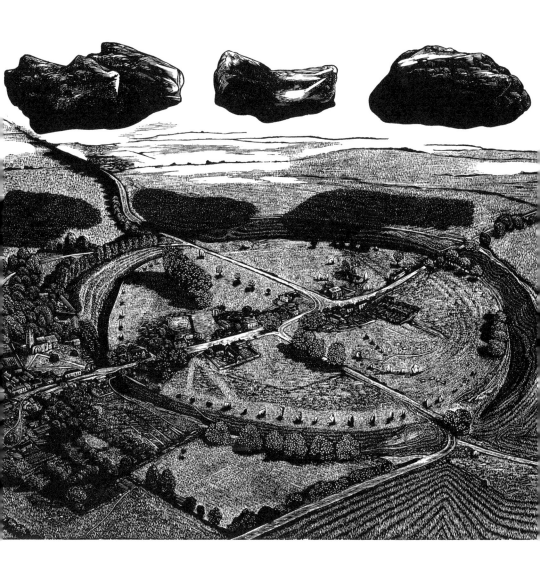

Chapter frontispiece: 'Stones over Avebury' (wood-engraving, Hilary Paynter)

This vivid engraving is an aerial perspective over the massive henge from the south-west, with the church and village to the left. The artist wrote of the engraving in her book Full Circle: Hilary Paynter Wood Engravings *(Woodend Publishing, 2010), 64: '[Avebury] is one of the most amazing places I know, and I keep returning ... I wanted to show how the stones dominate everything there and the only way I could do that was to have them hovering and casting their shadows over the [landscape].'*

Engraving: 1984, © Hilary Paynter (website: http://www.hilarypaynter.com).

It is just over sixty years since Stuart Piggott published his major work, *Neolithic Cultures of the British Isles*. This was the first comprehensive account of what was then known and assumed about the 'New Stone Age' in these islands, and it surveyed discoveries and summarized debates that had occurred over the previous century. This process of gradual accumulation of data and ideas has continued apace since Piggott was writing, not least owing to the precision with which we can now date much of the activity that characterizes the Neolithic. When Piggott was writing his book in the early 1950s an American, Willard Libby, was experimenting with the technique of radiocarbon dating as a by-product of the development of nuclear technology. This dating method uses the rate of decay of radioactive isotopes to measure the time that has elapsed since a sample of organic matter last exchanged carbon with its environment—in short, the time since an organism died. Application of the method has cumulatively transformed our understanding of prehistoric chronology. To illustrate the impact upon the study of Neolithic Britain, we have only to appreciate that in *Neolithic Cultures* Piggott imagined a British Neolithic period that lasted for around five hundred years, beginning in about 2000 BCE. This estimated span was based on a series of assumptions about the rate of cultural change, and the affinities between artefacts in Britain, continental Europe, and further afield. However, over the past half-century this inherited chronology has been swept away as radiometric dating has gradually been refined, and huge numbers of dated samples have accumulated. These now suggest that the Neolithic period began in Britain shortly before 4000 BCE, and 'ended' with the advent of a variety of objects made of metal instead of stone, from around 2400 BCE.

The implications of this transformed appreciation of the duration of the Neolithic are profound, for while Piggott and his contemporaries were dealing with periods of historical time that were comparable with those with which we are familiar from recorded history (the rise and fall of the Roman Empire, the emergence and spread of Islam, the development of capitalism), we now have evidence for human activity in the Neolithic of Britain that is dispersed across an expanse of time as much as three times longer than these major historical episodes. Over the past decade, moreover, the way in which we can calibrate the Neolithic has further been transformed by the widespread application of Bayesian statistical analysis to radiocarbon dating. Where a number of these 'radiometric' determinations exist for a particular site, and especially if they can be related to a sequence of archaeologically detectable events that took place in a known order, it is now possible to create a statistical model that reduces the error term on particular dates, and calculates the probability that specific events took place within what were often quite short periods of time (see Writing 'timescapes', below). The advent of this approach to achieving greater chronological precision has had an especially profound impact on the European Neolithic as we now have a prehistory that is reckoned in terms of decades and human generations rather than centuries or millennia. As a consequence archaeologists often find themselves confronted with brief bursts of activity set against the background of considerable periods of time during which not much *appears* to have happened, owing to the absence, or rarity, of archaeologically visible events from these times.[1]

Of course, the evidence for the British Neolithic is exclusively material in character, comprising pottery and stone tools, architectural structures, and the remains of the bodies of people and animals, unsupported by the kinds of clue provided by written records. The very muteness of this material has meant that archaeologists have been able to write a series of strikingly different narratives from closely similar material. As such it is inevitable, arguably even more so than in the work of documentary-focused historians, that these narratives have owed a great deal to the intellectual perspectives of their time, and the preoccupations of the writers themselves. New ideas about how societies develop and change have enabled us to recognize the significance of new forms of evidence, while placing existing evidence in a new light.

As a result, the history of writing about Neolithic Britain has involved repeated changes not only in the way that the significance of particular events has been interpreted, but also in understandings of what actually happened. Moreover, the phenomenon of 'the Neolithic' itself has repeatedly been re-evaluated, and still remains a topic for debate. For while the term serves to identify a particular period of the past, there is a general understanding that the period concerned was characterized by a distinctive process or phenomenon. So, unlike the Bronze Age or the Iron Age, which

---

1. The impact of this has been so great that it has been termed a 'third radiocarbon revolution' (the first such 'revolution' caused by the first introduction of this 'absolute' scientific dating method; the second being caused by the 'recalibration' of radiocarbon dates against organic material of known age, such as especially long-lived trees whose age is calculated by counting their annual growth rings, to counteract the effect of variable production of radioactive carbon in the upper atmosphere; this latter had the effect of rendering the Neolithic even 'older' than it had appeared from the first 'era' of radiocarbon determinations).

have traditionally been distinguished primarily by the appearance of specific kinds of metalworking technology, the Neolithic is often discussed as an entity definable in terms of the arrival or adoption of a *package* of traits, or simply as a development that overtook and engulfed particular groups of people. When Sir John Lubbock coined the term in 1865, he intended principally to separate a New Stone Age in which tools had been ground and polished from an earlier period in which they had been only chipped and flaked. Yet already in his *Pre-Historic Times*, in which he had first defined the period, Lubbock moved beyond this simple technological definition and suggested that the keeping of cattle might be an important characteristic of the Neolithic in some areas. In subsequent accounts, while some authors have defined the Neolithic primarily as being characterized by a particular economic system, others have emphasized its historical identity as a stage of social or cultural development. Still others have regarded the Neolithic as if it represented a form of social organization, or could be identified with a mode of thought developed, for example, around the idea of 'domestication'.

Although, therefore, there is general agreement that the Neolithic was the period during which domesticated plants and animals were first intro-duced to Britain from continental Europe, and in which people first used pottery vessels and polished flint and stone axes, built massive funerary monuments, and dug ditched enclosures, the significance of these develop-ments has been understood in radically different ways by different authors at different times. It is the nature and impact of such differences that we want to explore and explain in this chapter.

When archaeologists discuss the development of their own discipline, they often define a series of discrete periods or phases of investigation, very like the periods into which they divide the prehistoric past. This provides a useful heuristic, or shorthand, for describing the history of archaeological thought, but it is equally important to recognize that ideas and interpret-ations that were proposed many years ago, under intellectual regimes that we might now consider moribund, continue to have their reverberations in the present. Christopher Tilley has shown, for example, how use of the term 'megalith' has long outlived its utility, yet still today frames (or at the least influences) interpretive discussions about the purpose of Neolithic monu-ments in which large stones were deployed (see Fig. 1.1). In this way, writing about the British Neolithic has always involved making choices from the options that are available to us in the present, including drawing

Fig. 1.1 Bryn Celli Ddu passage grave (Anglesey) at night

The multi-phase chambered cairn at Bryn Celli Ddu ('the mound in the dark grove') has been the subject of a number of investigations, most recently in a project led by Ben Edwards, Seren Griffiths, Ffion Reynolds, and Adam Stanford. These still-ongoing investigations into the environs of the mound have shown that not only did the cairn itself have a complex developmental history (evident from previous excavations), but also the landscape in its immediate vicinity featured several other burial cairns, pits containing Neolithic deposits, and numerous examples of rock-art. The long passage that contains an example of 'Boyne' spiral stone carving and had a highly decorated monolith beyond its inner end is aligned on the summer solstice sunrise, the light from which penetrates down the stone-lined passage and into the interior. This photograph shows the kerb surrounding the front of the mound (also with echoes of the Irish passage graves) and light radiating outwards from the chamber and along the passage.

Photograph: June 2014, © Adam Stanford (website: http://www.aerial-cam.co.uk/).

on the past history of research, knowingly or unknowingly. For this reason, certain themes or tropes recur throughout the literature. For instance, there is a continuing tension between approaches that address artefacts and monuments typologically (seeking to classify and categorize, and to identify each tomb or stone tool as an example of a particular abstract 'type'), and those that attempt instead to place the object into its specific context, by concentrating on its place on an archaeological site, or in the broader landscape and its topography. These procedures lead to very different ways of representing the past, the former concentrating on the definition of particular kinds of entity at different scales of resolution ('cultures', 'traditions', or 'techno-complexes'), while the second focuses instead on social practices and lived experiences. Equally, some accounts of the Neolithic have sought to *explain* the changing relationships between people, technology, and the environment, while others have tried instead to *interpret* the meaning or significance of aspects of Neolithic culture. This important point underlines many of the arguments made later in this chapter.

Revolutions and emigrants

Piggott's *Neolithic Cultures* took some of its cues from the archaeologist Vere Gordon Childe, who had established much of the framework for European prehistory during the 1920s. Childe had brought together the Scandinavian tradition of detailed observation and classification of artefacts and the central European focus on identifying 'peoples' in prehistory. To this, he had added on the one hand a concern with transformative horizons of social and economic change (which he termed 'revolutions' in line with his Marxist interpretation of history) and on the other hand with how different cultural traditions accommodate themselves to particular regions and landscapes. Childe's 'revolutions' included the introduction of bronze metallurgy and the emergence of urban life, both of which he considered to be important preconditions for the eventual rise of modern capitalism. However, most fundamental of all was the 'Neolithic revolution', in which people ceased to be reliant upon food *collection*, and began food *production*. For Childe, this process had begun in the oases of the Near East, where the environmental conditions of the last glaciation had forced people, animals, and edible plants into a close proximity that gradually developed into a kind of symbiosis. Once human beings had domesticated cattle, sheep, pigs, wheat, barley, and lentils, they were able to relocate them out of their natural habitats and into new landscapes through the physical movement of populations.

While Childe took the view that cultural innovations (such as bronze metallurgy, the wheel, or horse riding) tended to have a single geographical origin and to 'diffuse' from one society to another, he also believed that the spread of the whole integrated set of elements that made up the Neolithic way of life was more likely to have been dispersed by folk movement. As he understood people generally to be culturally conservative and unwilling to change their material equipment without good reason, he believed the occurrence of similar kinds of artefact in different regions could be taken as an indication that the same community had passed through each separate area in the course of its migrations. This led him to the conclusion that a family of 'western Neolithic' cultures distributed across Atlantic Europe were linked like the branches of a tree, ascending from a single root. These people had been the bearers of a way of life based on domesticated species, and agriculture had been for them a cultural predisposition. Farming was a source of their identity as much as their sustenance, and the implication that farmers are a fundamentally different kind of person from hunters is one that has contributed an enduring undercurrent to subsequent discussions of the Neolithic: one that saw the adoption of farming as one of the great 'revolutions' that transformed society and moved it upwards along an evolutionary scale of increasing complexity.

Clearly, Childe's narrative of economic revolution sparking population movement and pan-European transformation is one that would have resonated widely in the immediate aftermath of the Russian (political) revolution and the First World War. History might easily have been understood by many of his contemporaries as a process in which radical transformations of economic life unleashed turbulence and dislocation on people who had little power to resist. However, a slightly different and more conservative inflection was placed on these ideas in Britain and Scandinavia during these same interwar years. In Britain, the notion that 'this island race' had been progressively enriched by the successive influxes of Romans, Saxons, Danes, and Normans had become a cornerstone of a colonial world view that sought to spread the virtues of (British) civilization around the globe. This was extended back in time to explain each new assemblage of artefacts throughout prehistory in terms of successive waves of Continental migrants: Beaker people, Urn folk, Halstatt invaders, and so on. At the same time, a 'scenic nationalism' was increasingly interested in the way that these different groups of people had created the foundations of the distinctive landscapes of Britain (and other countries), ultimately giving them the character that nurtured a unique national identity.

The popularity of this 'landscape and folk identity' perspective was most clearly reflected in the growing interest in proxy indicators of environmental change, especially through the study of microscopic pollen grains trapped and preserved in sediments and deposits such as those of peat bogs, and providing evidence of changes in the vegetation over long sequences of time. While this approach had initially focused on natural processes of landscape change, such as the recolonization of Britain by trees and shrubs after the last Ice Age, there was a gradual increase in attention paid to indications of human interference with the landscape. In particular, the evidence for episodes of deforestation during the Neolithic could be recruited to support a vitalist, post-Enlightenment narrative of venturous and adaptable humanity triumphing over brute, passive nature. Where Mesolithic hunter-gatherers had merely existed within the natural world, Neolithic people were able to subject nature to their will. So Neolithic migrants were not only the carriers of a farming lifestyle, they also brought with them a new spirit of striving and overcoming. In Britain and Denmark, studies of prehistoric pollen profiles from the 1930s to the 1960s developed increasingly sophisticated analyses of *landnam* (ground-breaking) clearances of the forests using stone axes to chop down trees, sometimes prefigured by a 'leaf fodder regime' in which stalled animals were fed gathered foliage.

It was a combination of Childe's archaeology of revolutions and this new landscape ecology that Piggott employed so systematically in *Neolithic Cultures*. His narrative envisaged groups of Continental migrants, the 'Windmill Hill folk', arriving by sea and adjusting their cultural repertoire and way of life to insular conditions, and in the process emerging as a distinctive strand within the cultural web of the European Neolithic. Yet the indigenous hunting people of Britain also found a place in Piggott's narrative: disrupted and archaeologically invisible for some centuries after the arrival of the Windmill Hill people, they eventually created, along with the newcomers, a series of 'secondary Neolithic cultures' of a distinctive insular kind. These unique cultures were made recognizable through the development of chisel-shaped arrowheads suited to wildfowling, a heavy stone tool assemblage used for grubbing flint nodules out of clay deposits, pottery decorated with cord and bird-bone impressions (echoing the 'Forest Neolithic' of the Baltic), and new mortuary practices and monumental forms. All these were added to the pre-existing Western Neolithic repertoire. But because these 'cultures' overlapped in some of their components, and even made use of the same kinds of monument, Piggott imagined a Later Neolithic in which a series of different kinds of community interacted, pursuing slightly different ways of life. Eventually, these groups were joined by small colonies of incomers from the Continent who brought with them small, fine, glossy Beaker vessels, copper daggers, and gold trinkets. The emergent characteristic Early Bronze Age of Britain was therefore seen by Piggott to be the outcome of the interaction and fusion of these different groups with varied cultural inheritances. Given the narrative coherence of his account, it is not hard to grasp why its arguments were such a strong influence upon the understanding of the dynamics of Neolithic 'history' in Britain in the second half of the twentieth century.

Ecology and social evolution

By the middle of the 1960s, the picture of Neolithic colonists whose pioneering spirit led them to tame and subdue the wildscape had begun to be implicitly challenged by a more overtly evolutionary approach to landscape change. This was more likely to focus on what was seen to be the direct evidence for the workings of a subsistence economy: animal bones, the charred remains of plant seeds, and the location of settlements in relation to favourable soils and other resources. Rather than identifying agriculture as the cultural preference of particular groups of people, this interpretive approach asserted that the way in which people acquired their food was simply a form of behaviour, no different in kind from the various ways in which other animals feed themselves. According to this perspective, people will generally adopt the most rational and efficient way of gaining sustenance within the ecological niche and climatic conditions that they find themselves in. The subsistence economy is, in this view of the world, primarily a tool with which to achieve successful adaptation to changing environmental circumstances. It followed from this that the adoption of agriculture in western Asia and its spread in Europe was not a 'revolution' in Childe's sense, but merely an intensification of the ecological relationships between people, animals, and plants. These relationships might wax and wane with time, and 'domestication' might have occurred many times in the distant past, in many different locations, in line with the environmental pressures that had acted upon human communities.

Directly or indirectly, these ideas have had a profound impact on the way that the British Neolithic was (and for some archaeologists continues to be) envisaged. The implications have been several, but two can be highlighted here to explain what could follow on from this way of thinking about, especially, how farming might have been adopted and developed. First, if farming was a way that people behaved, and which people could adopt or discard, rather than being an expression of cultural preferences, there was no reason to suppose that it might not have been adopted by indigenous hunter-gatherers who had been in contact with Continental neighbours from whom they could acquire cultigens and livestock. The many groups of migrants envisaged as having arrived from France and Belgium might therefore have been no more than a figment of archaeologists' imaginations.

Secondly, if Neolithic people had not been relentlessly imposing themselves on the natural world, but had been to some degree at the mercy of their environment, then their way of life might have proved fragile and subject to failure. A number of accounts published in the 1970s and 1980s argued that the apparent cultural disjuncture between the Earlier and Later Neolithic could be attributed to an episode of economic collapse, following which forest clearances regenerated and population declined. A Neolithic agricultural regime had overextended itself and had been overwhelmed by the effects of soil exhaustion and possibly also insect infestation. Only when society had recovered from this setback did a new (Later Neolithic) cultural formation emerge in Britain, characterized by henge monuments, elaborately decorated pottery, more diverse stone tools, and complex funerary rites.

This tendency to see the relationship between people and their environment as unstable and periodically subject to dramatic, negative change has been identified by Bruce Trigger as a feature of a growing anxiety amongst the Western nations from the 1970s onwards. Where the immediate postwar era had been characterized by optimism concerning technological progress, there was now increasing concern that humanity was faced with forces beyond its control, in the form of environmental degradation, population growth, and overexploitation of natural resources. These issues emerged at much the same time as the application of a completely different form of evolutionary thinking, ultimately derived from anthropological scholarship in the United States. This reintroduced the long-established idea, ultimately attributable to the European Enlightenment, that societies develop through time by passing through a series of characteristic stages of increasing complexity and sophistication, within which communities become progressively more internally differentiated and ranked. While the environment was, according to this model, still afforded an important role, it was nonetheless understood as existing in a dynamic relationship with population and technology rather than determining development. More complex and hierarchical societies were understood as managing and controlling these relationships more effectively than less formally structured ones by developing highly organized systems of leadership, redistribution, and economic specialization. A distinctive aspect of this approach was that it presented archaeological evidence as a correlate, or index, of the process of social evolution.

An influential paper on the archaeology of Neolithic 'Wessex' (the area of the modern-day counties of Wiltshire and Dorset, and parts of Hampshire and Somerset) published by Colin Renfrew in 1973 exemplified this approach. Renfrew argued that the increasing scale and centrality of monuments—from earthen long barrows in the Early Neolithic to henge enclosures, Silbury Hill, and the stone phases of Stonehenge in the Late Neolithic—reflected the growing size of populations whose labour was made available for massive projects owing to the development and workings of a new and more stratified social form (Fig. 1.2).

This latter was the chiefdom, distinguished by centralized heritable authority, the administered redistribution of resources, greater population and

Fig. 1.2 Stonehenge, viewed from the north-west
The famous structure is, as the result of the past two decades or so of work on the archive of past excavations and in its wider landscape, much better understood both in terms of its development as a monument, and contemporary activity in its environs. See Chapter 5 for details.
Photograph: September 2015, © Julian Thomas.

productivity, and the use of special forms of dress and monumental works to identify and to promote the interests of an elite. Later, Renfrew undertook fieldwork in the Orkneys, with the intention, at least in part, to demonstrate that a similar sequence of social hierarchization and centralization could be traced there.

Another important development associated with this social evolutionary school of thought lay in questioning the assumption that particular sets of artefacts automatically reflected the identities of distinct groups of people—Childe's 'cultures'. It had been pointed out, for instance, that a specific combination of stone tools might not be a manifestation of cultural preference or ethnic identity, but of what was required to conduct a particular set of tasks (such as hunting or butchering animals) within a specific ecological context. On this basis, Piggott's argument that a number of different cultural groups might have coexisted in Late Neolithic Britain came to be seen in a different way. Styles of pottery including Beakers and Grooved Ware and their associated artefact sets began to be described as 'special purpose assemblages'. These were not necessarily used by entire communities or even for a wide range of activities, and it was noted that they were often concentrated in specific kinds of site. Therefore, although 'coarse' or 'domestic' Beaker pottery was known, the preponderance of fine Beaker vessels and associated exotic items in graves led to the suggestion that they represented a status package of Continental origin, monopolized by the higher orders of society. Similarly, the discovery of large quantities of Grooved Ware at the massive henge enclosures of Durrington Walls in Wiltshire and Mount Pleasant in Dorset during excavations in the 1960s and 1970s led to claims that this form of pottery had been used to mark the presence, or rise, of a pig-herding subculture, or an astronomer-priesthood, or a social elite. This in turn gave rise to a 'prestige-goods' theory to explain elite control of increasingly centralized societies. That is to say, certain kinds of scarce or finely crafted artefacts were now understood as having been monopolized by socially pre-eminent groups, who were able to control their circulation, and in the process gather clients and followers.

Symbol and meaning

These arguments in some ways anticipated the developments of the 1980s and 1990s, which saw the presentation of a perspective in which artefacts came to be identified as material symbols that demanded interpretation, while social conflict and competition replaced environmental forces as the perceived causes of change. One important development of this phase of study and interpretation was that both objects and monuments were recognized as having had an active role to play in Neolithic societies, rather than simply having reflected the identities of groups of people in the past, or as having acted simply as emblems of power, rank, or authority. Richard Bradley described the stone axes that circulated from quarries in the west of Britain during the Early Neolithic, and also a range of exotic items including polished discoidal knives, jet belt fittings, finely polished adzes, stone maceheads, and carved stone balls that were in use from 3500 BCE onwards, as 'weapons of exclusion'. By this he meant that the exchange of these items amongst privileged people and their deposition in graves and other contexts both identified and amplified social differences. Similarly, John Barrett argued that the labour involved in constructing henge monuments and stone circles was not an index of the existing degree of social hierarchy and centralization so much as a means by which elites brought themselves into existence. In this view, these elites had actually created their own authority by inciting or coercing large numbers of people to work together to create massive architectural forms, in the process establishing privileged spaces that could be occupied only by the dominant few.

A further consequence of the characterization of material things as symbols that conveyed or constructed meanings was a greater attentiveness to the composition of archaeological deposits. It had long been recognized that groupings, sometimes spectacular, of certain materials occasionally occurred at Neolithic sites. Entire cattle skulls had been found in the flanking quarry ditches of earthen long mounds, while decorated chalk plaques and other unusual items had been recovered from isolated Late Neolithic pits. The excavation of the causewayed enclosure at Hambledon Hill in Dorset during the 1970s and 1980s revealed human skulls placed at the butt ends of individual ditch segments, while the similar enclosure at Etton in Cambridgeshire, dug at much the same time, contained rich and complex waterlogged deposits. These included a pottery vessel inverted over a mat of birch bark, a hafted stone axe, and bundles of cattle ribs. The unspoken assumption in prehistoric studies had always been that the bulk of the available evidence has accumulated in 'traps' such as pits and ditches in a random and haphazard fashion, normally as a by-product of the pursuit of everyday activities. Yet here instead, at sites such as Hambledon Hill and Etton and many others like them, there was growing evidence of an archaeological record that had formed to a significant extent through deliberate and purposeful acts. One reaction to this realization was the exploration of the concept of *structured deposition*, and a dawning recognition that although some deposits announced themselves as being out of the ordinary through their richness or sheer *oddness* (potsherds pressed against the sides of pits, or flint artefacts deliberately smashed immediately prior to burial, for example), some groupings of quite mundane objects appeared to be patterned or structured both in their selection and their careful placement in particular contexts—from the chambers of long mounds to the ditches of enclosures, but most commonly in pits dug into the ground and then immediately backfilled. In some cases there appeared to be particular objects and materials that were either routinely mutually associated with one another, or that were in contrast deliberately segregated from each other. Yet it has long been recognized that patterning in archaeological residues *can* be generated by entirely random processes. One way to accommodate this apparent contradiction is to suggest that there is a continuum between on the one hand highly formalized deposits of symbolically charged things, often within or near special places or 'monuments' of some kind, and on the other hand fortuitous accumulations of cultural materials that had been brought together owing to natural processes or routinized activities. Somewhere between the two are numerous Neolithic pits containing hearth-scrapings and potsherds, flint chips and animal bones, which may represent cleaning-up operations following short-lived episodes of habitation. These can nevertheless include occasional fine and clearly selected artefacts that have been deliberately incorporated into the placed material, and which enhance the impression that the assemblage as a whole represents the record, the marker, or the intentional trace of a human presence.

This phase in the study and writing of Neolithic Britain was also characterized by a heightened awareness of the inferential, fundamentally interpretive nature of archaeological investigation itself. Archaeological evidence is always fragmentary, and relates to a past time that is, to some degree, irretrievably lost. It follows, according to a then-emergent perspective, that simply presenting the available evidence in unalloyed form will inevitably result in something that is entirely inadequate in terms of the subtleties of past social practices and interactions. The traces of these past actions need therefore to be connected together by a narrative that renders them comprehensible and that is credible to its audience. Archaeology in such perspective is therefore a craft whose products are acknowledged as being constructed in the present, out of the scattered remains that past people have left behind them. Such a position is distinct from out-and-out relativism, in that it insists on the limitation on what can be said about the past imposed by the material evidence itself.

Writing the Neolithic as metaphor

One of the leading proponents of a semantic interpretation of archaeological phenomena, in which past objects and residues were legible as if they were texts, was Ian Hodder, who offered a distinctive perspective on the Old World Neolithic. For him, *domestication* was as much a symbolic or metaphorical relationship between humans and other species as a biological or ecological one, and it was grounded in the longer-term process of the domestication of society, through the development of the concept of *home*. Hodder's view was that in order for people to begin to cultivate plants and herd animals, they would first have had to appropriate the world conceptually, by distinguishing between the domestic domain of hearth and household and the external sphere of the wild. These he identified with the complementary principles of the *domus* and the *agrios*: the former encompassing the dwelling space, the domestic community, cultivation, nurturing and femininity, and the latter connoting the waste, the forest, masculinity, hunting, and violence. This opposition enabled living things to be drawn into and maintained within the domestic sphere (or shunned and repudiated), just as the agricultural labour force was constituted through ties of co-residence and consanguinity. Importantly, Hodder's perspective drew on the insights that he had previously developed into the meaningful constitution of material culture. He emphasized that rather than simply being a way of *thinking* about things, the *domus/agrios* distinction actually gave form to tangible reality, through the way that people habitually interacted with material entities that were imbued with significance. Yet this capacity to structure quotidian life was grounded on the way that the separation between home and the wild, life and death harnessed and mobilized people's fears and emotions to produce drama and the desire for change, towards sedentism and greater control over resources.

Hodder's book *The Domestication of Europe* described a long-term process in which the idea of domestication was gradually dispersed across Eurasia from the 'fertile crescent' of Iraq, southern Turkey, and the Levant, manifested in villages of substantial houses, fields of crops, herds of animals, and elaborate artefacts. However, towards the end of the fifth millennium BCE the *domus* ceased to be merely a framework for the organization of small farming communities and their immediate ecologies, and began to be applied to much larger social groups. Rather than the taming and subjugation of natural resources, it was now the direction and control of substantial groups of people and their labour that was at stake. From this time onwards, conspicuous domestic architecture faded from the record, and was replaced by massive monuments containing the remains of the dead. Nonetheless, these tombs and barrows often demonstrated similar organizing principles to the houses that preceded them, such as a linear and graded ordering of space. But ultimately, the scope of the *domestic* order to encompass larger and larger populations and more and more elaborate monuments reached its limit. The Later Neolithic saw a vengeful return of the *agrios*, in the form of warlike artefact styles and single grave burials, which together reinstated a concern with masculinity, violence, hunting, death, and the wild world beyond the house.

Hodder's account has been criticized for imposing onto the ancient past what amounts to a dichotomy between culture and nature, which is arguably an artefact of the modern Western sensibility. However, his intervention was critically important in two respects. First, it powerfully made the case that the Neolithic represented more than a cultural package or a particular subsistence strategy. For Hodder, the Neolithic was at once a way of thinking and a framework for social action. The Neolithic way of life was distinguished by a means of understanding the world as much as by access to a specific set of productive resources. Secondly, as much as any previous writer, Hodder drew attention to the different *kinds* of Neolithic that had developed in different parts of Europe. While *The Domestication of Europe* does not dwell on Britain to any great extent, it is clear from what he writes that the Neolithic of chambered tombs, long barrows, and causewayed enclosures was distinct in character from that of long-lived villages and cemeteries found in central and south-east Europe. Although we might disagree with his view that the essence of the Neolithic lay in conceptual structures rather than social relationships, it is abundantly clear that the pattern that he identified is one that demands explanation.

Writing the Neolithic creatively

The argument that narratives about the past are actively pieced together in the present resulted in a certain amount of reflection on the kind of writing that archaeologists have themselves routinely undertaken: too often the *reportage* is dry, timid, and unimaginative. The alternative might be a more creative kind of writing, which has the courage to experiment with narrative style and a combination of different media in order to elicit unexpected conclusions from the evidence. One of the most sophisticated examples of this approach was Mark Edmonds's *Ancestral Geographies of the Neolithic*. Published at the end of the 1990s, this book had first been conceived as a study of the causewayed enclosures of the Earlier Neolithic in southern Britain. However, the approach eventually taken was instead to place these monuments into the context of a series of specific and frequently attested activities that would have been played out across the Neolithic landscape. In particular, Edmonds chose to focus upon the management of woodland, the herding of animals, the acquisition and working of flint, and the relationship between the living and the dead, each of which is represented or implied by materials and objects found at the sites in question. The enclosures themselves were only directly addressed in the latter part of the book, by which time the themes of movement, exchange, consumption, and mortuary practice that were evoked at and through the monuments concerned were already well established. Moreover, Edmonds complemented his more prosaic discussion of the materials with evocative photographs of trees, of flint nodules, and of human remains, as well as a series of short imaginative vignettes, depicting moments of Neolithic life and the interactions of 'real' people. These had the virtue that, while prehistorians often find themselves discussing the past in abstractions, here Edmonds forced himself to imagine what everyday experience would have looked like on the ground. Equally, he was as much concerned with the grain and texture of Neolithic life as with historical events and processes.

Edmonds's visual images of tree bark, serrated stone, and pitted, grainy bones, and his word pictures of purposive Neolithic activity were perhaps a reaction against a discipline that had become increasingly removed from any kind of visceral or elemental engagement with material things, except through the practice of excavation itself. But at the same time, his imagined Neolithic episodes resonated with a growing concern with the *difference* of that once-living past. An increased familiarity with ethnography and the diversity of human ways of life on the part of archaeologists had given rise to a desire to resist the imposition of modern values and prejudices on the past. Ways needed to be found to allow the Neolithic to surprise us through its unfamiliarity.

These same issues were central to another key 1990s text focusing on the Neolithic of Britain, Christopher Tilley's *A Phenomenology of Landscape*. Tilley's point of departure was the observation that our written and visual representations of, and contemporary physical encounters with, prehistoric monuments tend to be both unnecessarily and unhelpfully remote from the lives of the people who built and used these structures. For example, tombs and enclosures are reduced to 'dots on maps', or are visited as 'heritage experiences', entering from the car park and exiting through the gift shop.

Tilley began his excursion by citing a range of ethnographic studies to suggest that in many non-Western societies the landscape is understood as animate in the sense of being imbued with the presences of ancestors and spirits. He then made reference to the work of a number of humanistic geographers, who had emphasized the experiential character of space and place. For these writers, human beings come to know their world through the body, haptically and sensorily (by touch, smell, and hearing) as well as visually, as they move across the land. In the attempt to develop a more immediate understanding of an otherwise distant Neolithic world, Tilley described his own field-based experiences of the chambered long cairns of the Welsh Black Mountains, the dolmens of Pembrokeshire, and the major linear earthwork structure, the 'Dorset Cursus', the latter in particular in reference to a lengthy walk across the landscape following its course over several miles. In a manner that can be compared with the practices of the German tradition of hermeneutics, Tilley then based his reading of the monuments he encountered on what he felt he had in common with their builders: a human body with its array of senses, and the landscape itself. For although vegetation has changed, fences have been built, and roads laid down, the 'bones of the land', the topography, is, he argued, broadly the same as it was in the Neolithic.

It is undeniable that Tilley's fieldwork resulted in a series of fresh insights into the location and configuration of prehistoric monuments that perhaps could not have been arrived at by any other means. Nonetheless, his work has been criticized for its assumption that the experiences of a late twentieth-century, white, middle-class man can somehow automatically have a significant amount to tell us about the perceptions of prehistoric people of diverse ages, genders, statuses, and degrees of ability. Equally, although Tilley explicitly denies this, there has been a suspicion that his approach demands an unacceptable degree of romantic empathy, attempting vicariously to think the thoughts and experience the feelings of past people. One plausible response to these criticisms is that an 'experiential archaeology' such as his was seen to be should be understood as no more than a contemporary analogue for the activities of people in the past, which may ultimately provide insights into presently existing landscapes and structures, but which affords no direct entry into the lived world of the past. It is, therefore, only the first step in the inferential process.

The writings of both Tilley and Edmonds have been viewed, sometimes very negatively, as representative of a 'hyper-interpretive' trend within archaeology, and it is arguable that as Western society has lurched into a pragmatic neoliberal era and a subsequent economic crisis, archaeology has to some extent edged away from sophisticated theorization, and any in-depth contemplation of its own ethical and political significance. This has coincided with an explosion of new scientific techniques that are of undoubted value to the discipline, and many of which are of particular significance to the study of the Neolithic. These include the investigation of ancient DNA, the use of stable isotopes in human bones to assess the predominant diets that people consumed during life (whether mammal or plant foods, maritime or terrestrial), the study of lead and strontium isotopes in human and animal teeth to determine how far people and their herds had moved from place to place during their lifetimes, and the analysis of the chemistry of residues from pottery vessels to identify the foods that they had contained, which has revealed amongst other things the extent of dairying in the Neolithic.

One response to this has been a retreat into a kind of naive empiricism: the view that techniques can now tell us all we need to know about the past, and that theory is therefore redundant. Such a view is ultimately unsustainable because archaeology cannot avoid being also a human and social science, at root an inherently inferential, interpretive discipline. Nonetheless, the appearance of new forms of evidence has sometimes occasioned a return to the explanatory frameworks that have been noted already, especially those that are social evolutionary in emphasis. So the tone of some recent interpretations of DNA and isotope data echoes the 'ethnic prehistories' of the 1920s and 1930s, with their folk movements and genetically homogeneous communities of 'hunters' and 'farmers'. While such interpretations are in themselves lacking in explanatory power in reference to how people live their lives and make their collective history, in defaulting to these models we ultimately run the risk of lending support to atavistic agendas in the modern world, which romanticize 'golden ages' of racial purity in the past.

Writing 'timescapes': new chronologies for the Neolithic

Besides the new narrative insights from creative interpretive writing and from the various novel laboratory-based, scientific studies, the greatest impact in recent years on our understanding of the Neolithic in Britain has, as we pointed out at the beginning of this chapter, come about as a result of the systematic application of Bayesian statistics to suites of more numerous and more accurate radiocarbon dates from more rigorously examined site contexts. The purpose of this new engagement in mature statistical study has been twofold: first, to introduce greater chronological resolution than has been possible in the past when isolated dates with their broad spans of probability were all that was available; and, secondly, to interrogate closely the relation between sequences of deposits and the kinds of datable material sealed within them. For instance, the clear preference now is that radiocarbon dates are obtained not only from precisely delineated site contexts where the circumstances of their deposition are certain, but also that they are from short-lived materials such as twigs, sapwood, seeds, or articulated bone that is unlikely to have been 'curated' (that is, saved from being entirely discarded and forgotten, but instead stored or buried in known locations for later retrieval and redeployment). This interrogative approach arose from a recognition of a past lack of rigour in selecting material for dating, and specifically the frequency with which already old organic material had been incorporated within later deposits, therefore erroneously making these latter deposits, and the structures and monuments they were part of, appear to have been created earlier in time than they had in fact been.

Towards the end of their monumental 2011 region-by-region Bayesian-based analysis of Early Neolithic site chronologies predominantly in southern and eastern Britain (*Gathering Time*), Alasdair Whittle and colleagues produced two chapters that synthesized the implications. In the first of these chapters, entitled 'Neolithic narratives', the south/eastern Early Neolithic (broadly mid fourth-millennium) enclosures were set (in 165 pages) in the context of their timescapes. These latter were explained in terms of the metaphor of an unevenly woven cloth with a pattern of threads marked by temporal gaps and intervals as well as continuities. This involved studying chronologies not only for sites in Britain and Ireland as a whole, but also for the use-lives of different materials such as the various kinds of pottery and stone axes. We shall return to issues concerning the longevity and periodicity of use of the enclosures, and the patterns of deposition they encompass, in Chapters 3 and 4; and how thinking specifically about the 'historical materiality' of axes and pottery can affect the writing of Neolithic history, also in Chapter 4. What interests us here is what Whittle and his associates thought such intensive comparative chronological study could make possible, in terms of what they termed 'narrative history'.

In brief, what was perceived was an uneven pattern of adoption of pottery-making, cereal cultivation, livestock farming, flint-mining, 'hall' construction and the first building of long barrows in the first two to three centuries from 4000 BCE, with the earliest activity focused upon Kent and the Thames Estuary. During the thirty-eighth century BCE, the pace of change was seen to have quickened, with a 'startling array' of innovations including both enclosure-building and long-distance trade arising perhaps 'within the span of an individual life-time', while a developed *package* of Neolithic practices spread beyond south-eastern England. Later, a peak in the creation of enclosures (for which most dates in southern Britain were obtained and studied) was traced in the final quarter of the thirty-seventh century BCE at the same time as a reduction in the number of long barrows being built. Then, in the early part of the following century, the pace of enclosure-circuit construction 'slackened', before a 'last main bout of fresh enclosure building' occurred in the middle of the thirty-sixth century BCE. There was then a decline in the creation of new enclosures 'in the generations around 3500 BCE', while at the same time the networks of contact that had facilitated the movement of axes and some pottery also wound down as new traditions of building, such as the creation of (southern British) cursus monuments, picked up. The conventions of 'rise' and 'decline' are tropes familiar from earlier eras of culture-historical writing, and therefore such historical writing exhibits continuities with British intellectual traditions first articulated in the 1920s. However, in the narratives of Whittle and his collaborators, these are given a new twist, with their fine-grained accounts of micro-variation and spatial variability in the various phenomena concerned.

The second of the two chapters of synthesis in *Gathering Time*, the latter of the two-volume work, examined 'the social dynamics of change' in reference in particular to the Mesolithic-Neolithic transition, consumption patterns, monument sequences, artefacts and their symbolism, and the close-Continental origins of practices of flint-mining, house-building, and enclosure-creation. Issues of sequence, contemporaneity, individual lifespans, and 'social time' were here seen as central to the process of writing history from site and artefact chronologies. The authors saw a social dynamic for the adoption of farming practices and a Neolithic world view in south-eastern Britain as potentially having arisen from economic pressures experienced by peoples on the near-Continent, together with a growing appreciation of the benefits of farming on the part of indigenous groups. Drawing upon the writings of American archaeologist (and specialist in the prehistory of migration on the Eurasian steppes) David Anthony, they saw the principal mechanism for such adoption as initial long-distance contact followed by migration led by pioneer individuals. These ideas will be discussed in Chapter 2 in some detail, not least because Anthony sees the process as both kin-dependent and a two-way process. This potentially places the whole concept of cultural adoptions and influences on the cusp of the earliest Neolithic in Britain in an entirely fresh light.

A key aspect of the particular kind of chronologically refined narrative of the Early Neolithic presented by Whittle and his associates was the recognition that there was great diversity among traditions of monument-building and the sequences of activity at different localities, while certain time-related changes affected wider areas within Britain. These phenomena demand satisfactory, necessarily complex, explanation. The final *Gathering Time* chapter identifies as especially critical, periods of apparently rapid change that marked transformations in the nature and pace of interaction between groups. The dramatic expansion of exchange networks from the mid thirty-seventh century BCE, along with the widespread appearance of Decorated Bowl pottery in the thirty-eighth century, was seen as a case in point, since it appears to correlate closely with the first appearance of causewayed enclosures.

The distinctive contribution of what we might term this timescapes approach to writing the Neolithic, therefore, has been not only to highlight the contrasting (and sometimes very narrow) timescales for activity that existed at different locations, nor only to help with the mapping of time-related changes spatially across Britain, but also to make evident the varied narratives that cut across one another. In other words, it is no longer tenable to suggest that there is fundamentally only one possible narrative of historical change within and across Britain through the 1,600–1,800 years of the duration of the Neolithic. Rather, each strand of evidence, each region, and also each similarly structured site across regions contributes its own narrative strand to Neolithic history across the decades and centuries concerned. Moreover, a single lived lifetime could intersect, and become bound up with, several such narratives.

Writing the Neolithic in a geographically balanced way

It is a truism to say that we write history from the evidence, but that various predispositions and biases affect the way that evidence is gathered as well as weighed.[2] In studies of Neolithic Britain the areas that were studied first and most intensively have tended to give us a view of the Neolithic period that is skewed geographically. We know far more about central southern England in the Neolithic than almost any other part of Britain, and certain sites in East Anglia, the Thames Valley, Anglesey, and some (albeit limited) areas of Yorkshire have, for example, also featured disproportionately in surveys of Neolithic phenomena. Similarly, what was known about the Neolithic archaeology of the Orkney Islands surpassed many times our understanding of most of mainland Scotland until very recently. That this situation needs to be redressed was first confronted explicitly in a polemical essay by Gordon Barclay published in 2001. This charted the nature and consequences of such particular biases, especially as regards the development of a 'research culture' that determined what was important, and where: in other words, how such imbalances were perpetuated.

That this imbalance is not just a feature of Neolithic studies in Scotland (and especially the mainland) is evident from the fact that other areas have only recently seen a level of activity even remotely matching the decades of

2. We are aware of a number of aspects of 'new writing' about Neolithic Britain that we have not touched upon in this historiographical chapter, emphasizing instead a different range of themes. One such alternative is the effort to produce a greater gender balance in accounts of the period, although few publications have emerged that do this systematically. Another concerns the use of anthropology to look at aspects such as gift-exchange, where the implications of inter-island contacts in Polynesia, for example, have been examined—again, nonetheless, by relatively few writers.

research and study invested in areas such as Wessex. An example of an area hitherto relatively neglected, the understanding of the Neolithic archaeology of which has been transformed in recent years, is Kent, which is ironically the area of Britain geographically closest to mainland Europe. This transformation can be attributed to economic development and the requirement for this to fund archaeological works in advance of destruction of sites. Even within Wiltshire, the bias resulting from a focus upon the principal chalk uplands has become evident as close to home as in the Vale of Pewsey, which is a low-lying area of country that actually separates the two parts of the Stonehenge and Avebury World Heritage Site. It has only been in the past five years that substantial new field research has begun in the area around Marden, despite the latter location having long been known to feature a massive Neolithic henge.

The impact of such imbalance on the entire historical narrative of the British Neolithic has arguably been fundamental. For example, although an intensification of archaeological activity in areas close to the eastern seaboard of Scotland from East Lothian near Edinburgh northwards up to Aberdeen has to a large degree addressed the deficit with north-eastern and eastern England (as chapters of a recent book edited by Kenneth Brophy and others demonstrate), the east–west imbalance remains. As Gordon Noble pointed out more than ten years ago, the Hebridean areas of Scotland have long been viewed as geographically marginal and their archaeology exceptional within, or somehow unrepresentative of, the British Neolithic as a whole. Among other reasons for this, the impact of the eighteenth- and nineteenth-century Highland clearances was to give subsequent generations (and especially from the early twentieth century) the impression not only that these areas had historically featured low population densities, but also that their lands had always been relatively unproductive.

Noble suggested that environmentally these areas were instead advantageous for farming in the Neolithic, with light, well-drained soils and long summer daylight (and therefore growing) hours. Moreover, once a maritime perspective is reintroduced, these areas can be seen as having been highly accessible by sea, in contrast to inland areas where both travel and transportation were arduous and time-consuming. The consequence of this was that travel and interactions were probably both more frequent and had greater impacts than for more easterly or central areas of Scotland. So although distinctions between east and west were a result of two separate sets of north–south routes that existed in prehistory, there is no inherently greater importance of east over west in terms of their relative contribution to the history of Britain in the centuries concerned. The differences are nonetheless profound, with one side of northern Britain interacting down the western seaboard southwards as far as Cornwall, and beyond ultimately to Iberia; and the other predisposed to interactions down to East Anglia, the Netherlands, and north-central Europe.

We need therefore to be mindful of the biases that are inherited and perpetuated, rather than simply inherent, in trying to write the history of Neolithic Britain; and also to be aware that we are still a long way from any 'complete' understanding of the Neolithic of *any* area of Britain. To illustrate, we can point to the various recent studies of the 'Stonehenge landscape', several of which are mentioned in this book. In this most-studied of areas, our understanding has been transformed in the last two decades by projects that have fundamentally dislodged received interpretations by locating and investigating new sites, in part as a result of asking fresh questions (for instance concerning early use of the River Avon) that had not previously been considered. The authors of this book, collaborating also on a major long-term field research investigation of a single site close to the Black Mountains in Herefordshire, are also acutely aware of areas where almost no research investigation had taken place until recent years. So, the Walton Basin in Radnorshire in eastern Wales has been shown to possess an extraordinary density of Neolithic sites, for example; while the Neolithic archaeological resource of Herefordshire has not only been shown to be both rich and extensive, but also to feature kinds of phenomena not so far witnessed in any other part of Britain. Had such areas been studied first, and more fully, some of the sites and regions perhaps thought of now as 'typical' might rather have been seen as less representative of other areas of Britain than they are currently perceived to be.

The grand narrative versus emergent causation

Throughout the Old World, the Neolithic is associated with a series of momentous changes: the inception of agriculture, the foundation of sedentary settlements, the construction of massive monuments, and the adoption of a series of new material technologies. This has meant that the period has always been central to long-term, large-scale accounts of human development. The Neolithic is often seen as a crucial stage in the journey from hunting band to advanced urban society. But at the same time, because the period is distinguished by elaborate material culture with potential symbolic significance, complex funerary customs, ceremonial architecture, and conspicuously non-utilitarian practices, it also became a focus for fine-grained analyses of social life at the micro level, as we have seen. This contrast between scales of analysis was the subject of an important discussion by Andrew Sherratt in the 1990s, who advocated a return to the 'grand narrative'. Sherratt held that reluctance on the part of archaeologists to address the 'big picture' of social and economic change through time denoted a loss of confidence. However, he also recognized the limitations of existing large-scale narratives, notably that they tend to rely on eighteenth-century archetypes of 'hunters', 'pastoralists', and 'farmers', which imply that social and cultural developments are determined by changes in subsistence practices.

The social categories that Sherratt refers to originated in the so-called 'conjectural histories' of the Enlightenment. While seventeenth-century writers had imagined a distant past in which human society had come into being through the establishment of a kind of contract to abide by a set of agreed rules of conduct, authors such as Rousseau, Montesquieu, and Adam Smith imagined instead a series of necessary stages that humanity must have passed through in order to arrive at its present condition. Importantly, these were narrative explanations of the human condition that dispensed with a reliance on the influence of God on worldly affairs. Yet they were entirely 'conjectural' in the sense that they made no use of material evidence: they stated *what must have happened* in order for the modern world to have come into being. Only with the work of the Danish antiquary Christian Thomsen in creating the Three Age scheme of Stone, Bronze, and Iron at the start of the nineteenth century did archaeological materials begin to be placed in the Enlightenment scheme. These imagined histories were *stadial*. That is, they were composed of a series of stages of development. Thus Adam Smith proposed successive phases of hunting, herding, farming, and commerce. While these were based on different forms of subsistence, Adam Ferguson suggested instead a progression of social types: savagery, barbarism, and civilization.

Enlightenment historical narratives were generally grounded in the notion that human progress is achieved over time through the application of reason and free will in order to transform the material circumstances in which people find themselves. However, while the Scottish authors took a predominantly optimistic view of this process, the French and Germans often argued that there was a price to be paid for progress. Becoming civilized might result in a loss of spontaneity and freedom, and growing inequality and conformity. In reaction against the progressive visions of the Enlightenment (and the revolutionary views that they inspired), the Anglican cleric Thomas Malthus presented a much more pessimistic world-historical narrative, in which successive technological innovations enabled human populations to grow to new levels. But the effect of this was only to press harder on resources, increasing human misery and challenging ingenuity to develop further solutions. During the nineteenth century stadial histories became rather more inflexible, generally assuming that progress from simple to complex social forms was a universal pattern. As Europeans became more familiar with the inhabitants of the regions that they explored and colonized, different peoples were identified as representatives of distinct stages of social evolution. Anthropologists such as Edward Burnett Tylor and Lewis Henry Morgan developed increasingly complex evolutionary schemes populated by existing human communities, and these were then retrospectively applied to the European past. Thus the Neolithic might be identified with the transition from hunting to farming, or from savagery to barbarism.

A common characteristic of grand narratives is that they often identify a single factor as the prime mover in human development. For the Enlightenment *philosophes* this might be the emergence of modern commerce, the growth of learning, the extension of human freedom, the increasing sophistication of science and technology, or the elaboration of religious beliefs. Inevitably, whichever of these is given the causal role, the others are relegated to the place of consequences and outcomes. In the case of archaeological grand narratives, Andrew Sherratt pointed to the 'premise of calorific priority', the understanding that the acquisition of food is always the first consideration for human beings, and that all other aspects of life are secondary and subsidiary to subsistence. By contrast, Sherratt advocated an approach to long-term processes that saw no inevitable priority for any particular factor. Rather, large-scale structures emerged from a concatenation of circumstances in unpredictable ways. For him, the complex global systems within which we now find ourselves enmeshed were the outcome of the progressive synchronization of phenomena that might originally have been independent and unrelated.

An elegant example of an archaeological grand narrative is David Miles's *The Story of the Axe: How the Neolithic Revolution Transformed Britain*. Although Miles is principally concerned with the Neolithic as a decisive episode in history, his account spans the entire period from the origins of humans up to the present. The Neolithic is therefore placed into a long-term sequence of developments, beginning with progressive increases in hominin brain sizes, which enabled social interaction and cooperation to grow in scale. Alongside this process, humans learned to make more complex stone tools, to use language, to cook food on fires, and eventually to make containers and projectiles and to process and store foodstuffs. Throughout his account, humans are nudged or bludgeoned into economic intensification or migration between regions by episodes of climatic change: amelioration provides opportunities, declining conditions demand adaptation. For Miles, the Neolithic is synonymous with 'farming', and its emergence and spread were the almost inevitable consequence of big-brained humans being confronted with population growth and environmental fluctuations. Farming was a causal process, rather than one element of the Neolithic alongside others. It arrived in Britain as a 'cultural and economic tsunami'. Yet once it was installed in the islands, he has rather less to say about the practicalities of agriculture than about the axes, tombs, enclosures, and henges that were supposedly the products of the new subsistence system. Late in his book, Miles acknowledges the arguments of Stevens and Fuller, who infer that the scale of cereal cultivation declined precipitously after an initial 'honeymoon' period, only to recover in the middle of the Bronze Age. But the implications of this possibility for a model of social and cultural development driven by economic intensification are not really worked through.

Like the conjectural historians, Miles sees the transition from one economic stage to another as both categorical and encompassing diverse aspects of human life. Mesolithic hunters and Neolithic farmers had different and incompatible world views. Where foragers dwelt in the midst of nature and treated their prey with respect, agriculturalists sought to dominate and control land, animals, and plants, and to forcibly turn raw materials into artefacts. Living things were transformed from fellow inhabitants of the earth to commodities and possessions. For Miles, farmers universally have a utilitarian view of plants, animals, and land, which he demonstrates with examples drawn from his home in rural France. Agriculturalists therefore have archetypal characteristics, and having crossed a crucial threshold six thousand years ago, Neolithic people became broadly comparable with Miles's modern-day neighbours. However, where fellow writers of grand narratives, including Jared Diamond, have presented the beginning of food production and the relinquishment of hunter-gatherer lifestyles as a terrible mistake that resulted in declining health and social inequality, Miles is more optimistic. He points out that most of the benefits and comforts of modern civilization (from telecommunications to healthcare) would have been impossible without the Neolithic revolution. Miles acknowledges that global agriculture is out of control: industrialized farming relying on excessive use of fertilizers, too much production of meat, destruction of soils and habitats and the poisoning of the seas, and too much focus on unhealthy processed foods. Yet he comes to the somewhat whiggish[3] conclusion that all is not lost, and that human ingenuity may yet enable destructive practices to be reformed.

It is instructive to compare Miles's global narrative with John Robb's article 'Material Culture, Landscapes of Action, and Emergent Causation: A New Model for the Origins of the European Neolithic'. Where Miles presents a highly readable text for a wide audience, Robb's is an academic journal essay, but this is not the limit of the contrast. While Miles identifies the essence of the Neolithic with agriculture, and therefore sees the other innovations of the period as being the *products* of economic change, Robb begins by stressing that physical things are more than just inert matter that human beings act upon. Rather, objects can influence, channel, and impact upon our lives, and his principal claim is that the Neolithic involved a new set of relationships between people and things. Human beings have the freedom to act in pursuit of their goals and desires, but they always do so in a world that that has been formed by the activities of past generations. So what any of us can achieve at any particular moment depends upon whether we find ourselves in a paddy field, in a modern city centre, or in a nuclear wasteland. This is what he calls the 'landscape of action', and in the Neolithic it became progressively more structured. For Robb, the paradox of the Neolithic is that it spread directionally from east to west across the Old World, and that communities rarely reverted to a Mesolithic way of life, but that the local processes involved were multiple and distinctive. In some areas, major movements of population took place, while in others the contribution of indigenous people was greater. Not all the elements of the Neolithic assemblage occurred in all areas, and the duration of change varied considerably. Robb argues that causal mechanisms such as population growth and climatic change that operate at a pan-continental level are inadequate, since quite different sequences of events can be identified in different parts

---

3. 'Whiggish': a view deriving from an eighteenth-century 'liberal' view of the world that holds that history follows a path of inevitable progression and improvement, and that judges the past in the light of the perceived manifest achievements culminating in the present.

of Europe. Yet the outcomes of these multifarious developments became gradually more alike as time went on. Thus in many areas the Neolithic 'package' of innovations did not appear all at once, but was gradually assembled from elements whose adoption was spread over a period of time. This might arguably have been the case in Britain, for one of the findings of the *Gathering Time* analysis was that pottery and timber buildings could be identified at an earlier date than monument building or domesticated animals.

Robb's answer to his conundrum is that the reasons why people adopted Neolithic things and practices were various: sometimes social, sometimes economic, and sometimes ecological. But one thing that they always had in common was a change to a more 'thing-heavy' world, filled with axes, pottery vessels, houses, garden plots, coppices, herds of domesticated animals, tombs, enclosures, and trackways (see Fig. 1.3 for the stone axe quarry at Great Langdale in Cumbria).

Fig. 1.3 The Langdale Pikes, Cumbria, from beside Blea Tarn

The view in this photograph is northwards over Blea Tarn towards the Langdale Pikes. It features Gimmer Crag and beyond it to the left, the pillar-like profile of Pike of Stickle, and conveys something of the rugged grandeur of Langdale Fell. The valley below the Pikes is known as Mickleden, and nearly all the surrounding peaks west to Bowfell bear at least some traces of Neolithic quarrying, although the concentration of working areas was on the Pike. (See also Fig. 6.1.)

Photograph: early June 2014, © Keith Ray.

Collectively, these things encouraged people to act in particular ways, often without having to think about it. Although people had been diversely motivated to place themselves in this position, their lives became increasingly similar. For Robb, the Neolithic was 'sticky' or 'funnel-shaped', easier to get into than to extract oneself from, because the accumulating landscape of action was one that encouraged more and more reliance on material things. There was no prime mover, no universal explanation for why Europe became Neolithic, merely a tendency toward convergence, a ratchet that worked more smoothly in one direction than the other. Causation was therefore *emergent*, growing out of a nexus of factors and events, but nonetheless pressing in a single direction.

Writing 'the transformation of social worlds'

In this book, we provide a perspective arising from our own 'living-through' the movements and moments within archaeology, of historicism (witness Piggott's prehistoric 'cultures'), processualism (exemplified by Renfrew's social evolutionary polities), structuralism and 'post-processualism' (especially Hodder's symbolic and semiotic archaeology), and post-structuralism (for example, Tilley's reflexive 'phenomenology'). These '-isms' are abstractions that to some extent represent intellectual fashions and, in archaeology, they have been worked through in often idiosyncratic ways. Despite this, theory is a necessary precondition, not an optional extra, to archaeological interpretation, and we have formulated our theoretical position in response to the emergence of real-world concerns with gender, cultural relativity, and philosophical thinking that have their roots in the early twentieth century. Concerns with human being and time, with the allusiveness of cultural expression (verbal, literary, material), with materiality and substance, with social reproduction and the negotiation of competing interests, with the person versus collectivities of people, and so on, are central, rather than peripheral, to a successfully holistic approach to history and archaeology. It is not possible to adopt a neutral, 'pragmatic', or 'objectivist' approach to the past.[4] Equally, our approach is not exclusively explanatory in the narrow sense. That is, we do not only wish to identify the processes of cause and effect that link the artefacts, resources, structures, and practices of the

---

4. For 'pragmatic' and 'objectivist', see Glossary.

Neolithic, bringing about change. We equally seek to evaluate their significance or meaning, and identify their place in the fabric of prehistoric life. We generally accept the view that historical change emerges from a cauldron of contingent and interlocking circumstances, rather than assuming the straightforward, law-like character of billiard balls colliding with one another.

Our perspective is avowedly interpretive and anthropological, therefore, and it builds upon a series of basic propositions concerning society, material culture, and history. We have expressed this perspective here as being concerned with 'writing the transformations' of the 'social worlds' of the Neolithic in Britain, with particular reference to the multiplicity of Neolithic societies and their history. Our point of departure in such a project is an understanding that connectedness through descent and alliance has, necessarily, long been fundamental to the ways in which human societies are organized according to bonds of kinship (both real and fictive—because, among other things, this is how 'strangers' become assimilated within social groups), and to how individuals understand and negotiate their place within society. The 'social', then, is time-bound, and the 'weaving' of narrative that Whittle and his collaborators see as being made possible by refining chronology is also a necessary *interpretive* corollary of a concern with social practice and social change.

We intend that this book should provide a particular lens, therefore, through which we seek to view the distant cultural worlds of one period of British prehistory. Its theoretical bearings will nonetheless become more apparent in practical narrative and commentary in the pages that follow. We have attempted to isolate the principal social, economic, and cultural developments through a period of profound change in the landscape, physical and cultural, of Britain, lasting from the end of the fifth to the middle of the third millennium BCE. This account is deliberately more interpretive than descriptive, not least because there are already several excellent texts that provide an introduction to the monuments and artefacts of the period, and more will no doubt appear in the years to come. We focus in particular upon the key themes of social practice, kinship, and descent, and in doing so we hope to privilege neither the analytical framework of modern science nor the immediacy of experience. Given that our perspective is an anthropological one, we view the acquisition of sustenance, the conduct of relationships with animals, of ceremonial life, and of craft activities (for example) as aspects of an integrated way of life, rather than separate spheres to be investigated by different kinds of archaeologists. We have in a way dipped into the stream of stories that together made up the lived millennium and a half of the human past of Britain that we term 'Neolithic'. We have selected, and our 'samples' are necessarily partial. We hope, nonetheless, that the journey will prove interesting.

TWO

4000 BCE: a cultural threshold

Chapter frontispiece: 'White Arch, Rhoscolyn' (wood-engraving, Hilary Paynter)

This engraving features a clifftop on the southern end of Holy Island, off the western end of Anglesey. It is evocative of the rugged western coastlands of Britain, within walking distance of which were created many of the most impressive of the monuments of the Neolithic period. They were also close to the sea-lanes and coastal routeways used by prehistoric seafarers from the Mesolithic period onwards that sustained links between the littoral communities from Portugal northwards to the Shetland Islands across several millennia. The Early Neolithic houses at Llanfaethlu were built only ten kilometres or so away, on the west coast of Anglesey facing the northern part of Holy Island (see Fig. 3.3).

Engraving: 1990, © Hilary Paynter (website: http://www.hilarypaynter.com).

The archaeological evidence that has accumulated over the past five decades demonstrates that two very different situations existed successively in Britain in the centuries on either side of 4000 BCE. While this is in some ways an arbitrary date, it is nonetheless a convenient one, since there are very few indications that 'Neolithic' artefacts and structures existed in Britain for long before the turn of the fourth millennium. Up until 4000 BCE (or perhaps a century or two earlier), the mainland and islands were populated by people who were heavily dependent upon hunting and gathering; afterwards the population lived a way of life that to a greater or lesser extent relied on herding and cultivating. Further, whereas the technology of the hunting societies had been skilfully made but was highly portable, more durable artefacts and architecture now proliferated, creating a much denser world of crafted things. However, the available evidence can be cast in a number of different ways, with the material before and after the critical date being capable of sustaining either maximal or minimal interpretations. As a consequence, the ways in which the character and degree of change across the threshold can be understood are also multiple and varied.

Differing views of a threshold

As we saw in Chapter 1, the archaeologists of the 1920s to 1960s emphasized the contrast between the Mesolithic and the Neolithic. Before the 'transition' between the two, Britain was home to a sparse population of hunter-foragers who followed game (including deer, wild pig, and wild cattle) and collected plants, nuts, and berries, and, for those near the sea, exploited marine resources. They had few, often simple artefacts, although it was acknowledged that significant skill was invested in some of them. They lived in informal campsites composed of rudimentary shelters while pursuing a transient way of life. Afterwards, in contrast, there were settled agriculturalists living in stable communities, in well-built houses, enjoying a mixed farming subsistence base. They were capable of building barrows and tombs for their dead, which may have demonstrated their incorporation into a widespread megalithic cult. The dichotomy between these two ways of life demanded that some fundamental change must have separated them, of whatever kind. Gordon Childe initially imagined that this involved a transformation in the way of life of the native people, with only monumental architecture being introduced from the Continent. Later, he and others preferred the explanation that agriculture had been brought to Britain by immigrants, who had established pioneer communities in a new island setting. The indigenous Mesolithic people of Britain had meanwhile either died out or, as we have seen, been later drawn into the new way of life, contributing to the formation of Stuart Piggott's Secondary Neolithic Communities.

The accumulation of evidence since this time has created a situation that is messier and more complex. In the first place, new investigations, including scientific analyses and insights gained from researching old data anew, are cumulatively revealing these Mesolithic people to have been more sophisticated than previously imagined, in several ways. Recent studies have shown that Mesolithic communities were able to achieve a variety of outcomes that once would have seemed unlikely for them. Among other things, they were capable of colonizing Ireland, the Scilly Isles, the Hebrides, and Shetland by sea, while the genetics of modern snails indicate that there was maritime contact between Ireland and Iberia during the Mesolithic. It has also been suggested that the Isle of Man must have been in frequent contact with Britain or Ireland during the period in order to maintain a viable human population. Such was the degree of logistical sophistication amongst Mesolithic people that they were capable of introducing red deer to offshore islands by sea, and perhaps also of bringing wild pigs to Ireland. Furthermore, Mesolithic communities raised substantial pine posts to mark particularly significant locations. As recently as 2012, moreover, an oak post bearing complex geometric carvings on its side was found buried in peat at a site near Maerdy overlooking the upper Rhondda Valley in south Wales (Fig. 2.1). It has been convincingly dated from dendrochronological samples of its sapwood to around 4175 BCE, and this suggests that late Mesolithic peoples living in Britain were capable of producing elaborate designs that echo similarly complex contemporary patterns carved in wood in Scandinavia by similarly 'Mesolithic' people, and that prefigured those known in stone in British passage tombs from several centuries later.

Indeed, the Maerdy decoration has also been compared with that on the stones of the large passage tomb of Gavrinis in the Gulf of Morbihan. If so, this would be an indication that the Mesolithic people of Wales had some contact with Neolithic communities in Brittany, a theme to which we shall soon return. These hunter-gatherer people occasionally built structures as robust as any of the small-scale domestic dwellings built by later inhabitants, and in the earlier part of the period substantial houses are known from Howick in Northumberland and Star Carr in Yorkshire. They worked flint

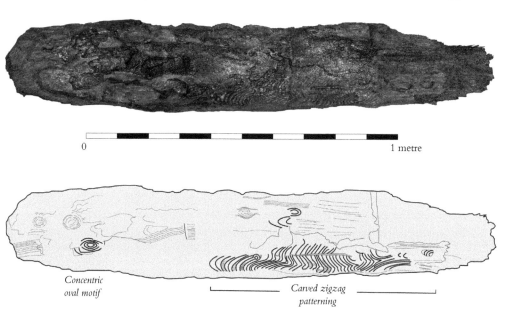

0   1 metre

Concentric
oval motif   Carved zigzag
                                             patterning

Fig. 2.1 The Maerdy (Rhondda) carved oak post
The oak post retrieved from waterlogged ground during archaeological excavations in advance of the construction of a wind farm on the slopes above the upper Rhondda valley features a series of zigzag lines carved carefully into one side. The surprise is that such elaborate carving appears to date to the Late Mesolithic rather than the Neolithic period. The pattern of curving zigzag or 'rippling' lines has resonances with contemporary passage-tomb art in Neolithic Brittany.
Images: © and courtesy of Richard Scott Jones (HRS Wales).

nodules to make and exchange stone axes and adzes that could in turn be used to work wood. And they made and used stone maceheads (pebble-like stones with drilled perforations presumably for hafting) that were either used as weapons or were emblems of power (or both), thereby marking and maintaining personal social authority or seniority.

The precise level of population toward the end of the Mesolithic is diffi-cult to ascertain, given that the archaeological visibility of *any* pre-Neolithic community in Britain is modest. The reasons for this are easy to appreciate: not only are hunting and gathering societies often mobile, minimizing their belongings to facilitate portability, but they also often observe cultural prohibitions against the accumulation of possessions. At the same time, the comparative scarcity of cut features such as pits, ditches, and post-holes dating to the Mesolithic that might serve as 'traps' for artefacts appreciably reduces the extent to which activity can be recognized by archaeologists, while also restricting the opportunity to recover samples suitable for dating. Mesolithic use of caves and rock shelters has been demonstrated in several regions, prefiguring Neolithic (and later) use of these same, or similar sites for the disposal of the dead.

Other new discoveries offer the prospect of a significant rethinking of the whole organization of society in Late Mesolithic Britain. One example derives from the investigation of a pit containing cremated human bone during the construction of a pipeline at Langford near Maldon in Essex late in 2014. The pit was assumed to be Bronze Age in date by its excavators, since its form was identical to myriad similar others when revealed, investigated, and recorded. That is, until the report on the radiocarbon dating of the cremated bone early in 2015 revealed that the bodies concerned had been committed to the pyre around 5600 BCE. Meanwhile, the extreme scarcity of sites dating to the final Mesolithic, and the perceived chronological 'gap' between Mesolithic and Neolithic is starting to be eroded. Locations such as the tree-throw hole (the ragged-edged, often crescent-shaped pit produced by the lifting of the root-bole of a tree blown or pulled over) containing Mesolithic flints at Irthlingborough Island in Northamptonshire, and Pennine sites such as March Hill and South Haw, are now producing dates in the late fifth and early fourth millennium BCE, actually overlapping with the earliest Neolithic presence in Britain. Furthermore, recent excavations by Oxford Archaeology North at the site of Stainton West near Carlisle in Cumbria have revealed a large occupation dating the period to around 4300 BCE, immediately before the start of the Neolithic. This produced an assemblage of over 300,000 flaked stones, which included pieces of pitchstone from the Isle of Arran, till flint from East Yorkshire and pebble flint from the Cumbrian coast, radiolarian chert from the southern uplands of Scotland, Carboniferous chert from the Pennine Hills, and volcanic tuff from the Lake District. Evidently, this was a location at which substantial gatherings took place, and that demonstrates social connections and patterns of movement spanning a vast area of northern Britain.

On the other hand, during the first few decades or centuries of the Neolithic period in Britain, people constructed very few substantial monuments of earth or stone, and the scale of their cereal gardens and animal herds may have been quite modest to begin with. And although it is difficult to specify what the balance was between hunting and gathering on the one hand and farming on the other, there is appreciable evidence to support the notion that animal hunting and plant collecting, if not sea fishing (and as practices, rather than an 'economy'), remained integral to the subsistence concerns of people living in Britain after 4000 BCE. Initially at least, the contrast in the scale of activity between Mesolithic and Neolithic may not have been as great as it is sometimes portrayed.

However much this may be the case, the attraction of interpretations that rely on a complete discontinuity between the two periods remains considerable. The past two decades have seen new finds of timber-built houses dating to the earliest Neolithic, and a refinement of dating techniques has enabled us to chart for the first time the earliest appearance and subsequent geographical dispersal of Neolithic innovations. These developments have contributed to a reinstatement of arguments attributing the initiation of the Neolithic to a process of large-scale population movement from the Continent. However, one issue that remains unclear is the extent to which the various novelties that were introduced during the period constituted an integrated 'package', occurring alongside each other from the start.

In *The Tale of the Axe*, already discussed in Chapter 1, David Miles has clearly restated the case for a transition from 'gathering' to 'farming' that was wholly attributable to the movement of distinct (and implicitly ethnically homogeneous) groups of people on a substantial scale. In the book, Miles asserts that a new orthodoxy has increasingly held sway since the 1970s. This is that the transformation into a 'fully' Neolithic Britain could not have been as abrupt or as wholly externally inspired as was previously thought. He says, 'until recently, it has been fashionable among English archaeologists to dismiss the idea of wholesale migration from the Continent and instead emphasize the role of the, *albeit invisible*, indigenous population' (p. 226, our emphasis). He continues,

> According to this view of the origin of the Neolithic, British hunter-gatherers gradually selected and adopted elements of the Neolithic package. Domestic animals could fit relatively easily into the mobile, Mesolithic way of life. Continued mobility would explain the flint-scatters, the limited evidence of cereals and, above all, the absence of continental-style houses.

Miles then goes on to demonstrate what he sees as the limitations of such a view, by describing his visit to see an Early Neolithic hall-like rectangular building being excavated a few years ago at the White Horse Stone site in Kent. This structure was found—somewhat amusingly, it has to be conceded—as a result of the construction of a high-speed rail link to Europe through the Channel Tunnel. His account of that visit and his interpretation of what it signifies for the transition period are worth considering at some length, and we shall therefore return to a discussion of it later in this chapter.

This is not least because re-examination of what was actually found at the White Horse Stone site poses some interesting, perhaps even fundamental, questions regarding the nature of the evidence for the earliest Neolithic in Britain and what it tells us about what was novel and what persistent in island culture in the years following 4000 BCE.

Yet what remains undisputed is that there was a relatively rapid transformation in the outward appearance and seemingly also the basic concerns of communities in Britain between 4100 and 3800 BCE, that was made manifest for example in the use of pottery, polished stone axes, certain kinds of flint tool, the planting and growing of several kinds of grain, and the keeping of domesticated animals such as pigs, sheep, goats, and, above all, cattle. In the midst of all this, these post-4000 BCE inhabitants of the British mainland, and some islands, also began constructing sometimes massive rectangular timber halls, and some while later started burying some at least of their dead in purpose-built repositories. In this context, it is not at all surprising that the people who did all these things were presumed to have been, wholly, exclusively, and from the start, immigrants from the continent of Europe where many of these cultural attributes had long existed. Yet this is not the only interpretation that has been proposed, and even those arguments that presume some form of population movement are highly varied in character. With these points in mind, we need to explore and explain the complexities of the processes involved in the establishment of a radically different set of cultural practices, unquestionably evident in the archaeological record of Britain sixty centuries ago.

To that end, it is important not to assume that the structures, artefacts, species, and practices that manifested themselves in Britain during the fifth to fourth millennia BCE necessarily represented an invariant and closely bounded package of elements that could only travel through space and time alongside closed groups of pioneer people with a uniform ethnic or genetic identity. But equally, we should not imagine that these innovations were simply cultural 'traits' that could be readily exchanged between social groups living in different locations and leading different kinds of lives. Whatever the mechanisms involved, the arrival of the Neolithic involved both a transfer of technology and a transformation of everyday practices and social relationships, potentially achieved in a variety of ways, but the ultimate outcome of which was comprehensive and irreversible. Appreciating the character of these developments demands a recognition that they involved a complex combination of continuity and change.

Continuities across the threshold

It is one thing to assert persistence within a pattern of change, and quite another matter to be able to document it closely. We think, however, that in order to achieve this we must look at changes and continuities in *practices* as attested in the archaeology we encounter, rather than simply focusing upon objects or structures that we can all too easily regard as somehow emblematic or representative of those changes or continuities. For example, people living in diverse locations across Britain well before 4000 BCE had repeatedly met at particular places to share collective meals, and to make and exchange objects including flint tools and (sometimes) axes, while at the same time they quite probably spent much of their time in small family or task groups, or even individually, ranging widely across the landscape. It is of more than passing interest in this context that one of the main ways that we know about these occasional meeting places is that traces of Mesolithic activity have been identified sealed beneath substantial monumental structures of Neolithic date. At both Hazleton North in Gloucestershire and Ascott-under-Wychwood in Oxfordshire, chambered long cairns were constructed in locations that contained both concentrations of Mesolithic chipped stone tools and midden deposits indicating gatherings of people and the collective consumption of food in the earliest Neolithic. At Gwernvale in south Wales, another such long cairn had been built over a prominent boulder that had served as a focus for the deposition of flint burins and microlithic tools during the Mesolithic, and pottery, axe fragments, and leaf-shaped arrowheads at the start of the Neolithic. At Crarae in Argyll, and Glecknabae on the Isle of Bute, chambered tombs had been constructed over heaps of marine shells and other debris of Mesolithic date, known as 'shell middens'.

In other cases, human bones of Neolithic date had been introduced into these shell middens, or into rock shelters that had been occupied in the Mesolithic. Examples include An Corran on the Isle of Skye, and Raschoille Cave near Oban. At Cnoc Coig on the island of Oronsay the situation is more complex. Human bones began to be inserted into the midden there around 4000 BCE, but have produced stable isotopic signatures (see Glossary) suggesting a predominantly marine diet, generally considered a hallmark of a Mesolithic way of life. So did the change of mortuary activity amongst these indigenous people at the dawn of the Neolithic

Fig. 2.2 Down Farm shaft, Cranborne Chase

This photograph shows the natural solution-hollow that was used as a place for depositing cultural items, and possibly also 'waste' materials, in the fifth and fourth millennia BCE. As is standard archaeological practice, only one side of the hollow has been fully excavated at this stage, so that the 'section' can be drawn to illustrate the pattern of infilling.

Photograph: © Martin Green.

period indicate that they were being drawn into a new world, emulating the practices of other communities?

Other kinds of sites also see the coincidence of Mesolithic and Neolithic activity. At Fir Tree Field on Cranborne Chase in North Dorset, a deep natural solution shaft descending through the chalk underwent a process of gradual infill from the seventh millennium BCE onwards (Fig. 2.2).

Two roe deer appear to have fallen into the shaft in the later fifth millennium BCE, indicating that it was open at that point. Shortly afterwards, probably in 4240–4100 BCE, as the shaft was becoming infilled naturally, a group of small flints which probably represent the barbs of a compound weapon (an arrow or spear) came to rest in a layer that also contained fragments of disarticulated animal bones. The presence of a scatter of Mesolithic flints and pits containing burnt flints nearby indicates that the immediate area had been sporadically visited by hunters throughout the Mesolithic period. A little higher in the shaft, bones of domesticated cattle and pigs, Neolithic pottery and a ground flint axe fragment occurred, yet these may have been deposited a century or two after the Mesolithic remains.

At Spurryhillock in Aberdeenshire, a pit that produced a radiocarbon date of 4900–4300 BCE was identified in the midst of a scatter of Early Neolithic debris, while at Chapelfield near Stirling a group of Mesolithic pits had been re-dug in the Neolithic. Finally, at Perry Oaks in Greater London the central earthen bank of a massive linear monument known as the Stanwell Cursus sealed a group of pits containing burnt flints that had been dated by thermoluminescence methods (q.v.) to the seventh millennium BCE. A possible Mesolithic midden may have lain nearby. A little to the south, a group of substantial post-holes which might have been either Mesolithic or Neolithic in date was also incorporated into the monument. The excavators conjectured that the cursus had been deliberately constructed in such a way as to connect these groups of earlier features together.

In none of these examples is there compelling evidence for unbroken continuity of activity across the temporal boundary between Mesolithic and Neolithic, and sometimes the chronological gap between the two may be one of hundreds of years. What seems undeniable is that these locations were identified as places of enduring ancestral significance, which were memorialized, revered, and venerated over many generations. They attracted later activity of various kinds, owing to the occurrences and ceremonies that had occurred there, time out of mind. They formed parts of the collectively remembered geography that enabled people to make themselves at home in a landscape. It is difficult to imagine how these places would have been recalled and returned to if one population, of indigenous hunter-gatherers, had been replaced by another, composed of pioneer colonists who were entirely unfamiliar with the land, with complete discontinuity. How, then, would their cultural importance have been appreciated and transmitted through time?

While it is supposed that a wide range of gathering- and foraging-related subsistence practices continued throughout the period concerned, some specific foodstuffs and their residues appear to have had a continuing resonance over and above their calorific value. Gathered substances such as crab apples are well represented among the surviving traces of such collected foods, but pre-eminent among them are hazelnuts. This is due to some degree to their durability when carbonized, which leads to greater archaeological visibility in early fourth-millennium deposits. By the by, this also renders them more important to archaeologists owing to the capacity of their shells to be preserved, while also representing short-lived organic items that can therefore provide radiocarbon dating precision for the contexts concerned (see An outline of chronologies). Significant numbers of hazelnut shells have been found in several late Mesolithic contexts (for example at two sites at Goldcliff, just to the east of the Usk estuary in south Wales), but they are also remarkably common in the more frequently encountered Early Neolithic deposits. Such ubiquity is, for instance, to be gauged by the discovery of hazelnut shells among the debris of most of the known early timber halls in Scotland, and especially at Claish Farm in Perthshire.

Although the presence of hazelnut shells in such deposits is well known and well documented, their significance has rarely been debated among archaeologists. It is broadly acknowledged that they constituted such a readily available foodstuff that they would have provided an obvious dietary supplement. However, the 'wild' status of hazel trees in the fourth millennium has occasionally been questioned, given the widespread evidence for hazel coppicing from an early stage in the Neolithic. It may of course be the case that such coppicing was practised in the Mesolithic also, although this has been remarked upon less often. Be that as it may, the key point to be understood here is that hazelnuts were important to the Early Neolithic communities just as they had been to the preceding fifth-millennium people in Britain. Moreover, given an apparent decline in hazelnut consumption (and more especially in their deliberate inclusion in buried deposits) by the end of the third millennium BCE, it is likely that there was a cultural and symbolic significance for these nuts in the Mesolithic and through much of the Neolithic that was just as fundamental to explaining their ubiquity as any 'economic' consideration.

Equally, the raising of wooden posts, and possibly also in some places of tall stones, is a practice that has only recently been realized was a feature of the life of some Mesolithic communities. At Stonehenge, immediately north of the location where the circles and arcs of standing stones were later to be raised, this involved creating a line of three posts, perhaps dug sequentially in the period between the ninth and the seventh millennia BCE. A fourth feature nearby may have been a treehole, while a fifth was revealed about 100 metres further east in 1988. This implies that the people who raised them (or whose forebears had done so) returned to the site at intervals to renew their marking of the place or to commemorate ceremonies conducted there. That these are by no means alone is indicated by the eighth-millennium dating of a pair of similar posts at Hambledon Hill in north Dorset. At this site, these features were 'submerged' under a welter of traces of subsequent Early Neolithic activity (see Chapters 3 and 4), and it is only because there was a major programme of excavation, and in recent years a significant amount of analysis of dating evidence, that their presence there was detected. The posts at Hambledon Hill would have been a very visible feature of the landscape both on the hill itself and beyond. A further group of six less substantial timber uprights, dating to the middle of the fifth millennium BCE, was recently located on the Thames foreshore at Vauxhall, close to the present-day home of UK government intelligence services. These may originally have stood on dry land, potentially forming a monumental structure, platform, or bridge of some kind.

At the time when the pine posts at Stonehenge were first discovered and dated, there was very little evidence of Mesolithic activity in the near environs. However, in recent years fieldwork at Blick Mead, Amesbury, on the banks of the River Avon only a mile to the east of Stonehenge, has transformed appreciation of the local cultural context. This work has revealed a location close to a spring, with evidence of intense episodes of deposition during the Mesolithic period, in a pool whose active use apparently extended from the mid eighth millennium BCE right down to the late fifth millennium. The scale of deposition involved, and the fresh condition of much of the flintwork retrieved in the excavations, imply that the deposits derive from large-scale gatherings at, or very near to, the locality in question. This was a large, dense, and long-lived site, at which the meat of large animals, and particularly wild cattle, was consumed on a considerable scale. Stone tools were manufactured on site, implying that it was occupied for appreciable periods of time. The tooth of a dog recovered from the site has produced isotopic measurements (see Glossary) that indicate that it may have been raised in the Vale of York, while some of the stone tools on the site derived from sources as far away as Wales and the Midlands. Like Stonehenge after it (and Stainton West at much the same time), Blick Mead was a place that was connected to a much wider world through the movements of people, animals, and things. In the immediate region, concentrations of Mesolithic stone tools have also now been identified just west of Stonehenge, and beside the River Avon at Durrington Walls, West Amesbury, and Countess Farm, as well as downriver at Downton. As we will see in Chapter 5, there is now good reason to believe that Stonehenge was eventually constructed in a landscape that had been intensively occupied from the Mesolithic onwards. At Stonehenge itself, the recovery of a fragment of bovid bone radiocarbon-dated to the fifth millennium BCE from the packing of Sarsen stone 27 may indicate that large mammals such as aurochs (wild cattle,

Bos primigenius) were hunted over a significant area of Salisbury Plain, whose comparatively open landscape was partially maintained by the browsing of the animals themselves.

Meanwhile there is also evidence, supported by radiocarbon dating, that gatherings that involved the digging and filling of pits were taking place in the later Mesolithic period close to the spectacular outcrops of stone jutting out of the hilltop on Carn Menyn on the top of the Preseli Hills in north Pembrokeshire. We now know from excavations in the Brynberian/Nyfer valley at Craig-Rhosyfelin and at nearby Carn Goedog on Mynydd Preseli that long tabular-shaped stones were prised from similar natural stone outcrops and were being shaped nearby, during the fourth millennium BCE (Fig. 2.3). This of course again has a Stonehenge resonance, in that the

Fig. 2.3 Carn Goedog, Preseli: stone quarry

Carn Goedog is located to the south of Newport near the north coast of Pembrokeshire. The opinions of geologists differ slightly over the processes whereby these massive stone outcrops came into being in the Ice Ages. Their craggy, almost spiky appearance today, however, is probably much as it would have been five and a half thousand years ago in the Neolithic. This view is northwards towards Newport Bay with Carn Ingli to the left and the valley of the Afon Nyfer behind the Carn. The excavation in progress on the southern margins of the Carn in 2016 was one of a series of exploratory investigations in the locality being undertaken as part of a project led by Mike Parker Pearson looking for the sources of the Stonehenge bluestones.

Photograph: September 2016 by Keith Ray, with thanks to Professor Mike Parker Pearson and Adam Stanford (pictured undertaking drone-based photography at the site).

bluestones from Preseli were subsequently a considerable feature in the early 'stone-built' phases of that monument in the early third millennium BCE (see Chapter 5). So several aspects of the Stonehenge story had Mesolithic antecedents.

It would seem, then, that this kind of gathering, and the erection of structures composed of timber and possibly also of stone, and quite probably also long-distance contacts, were a feature of the 'Mesolithic world' in Britain. The distances involved in such contacts, including by sea, have been confirmed by discoveries in the Isles of Scilly, again very recently. So, during recent excavations at Old Quay, St. Martin's, a Mesolithic worked flint assemblage was retrieved, the closest affinities of which appear to be from the Rhine-Meuse-Scheldt region in modern Belgium and Holland. This is over 861 km (535 miles) on a direct line over the sea, but up to half as long again if, as was likely, such a journey was made close to the coastline of southern Britain (which extended slightly further southwards than it does today, given that the post-glacial Holocene coastal inundations had yet to reach their modern extent). In discussing marine journeying around Britain and Ireland in the fifth and fourth millennia BCE, Duncan Garrow and Fraser Sturt have suggested that it may be unhelpful to identify this activity as distinctively or exclusively Mesolithic or Neolithic in character. Instead, this may be another area of continuity across the boundary: a maritime culture that was not closely linked to a particular terrestrial subsistence pattern.

The practice of raising timber posts, again, is something that became ubiquitous in the Neolithic in Britain, and the post-holes marking lines of such posts have been found in locations ranging from Hampshire to the Scottish lowlands. One difference, however, is that instead of being isolated standing forms, or single lines, as in the Mesolithic, these posts formed, from an early stage in the fourth millennium, parts of more complex arrangements. In some cases, as at Douglasmuir, Kinalty, and Inchbare in Scotland, these constituted rectilinear enclosures defined by free-standing uprights, sometimes with internal divisions, and possibly vaguely evocative of domestic architecture. These have been referred to as post-defined cursus monuments, and are discussed further in Chapter 3. Other arrangements of posts formed screens or façades, as with the structure associated with a hearth, a concentration of flint and animal bone, and human skull fragments, beneath the Hazleton North barrow. A further linear group of large posts was associated with an elaborate sequence of mound construction, early pottery vessels, and the placing of human remains in rudimentary chamber structures at Eweford West, east of Edinburgh in East Lothian. These various structures can arguably be identified with indigenous traditions as much as with Continental inspiration.

Perhaps equally significant, though documented in fewer places as yet, is the digging of lines of pits across the landscape. One site where this has been closely documented is at Warren Field, Crathes, in the Dee valley west of Aberdeen. Here, an alignment of thirteen pits (some of which may have held posts) was spaced between two and three metres apart. The line ran along the base of a slope on an orientation set obliquely towards the north bank of the River Dee. Six of the pits had fill-sequences that were radiocarbon-dated: the initial digging of three of the pits was found to have taken place around 8000 cal BCE, another was found to date to around 7500 and another to around 7000. This latter pit was apparently re-dug on a number of occasions (as were three others in the line), the penultimate fill being dated to the middle of the sixth millennium, and the latest fill early in the fourth millennium. The upper fill of an adjacent pit produced an exactly similar date. The significance of this is the continuity of practice that it demonstrates, albeit at intervals, throughout 4,000 years; as well as the fact that the later dates bridge the Mesolithic/Neolithic divide. Similarly, at Nosterfield Quarry in Yorkshire a double line of pits has produced a radiocarbon date in the mid fifth millennium, in a location close to fourth-/third-millennium Neolithic cursus monuments and henges at Thornborough. A similar alignment of pits, also running obliquely towards (and in this case across) a river, has been found by geophysical survey in the Golden Valley in Herefordshire, close to Dorstone Hill and the Neolithic chambered tomb known as Arthur's Stone, also in Dorstone. At this location one of only two pits (out of a line of at least ten pits) that were subsequently sample-excavated produced a diagnostic fourth-millennium worked flint from its upper fill, leaving open the possibility that, as with the Crathes situation, the pits were initially dug during the Mesolithic period.

The way in which animals were exploited changed markedly between the late Mesolithic and the Early Neolithic, in that there were no domesticates in the subsistence repertoire before 4100 BCE (although domesticated dogs had long been the companions of hunting people), but after 3800 their bones dominate the great majority of contexts examined. And yet there were continuities of practice that indicate that many of the habitual relationships between people and animals continued across the threshold, and that the wild animals of the preceding period continued to be preyed upon by, and potentially to have had a special relationship with, the people of the later period. For example, late Mesolithic communities hunted certain kinds of animal, such as deer and wild cattle, that lived at least some of the time in herds. These indigenous communities also deliberately intervened in the landscape to create or enhance clearings to improve grazing for such wild animals, and would have monitored their movements closely.

Red deer and roe deer were likely to have been 'harvested' in this way, but their herding and feeding patterns contrasted markedly with those of wild cattle, which were also subject to specialized hunting. Wild cattle, a considerably larger and more robust animal than the domesticated cattle that derived ultimately from the area of modern Turkey, were only seasonally a herd animal, and then only in herds of thirty or so individuals. They were grazing animals that inhabited wetter parts of the landscape in Britain, as opposed to deer that were browsers inhabiting mostly wooded areas. Bones of wild cattle have been recovered in quantity at Mesolithic sites such as Goldcliff on the Severn Estuary and, as we have seen, at Blick Mead, Amesbury, and this indicates both that they were a favoured source of meat and other products such as hide, and that the consumption of their flesh often took place in the context of significant gatherings of people. They continued to be hunted in the Early Neolithic period and beyond, as is attested by the fact that their remains have been found in small quantities at some sites, often alongside domesticated cattle and deer, including during the transitional period.

Both red deer and roe deer bones were found together with a substantial quantity of other bones, predominantly of cattle, and broken objects, in a large Early Neolithic pit at Coneybury near Stonehenge. The nature and condition of the bones from this pit (many were those of young animals, and fine butchery marks on the bones indicated the processing of carcasses for immediate consumption) point to the likelihood of early summer gathering and feasting—again linking positively with the evidence of communal Mesolithic feasting at Blick Mead less than a mile away. That there was a close familiarity with, and attachment to, red deer among these very early Neolithic communities is evident from the numbers and careful arrangement of red deer antlers in the backfilling of the shafts and galleries of flint mines in Sussex (see Chapter 4). On the near Continent, such mines had primarily been dug using stone axes, whereas in southern Britain, only collected and carefully prepared shed deer antlers were used as digging tools in such locations. Both the restriction of the use of objects made from flint

Fig. 2.4 'Bluestonehenge', Amesbury Riverside site, Wiltshire: antler-pick
This antler used as a pick is shown as found: lying on primary infill deposits close to the base of the quarry-ditch surrounding the henge that was built on the west bank of the Salisbury Avon river in the early fourth millennium BCE, now just to the south of Amesbury, Wiltshire. The Preseli bluestones formerly located here were probably removed to Stonehenge within a generation or two. The remains of the henge were levelled most probably in the medieval period. This pick was one of a number of almost-complete specimens from the site, shown here being excavated by Ellie Hunt. Unlike those from fourth-millennium BCE sites that were rarely modified before use, Late Neolithic antler-picks from sites such as Grimes Graves and Durrington Walls were frequently so prepared, as in this case with the deliberately blunted tines. In most cases throughout the Neolithic, the picks were made from shed antlers rather than from those still attached to skulls.
Photograph: © Adam Stanford and the Stonehenge Riverside Project.

available within these mines and worked into axes on the surface, and the careful deposition of the antler-picks, indicate a deliberate choice to use the antlers. In turn this suggests that the people concerned had a close connection with these animals, which may have involved a recognition of their importance to people in the by-then receding past (see Fig. 2.4 for the discovery of a later example of an antler-pick).

Innovative communities and their practices

To talk of a threshold at a particular point in time emphasizes the transition that certainly occurred at the end of the fifth millennium, but it also potentially telescopes the timescale too much. There were more than two centuries during which change occurred, and Neolithic things and practices were established in the south-east of England considerably earlier than in Wales, Scotland, or the south-west peninsula. Moreover, these were centuries in which there was experimentation, and a certain amount of diversity, based upon emergent practices and already existing cultural differences. This was a period of contact and transformation occurring at various rates of change at different places. It is therefore open to question how much of this change would have been perceived as 'revolutionary' by those actively caught up in its midst. Nonetheless, innovation there undoubtedly was, and along with it a significant cumulative shift in identity. It is therefore not unreasonable to talk of innovative, or innovating, communities.

Such innovation included the manufacture and use of some kinds of object that became ubiquitous in the earliest Neolithic of the British Isles but that had no discernible presence in the later Mesolithic. A prime example is leaf-shaped flint arrowheads. These are oval-shaped or pear-shaped wafer-thin flints, the 'blanks' for which had been struck from flint nodules or pebbles.[1] These blanks were then carefully subject to further subtle chipping on both sides of the flake. They occur in a variety of nonetheless closely similar shapes (pear-shaped, tear-shaped, ogival, diamond-shaped, and so on, as well as and perhaps more so than leaf-shaped), often with very narrow pointed ends and rounded bases (where they were hafted into wooden shafts). Whether used to intercept deer, bring down birds, or slay semi-domesticates such as pigs, these arrowheads testify to the practice of hunting, and in these terms are markers of continuities of practice with those of the fifth millennium. That said, similar, though not identical, flint arrowheads were an innovation among groups in Belgium in the later fifth millennium. These latter arrowheads lack the fine 'invasive' retouch found on the British examples, and are found in assemblages that also include triangular and chisel-shaped projectile points, which do not occur in Britain at this date. While their character in Britain diverged markedly from those in continental Europe, their adoption and use clearly signalled new practices within the hunting repertoire and a break with former practices of arrow hafting and traditions of flintworking.

---

1. Although it should be noted that Roger Ellaby (see Bibliographical commentary) has suggested that an apparent decline in the use of microliths towards the end of the fifth millennium could be ascribed to a possible *Late Mesolithic* indigenous 'invention' of this distinctive form of insular arrowhead (see also Anderson-Whymark and Garrow (2015, 70) for a discussion of how the otherwise similar 'Michelsberg' Continental arrowheads feature a different technique of production).

The wide dispersal of leaf-shaped arrowheads in the British landscape not only testifies to the lengthy span of time that they were subsequently in use during the Neolithic period, but also the extent of the territories across which individuals and groups of people ranged on foot over the terrain on hunting and other expeditions. These arrowheads were not necessarily more capable of killing or wounding larger game animals than the composite points, with multiple microliths inserted into the arrow-shaft, that were used in the Later Mesolithic. However, they were perhaps easier and quicker to make and to haft. They also, perhaps incidentally, facilitated the use of arrows in conflicts between human groups, and this is a subject that will be returned to in Chapters 3 and 4.

Nor were these arrowheads the only flint artefacts to represent innovation in the transitional period. While the scrapers, awls, 'fabricators', and borers that were a feature of late Mesolithic toolkits continued to be made, and narrow-blade-based technologies continued in use, new forms such as 'plano-convex' knives (with one side flat, the other curved), sickles (curved flakes, sometimes with indications of use for cutting plant stems), and laurel leaves (elongated bifacially-worked flint objects) were rapidly brought into the repertoire. Furthermore, it was not only the forms of flint manufacture that were innovative, but also some of the means by which the raw materials were obtained. Flint from beach and river pebbles, and from river gravels, or from nodules collected from clay-with-flint surface deposits covering chalklands, continued to be used for everyday items and 'expedient' working to create task-related toolkits in the very early Neolithic, as they had done in the Mesolithic period. In marked contrast, however, nodular flint was quarried, and even mined, at an early stage in the Neolithic, to obtain material that could be worked specifically to create objects for exchange— and especially axes. Although in some cases flint cores may have circulated as exchange items, more commonly the early stages of working axes will have occurred in the vicinity of the mines, creating flaked axes that had not yet been ground and polished. A group of such axes, flaked but unpolished, was discovered at Peaslake in Surrey in 1937, for instance.

It is likely that the flint mines of the Sussex Downs (the character and significance of which are described in greater detail in Chapters 3 and 4) were in use by 3900 BCE, while recent radiocarbon results raise the possibility that some of them may be even earlier. This places them amongst the earliest substantial Neolithic works in southern Britain. It is therefore arguable that their creation was not simply a side-product of the establishment

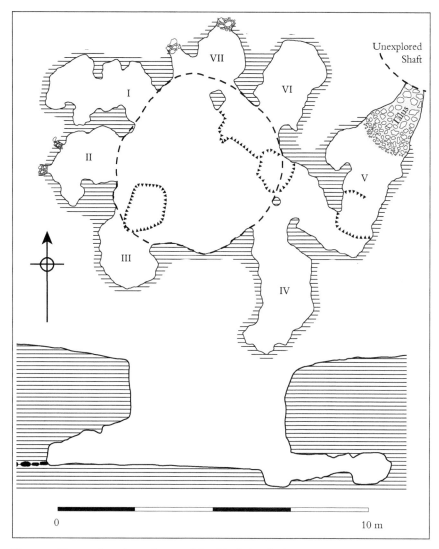

Fig. 2.5 Plan and section of one of the Black Patch flint mines, Sussex

The plan shows the location and extent of the seven radiating galleries leading from the base of the 7-m-wide shaft dug up to 5 m down into the chalk. The east–west cross-section extends from Gallery II to Gallery V, and indicates the often less than 2-m height of each gallery. The interconnection with an unexplored shaft to the north-east demonstrates the intensity with which productive seams of flint nodules were exploited.

Redrawn by Julian Thomas from original plan by Goodman, Frost, Curwen, and Curwen.

of agricultural settlement, but may actually have been instrumental in bringing about economic and cultural change. The flint mines were often dug deep, and through bands of flint nodules as well as chalk, to reach the higher-quality floor-stone (Fig 2.5).

It was this material that was chosen to make axes. The axes travelled from the Sussex mines in an unpolished state, and the very fact of that travelling, and the distances involved (far into the north and west of Britain), implies that the scale of long-distance exchange networks had continued to expand from those hinted at during the later Mesolithic. This in turn implies not only that the acquisition of exotic items became more important to communities widely dispersed across Britain, but also that existing networks of contact were being stimulated more intensely during a period of rapid cultural change.

Perhaps the most remarkable innovation of the transitional period—in Britain at least—and the most overt indicator that the communities concerned were wishing to accentuate the degree of cleavage from past traditions of practice, was the making and using of pottery. During the Mesolithic period, wooden (including birch-bark) containers, woven baskets, and leather vessels and bags would have been widely used, but, unlike in Denmark and southern Sweden (for instance), there were no ceramic vessels in use. However, from the turn of the fourth millennium onwards, broken pottery is found in a variety of contexts in Britain, and often in highly formalized deposits.

The advent of pottery brought to Britain not only the bonfire-kiln technology necessary for its production, but also the introducution of new ways of food preparation, storage, and consumption. The simple bowl-shaped vessels that characterize the earliest pottery used in Britain have close Continental antecedents, like the flint axes or quarries and some flint tool types. Recent work by Hélène Pioffet has shown that assemblages in the south-east of England have both stylistic and technological affinities with pottery from Belgium and north-east France, while those in the south-west are more reminiscent of ceramics from Normandy and Brittany, although in both cases the distinctive form of the carinated bowl was abstracted from a wider range of vessel shapes. Notably, the eastern vessels have more open profiles, while their carinations were formed using distinctive techniques. The legacy of this 'technology transfer' was that some of the practices of potting endured over time, although stylistic change soon took place within the insular context, with pots in the east becoming progressively more open and flaring. Paradoxically, some of the earliest pottery was also some of the finest produced in the fourth millennium. The vessels with the sharpest carinations were, for example, some of the thinnest-walled and were made using the finest clay pastes. That some of the later pottery was rougher and coarser in execution could be taken to indicate that the skills necessary to the making of fine Continental wares were gradually lost as contact with the parent communities was lost. Another view, however, is that the finest pots were made as an overt statement about how distinctive such a new practice was, and how it exemplified the condition of 'being Neolithic'. Soon afterwards, such distinctiveness was no longer deemed essential to the processes of manufacture.

The restricted range of vessel types that characterize the numerically small groups of pottery made and used in the very early fourth millennium suggests that there was a deliberate attempt to restrict the repertoire and to signal both rarity and value in this new form of technology. Such pottery was likely initially to have been used only in a restricted range of social circumstances, and perhaps principally for the communal serving and eating of food rather than in its preparation. This serving, however, may have been highly performative, or ritualized, since the study of lipids in the food residues absorbed into the fabric of the vessels shows that they were often used to contain milk, while at the same time the vessels were mostly too small to have been useful in the storage of this foodstuff.

The number of find-spots of the earliest pottery is so far relatively small, but the range of contexts involved is broad, including pits and shafts (and middens associated with their infilling), other middens spread out across the ground-surface, early burial contexts, and large timber-built halls. The earliest halls will be discussed separately in the next section and in Chapter 3, but the other contexts are worth describing here. Finds of carinated bowl sherds are known from pits at Roughridge Hill in north Wiltshire and Rowden in south Dorset, as well as the pit immediately beside a small megalithic chamber later enveloped in a large long cairn at Dyffryn Ardudwy in north Wales. Alistair Barclay and Oliver Harris have pointed out that most of the richer pit assemblages containing carinated bowls occur in areas that do not have timber halls or houses of the same date, suggesting that they relate to alternative modes of social gathering. Comparably, a natural shaft at Cannon Hill in Berkshire had infills in its upper levels, dated to shortly after the beginning of the fourth millennium, that included pieces from six carinated bowls and three cups.

We have seen that, in two places in the Gloucestershire and Oxfordshire Cotswolds that were later to become the sites of long cairns, middens have been dated to the earliest Neolithic period. Among other items found in these spreads of discarded (mostly food) debris, there were sherds of carinated

bowls and, again, small cups. Whether similar middens were associated with
the earliest timber buildings is uncertain. At Gwernvale, for instance, a line
of timber posts was partially cut through a possible midden deposit, but
since only a pit also sealed by the later long cairn is closely dated, the date
of neither the midden nor the posts is certain (although they certainly pre-
date the period, probably not later than around 3600 BCE, when the stone
cairn sequence begins).

Carinated bowl pottery has also been found in some form of association
with other long cairns on the Gloucestershire Cotswolds at Cow Common
Long and Sale's Lot, but not at Burn Ground, where apparently early phases
of mortuary practice are suggested by radiocarbon dates, and yet the ceramics
that were recovered are of later styles. The structurally less complex burial
in a wooden coffin at Yabsley Street (next to the River Thames opposite the
O2 Stadium/Millennium Dome in east London), dated to around 4000 BCE,
is clearly extremely important. This is owing to the direct association of the
burial with at least four, and possibly more, very fine carinated bowls (sherds
of which had been carefully placed within the grave) that had in their
manufacture been finely rubbed, or burnished, on both the inside and outside
of the vessel(s).

Building in timber must have been a commonplace of Mesolithic
societies, but it would appear that the multiple felling of substantial trees and
the cutting of timber for significant construction was another innovation
of the 'transition' period. This is marked by the evidence in the landscape
for the swift removal of tree cover in many localities, on a scale that was
hitherto possible only by controlled burning. In the Early Neolithic, dated
pollen sequences from closely sampled individual locations has indicated
the clearance of broad areas of, for instance, oak woodland in places such as
Rough Tor on Bodmin Moor in Cornwall (see Chapter 4). In parallel, the
excavation of extensive tracts of land, for instance in the river valleys drain-
ing into the southern Fens, where trees had been deliberately removed by
being rendered vulnerable to wind-throw, and where the resulting hollows
have contained material that has yielded radiocarbon dates, or worked flint
tools from the same hollows, indicates the same phenomenon.

While it is no doubt the case that such clearance was chiefly undertaken
to open up ground for grazing, the resulting crop of timber, and especially
of oak wood, produced material for building in wood on a scale that previously had not existed. The final innovation to be discussed here, then, was
the creation of rectangular-plan structures that were used, probably, for a

variety of purposes from the venues for gathering and feasting through to places for storage of a variety of goods and substances, and the enacting of a variety of exchanges (cementing of alliances and so on). A number of buildings that were larger than would be anticipated for a single household, and that have therefore been termed 'halls', have been found and excavated in recent years.

Halls, migration, and complexity: a White Horse Stone tale

What is so far the earliest known amongst such buildings, again apparently associated with small quantities of carinated bowl pottery, was, as we have noted, found a few years ago at White Horse Stone near Aylesford in Kent. This structure, with dimensions 17.5 m long by 8 m wide, featured four rows of posts and a series of foundation-slots into which the two outer rows of posts appear to have been inserted (Fig. 2.6).

The inner two lines of posts were larger and could have supported a central aisle, although some central posts may also have held up a ridgepole. Another, slightly smaller building apparently dating to this same early period was excavated at Yarnton near the River Thames north of Oxford, while a group of three potentially early halls has been excavated at Dorstone Hill in Herefordshire. We will argue that these structures played a foundational role in establishing Neolithic communities in Britain, and we will discuss their place in the proliferation of new forms of life in the earliest centuries of the fourth millennium in Chapter 3.

For the moment, we can explore the White Horse Stone structure in a little more detail, not least because of the central place that it has assumed in recent accounts of the process of Neolithization in Britain. According to the available dating evidence for this longhouse or hall, derived from samples from those of its upright posts made of oak, it was probably built at the very start of the fourth millennium BCE, that is, precisely upon the threshold-point we have been considering in this chapter. Its active use ceased around three hundred years later. In *The Story of the Axe*, David Miles's account of the 'Neolithic Revolution' discussed in Chapter 1, the author points to the critical importance of the building to its time: 'this is the earliest-known Neolithic building in Britain: the imprint of the first farmers'. And he quite properly asked (p. 228), 'Were these people strangers

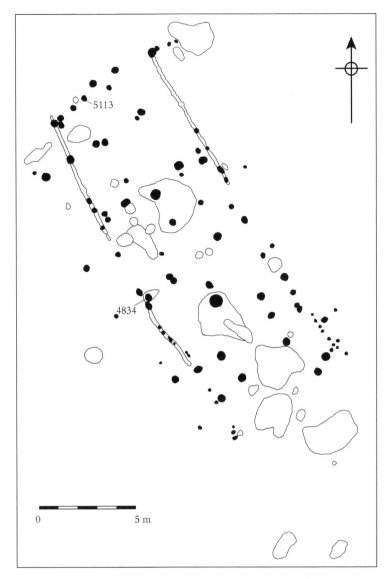

Fig. 2.6 White Horse Stone, near Maidstone, Kent: plan of 'hall' 4806

This plan shows 'context 4806', which is how the excavators at the WHS site referred to the hall-like structure built around a rectangular arrangement of earth-fast oak posts that was built in the period around 3900 BCE. The linear slots were presumably where the side-walls stood, and the building was essentially an aisled structure approximately 8 m wide (central aisle 4 m wide) and at least 15 m long. The eaves may have extended almost to ground level beyond both the longitudinal walls.

Redrawn by Julian Thomas from an original plan published by Chris Hayden.

in a strange land? Was the White Horse Stone house built by innovating natives or by immigrants arriving from across the sea?' His suggestion that the White Horse Stone building bears no resemblance to anything seen before in Britain certainly appears correct, but his related statement that 'In this part of Kent there is scarcely any evidence of late Mesolithic activity' is more open to question. It might be more accurate to say that the prehistoric archaeology of the area is presently under-explored. However, there are at least three known individual find-spots of diagnostically Mesolithic (though not precisely dated) tranchet axes within three or four kilometres of the White Horse Stone site, and there are also several flint-scatters including Mesolithic items within a ten-kilometre radius. In contrast, the nearest site that has produced Early Neolithic finds in quantity is sixteen kilometres to the north-east at Milton-next-Sittingbourne. In general, the likelihood of discovering Mesolithic sites that have no above-ground signature and are composed principally of small flint artefacts, in a landscape that has been heavily developed, densely populated, and subject to intensive agriculture, is limited in the absence of high-quality archaeological investigation. Despite this, recent work has begun to demonstrate that Late Mesolithic activity in south-east England was considerably more intensive than previously imagined. Substantial lithic assemblages have been identified at sites that include Ranscombe Woods, Cuxton, and Westcliffe and Finglesham near Deal, some of these revealing evidence for the manufacture and maintenance of tranchet axes. More pertinently, in advance of the recent construction of the Bexhill to Hastings link road, a total of 140 scatters of Late Mesolithic artefacts were encountered. This perhaps gives us an indication of the potential density of hunter-gatherer occupation in the region.

Miles then correctly observes that 'Jonathan Last has suggested that by 4000 BC the house was no longer so fundamental to the way farmers across the Channel saw themselves; houses were smaller, more varied in style and construction, often not built to last. By 4000 BC, northern farmers had downsized' (*Story of the Axe*, p. 230). It is important to note at this point that if people were migrating to Britain and, having arrived, returned to the practice of building large houses, some explanation is required for this change in behaviour.

One interpretation that has been proposed is that these 'big houses' amounted to a means of providing shelter from potentially unfriendly natives for newly arrived immigrants in a hostile land. This is possible, although if these grand structures were built as secure enclaves we would still need to ask why these new arrivals chose to reproduce a kind of structure that had not been in general use for some centuries, rather than some form of protective enclosure. David Miles preferred instead to link the builders of the White Horse Stone to their close Continental neighbours through a comparison of the building techniques and structural forms that they employed. He went on to say, 'However, archaeologists have found houses in northern France and on the North Sea Coast as far as Denmark that bear a resemblance to White Horse Stone and other British examples,' while nonetheless conceding that 'The White Horse Stone building—and its companion—cannot be precisely matched in the near Continent. This is hardly surprising at a time when people did not work to a blueprint. We also seem to be looking at a pioneer site...' (ibid.).

In order to expand on the implications of why the White Horse Stone building, with its few associated traces of fragmentary pottery and cereal grains, was nonetheless fundamental to the migration story, Miles proceeded to paint a picture of the details of the process. To begin with, he suggested, 'scouts' would have been sent ahead to establish the lie of the land and familiarize themselves with coastal waters. Evidently finding their way into the Thames Estuary and up the Medway, they then followed a route inland, exploring the area around modern Maidstone, to the east of which the White Horse Stone site lies. Despite the alleged near-absence of a local Mesolithic population, 'perhaps they had local guides who saw potential advantages to be gained from cooperation with the newcomers'. Miles speculated that his 'Neolithic arrivals' may have comprised small kin groups, which, appearing in a handful of boats, must have had to find landfall and (again, surprisingly, given their apparent rarity) 'negotiate with the local inhabitants'. To be fair, Miles was only suggesting that it was the Maidstone area that was devoid of resident Mesolithic indigenes, but the picture he draws of pioneers establishing themselves into the landscape is one familiar to us from the stories of the Pilgrim Fathers, told and retold to generations of Britons and Americans (and French and Germans) alike. Miles proposes that, having established their novel structure in a location hidden from view and full of sarsen stones that may have recalled their homeland, 'The White Horse Stone people moved inland. They did not stay by the River Medway...' (ibid., 231). This sequence of events would arguably be at odds with the longevity of the structure, and this is one of a number of inconsistencies that collectively make it harder to sustain the view that this was the dwelling of a group of pioneer settlers. These also include the location and constructional details of the hall, its relationship with a second building close by, and most importantly the presence of a series of features on the same site that appear to prefigure the Early Neolithic activity.

The White Horse Stone building is a remarkable construction, made all the more so by its early date. Its creation and use are of the greatest possible interest, but they need to be contextualized in relation to its immediate topographic setting and its longer history. This can be achieved by reviewing aspects of the excavation record, which is possible thanks to the prompt report of the site by the project director, Chris Hayden, and the availability of archive material online through the Archaeology Data Service hosted by the University of York.

The White Horse Stone structure was referred to prosaically, and for shorthand, to its excavators as 'context 4806'. Building 4806 had a companion structure 140 metres to the south, and set at right angles to it. The temporal relationship between the two remains unclear. Hayden, the excavator, like David Miles, argued that although these buildings found no close analogues amongst contemporary European timber-built structures, they possessed broad family resemblances. On this view, we should not expect them to be identical, given that the Continental structures were themselves highly variable, although aspects of the constructional techniques employed, such as post in slot arrangements, are paralleled.

Eleven radiocarbon determinations were obtained from the post-holes that constituted the footprint of this structure. Nine of these dated samples were regarded as significant to an understanding of the date of the initial construction and subsequent use of the building. The dates indicate that the raising of the hall was undertaken in the period 4065–3940 BCE, and that it continued in use potentially until 3745–3635 BCE : in other words, for at least 200 years. These dates were mostly obtained from samples of oak wood from the post-holes. However, two of the other features among the 60-odd post-holes making up the structure also yielded carbon that successfully returned dates. Remarkably, these samples (from post-holes 5113 and 4834) produced dates of 8530–8250 BCE and 7600–7520 BCE, that is, at two different times in the *Early Mesolithic* period. These samples were therefore dismissed as being from residual charcoal: as such they were deemed to be unrelated to the hall. Structurally, given the length of time that appears to have elapsed between these early dates and the building of the hall, it is without doubt the case that these posts could hardly have still been standing when the Early Neolithic hall building was created.

Nonetheless, the setting aside of this evidence for precedent activity, and especially the possibility that posts had been raised to mark the site (although not to form a coherent structure), means that the significance of one further detail that is crucial to an understanding of the time-depth of activity at the site was consequentially omitted. This is that the charcoal concerned was of *pine*, a tree that no longer existed locally by the fourth millennium. Because of this identification, it was assumed that the charcoal concerned *must* have been residual, given that there was no other demonstrable Mesolithic presence at the site: the pine charcoal had to have simply been lying about in the area where the later building was constructed, becoming swept into two of the post-holes. Yet this conclusion may have been premature, because there were actually *five* post-holes that contained recognizable quantities of pine charcoal. It follows that although the posts concerned had no connection with the structure itself, they might potentially alert us to the character of earlier activity on the site.

The presence of pine uprights here in the Medway valley echoes closely in date the pine posts erected in a row found close to Stonehenge, and those raised at Hambledon Hill, which we have already discussed. Post-hole 4834, moreover, arguably had a ramp to one side to enable a tall post to be raised, just as at least one of the Stonehenge posts had. What are we to make of this? If two of the posts present were actually raised several centuries before the Early Neolithic house/hall was built, it is possible that more of the posts evident in plan might have actually belonged to a setting of timber uprights of pine that marked the place as having been of some significance to Mesolithic communities over a long period. It may not be irrelevant that the two dated pine posts form an alignment similar to, but not precisely the same as, the orientation of the Early Neolithic hall. They might therefore have established a practice of marking place, and an orientation, that was subsequently recalled and referred back to by the builders of the hall long afterwards. This might even explain why the building was fully 1.5 m higher at its northern end than at its southern end. Even with the kind of plank-flooring that we now know (from the Dorstone Hill excavations, see Chapter 4) was present in at least some examples of this kind of structure, it was surely somewhat inconvenient to have to raise up the southern end of such flooring and attach it to the side-walls if the users of the structure wanted an approximately level floor (there was no indication of levelling down into the chalk of the hill for this purpose)?

Finally, it is worth noting in passing that although the White Horse Stone building went out of use by 3635 BCE, the idea that the people concerned 'moved on' fairly quickly is open to question, and not only in relation to the use-life of the building itself. More broadly, the site produced enough evidence to make a reasonable case for continuous (or at least recurrent) activity there throughout the Neolithic period, in the form of the presence of pits containing Decorated Bowl pottery dating from the middle of the fourth millennium, Peterborough Ware from slightly later, and Grooved Ware from a variety of contexts dated to the third millennium (see, especially, Chapters 3 and 5 for the relevant chronologies and histories). It could, perhaps, be argued that the Early Neolithic occupants of this site above the Medway valley sent some of its earliest (or even later) occupants to colonize adjacent areas of Britain. Yet it nonetheless appears that this was a favoured location for activity across a broad span of time, from the Mesolithic through into the Bronze Age. The existence of traces of habitation relating to a series of different periods could be argued to be coincidental, but we would choose to place this alongside the numerous examples of the spatial coexistence of Mesolithic and Neolithic remains that we have already cited. This was clearly a *place* that had been persistently, or at least recurrently occupied over the long term, whether by the same people or by successive groups who acknowledged its accumulated history. In some cases, this process would doubtless have involved the incorporation of 'outsiders', perhaps with connections across a wide span of Britain and Europe, into an existing community with a long history and a strong folk attachment to the distinctive locality on the rolling hills to the north of (modern-day) Maidstone that can still be visited today, together with the 'White Horse Stone', itself a massive sarsen boulder, just up the lane.

New preoccupations, new histories . . . new people?

What we hope to have demonstrated in this extensive excursion into the archaeology of a single site, albeit standing as exemplar and metaphor for aspects of the 'transition' more widely, is that the evidence for the earliest Neolithic presence in Britain is highly malleable. This evidence can easily be read in a variety of different ways, often underwritten by quite different philosophical and methodological preoccupations. Most archaeologists are agreed that the various innovations that made up the Neolithic way of life were transmitted from the European continent to Britain towards the end of the fifth millennium BCE, but they differ in imagining very different mechanisms by which this may have been achieved. To the non-specialist the differences between the three main competing 'models' of change may not appear especially great, since all three find a role for both 'new people' from the Continent and the established Mesolithic population. Moreover, all agree that from some time before 4000 BCE the people living in Britain shared a new set of preoccupations, in terms of subsistence practice and diet; and that the process either of adopting or of insinuating a Neolithic way of being in(to) these islands meant the creation of new histories. Yet the respective roles of two communities involved, and the character of relations between them, differ considerably in the competing readings of the evidence.

One influential perspective is that offered by Alison Sheridan, which emphasizes the comparative isolation of Britain after the flooding of the English Channel in the period following the retreat of the ice sheets, and the submerging of the large island of Doggerland in the North Sea. British Mesolithic people had different material traditions from their European coun- terparts, and none of the innovations of the Neolithic appeared precociously before the arrival of groups of colonists, in contrast to the situation in southern Scandinavia. Small communities of pioneer agriculturalists, who would have had little or no prior contact with the indigenes, introduced the Neolithic assemblage to the 'northwest European archipelago'. These groups arrived by boat, bringing all the necessary paraphernalia of farming settle- ment with them: seed corn, trussed-up animals, pots, and axes. Sheridan proposes a series of discrete episodes of colonization, each having a separate place of origin and destination, and each occasioned by a specific set of causal factors. The first of these was an abortive attempt on the part of people from western France to establish agricultural settlement in the west of Ireland, manifested in a group of bones of domesticated cattle found at the mid-fifth-millennium BCE Mesolithic site of Ferriter's Cove in Co. Kerry. Sheridan reasons that the animals concerned must have escaped or been pilfered from a Neolithic farmstead that has left no other material trace. A second burst of migration issued out of the Morbihan region of Brittany in the period 4300–4000 BCE, and is represented by a number of small tombs with simple polygonal megalithic chambers, dispersed in coastal regions surrounding the Irish Sea. One such chamber, at Achnacreebeag in Argyll, contained a small, closed, carinated bowl bearing incised decoration in the form of a series of sets of nested arcs, which Sheridan compares with the 'late Castellic' pottery of north-west France, and suggests may be ancestral to the Beacharra-style ceramics of Scotland. Yet a number of authors have noted that the similarity of these tombs to those of Brittany is general rather than diagnostic, that none have produced particularly early radiocarbon determinations, and that if the pottery vessel were indeed of Castellic type this tradition continued until a time when Neolithic activity had in any case spread northwards into western Scotland. Sheridan argues that the scattering of groups of Breton farmers around the Irish Sea basin was a facet of a period of social dislocation in which a cultural order that was represented by large standing stones and massive long mounds was eclipsed by a new pattern of tombs containing megalithic chambers accessed by long stone passages.

The third and most significant of the incursions that Sheridan has hypothesized was the 'Carinated Bowl Neolithic', originating in north-east France and Belgium in an area influenced by the Chasséen and Michelsberg cultural groupings. From this region came people bearing the eponymous carinated pots, leaf-shaped arrowheads, polished flint and jadeitite axes, and timber buildings, as well as cereals and livestock, to settle along the coasts of eastern and southern Britain, and ultimately to penetrate into Ireland. These groups crossed the Channel and the North Sea around 4000 BCE, propelled by growing population pressure in the Paris Basin and a disruption and displacement of settlement that followed the emergence of the Michelsberg group in the Low Countries after 4300 BCE. Finally, Sheridan has proposed that in the period between 4000 and 3750 BCE, another wave of colonists left Normandy, bringing pottery of Chasséen affinity and building cairns containing megalithic or drystone chambers. This she saw as demonstrated at the small round cairn at Broadsands in Devon, and in the 'rotunda', which (if indeed they existed as separate primary structures) represent the earliest elements of some long cairns in the Cotswold and Severn regions. These movements are explained as being the consequence of some form of depopulation taking place in north-west France at this time.

Sheridan's arguments are generally based on the apparent similarities between individual artefacts and structures identified in different regions. Those between pots and stone tools found in Britain and the Continent are often striking, but the European examples generally form elements of more extensive assemblages, other aspects of which are not represented in Britain at all. This suggests that specific material forms were being selected by the first Neolithic generations from more extensive repertoires rather than simply being transferred as a whole. By contrast, the earlier Neolithic monuments of Britain and Ireland have more of a general 'family resemblance' to those on the Continent. While Sheridan is undoubtedly correct that where similar items occur in different regions it is reasonable to infer that there was some connection between the two, she also relies on the reverse argument: that where two areas do not share artefactual forms, there can have been no contact between them. Yet this is harder to sustain: different communities often maintain their separate identities by dressing differently and using different styles of objects, irrespective of the degree of contact between them. So the 'isolation' of Mesolithic Britain from the mainland may be a chimera.

Alasdair Whittle, Frances Healy, and Alex Bayliss, arising from their evaluation of the dating evidence presented in *Gathering Time*, propose a second point of view. They are sceptical of Sheridan's multistranded view of the Neolithic transition, and reject the notion of separate movements of population into the Irish Sea area or south-west England in favour of a single episode of migration into the area surrounding the Thames Estuary (Kent and Essex) towards the end of the fifth millennium BCE. This they see as being composed of a small founder pool of population which fissioned from a parent community in the Low Countries or north-east France over a period of only one or two generations. Thereafter a pattern of *chain migration* was established, with a stream of movement back and forth between the colony and its homeland gradually building up the scale of the Neolithic presence. While the earliest generations of farmers were exclusively migrants, more mixed populations would have begun to develop later on, as local people began to be integrated into the new way of life. The consequence of this pattern was that the beginning of Neolithization was slow and small-scale, but the process gradually gathered pace, and Neolithic things and activities began to penetrate into Sussex, Wessex, the Cotswolds, and the Upper Thames Valley. From around 3800 BCE there was an abrupt shift in the tempo of change, as Neolithic activity spread more quickly into northern England, southern Scotland, the south-west peninsula, and Ireland. This may have constituted a 'domino effect' in which indigenous communities swiftly gave up their resistance to change and were integrated into new patterns of social relations and economic practices.

Both Sheridan on the one hand and Whittle, Healy, and Bayliss on the other propose that indigenous hunter-gatherers would eventually have been absorbed and assimilated into Neolithic social networks and ways of life, ultimately becoming indistinguishable from the incomers. But both perspectives identify the earliest Neolithic communities as *enclaves* that were internally homogeneous, having come from specific locations on the Continent, and existed completely separately from the native Mesolithic groups. David Miles's description of a 'White Horse Stone people' power-fully evokes this sense of a group that shared a common origin and perhaps an ethnic identity. For Alison Sheridan, these founder communi-ties were diasporic in character, linked both to each other and to their respective homelands.

It is this notion of the homogeneous founder enclave of pioneers in an unknown land that we question within these accounts of the earliest Neolithic in Britain. We would suggest that it tacitly relies on a parallel with the European colonization of the New World, and that it implies that Mesolithic hunter-gatherers and Neolithic farmers had world views and ways of life that were as incommensurate as those of Native Americans and Pilgrim Fathers. The maritime colonization of an unfamiliar landscape by agriculturalists is at the least an extremely dangerous pursuit. Early colonies in the Americas, supported by the technology of iron, steel, and gunpowder and with galleons full of supplies, nonetheless often died out during their first winter. In recent years, archaeologists and anthropologists have stressed the notion of *landscape learning*, the importance of acquiring an understand-ing of soils, vegetation, wild animals, prevailing winds, precipitation, water sources, growing seasons, and communications routes before transferring one's way of life into a new environment. Hunter-gatherers are good colon-izers, flexible and adaptable in the way that they can accommodate their way of life to new conditions. But this is less the case for farmers, for whom minor variations in ecological conditions can mean the difference between life and death. Having first made landfall on an unknown coast, through unknown currents, and avoiding submerged rocks and other hazards, and having found a suitable location for settlement, Neolithic pioneers would then have had to construct shelters and create gardens while living off the land until their first harvest, if it came at all. Various writers, from Humphrey Case in the 1960s onwards, have suggested that 'scouts' may have recon-noitred target areas prior to colonization, but it is unclear whether they could have acquired the necessary information without protracted experi-ence of a given landscape.

In *The Birth of Neolithic Britain*, one of the present authors outlined a third view of the what happened around 4000 BCE, which proposed that the British Neolithic was a 'co-creation' achieved through contact and interaction between Continental Neolithic people and the indigenous British population. Rather than one group of people immediately and comprehensively replacing another, the principal process involved was one of *transformation*, in which one kind of society evolved into another. It was recognized that this was not simply a matter of Mesolithic people acquiring a set of innovations from a distance and 'becoming Neolithic', and that there would have been an appreciable exchange of personnel: population movement perhaps, but not simply between parent and founder communities. It is important to note at once that the model of Britain cut off from the Continent during the Mesolithic, and of Neolithic pioneers arriving on a mysterious, mist-shrouded shore is one that has been increasingly eroded in recent years. We have seen that Mesolithic mariners found their way from the Low Countries to the Scilly Isles, as well as accessing the offshore islands of Britain by boat. Recently, the DNA of wheat was identified from a palaeosol containing Mesolithic artefacts and dated to around 6000 BCE at the offshore site of Bouldnor Cliff near the Isle of Wight. This, and the cattle bones from Ferriter's Cove, are perhaps best attributed to the activity of Garrow and Sturt's 'maritime culture', neither exclusively Mesolithic nor Neolithic. Similarly, it is possible that some of the jadeitite axes found in Britain, of styles made centuries before the start of the local Neolithic, were not heirlooms brought from the Continent by colonizing groups (where they were often taken out of circulation by burial when they went out of fashion and were replaced by new forms) (Fig. 2.7). Instead, their exchange may have represented a means of establishing or maintaining relationships between communities on either side of the Channel during the later fifth millennium. Significantly, few of the British examples have been found in contexts that were unambiguously Neolithic in date. Finally, as we have seen, the decorated oak timber found at Maerdy in Wales may represent evidence of Mesolithic people in Britain emulating the designs found engraved on the stones of megalithic tombs in Brittany.

It seems reasonable to deduce, therefore, that there was at least sporadic contact across the Channel and the North Sea before, during, and after 4000 BCE. Mesolithic communities in southern coastal Britain would have been at least vaguely aware of the existence of domesticated plants and animals, and of new forms of material culture across the sea, once a Neolithic presence had been established in Normandy in the earlier fifth millennium, and in the Pas-de-Calais around 4300 BCE. This knowledge may, of course,

Fig. 2.7 Histon jadeitite axehead, Cambridgeshire

This fine example of a jadeitite axehead was found by chance in the late nineteenth century at Histon, a northern suburb of Cambridge. All but two of the 119 jade (mostly jadeitite) Continental axeheads with known find-spots found in Britain by 2013 were similarly discovered by chance and not retrieved from secure archaeological contexts. The elongated form and 'bulbous' body of the Histon axehead is indicative of the Durrington-style of such axes, although this is not the commonest form in East Anglia, where most known examples are of the thinner Greenlaw type with a more pronounced triangular shape, as one retrieved along with another, miniature form from nearby Burwell Fen (K.Walker 2015: cat. 56). (See Bibliographical commentary for full reference.)

Photograph: © Cambridge University Museum of Archaeology and Anthropology.

have taken the form of travellers' tales, describing monstrous animals, magical seeds, and enchanted artefacts. Nonetheless, we suggest that the beginning of the Neolithic in Britain is as likely to have involved the overcoming of a resistance to innovation on the part of indigenous populations as it is the sudden appearance of groups of people bearing new species, artefacts, and practices. However, as we have already noted, this is not to say that the movement of population had no part to play in this process. In *The Birth of Neolithic Britain*, reference was made of Continental people 'filtering in' to indigenous British societies through a variety of mechanisms, bringing new knowledge and skills with them, and perhaps achieving social advancement of various kinds as a result. Here, we would like to expand on the role that such people might have played, whom we might be happier to describe as *migrants* rather than as *pioneers*, and still less as *invaders*.

In the contemporary world, migration is a more or less constant process that we are all familiar with. On the nightly television news we see images of mass population movements caused by wars, droughts, and famines. But far more common is the steady trickle of individuals and family groups moving in multiple directions, seeking new opportunities for innumerable reasons. Our view of migration in the past has perhaps been coloured by the European colonization of the Americas, already noted, and the great invasions that coincided with the collapse of the Roman Empire. Massive geopolitical forces that arguably had no parallel in prehistoric Europe occasioned both. Abrupt folk migrations of the kind imagined by the pre-historians of the 1930s may be quite uncommon, and Stefan Burmeister has argued that it is often necessary to 'replace the supposition of prehistoric mass migrations with the recognition of a process of infiltration that took place over centuries'. The outcome of this kind of process might be equally significant in genetic terms, but the way in which it might have been lived and experienced at the time is another question.

The initial arrival of agricultural societies north of the Alps and the Carpathians in the late sixth millennium BCE, in the form of the longhouse communities that are referred to as the *Linearbandkeramik* (after their pottery, decorated with incised bands), almost certainly did involve the displacement of entire communities. These probably spread by 'leapfrog migration' up the valley systems of central Europe, seeking out plateau-edge locations on the light, wind-blown soils of the loess. Thereafter, things became more complex, and the degree and form of migration, and the extent of indigenous involve-ment in Neolithization varied from region to region. As David Anthony has argued, 'cultures don't migrate, people do', and in general it is only a very restricted and self-selecting subgroup within any population that is motivated to leave home and change its circumstances. In non-state societies, people are only rarely forced to relocate *en masse* by environmental catastrophes, resource crises, or conflicts. Far more often they fission or fragment owing to interpersonal conflicts: disputes over marriage partners or inheritances, killings, thefts, witchcraft accusations, feuds, and rivalries. The number of people who opt to leave a community for these reasons may be quite small: individuals, pairs of siblings, family groups, or aspiring leaders and their immediate followers. They will often represent the disaffected and disgruntled, outcasts and adventurers, or low-status persons seeking to establish themselves and acquire wealth. These episodes of leave-taking may be sporadic but ongoing, rather than forming large synchronized waves.

Migrants of this kind rarely travel to places that are entirely unknown to them: they generally exit from one familiar set of social relationships and enter into another. It is possible that this is the form that much of the movement of people in late-fifth-millennium north-west Europe will have taken. Individuals or small groups will have moved between communities amongst whom relationships had already been established. The most obvious example of this kind of movement would be the exchange of marriage partners between British and Continental societies and vice versa. Such people may have brought with them the skills of potting, cultivation, and animal herding, and this may have given them positions of authority and esteem in the groups that they joined. Some may simply have sought to attach themselves to indigenous groups in an opportunistic way, exploiting the possibilities offered by a society on the cusp of profound change. Others may have travelled in order to establish flint mines, drawing on local labour. Yet others again may have set themselves up as leaders or household heads, recruiting followers from the local population by offering the novel attractions of the Neolithic way of life. In some cases, the skills and resources that the newcomers brought with them will have facilitated the transformation of indigenous societies. In others, these arrivals may have been a catalyst for change. It follows that the beginning of the Neolithic in Britain may have been a time of upheaval, when social groupings were in flux, and communities were being refounded from disparate fragments. Describing the contemporary situation in southern Scandinavia, Douglas Price conveys this well, by saying that the Neolithic transition was a time of chaos and disorder, in which new social and economic options were being 'auditioned'. The social groups that emerged from this turmoil differed from the hunting bands that preceded them in being more bounded and defined, and exercising exclusive rights to collective property in the form of cultivation plots, animal herds, and prized artefacts. They may have understood themselves as *households*, and we argue that timber halls such as that at White Horse Stone were both the symptom of this new kind of collective identity and the means by which it was established. *Building the house* was in part the mechanism by which house-based groups were brought into being, labouring together to prod-uce the material symbol of their shared selfhood. Later, the construction of monumental tombs containing the remains of a community's ancestral dead expressed the same idea in a more enduring fashion.

This argument implies that the first Neolithic societies in Britain were *hybrids*, composed of a mixture of 'new people' (perhaps initially modest in number) and indigenes. Moreover, the newcomers within any such group need not all have come from the same parent community. The movement of people between communities is a normal feature of social life, and they would have brought with them diverse cultural traditions, skills, techno-logical know-how, and social expectations. In our view it may be hard to define a particular moment when the Neolithic 'arrived' in Britain and there may have been no clear period during which 'pure' Neolithic societies stood apart from 'the locals'. Instead, the process may have been one of Continental and British societies progressively interpenetrating. The British Neolithic became archaeologically visible at the point where new kinds of community were brought into being, adopting a new material assemblage, new social relationships, and new subsistence practices. We believe that this interpretation best explains two of the most significant aspects of the Neolithic transition in Britain: the combination of continuity and change that we have already dwelt on at length, and the conspicuous pattern of cultural mixing and syncretism, what the French anthropologist Claude Lévi-Strauss referred to as *bricolage*.

Numerous previous accounts of the beginning of the Neolithic have pondered the problem that it is impossible to identify a single Continental homeland from which all of the cultural elements found together in Britain could be derived. A famous exchange on the subject took place many years ago between the archaeologists Jacquetta Hawkes and Stuart Piggott, debat-ing whether the origins of the 'Windmill Hill culture' should be sought in the east or the west, central Europe or Iberia. Much more recently, Hugo Anderson-Whymark and Duncan Garrow have contemplated the earliest

Neolithic ceramic and lithic assemblages of Devon and Dorset. Here, pottery shows affinities with both the carinated bowl tradition of eastern England and the baggy, lugged, and knobbed vessels of contemporary north-west France (see Chapter 3). Yet the tranchet arrowheads and decorated *vase supports* (cylindrical ceramic objects with dished upper surfaces, which may have been incense burners) commonly found with the latter are missing. Similarly, the earthen long barrows of eastern and southern Britain have close (if not precise) parallels in Denmark, but the pottery associated with them is quite different from the early funnel beakers found in the latter. The long cairns of the Cotswolds and south Wales have structural similarities to the passage tombs of Lower Normandy, but their chambers are more like those found in Brittany, while the presence of deep forecourts is perhaps borrowed from the earthen long mound tradition. And again, they are often associated with the 'wrong' pottery and stone tools. Chris Scarre has put it rather well in stating that the relationship between Continental and British megalithic structures is one of translation rather than transmission. These patterns of mixing, matching, and selective rejection are ones that can be better explained in terms of social flux, reformulation, and interaction than the simple transfer of populations from one region to another.

Genes and migrants

For some while it has been maintained by some archaeologists that the debate between these three models of Neolithization (broadly, 'multi-stranded colonization', 'chain migration', and 'interaction and migrant exchange') will eventually be resolved through the building up of a suffi-cient database of reliable aDNA (ancient, 'preserved' DNA, extracted from the bones and teeth of past people) samples, and their believable linkage to 'modern' populations defined using mtDNA (mitochondrial DNA) from present-day populations. One of the first successful examples of this kind of work in the context of the Neolithic of Britain and Ireland was the report-ing in 2016 of genome data for the remains of a woman from a passage tomb at Ballynahatty in Co. Down, dated to 3343–3020 cal BCE. Her ancestry appeared to be of predominantly Near Eastern origin, but what proved remarkable and unexpected was that her closest affinities appeared to be with Spanish Neolithic groups, rather than those of central Europe. More recently, in a paper that is primarily concerned with rather later Beaker-age populations and their genetic relationships by Iñigo Olalde and colleagues (discussed further in Chapter 5), it is suggested that this pattern may be more widespread. This study compares Beaker-associated genetic material with that of various Neolithic groups in Europe, and indicates that the available sample of remains of British Neolithic people is genetically distinct from existing results drawn from Mesolithic people. These people also show a greater biological affinity to Iberian Neolithic groups than to central European ones, and it is argued that some portion of the ancestry of Neolithic communities in Britain must have been derived from the Atlantic zone. The extent of any contribution from either native Mesolithic people or central European Neolithic groups is not quantified. It is perhaps premature to comment in too much depth on the limited evidence presented in the Olalde publication, but as a kind of 'thought experiment' we seek here to demonstrate how the emerging pattern might articulate with the arguments that we have been discussing in this chapter.

The Ballynahatty result and the Olalde paper are challenging for all three existing models of Neolithization in Britain, since they imply that there was at some point a significant influx of population into Britain from the west, presumably ultimately connected with the spread of Neolithic things and practices westwards along the Mediterranean basin from the Near East. There are indications that this strand of dispersal had had some impact on the west of France during the fifth millennium BCE, manifested in the presence of Cardial and Epicardial styles of pottery, and perhaps connected with the first emergence of megalithic funerary structures. This process was quite separate from the spread of *Linearbandkeramik* communities and their successors through central Europe from the Hungarian Basin, ultimately into Belgium, Holland, the Paris Basin, and Normandy.

For Whittle, Healy, and Bayliss, it is north-east France and Belgium that are identified as the probable source of a founding migrant population in south-east England, who might be expected to carry a genetic signature connected to this central European route, while for Sheridan the same area was the origin of the Carinated Bowl Neolithic, dispersed over much of Britain and Ireland. The aDNA results are potentially at variance with this: even in the Paris Basin, according to recent aDNA analysis by Maïté Rivollat and colleagues, a central European genetic element was present throughout the Early and Middle Neolithic. There are, however, several reasons to treat the existing results with a degree of caution at this stage. First, it appears that the findings are based on quite a small data set, since the Olalde study mentions a total of eighty individuals (nineteen of them of Beaker date) sampled in Britain for the entire period between 3900 and 1200 BCE, from the start of the Neolithic until well into the Bronze Age. Those that date to the Early Neolithic are presumably derived principally from chambered tombs, earthen long barrows, caves, and causewayed enclosures. As will be made clear in Chapter 4, these represent only a very small minority of the people who lived and died in Neolithic Britain, and the means by which the majority of the dead were disposed of throughout the period remains a mystery to us. It is entirely possible that burial in funerary monuments was the prerogative of privileged lineages of Continental origin (while cave burial may have been reserved for people who were in some way 'aberrant'), and that a more diverse population is not registering in the data set. Secondly, the available skeletal material is likely to be skewed toward particular periods, with something of a gap over the period of 'transition' itself. Mesolithic burials in Britain are concentrated in the ninth to seventh millennia BCE, while those human remains attributable to the fifth millennium are found principally in western Scotland, and may not provide a representative picture of cross-Channel interactions in the south of England. Those of Neolithic date are likely to be more numerous after the proliferation of funerary monuments of various sorts, from 3800 BCE onwards. In other words, it is probable that the aDNA evidence will present us with a 'before' and 'after' picture and that, as with other categories of archaeological evidence, it will be possible to read this in a number of different ways. For instance, it may be difficult to demonstrate whether any genetic change was sudden or gradual.

However, if, for the sake of argument, future work demonstrates that the population of Neolithic Britain had a genetic profile primarily similar to that of Neolithic Iberia, and contained a significant component ultimately derived from western Asia, then one straightforward explanation would be that such a population entered Britain at the start of the Neolithic, bringing a full suite of novel resources and artefacts with it, and swiftly displaced the indigenous hunter-gatherers. Nevertheless, we submit that such a model cannot easily account for several aspects of the evidence that we have been emphasizing in this chapter: the various forms of continuity from Mesolithic to Neolithic that we have identified, most notably the enduring significance attached to particular locations; the selectivity involved in the creation of British Neolithic artefactual assemblages, in contrast to those on the Continent; and the mixing and merging of multiple Neolithic cultural traditions of diverse geographical origins from the start of the period.

Can our focus on interaction and 'co-creation' provide an alternative perspective? We believe that it can. The points that we continue to emphasize are: that particular economic practices and forms of material culture were not necessarily the exclusive prerogative of people with a specific genetic signature; that Mesolithic and Neolithic people were essentially similar in their capacities and achievements, and that the former were sufficiently sophisticated and organized to have not been immediately displaced by an incursion of modest size; that it would be difficult for maritime pioneers to establish a Neolithic way of life in Britain without the active cooperation of indigenous people; that there appears to have been a transmission of cultural knowledge and understandings of various kinds across the boundary between Mesolithic and Neolithic; and that the British Neolithic was, for whatever reasons, materially distinct from its Continental counterparts from the beginning.

In one possible scenario, the first few generations of Neolithization in Britain were messy and complex, with new kinds of hybrid community forming predominantly in the south-east of England, drawing on both indigenous people and incomers from diverse points of origin. In this chaotic situation, local and exotic traditions were mixed together, and new social relationships and patterns of exchange began to fall into place. If the indigenous component of this formation was modest in size, the number of incomers from north-east France, Belgium, and other regions may also have been limited, so the composition of these groups may have changed over time. In this initial period, pottery assemblages were small, and contained few vessel forms. The use of domesticated plants and animals may have been quite limited in extent. Very few if any monuments were constructed, but flint mines may have been a focus of considerable interest and activity.

As a stable pattern of Neolithic societies began to emerge, external contacts shifted toward the west, bringing new cultural influences (manifested in western French pottery forms progressively added to existing assemblages, and megalithic architectural devices) and establishing an enduring migration stream. Ceramic assemblages now became larger and more diverse, cereal cultivation became more common, and labour began to be invested in large monumental structures. In this version of events, migration was not synonymous with Neolithization; rather, it was the *consequence* of the foundation of hybrid Neolithic societies that served as *attractors* for external migrants, who progressively swelled their numbers. Equally, migration was not a discrete event, but a protracted process played out over many generations, which may have begun to escalate toward the thirty-eighth century BCE. This might explain why Whittle, Healy, and Bayliss identify an abrupt acceleration in the spread of Neolithic things and practices through Britain and Ireland from 3800 BCE onwards. In their argument, this was the point where indigenous people were drawn into the expanding Neolithic network, but we are effectively suggesting the opposite. As the number of incomers increased, indigenous people may have been progressively squeezed out and marginalized: perhaps deliberately excluded, but equally perhaps as a population of finite size, simply genetically out-competed by one that was being continually 'topped up' from outside over a period of centuries. By the mature stages of the Early Neolithic, the population of southern Britain may have been predominantly similar to groups in Atlantic Europe in biological terms. Nonetheless they had been fundamentally transformed by their encounter with the Mesolithic societies that they had gradually displaced. Indeed, they may even have understood themselves to be 'native' to their regions, able to cite connections and continuities back to a distant past. Even if the indigenes had now wasted away, they had left an indelible mark on their successors, in the same way that North Americans of European descent today use Native American place names, eat beef jerky and pot roast, play lacrosse, wear parkas and buckskins, and use snowshoes, canoes, and lassoes.

The complexity of the population dynamics that may have been involved in the beginning of the Neolithic period in Britain is well illustrated by a recent analysis of strontium isotopes in human remains from two long cairns in the Black Mountains of Wales. At Ty Isaf, all the skeletons investigated belonged to people who had apparently spent their childhood in the immediate vicinity, ingesting water containing the local strontium signature. But at Penywyrlod, ten bodies were of people who had grown up a little distance away, perhaps in modern Herefordshire or Worcestershire. This might be an indication that the community had migrated locally during their lifetime, but more likely it suggests that the two areas were linked by habitual patterns of movement. The final skeleton from Penywyrlod, radiocarbon-dated to 3770–3630 cal BCE, had potentially been born in a rather more distant location, perhaps north-west France. The Penywyrlod burials were not a founder community that had come directly from the Continent. The single person of exotic origin was somewhat later in date than any of the colonizing movements that have been hypothesized. This therefore vividly demonstrates that the large-scale processes of transformation were punctuated by periodic comings and goings that may have been more personal and intimate in character.

Into fourth-millennium 'history'

The story of what has come to be known, inelegantly, as 'the Mesolithic-Neolithic transition' has preoccupied prehistorians for several decades, as reflected in the lengthy discussion of the question in this chapter. The divide between what are routinely seen as two highly divergent economic systems, or at least lifeways, has, as we noted in Chapter 1, arisen to some extent from the existence of two contrasting traditions of research into prehistoric peoples, arguably exacerbated by the nature and history of modern ethnography. There have traditionally been those anthropologists who study 'hunter-gatherers/foragers', those who study agriculturalists (including so-called 'shifting' agriculturalists and horticulturalists), and those who study pastoralists and nomads. We need now, for the purposes of the present book at least, to lay these questions aside and to begin to trace the history of these new Neolithic communities forward from the earliest centuries of the fourth millennium BCE. Before doing so, however, we want to conclude this chapter with a renewed emphasis on what was different, that is, what was truly transformational, from the period of 'transition'. This of course comes down to more than a matter of how livings were made.

We have noted the variety of innovations in material culture that occurred at or near the beginning of the fourth millennium BCE, and how these innovations represented a subtle change in both indigenous and 'imported' practices. While milk residues in pottery point to one of the consequences of the adoption of animal husbandry, the wholesale change in lifestyle that came with the keeping of domesticated animals was not simply innovative—it was transformational. While pigs, sheep, and goats could be 'run' in areas beyond the living-places of each Neolithic human community provided that they were protected from predators, it was the keeping of cattle that most tied those communities to their animals. And cattle provided a source of accumulation of social and economic capital—of wealth—that no Mesolithic community had enjoyed. Archaeological deposits right from the start of the fourth millennium reflect the new preoccupation with cattle, and not only in the sense that these animals became ubiquitous and demanded so much caring for. Finds of cattle bones are both pervasive and often numerically dominant in early fourth-millennium (as well as in many later) deposits, such that it is clear that they were regarded as a, or perhaps even *the*, dominant individual food source in certain situations, and especially for feasting. So, for example, while red deer bones were present in the Coneybury pit, near the later site of Stonehenge, and roe deer bones were abundant, there were more bones of cattle in the deposit than of any other species.

But it is not only how numerous such bones were, but also how they were treated, and with what other materials they were associated, that provide an indication of a different aspect of human preoccupation with cattle. Time and again the bones of cattle are associated with human remains in a wide range of contexts, and this association continues throughout the Neolithic period. While such repeated associations could simply be symbolic of the centrality of cattle to the new farming economy, and there could be aspects of the keeping of cattle and the intimacy with which it was necessary to coexist, as a social resource they also had some other important potentials. These latter will be explored further in Chapters 4 (concerning capital) and 6 (concerning history).

Equally, the creation of buildings that were large enough to be used collectively signalled a fundamental change in the way that societies were ordered. 'Being Neolithic' involved more than the use of new classes of material item and subsistence resources and the performance of new practices. Rather, it concerned different ways of behaving, socially, and different conceptions of social and material value. New kinds of social relations became possible, expressed through new ways of creating and sustaining obligations, including the formation of alliances. Investment in more permanent, or at least more labour-intensive, constructions meant an investment also in place and in the marshalling of physical resources that were of a different order than hitherto. And yet there is evidence—if only we are able to look adequately closely, with an eye to the importance of too-easily dismissed observations—that the communities concerned were well aware of the importance of their own histories *as* communities.

This phenomenon of a Neolithic awareness of history and its unfolding is only just beginning to be recognized, and to explore its implications we shall return to a further very brief discussion of Warren Field, Crathes (see Fig. 3.2). The recutting of the tops of the 'Mesolithic' pits either side of 4000 BCE was not an isolated act, because just over 100 m to the east a timber hall some 22 m long by 8 m wide was built very close to 3750 BCE. Associated with this hall that was deliberately burnt down less than fifty years after its construction was a small but striking assemblage of open carinated bowls. Intriguingly, the hall shared a broadly similar orientation to the pit alignment, and it is difficult to see how this represents anything other than direct continuity of tradition and awareness of ancestral presence and place. And on final reflection, it is noting the way that a Mesolithic presence had shaped the way in which Neolithic people inhabited the same locality, even though by this time their mode of existence had become quite different.

THREE

Narratives for the fourth millennium

Chapter frontispiece: 'Snowdonia' (wood–engraving, Hilary Paynter)

The rocks of the northern flanks of the mountains of Snowdonia, facing the Irish Sea between the north-eastern tip of Anglesey and the Great Orme headland, were exploited during Neolithic times to quarry stones at Graig Lwyd that were used to make the (frequently) light-grey-coloured coarse-grained 'Group VII' stone axes (as defined by the Implement Petrology Group). This engraving evokes the wildness of the mountain valleys that the roughout axeheads may have been taken to for grinding and polishing before being transported individually or in batches across Britain and Ireland.

Engraving: 2007, © Hilary Paynter (website: http://www.hilarypaynter.com).

The story of the Neolithic period in Britain as we so far understand it has been compiled from myriad individual archaeological encounters with the traces of human activity from the centuries concerned in different places within the landscape. These traces include the remains of partly earth-fast timber structures which often consist of recognizable features representing where the timbers had been pulled out of the ground, or had rotted *in situ*, or had been burned; areas of burning of ground-surfaces where hearth-fires had been laid; spreads of decayed materials that were formerly rubbish dumps or 'middens'; large holes (usually referred to as 'pits') dug and backfilled with various deposits including whole or broken artefacts thrown or placed within them; and ditches that had been infilled or had silted up, and sometimes re-dug and redefined. The different episodes of construction and deposition that led to the formation of these traces are differentiated by those investigating them through the identification of thousands of isolable 'events'. Some of these events were almost momentary (the digging of a pit, the removal of a post), while others (such as the gradual silting of a ditch) took place over an extended period. Archaeologists describe the isolable actions, events, and deposits resulting from such occupation of the land as 'contexts'. Some materials retrieved from some of these contexts have been carefully selected by the archaeologists during their investigations to be datable using a variety of scientific dating techniques, and they provide individual site chronologies linked closely to the stratigraphic sequences involved. Repeated observed associations of different kinds of artefact with reliably dated contexts and site sequences allow comparative chronologies to be painstakingly constructed, and it is from this process that the possibility of a chronologically sound historical narrative for the Neolithic is gradually being built up.

In these chapters entitled 'narratives', however, we are not only talking about the sketching out of a historical sequence, extremely important though it is. We are speaking also, if to a limited extent, about the teasing out of multiplicities of story from the material evidence. So, the presence and course of individual lives is immanent in the individually made, broken, and placed items, and the residues of immediate action, that are encountered. Equally, the places of habitation each have their own narrative that encapsulates aspects of the history of the communities that created them and extended their use-life through time. Moreover, the stories of interaction between communities are embodied in the locales, the substances, and the made items through which social relations, interactions, and exchanges were enacted.

Fig. 3.1 Location of fourth-millennium sites
Map: 2017, © Julian Thomas.

The fourth millennium BCE in Britain:
a broad-brush perspective

One way of perceiving the history of the fourth millennium BCE in Britain is to see it in terms of a big picture comprising the grand narrative of the arrival and spread of a Neolithic 'package', along with Continental culture-bearers. As we have seen, this is much as David Miles has recently proposed in his book *The Tale of the Axe*. While this can be understood basically as a social evolutionary approach, it has become nuanced by a new attention to the transformation in world views as well as subsistence practices that occurred across the span of time involved, and it has been finessed in respect to new fine-scale chronology. It is more generally understood, and is acknowledged by Miles and others, that there is manifestly much variation among the sites and artefacts encountered from the first centuries of the Neolithic period in Britain. It is now widely acknowledged that this must have implications for our awareness of regional trajectories of change and the processes of cultural differentiation that were likely to have occurred at different points in the millennium concerned. Curiously, such writers appear to have brought us full circle, since it is clear that this much was recognized also by Stuart Piggott back in 1954. So how far have we really moved on, interpretively, in the intervening sixty years?

Despite the evident variability, there are clearly a number of themes in common across the centuries concerned from region to region, and also some broad horizons of change. These horizons are registered in the adoption of practices that recurred across sometimes (we now understand) relatively short spans of time, and in the subsequent 'referencing' of earlier activity by later activity in the same locations. A first horizon, for example, saw the appearance of some of the earliest manifestations of Neolithic practice, which occurred within a landscape that had perhaps been more extensively occupied by a late Mesolithic population than is sometimes acknowledged, and often employing ancestral locations. These phenomena included sequences of acts that would culminate in the construction of some of the earliest long barrows, fine bowl pottery, pit-digging and deposition, polished flint and stone axes, individual inhumation burials, and other distinctive workings and structures (including some of the Sussex flint mines), large and complex pits, timber 'halls', and some houses, in the period between around 4050 and 3750 BCE. The decades around 3800 BCE saw these same entities rapidly appearing for the first time in the north of England, southern Scotland, Wales, and the south-west peninsula, even as some of the practices concerned began to wane and to be supplanted by new innovations in the south-east.

A second horizon is marked, broadly from 3750 to 3600 BCE (with again the earliest dates from the south of England), by the appearance in pits and other locations of more items than previously that had travelled over some distances (including, only now, pots from the south-west peninsula), and novel kinds of site including, especially, the distinctive 'causewayed enclosures' discussed at some length later in this chapter. Meanwhile, other structures such as the early halls ceased to be built, and the production and use of fine carinated pots gradually declined. The latter were supplemented and before long apparently supplanted by the use of distinctive shouldered vessels and deep bag-shaped bowls in a variety of coarser fabrics. From around 3700 BCE, long mounds became more numerous and more varied in form, with whole traditions of construction mushrooming across the British mainland. As causewayed enclosures became more numerous, and the repertoire of deposition more varied, the forms of pottery in use included an increasing variety of surface decoration. In the earlier part of this 'phase' of activity, kinds of site not previously seen, such as post-defined linear monuments, made their appearance in Scotland.

A third horizon is represented during a later stage in the use of causewayed enclosures from 3500 to 3300 BCE by a pronounced shift in the pattern of 'exchange' linkages, most dramatically evident at sites such as Hambledon Hill in Dorset. In the same period, the enclosures themselves were often reconfigured and reused, and long mounds were often monumentalized before being abandoned. Coarse pottery became yet more elaborate and highly decorated, and signs of warfare occur at several sites, with cases of trauma showing up in skeletal remains. Parallel-sided embanked cursus monuments became common in many parts of southern Britain, in several instances built across the abandoned earthworks of causewayed enclosures. Further changes ushered in a period that extended down to 3100 BCE and beyond, during which in some places individual burial was monumentalized while elsewhere timber 'palisaded' enclosures and cremation cemeteries appeared for the first time.

This rapid overview has necessarily suppressed much of the complexity and variability of fourth-millennium history. The rest of this chapter is therefore devoted to exploring something of that richness as revealed through different dimensions of the evidence and as expressed here through a series of overlapping narratives vested in contrasting traditions of practice. Inevitably, we focus most closely on those locations, kinds of site, and artefacts, the remains of which have survived most extensively and are best-preserved and more frequently encountered; although exceptional survivals and some individual remains and artefacts provide insights disproportionate to their number.

In the beginning, there was fine pottery...

As we have already argued, the story of the first efflorescence of the Neolithic in Britain is one characterized by relatively abrupt change in cultural practices against a background of continuity, both insular and Continental. The trans-formations that took place within Britain across the span of time running from the last centuries of the fifth millennium through to the first quarter of the fourth millennium BCE can be identified as much with the rapid development of a radically different way of defining community as with a switching of mode of subsistence. In constructing a narrative for this period, we will inevitably consider in more detail some of the strands of cultural practice that emerged, and identify the various trajectories of change that can be traced through the first centuries of the fourth millennium. Such a narrative takes us onwards to an era in which the interactions and linkages between communities became much more clearly manifest, and the tempo of change appears to have quickened.

Some of the earliest dated traces of the people whom we could identify as 'Neolithic' are found in contexts that would at any point and in any place in the following 2,000 years be regarded as unusual. So, for example, by the side of the River Thames at Yabsley Street, Blackwall, downstream from modern London, a timber-lined elongated pit had been dug most likely sometime in the period 4028–3990 cal BCE (as mentioned in Chapter 2). The pit was evidently a coffin-like grave in which the body of a woman had been placed. Close to her head had been placed a large sherd from a fine, angular-shouldered, thin-fabric, highly burnished carinated bowl, while pieces from further vessels were found elsewhere in the grave. Near St Albans the cremated remains of another adult had been placed, some-time around 3900 BCE, in a hollowed-out canoe-like tree trunk at least five metres long within a grave full of traces of burning. On Cranborne

Chase near Blandford in Dorset and near Maidenhead in Berkshire, deep shafts have been found, dated to shortly after 4000 BCE, into which pieces from similar pots, worked flints, and in one case fragments of stone axes had been tipped.

One of the most common kinds of location from which such early pottery has come, however, is the ashy organic spreads of debris that we have already referred to as middens. The character of such accumulations, in which apparent food waste (mostly animal bone), broken pottery, and worked (and sometimes burnt) flint are regularly found, has been much debated. For instance, were these objects incidental to domestic activity, or were they being deliberately curated (that is, purposefully stored within maintained piles from which they could later be taken and reused)? Certainly, there is growing evidence that material of various kinds had been retrieved from these piles after a period, and then intentionally re-entered into circulation. It also appears that sequences of deposition and the creation of structures within and around which such material accumulated were a recurring feature: in some cases these were light timber structures, and in others stone-slab defined boxes.

Elsewhere, parts of several pottery vessels, including five carinated bowls, were found in two successive fills of a substantial Early Neolithic pit at Eweford West, near Dunbar, to the east of Edinburgh. Close by, a mound of turves and earth represented an enlargement of a primary mound and pit, and over this turf mound had been spread individual pieces of similar pottery. Timber-lined chambers that had been burnt, and that were associated with human remains, were then inserted on either side of this mound. In this way, spreads of material usually thought of as accumulated 'occupation debris', often apparently from deliberately reworked middens, recur at a series of different locations. While such occurrences have in most cases been dated, the principal place accorded them within conventional narratives of 'the development or spread of the Neolithic' has been as *indicators* of a stage reached in the process of 'becoming Neolithic'. We would consider them instead to represent instances of lived practice in the past. Each example constitutes part of the unfolding history of these practices, which cumulatively brought about the transformation of the social worlds that people inhabited.

However, our awareness of time and its passing during the Neolithic has been transformed by the development of finer chronologies. As we have seen, these have often been based on the Bayesian statistical approach that brings together absolute dates and finely scrutinized contextual information:

identifying whether the sampled material was encountered in its original place of deposition, for instance. While the dates concerned can still be used to 'map' the adoption of Neolithic ways of life, they can also facilitate a focus upon the cultural significance of different social practices and their material outcomes. One aspect that we have already touched upon is the role of 'the house' in the establishment of distinctly Neolithic communities, and a sense of collective identity amongst the groups concerned. We would argue that this involved rather more than an awareness of 'being Neolithic', and indeed there is no guarantee that such a notion would have been comprehensible to these people. Instead, we suggest that a new way of life was facilitated by the formation of what one of us has previously referred to as 'house societies', and for which we will here coin the neologism of 'invested lineages'.

A narrative of Neolithization, and the creation of houses or halls

As more dates from a variety of contexts have accumulated, and more particularly since it has become possible to model these convincingly using both sophisticated statistical techniques and stratigraphic arguments, it has been possible to trace the introduction of Neolithic innovations and practices as a process that began in the Thames Estuary region from as early as 4100 BCE before expanding over the subsequent three centuries towards the outer limits of the mainland of Britain. This is a model, and by definition a simplification of reality. The danger in expressing such an argument in graphic form, as a map of the 'spread of the Neolithic', is that it appears to be based upon data that is entirely solid. But in reality, it is based upon *indicative* data, which means that it glosses considerable disparities in the amount of reliable information available for different regions. This point is explicitly acknowledged in the *Gathering Time* study, but there is a danger that the results might be employed without acknowledging its limitations. Most notably, there are crucial lacunae that to some degree compromise its general utility beyond the comparatively data-rich areas: in several parts of the British mainland, there is a notable paucity of reliable evidence. In the north of England, meticulous modelling has been undertaken by Seren Griffiths with important results, but the overall number of dates on which it is based remains modest. Still more limited is the data for Wales and the

Marches, which relates to only a handful of sites, and as we shall note later in respect of places such as Herefordshire, such areas will undoubtedly yield dating 'surprises' in the years to come.

We could arguably produce some form of alternative rendering that attempted to express these uncertainties in a visual form, but the result would probably still mask the lived complexities and reinforce the impression of a straightforward spatial and temporal progression. The messy reality of lived experience alternatively informs us that such simplicity is the exception and not the rule, that the spread or adoption of change is only very rarely a linear process, and that 'Neolithization' will not inevitably occur in a 'wave-like' manner, as proposed by Ammerman and Cavalli-Sforza back in the 1970s. A variety of factors will condition the dispersal of things and practices (and their transformation in the process), ranging from topography, vegetation, and established routeways, to collective knowledgeability, sociality, and the interconnectedness of communities across sometimes considerable distances, separated by other groups that do not necessarily share the same networks of contact. As this process was lived out, it would produce a variegated pattern in the emergence of Neolithic societies, and we should not be surprised to find that the adoption, introduction, or adaptation of new ways of living leapfrogged its way across the landscape. This is important, because advocates of the *wave* model of change will tend to attribute an early date for 'Neolithic' activity from a site, say, in south Wales, to scientific, sampling, or investigatory 'error', because it does not fit the preferred model of orderly spatial progress. This is a much simpler, if less rigorous, reaction than to take the evidence in the first instance at face value, and accept that it indicates that the process was both dynamic *and* stochastic. The precise pattern of appearance, adoption, or change is likely to have been affected to some extent by links of various kinds that preceded the commencement of the adoption of farming and/or the first appearance of Neolithic artefacts. These connections might include consanguinity and kinship, or networks facilitating the circulation of objects or information.

It seems possible that in the fullness of time we will be able to offer a more sophisticated account of the dispersal of the Neolithic in Britain, but for the moment there are several other narrative strands that we might follow through this earliest Neolithic period. We will explore just two of these that appear to us to be significant, but first we should pause and note that the exploration and interpretation of the earliest Neolithic of Britain also have the capacity in future to change the nature of the question itself.

It is open to question how far 'arrival and spread' will remain the most important dimension of narratives of Neolithization, and it might be concluded that this is a rather old-fashioned way of thinking. As such it may be replaced with one that focuses not upon a totalizing *process* as much as upon the ways that innovations were introduced locally, promoting specific ecological, economic, and social trajectories in the centuries that followed.

We would suggest that it is through an exploration of these various alternative narrative subjects that we can begin to see the outlines of just such a more historically literate kind of approach to the earliest period of Neolithic history. The first of the two subjects we have chosen to highlight here is the creation of 'houses' in both the physical and the social sense. The focus is not so much upon the relative dating of the initial construction and subsequent use of the different examples excavated in recent years, which we have already addressed in Chapter 2. Rather, it is what their building, and in particular their narrow temporal horizon, can tell us about their significance in the broader historical sense. The second subject concerns burial and the creation and use of bone repositories, and the historical moment encapsulated in the creation of the first examples.

We have already introduced the large timber halls that have been identified in southern Britain and in lowland Scotland and north Wales, but we have not yet expanded upon their character and significance, beyond emphasizing that they were both an early and a distinctive phenomenon. Not all of the early halls had the aisled layout that we have observed at White Horse Stone, but all were rectangular or sub-rectangular in plan (Fig. 3.2).

Most were post-built, but some may have had solid wooden side-walls comprising upright timbers, and at Dorstone Hill in Herefordshire the walls were apparently infilled with dung- and clay-based daub. These halls at Dorstone were deliberately burnt down, and this was also the case at Claish Farm, at Lockerbie Academy, at Doon Hill, and at Warren Field and Balbridie (on opposite sides of the Dee valley west of Aberdeen). This burning was not ubiquitous, however: similar buildings that were *not* burnt have been excavated at Yarnton in the Thames Valley, at Llandygai in north Wales, and at Lismore Fields near Buxton in Derbyshire.

One aspect of the building of these halls that may be significant is that there had sometimes been more than one such structure (or at Horton near Reading, smaller rectangular, post-defined buildings referred to as 'houses') at a location. It is rarely the case that the footprints of different

Fig. 3.2 Warren Field Early Neolithic hall: excavation in progress, 2005

The timber hall at Warren Field, Crathes, near Banchory, was some 24 m long by 9 m wide and featured a central aisle and three (or four) partitions creating a series of bays along the inside of each side-wall of post-and-slot construction. Its proportions were therefore similar to those excavated at Balbridie (just across the River Dee) and at Claish Farm near Stirling. The hall was in use between 3820 and 3690 cal BCE, and was deliberately destroyed, it would appear, by burning.

Photograph: © and courtesy of Charles and Hilary Murray.

buildings are superimposed upon each other, so it is difficult to assess whether these structures had been constructed sequentially, or had existed contemporaneously. Thus chronological succession is possible, but so too is social segmentation, with the buildings having been 'owned' by different kin- or clan-groups. Multiple structures have been recorded at Llandygai near Bangor, at Llanfaethlu on Anglesey, at Lismore Fields in Derbyshire, and now at Dorstone Hill in Herefordshire; and possibly also at White Horse Stone in Kent (Fig. 3.3).

As previously explained, the period during which such structures were built and used was relatively brief. In any one place where they occur, the span of their construction and use can probably be fitted within a period of anywhere from less than a decade to 150 years. So the refined chronology that we are now developing indicates that there appears to have been a time in each region when no such buildings were known, followed by a brief interval in which they were built and used, before the practice was again abandoned. In the comparable situation in Ireland, where the structures are much more numerous than in Britain but are predominantly smaller houses rather than large halls, all may have been constructed within a period of fifty-five to ninety-five years, a generation or two after the first Neolithic activity there.

This brevity of use may mean that the halls and houses concerned had a specific role (or roles) at a particular point in time, and that subsequently their construction ceased to be important to the communities concerned, or their purpose was met by other means. One way of explaining this is to argue that the craft-skills of the initial immigrant communities in building such structures died out, so that the successor communities were no longer capable of raising such sophisticated buildings. Alternatively, it could be maintained that living together in robustly constructed shelters might have been an important source of collective security for newly arrived colonists. However, the people in Britain responsible for the earliest structures were soon building other structures in wood, earth, and stone that were at least as sophisticated as these 'foundational' halls and houses. Moreover, as we saw in Chapter 2, with the possible exception of the site at Mairy in the Ardennes region of Belgium, closely similar structures are uncommon amongst communities on the near-Continent at the relevant period. It follows that the reasons for the rise and fall of hall-building should be found in the immediate conditions of the first Neolithic communities of Britain, whether we

Fig. 3.3 Llanfaethlu houses, Anglesey, under excavation

Two of the three buildings revealed during excavations in 2015 in advance of the building of a new school just to the north of Llanfaethlu village are visible here. The largest of the buildings is visible furthest from the camera, built on a north-east to south-west axis and measuring more than 17 m long and 7 m wide. The clustering of house-structures in this way is strongly reminiscent of the grouping of houses in Ireland. The west coast of Anglesey is visible in the background. Another building comprising wall-slots surrounded by massive post-holes was revealed and partially excavated in 2016.

Photograph: Adam Stanford; project by Catherine Rees and Matt Jones, CR Archaeology.

consider these to have been migrants, indigenous people, or some combination of the two.

So rather than being a circumstance forced upon these early groups, the innovation and the cessation of building such large and sophisticated structures were deliberate acts, intended to have specific outcomes. After a period of some decades it was apparently no longer necessary or appropriate to raise such structures. It is therefore our strong inference that *building the house* was at once an undertaking that drew people together in an act of labour, and one that established their solidarity and collective identity in a tangible and enduring form, *building the household*. The physical act of creating the structure bound the builders together into a new kind of community, which anthropologists refer to as a 'house society'. This is a kind of social unit in which the right of residence in a dwelling structure, and shared ownership over resources, artefacts, and intangible goods such as names and rituals, define who is and who is not a member. This is not to say that these Neolithic halls and houses had only symbolic importance. They undoubtedly had practical uses as places for living (whether permanently or seasonally), for meeting, and for storage. But their sometimes impressive size and robust construction and their concentration in a particular horizon of time indicates that they encapsulated the idea of the inception and assembly of a new kind of community, whatever the origins of its individual members. In particular, we would emphasize that during this period the communities concerned defined themselves as entities capable of collectively owning and disposing of wealth. This was an arrangement that was essential both to facilitate the cultivation of plant foods and the keeping of stock, and to enable the accumulation and inheritance of resources between the generations. These groups thereby became what we have termed 'invested lineages', insofar as investment in capital projects (at this stage, halls and houses), and the collective organization of subsistence production, became fundamental features of their existence. Although the process itself occurred across a brief span of time, once these social and material investments had been made, and the necessary relations of gifting and intergenerational transfer had been entered into, it was impossible to go back to looser social and material arrangements. This question of the loss of options is one that it is important to understand in reference to a new 'Neolithic' way of comprehending the passage of history, and it is a point that we shall return to in particular in Chapter 6.

Fig. 3.4 Hambledon Hill, Dorset: north long barrow

Hambledon is a large isolated, steep-sided hill that stands apart from the chalk escarpment looking northwards over the Blackmoor Vale in north Dorset. This view northwards across the Iron Age hillfort occupying the northern spur of the hill shows the massive bulk of the more northern of the two Neolithic long barrows located on the hill. Although not proved, it seems probable that a third causewayed enclosure occupied the upper slopes of the spur, hinted at by the line of pits above the Iron Age ramparts at left.

Photograph: early June 2017, © Keith Ray.

A narrative of human burial, and the first creation of bone repositories

Earthen long barrows and 'megalithic tombs' (the latter better described as barrows or cairns that featured the 'architectural' deployment of large stones) are arguably the most distinctive monuments of the Earlier Neolithic, not least because of the use in many of them of whole or split tree trunks or unworked boulders as major structural components (Fig. 3.4).

As we have related in Chapter 1, it was once conjectured that these monuments were created from the beginning of the period as territorial markers that were dominant and durable presences in the landscape. However, we now know that the earliest structures built in part at least to contain ancestral human remains were not always as prominent as they later became. To begin with, these barrows were few in number relative to their later ubiquity in some regions at least, and while the earliest structures possessed elements that prefigured later elaborations, some of these were relatively small in scale, even though they were occasionally strikingly complex.

Only a small minority of these sites have produced series of dates that place their beginnings clearly in the period before the thirty-eighth century BCE.

The stone-lined chamber set within the earthen barrow at Coldrum near the Medway river in Kent has possibly the best claim to be the earliest such structure so far known, perhaps dating to sometime in the fortieth or thirty-ninth century BCE, with the circular stone tomb at Broadsands near Paignton in Devon being built a century or more afterwards. Potentially early dates have also been returned on bones from stone cairns in the Cotswolds at Burn Ground and Sale's Lot, although the margin of error is sufficiently wide that either might have been constructed around 3800 BCE or later, along with cairns at Notgrove and West Tump. Nearby, the earthen so-called 'Banana barrow' sealed beneath the bank of the later causewayed enclosure at Crickley Hill may also be early, although its precise character is unclear. An earthen mound at West Cotton in the Nene valley in Northamptonshire appears to have been some form of burial site or cenotaph that has also produced early dates.

All these sites, apart from the latter two, were the subject of early excavations; and for this reason, where the radiocarbon dates have been obtained from human remains the contexts from which they derive are not as clearly related to the construction of the monument as we might prefer. However, all the bones appear to have been associated with primary structures at each site, even if, as in the case of Burn Ground, it is possible that the human remains had been curated in some other location before 'final' deposition in the contexts in which they were found. The site at Yabsley Street by the Thames east of London (already mentioned in this chapter and in Chapter 2) is also extremely important here, because it indicates the existence of a contrasting tradition of inhumation burial in coffins at exactly the same time

that repositories for the remains of multiple individuals began to be built in
southern Britain, shortly after the start of the Neolithic period. Furthermore,
the existence of cremation burials associated with fine carinated bowl
pottery at Bishop's Cannings in Wiltshire, at Yeavering in Northumberland,
and at Midtown of Pitglassie in Aberdeenshire indicates that this diversity of
practice was maintained through the early centuries of the Neolithic. What
it suggests is that the deceased were in some cases afforded a burial that
placed them outside the orbit of continuing daily life, while in other cases
their remains began to be used as a kind of resource, possibly understood
collectively as matter that was imbued with the presence of the ancestral
dead, and which could be employed in a variety of activities that deliberately
evoked the past.

When we turn to the more numerous long barrow and long cairn
monuments that began to be constructed from 3800 BCE onwards, our
understanding of their individual histories has been transformed by the
development of more fine-grained radiocarbon chronologies over the past
decade or so. A detailed study of the construction-, use-, and decay-sequences
of five long mounds in central southern Britain was the first archaeological
excursion into Early Neolithic close chronologies. This series of studies
found that the excavated one of two Ascott-under-Wychwood barrows
north of the Thames in west Oxfordshire was most likely the earliest of this
group of five closely studied monuments to have been built, and that its
entire span of use was probably less than fifty years either side of around
3725 BCE. Its construction may have been contemporary with the timber
mortuary structure that was the first element in the development of the
Fussell's Lodge long barrow in Wiltshire. However, the elaboration of that
structure and its subsequent transformation into a timber-revetted long
mound was not completed for another century or more. It was not until as
much as seventy-five years later than the start of building at Ascott that the
primary elements of the Hazleton long cairn in the western Cotswolds
were put in place. Another generation on saw the raising of the West Kennet
long barrow near Avebury (but not its subsequent elaboration as seen today)
around 3670–3635 cal BCE (Fig. 3.5), while the first burials were placed in
the chamber of the earlier of the two successive barrows at Wayland's Smithy
on the Ridgeway overlooking the Vale of the White Horse in Oxfordshire
(formerly north Berkshire) at about 3610–3550 cal BCE.

What is remarkable is that the entire sequence of interment in the first
chamber at Wayland's Smithy extended over a period of one to fifteen years.

Fig. 3.5 West Kennet long barrow, Wiltshire

The huge long barrow at West Kennet is seen here from the north-east. It was built long before Silbury Hill, which it now overlooks from the south. The colossal 100-m length of the earthen barrow is due to deliberate enhancement some centuries after the initial construction. The layout and excavated contents of the 'transepted' chambers are shown in Fig. 3.12. The later history of the site involved the blocking of the entrance and the infilling of the centre of the original façade, visible here at bottom left of the photograph.

Photograph: May 2017, © Adam Stanford (website: http://www.aerial-cam.co.uk/).

So the use of this structure for burial was brief, and limited to a few short episodes.

More recent research has demonstrated that the construction of the mortuary enclosure beneath the long mound of Wor Barrow on Cranborne Chase in north Dorset probably took place between 3685 and 3645 cal BCE, much the same time as the construction of West Kennet. A turf mound was

probably raised over the burials in 3650–3630 cal BCE, and the ditch surrounding the mound was probably completed in 3630–3540 or 3585–3515
cal BCE. The mortuary activity at this site is likely to have lasted for a little
more than two generations. Aside from Wor Barrow, the refined dating of
the initial five barrows is not yet closely replicable elsewhere because we do
not have the same number of closely dated samples from other barrows:
so the extent to which this sample of sites is representative of the wider
picture is so far unclear. This is the case even elsewhere in the same regions
as those barrows, although a further four sites in the Avebury area in which
West Kennet is situated do provide some clues as to the likely variability
among the twenty or so others known in and around the North Wiltshire
Downs. These less detailed results indicate that the construction of barrows,
some of them simpler in form, continued alongside the period in which
causewayed enclosures were in use locally, which we discuss later in this
chapter. Thus the long mound on Easton Down was probably raised between
3485 and 3385 cal BCE, while that at South Street was almost precisely
contemporary, with a likely build-date somewhere between 3495 and 3385
cal BCE. An interesting feature of the latter site is that marks apparently made
by an ard plough were scored into the pre-barrow turf sealed beneath this
barrow, perhaps indicating that ploughing had taken place in two directions
here not long before the barrow was raised. The stone-chambered long
mound at Millbarrow appears to have been constructed late in the millennium, between 3390 and 3200 cal BCE, while the barrow at Beckhampton
Road west of Avebury, which may have contained no burial chamber at all,
was built at much the same time. This tends to support the long-held con-
viction that long barrows built after the zenith of this kind of monument
(which now appears to span a roughly 250-year period from around 3700 to
3450 BCE) may have become increasingly divergent in form.

It has long been recognized that although earthen long barrows and long
cairns generally contained multiple burials, these were far from numerous
enough to represent the majority of the people who lived and died during
the period. Given that the remains of men, women, and children are often
represented, the criterion for selection was clearly neither age nor gender,
and it has been speculated that these dead might have been drawn from a
chiefly lineage, might represent persons who had died in inauspicious
circumstances, or might simply be representatives of a larger community,
deposited at infrequent intervals. The implication in each case is that aside
from the few people who were cremated, buried in pits and flat graves, or

deposited in caves, most of the deceased had been dealt with in some other manner that left no archaeological trace, whether exposed on platforms, consumed by scavengers, or immersed in rivers.

In both wooden and timber chambers, human remains have often been encountered in a state of disarticulation, with skulls often placed alongside each other and longbones bundled together. At Wor Barrow in Dorset, two bodies, at least one of them a young man, were laid out in a timber box chamber, before a third, partially articulated corpse was added. Later, three 'bundled' skeletons were added before the chamber was encased in turf. Later again, the bodies of a man and a child were introduced to the ditch surrounding the mound. Although the former of these was found in articular order, radiocarbon results indicate that he had died somewhere between 30 and 165 years before the ditch had been dug. Evidently, his remains had been curated, either tightly bundled or actually mummified. These findings highlight the importance that was sometimes afforded to remains regarded as ancestral, and indicate that not all the bodies interred in long barrows and long cairns need have been those of the recently deceased. People who were especially significant in relation to kin ties and descent may have been prioritized for inclusion in certain mortuary deposits at particular junctures. We will discuss the implications of these funerary practices further in Chapter 4.

Outside southern England the dating of long mounds and cairns is so far somewhat less precise. In Yorkshire, long barrows at Kemp Howe, Wold Newton, and Burythorpe were all probably built in the thirty-eighth or early thirty-seventh centuries, anything from a few decades to more than a century after the first Neolithic activity in the region. At Whitwell in northern Derbyshire, human remains probably began to be deposited in a linear mortuary structure in 3780–3720 cal BCE, and this was later incorporated into a trapezoidal long cairn, following the construction and extension of a smaller oval cairn (see further discussion in Chapter 4). In the Scottish lowlands, long barrows may have first been built around 3800 BCE, almost as soon as any other Neolithic activity has been identified locally. By contrast, Vicki Cummings has argued that many of the chambered tombs of western Scotland may have been no older than 3700 BCE (Fig. 3.6).

This suggestion chimes with recent work by Rick Schulting and colleagues, which indicates that the court cairns (or chambered long mounds) of Ireland were first built in the mid thirty-seventh century BCE, shortly after the climax of house-building, and more than a century after the beginning

Fig. 3.6 Cairnholy I chambered cairn, Kirkcudbright, façade

The impressive long cairn constructed overlooking Wigtown Bay from the north was probably a multi-stage construction, starting with a small closed, stone-lined box within a small mound, and then expanded to create a long mound with a façade of tall, thin stone monoliths linked together by low stone walling. The imposing stones were the equivalent in stone to timber uprights in the façades of long barrows in Yorkshire, Lincolnshire, and central southern England. Cairnholy I was excavated by S. Piggott and T. Powell in 1949 and is only one of two sites in Britain (the other being the Sweet Track in Somerset) where a jadeitite axe has been retrieved in situ during an archaeological project. This tomb, and the nearby Cairnholy II, are examples of the Clyde group of long cairns in western Scotland, which Vicki Cummings and others have suggested began to be constructed around 3700 BCE.

Photograph: 2002, © Julian Thomas.

of the Neolithic there. This raises the possibility that in some areas mortuary monuments became common only after houses or halls began to go out of use. The implication is that these 'houses of the dead' took on some of the functions of the houses of the living, as a tangible feature of the landscape tied to the persistent identity of a particular human community.

It is now widely accepted that the mortuary practices manifested in long barrows and long cairns often took the form of protracted rites, in which fleshed bodies were laid out in a defined space such as a chamber and allowed to rot down, before the skeletal remains were subsequently reorganized. This has sometimes been interpreted as a means of expressing the person's gradual incorporation into an ancestral community after death. However, it would be a mistake to extrapolate from these extended mortuary activities to imagine that the resulting deposits had accumulated over a period of several centuries. Instead, it has recently become apparent that the period of funerary activity was probably limited to a few generations at most. At Hazleton and at Ascott-under-Wychwood in the Cotswolds, for example, the refined radiocarbon chronology indicates that human remains were deposited over an interval of about a century. At West Kennet near Avebury in Wiltshire, the period of activity was limited to less than thirty years, and in the small earthen barrow that preceded the massive stone-bounded long mound at Wayland's Smithy in Berkshire, it can have been no longer than fifteen years. Yet in most cases there are indications that the monuments concerned continued to be visited and venerated by their host communities over much longer periods. Animal remains or artefacts were introduced to the chambers or flanking ditches, and the mounds themselves were sometimes altered or enlarged, in various ways.

Perhaps the best way of explaining this is to relinquish the idea that long barrows and long cairns were the equivalents of modern cemeteries, that is, that they were spaces that were reserved for the accumulation of the dead over a lengthy period. Instead, inhumation was practised over a relatively short timespan integral to the construction and/or earliest use of each monument. So, rather than barrows and tombs serving as facilities for housing the deceased, it was the actual but in some senses token presence of the ancestral dead that conferred a particular social and historical status on these structures. In this way, it may be preferable to think of these works involving communal investment as commemorative structures, continually bringing to mind among the living their lineage stretching back to the foundational progenitor-groups: in other words, to significant ancestors. Long barrows and cairns embodied the community and its history in this way, because they contained the remains of that community's founding generations. If 'being Neolithic' involved maintaining new mindsets, practices, and habits, as well as living in new ways alongside plants and animals, these were the people who had first dwelt in this manner. They constituted a point of origin for their descendants, who both reckoned their descent and drew their identity from these ancestral generations.

Often, nonetheless, the construction of long mounds containing chamber spaces for the dead followed on from earlier activity in the same location, which may not have been strictly funerary in character. In many earthen long barrows, the chamber took the form of a linear, trough-like space flanked by banks of clay or stone and bracketed by two massive upright posts (sometimes with a third, medial post). These posts were generally derived from the trunk of an oak tree, which had been split in two longitudinally, with the two flat sides facing inwards. In some cases, as at Street House in North Yorkshire, and at Haddenham in the Cambridgeshire fens, these timber uprights are now thought to have been decades or even centuries older than the rest of the chamber to which they later became integral. The implication is that pairs of posts originally constituted free-standing structures of some kind, and that their funerary use was a later and secondary adaptation. Interestingly in this context, pairs of oak uprights often form an element of the large timber halls that we have already discussed, and it may be that these pairs of posts were regarded as timber shrines which connected the ancestral community with the subsequent creation of structures associated with mortuary and commemorative rites. The raising of posts bedded in the earth in this way may have made a powerful foundational statement that was both sustained and at the same time reinforced by the transposition of the posts and their symbolic enclosure of human remains.

Regionalization and exchange networks

If the early part of the fourth millennium saw the establishment of a Neolithic way of life in Britain, aspects of this came to be transformed in fundamental ways during the thirty-seventh century BCE. One indication of the nature of such change is registered in pottery production and use. Over time, the fine carinated bowl pottery of the earliest Neolithic occurred within more varied and larger groups of pottery vessels, became more regionally diverse, and may have begun to be used for a wider variety of purposes (Fig. 3.7).

The 'developed carinated bowl' at the end of this series is notably thicker and coarser, and manifests in a wider range of vessel forms. Meanwhile, in the south and west of England assemblages occurred that combined coarser carinated bowls with other forms, apparently drawing on west French prototypes. Subsequently, throughout much of Britain, 'heavy bowl' assemblages developed, with a variety of hemispherical bag-shaped and shouldered forms, thicker walls, and heavy rims. It is hard to avoid the conclusion that pottery had by this time lost something of its exotic and exclusive character,

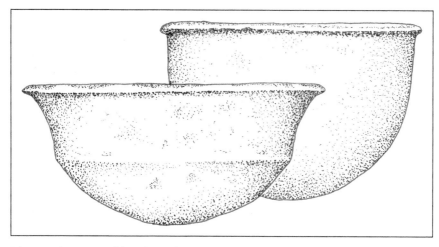

Fig. 3.7 A carinated bowl vessel and a plain bowl vessel (not to scale)
These pottery vessels represent two distinct, but chronologically overlapping traditions of Neolithic pottery from the first half of the fourth millennium. The drawing of a carinated bowl is derived from a vessel, some of the sherds of which were found at Eweford West, Dumbartonshire (rim diameter 26 cm), while the plain bowl vessel behind it was excavated at Ty Isaf, Breconshire (rim diameter 22.5 cm).
Drawing: Tim Hoverd.

although its increasing ubiquity occurred at the same time as the emergence of a series of decorated wares. These latter were often no finer than the plain pottery, and assemblages frequently combine the two, in proportions that vary from region to region. However, what is notable is that one particular vessel form, the shouldered bowl, was repeatedly singled out for decoration, and this was generally concentrated on the rim and the upper part of the body. Joshua Pollard has recently pointed out that the burnished surfaces and subtly rippled decoration of the earliest pottery suggests that it was engaged with in a tactile and intimate manner, perhaps by small groups of people. In contrast, the introduction of decoration indicates that pots may have increasingly been apprehended visually, amidst larger gatherings, and their significance appreciated from a distance.

It is with the development of decorated pottery that distinct regional identities begin to be clearly discernible in Neolithic Britain. It may be that groups of people living in different parts of the country had gradually and unintentionally developed separate traditions of ceramic manufacture, in the manner of what has been termed by anthropologists 'cultural drift'. However, studies of near-contemporary but essentially pre-industrial technology demonstrate that people are generally acutely aware of the differences between their own handiwork and objects made by neighbouring groups. Moreover, they actively use these differences to establish and maintain boundaries of one kind or another. However, these 'decorated wares' actually tend to blur into each other to some extent, and their ornamentation may have had as much of a role in marking out places and practices as separate groups of people. In most cases, the new mid fourth-millennium decorated styles of Neolithic pottery in Britain clearly developed from, but involved an elaboration of, existing vessel forms. For example, the Whitehawk Ware of south-east England featured open, S-profiled, round-bottomed bowls closely related to the earlier fine carinated bowl assemblages, but with decoration on the upper body above a horizontal cordon. Meanwhile, the Windmill Hill Ware of northern Wessex included among its variety of forms decorated versions of shouldered bowls apparently inspired by pots that were in use at broadly the same time in western France.

This proliferation of ceramic traditions and growth of decoration coincided with the occurrence of a series of indicators of social stress and enhanced competition. One of these was a growing number of human bodies showing signs of either healed or fatal trauma. These include the tips of flint arrowheads embedded in human ribs, and depressed fractures in skulls, suggesting the impact of a blunt weapon. Observations of these traces of body traumas are now numerous enough and are sufficiently closely dated as to indicate the existence of endemic warfare, although the probability is that this generally took the form of raiding and feuding, and that pitched battles were infrequent events (see Chapter 4 for further commentary). This picture echoes the evidence for a number of massacres earlier in the Neolithic era in continental Europe, and indicates that the period more generally was not necessarily one of widespread peace and cooperation. Rather, the periodic threat of violent interactions formed part of the background to everyday life in the Early Neolithic. This was nonetheless the counterpart to practices that increasingly emphasized the importance of alliances, collective hospitality, and convivial relations. We might therefore suggest that social life was becoming more intensive, in various ways and at several different scales.

This accords well with the way that the growth of regional identities from the thirty-seventh century BCE onwards is matched by increasing evidence for interregional contact and exchange. Such is the range of artefacts and materials that was being circulated over considerable distances from this time onwards that it can surely be inferred that a set of more extensive exchange networks was in the process of being established. Good-quality flint from Beer Head in Devon, and dark chert from the Isle of Portland in Dorset, for example, were transported into central southern Britain, as were pottery vessels gritted with fragments of igneous gabbroic rock from the Lizard peninsula in Cornwall, and with oolitic limestone from the area between Bath and Frome. More widely distributed still were ground and polished stone axeheads from quarry sites in the west of Britain. These might arguably have emulated the axes of jadeitite that had been quarried in the Italian Alps from the sixth millennium BCE, small numbers of which had found their way to Britain. It is likely that one of the earliest of the British stone sources to be exploited was the distinctive blue-green volcanic tuff of the Langdale valley in Cumbria, where radiocarbon dates for the working are concentrated in the period between 3800 and 3500 cal BCE, but continuing sporadically for a further five hundred years thereafter. The appearance of the Langdale axeheads was not entirely unlike those made in jadeitite stone from Alpine quarries, and similarly the Langdale stone itself was found, as with the jadeitite source-locations in the Alps, in a relatively inaccessible upland location. Moreover, the most common source-location was distinguished by its occurrence close to or on the visually arresting Langdale Pikes.

Fieldwork in the Langdales by Richard Bradley and Mark Edmonds has demonstrated that the earliest quarrying for axes may have been relatively unskilled, resulting in numerous failed axe preforms, and waste flakes of variable size and thickness. Over time, it seems that the manufacture of axes became more accomplished, and was concentrated in a smaller number of locations, which tended to be more difficult to access, and to command more spectacular views. This is most clearly the case with the quarrying on the buttresses of the Pike of Stickle, where fires were lit to loosen the rock from the quarry face (Fig. 3.8).

It is probable that while the earliest stone axes from Langdale were made by non-specialists who visited the valley seasonally, perhaps grazing animals on the slopes and in the nearby valleys, over time more skilled people took over, presumably making axes intended for long-distance exchange. Indeed, the densest concentration of Langdale axes found at some distance from their source-area is located in the Wolds of East Yorkshire, where there is abundant flint that could be, and was, used to make perfectly serviceable polished axes. The implication is that axes which came from a remote and

Fig. 3.8 Great Langdale, Cumbria: the view looking up the south screes

The south-west-facing stone screes beneath the Pike of Stickle crag (one of the Langdale Pikes at the head of Great Langdale in the central Lake District) appear at first glance to be, like so many other such accumulations of exfoliated rock debris, the natural product of erosion of exposed rock-faces. At the Pike of Stickle and other prominent crags in the immediate area and over towards the Scafell Pikes, however, while such screes do contain naturally occurring erosion products, in among their mass are often considerable amounts of working debris derived from fire-setting and quarrying of the rock in the Neolithic period.

Photograph: 2016, © Julian Thomas.

special location, and which had a distinctive appearance, had a value over and above any everyday utility they may have had for felling trees, splitting logs, or clearing brush.

Valuable objects acquired from a distance and limited in their supply might have had a number of important roles. Secured in a wooden haft and carried around, a finely polished stone axe would have announced its owner's importance or identity, and drawn attention to their access to connections with distant communities and places. As a gift, it would have enhanced the giver's prestige, attracted followers, or secured alliances. As a payment, it might have procured a marriage or compensated for a killing. It is therefore easy to see the attraction that goods of this kind may have had in the increasingly violent and competitive world of the earlier fourth millennium. Indeed, the fine but nonetheless strong stone axeheads that have in rare circumstances been found along with their elaborate wooden hafts may themselves have been weapons of both display and actual warfare.

In time, the axes from the Lake District were complemented by those quarried at, and procured from, stone sources elsewhere in Britain, for instance in Cornwall, north and south-west Wales, and western Scotland. Even axes of the distinctive dark porcellanite stone from Tievebulliagh in Antrim and from Rathlin Island off the north-west coast of Ireland sometimes occur on the British mainland. What all these source-locations share in common is remoteness, and frequently an association with dramatic crags or mountainous outcrops, several among which directly overlooked the sea.

This rapid 'uplift' in the tempo of the interregional exchange of readily identifiable stone items was accompanied in all likelihood (albeit as gauged from so far only exploratory studies) by the use of certain rocks, after deliberate crushing, as tempering agents in pots, including the gabbroic and oolitic sources noted already. That these pots themselves had in some cases travelled some distance from their location of preparation or production tells us something about the nature and purpose of the supra-community interaction that was occurring at this time. So although regional identities had become more distinct by the middle of the fourth millennium, they were cross-cut by channels of exchange contacts that extended over very considerable distances. This may have resulted from, but may also have partially facilitated and fuelled, more localized competition for personal or kin-group-based accumulation of wealth, prestige, and the acquisition of followers.

A narrative of changing subsistence practices

The development of new ways of circulating desirable and exotic artefacts and materials was complemented, perhaps not entirely surprisingly, by changes in the way that food was acquired. We have seen that at the beginning of the Neolithic domesticated plants and animals were introduced to Britain from the Continent. To begin with, the cultivation of cereals was seemingly adopted enthusiastically throughout much of Britain, although probably in very small 'garden' plots, and alongside the continued exploitation of wild plants such as hazelnuts, acorns, berries, and crab apples. However, from the thirty-seventh century onwards the representation of directly dated charred cereal grains and threshing residues in archaeological deposits on the British mainland begins to fall away abruptly, becoming all but invisible by 3300 BCE.

There is strong circumstantial evidence that cultivation did not cease altogether, but its scale and intensity almost certainly declined. The remains of wild plants, however, continue to be present among the dated samples that have been recovered from this time horizon. A similar pattern has been observed in Ireland, and here it has been noted that the apparent decline in cultivation coincides with the disappearance of the numerous rectangular timber houses that, as we have seen, were built during a short period in the earliest Neolithic. One interpretation that has been put forward for this phenomenon is a 'boom and bust' of pioneer agriculture. It has been noted that the yields achieved from early, unimproved grain species were generally low, but that for a short while after their introduction into a given area they would have been relatively productive. However, after this 'honeymoon' period, local pests and diseases would have begun to attack the new domesticates, while soil exhaustion may also have started to set in. The consequence of this will have been a collapse of arable farming, and a rapid decline of population, which only recovered in the Later Neolithic.

The flaw in this argument is that the period between, say, 3650 and 3300 BCE actually coincided with a major increase in the scale and number of the monuments being built in both Britain and Ireland. In Ireland, the supposed agricultural crash corresponds with the development of the passage-tomb tradition. On the basis of a project devoted to dating the bone pins from the Carrowmore passage-tomb cemetery in Co. Sligo, Robert Hensey has argued that small, simple tombs with polygonal chambers, surrounded by a boulder kerb, may date to the thirty-eighth or thirty-seventh century BCE, shortly after the start of local Neolithic activity. After 3600 BCE, much more numerous and more substantial structures developed, like those in the Loughcrew and Carrowkeel cemeteries, with substantial covering mounds and more developed passages and entrances. The process of elaboration in scale and complexity culminated with the construction of the three massive tombs of Knowth, Dowth, and Newgrange, in the 'bend in the Boyne' in Co. Meath, between 3200 and 3000 BCE. This development, demanding the investment of progressively greater quantities of labour, was played out over the period during which the supposed economic decline took place.

In southern Britain, the same period saw the creation of two of the country's most monumental prehistoric structures, the Dorset Cursus and the Hambledon Hill causewayed enclosure complex, each of which is discussed further in this book. If large numbers of people could be mobilized to work on the creation of these edifices, the notion of a catastrophic fall in population is probably not tenable. Equally, while the evidence for cultivated plants begins to fall away at this time, the same is not the case for domesticated animals. This evidence suggests, on the contrary, that there was an increasing emphasis on raising cattle: it has been argued that at some enclosure sites the animal bone assemblages indicate the culling of older cows from large herds that were not concentrated in the immediate vicinity year-round. Chemical analysis of residues from pottery from the start of the British Neolithic onwards has not only shown that it is highly likely that dairy products were regularly being consumed, possibly including cheese as well as milk, but also that this consumption seemingly continued after the thirty-seventh century BCE. Moreover, strontium and oxygen isotope values from the tooth enamel of people buried in this period are such as to suggest that they had often repeatedly moved during their youth between areas some distance apart, and with different geological characteristics. New analyses of bodies dating to the thirty-seventh century BCE from Wor Barrow in Dorset, for instance, suggest seasonal movements (or perhaps resource acquisition) between different regional environments. Comparable work on remains from Hazleton in the Gloucestershire Cotswolds indicates more extensive peregrinations, as far as Herefordshire or south Wales.

One plausible way to explain all this evidence is as representing a change of emphasis from arable to pastoral farming, with at least a proportion of the population following large mobile herds between seasonal pastures. Probably both wild and domesticated plants continued to be exploited, although there are hints that the plots where the latter were grown were less intensively manured as time progressed. Nonetheless, the centre of gravity of subsistence activity seems to have shifted markedly towards meat and dairy products. It may be that a decline in cereal yields provided a 'push' factor behind this change, but the 'pull' of livestock was probably the more important factor in promoting the shift.

A key reason for this is, we think, that while plant foods are reliable staples that feed people and keep them alive, livestock represent mobile *wealth* as well as simply nutrition. Herds of cattle, in particular, can be accumulated by prominent people or powerful groups, and constitute 'capital', the use-value of which can be realized in a variety of different ways. While milk and a certain amount of meat can contribute to the everyday diet, meat is much more valuable than grain as a feasting food, and the provision of feasts is a powerful means of enhancing prestige and social standing and recruiting followers. Cattle are also better suited than cereals for use as dowry or bridewealth payments, and as gifts they can establish relations of debt and obligation between donor and recipient. By building up increasing numbers of cattle, it would have been possible for particular people to actively manage and steer their social interrelations in a variety of ways, thereby increasing their influence and authority. It is probably no accident, in this light, that the start of this shift from cultivation to herding appears to have coincided with the growing evidence for regionalization, violence, and the exchange of prestige valuables. This is because all these developments denote the emergence of a more competitive society and increasing social inequality. Indeed, it is entirely possible that some at least of the violent episodes noted earlier could have occurred during cattle-raiding expeditions.

However, in one part of Britain a very different pattern of settlement activity was developing at this time. In the Orkney Islands, Neolithic activity began a little later than on the mainland, and a decline in cereal cultivation from the thirty-seventh century is not evident at all. While the large timber halls and smaller houses were a short-lived phenomenon elsewhere in Britain, there is a virtually unbroken sequence of the building of walled and roofed structures throughout the Orcadian Neolithic, beginning with scattered post-hole-built timber houses and developing into nucleated villages of cellular stone buildings. This was not simply a consequence of the existence of suitable building materials on the islands, since areas such as Caithness that have precisely the same flagstone and sandstone geology have (so far) not revealed any settlements of Neolithic stone houses. While much of Britain moved towards a semi-mobile way of life, based on the accumulation of cattle herds, this may not have been practicable on the islands, where ecologically distinct and spatially separate seasonal pastures were not available, and stands of hazel were minimal. In its place, a distinctive social and economic forma-tion developed, based on household groups with fixed horticultural plots and small numbers of livestock. The emergence of this very distinctive Orcadian framework of economic and social life was, remarkably, and as we shall see, to have far-reaching consequences across Britain later in the Neolithic.

Building long mounds and chambers, variously

One of the problems highlighted by the development of a more accurate chronology for the Neolithic is that although individual mortuary monuments may have been constructed and used over a relatively short period of time, broadly similar kinds of structure may have been built over several centuries. It follows that neat sequences in which one morphologically defined 'type' is replaced by another are often less accurate than previous generations of archaeologists would have assumed.

Indeed, the very structural features of long barrows that were once thought to have indicated that they were built and used at the same time as one another may instead denote the recurrence of motifs and practices that had their heyday and then became part of a repertoire that enabled them to

Fig. 3.9 Capel Garmon chambered long cairn, Conwy, north Wales

The long cairn south of Capel Garmon, sited above the middle reaches of Afon Conwy near Betws-y-Coed, was excavated in 1927 and subsequently restored (now in the guardianship of Cadw, the Welsh Government's historic environment service). The cairn features a pair of chambers, one of which retains its large capstone, both accessed from a central passage, and structurally it has affinities with the 'Cotswold-Severn' long barrows. The bulk of the cairn was once entirely covered over with stones. The view here is north-westwards towards the peaks of the Snowdonia massif, and in particular Carnedd Llewelyn and Glyder Fawr.

Photograph: March 2007, © Adam Stanford (website: http://www.aerial-cam.co.uk/).

be redeployed in distinctly later monuments. Only the kind of fine-grained chronologies already mentioned will enable us gradually to unpick these complexities. Some broad patterns are nonetheless emerging. We have seen that long mounds and cairns containing stone chambers first occurred quite early in the British Neolithic sequence. However, their appearance in different regions was not precisely synchronized, nor was their occurrence prefigured by a uniform elapse of time after the first manifestation of Neolithic things and practices locally. In general, there appears to have been escalation of monument building from the thirty-seventh century onwards, which involved both a proliferation of existing kinds of structure and the emergence of new traditions. Long mounds and cairns in areas such as southern England, eastern Scotland, and eastern Yorkshire continued to be constructed until after 3500 BCE, although, as we have seen, the primary use of any particular barrow for the deposition of the dead often lasted for less than a century.

Yet there is some indication that as the long-mound tradition progressed, it became more diverse. Some mounds that have produced relatively late radiocarbon dates, such as the Amesbury 42 long barrow located beside the Great Stonehenge Cursus, are exceptionally large. Other massive long barrows, such as Tilshead Old Ditch on Salisbury Plain, may have encapsulated smaller, earlier long mounds.

In addition, prodigiously long mounds known as 'bank barrows' developed, such as the potentially two-kilometre long Tom's Knowe/Lamb Knowe structure that crosses the White Esk in Dumfries and Galloway. At Maiden Castle in Dorset another bank barrow runs across the banks and ditches of the Neolithic enclosure, demonstrating that it dates to a mature phase of the Neolithic. Bank barrows are of consistent height and width along their length, and contain no obvious mortuary structure or chamber. Like the equally late South Street and Beckhampton Road long barrows in the Avebury area that we have already mentioned, they rarely produce any human burials. Towards the end of the long-barrow tradition, then, mounds appear to have been built whose sheer imposing monumentality was more significant than their potential role as containers for (some or all of) the dead of each relevant community. Other late long mounds, of which the Alfriston long barrow in East Sussex is a good example, contained small numbers of articulated burials in individual graves or small-group interments, rather than featuring any kind of collective mortuary structure within the mound. This suggests a form of funerary activity of yet shorter, rather than

Fig. 3.10 The 'Cotswold-Severn' chambered tomb at Parc le Breos Cwm, West Glamorgan

This aerial view of the stone-built cairn shows very clearly the trapezoidal shape of such tombs, the particularly deeply recessed forecourt here, and the prominent flanking 'horns'. Far from being prominently located, however, the Parc le Breos Cwm structure lies in a dry, narrow, flat-bottomed and steep-sided limestone gorge (the Cwm in question), where the Cathole Cave, occupied in the late Upper Palaeolithic period, has also produced evidence for Mesolithic activity. Parc le Breos Cwm is (probably) one of a whole series of such structures featuring 'extra-revetment' blocking materials representing formal closure and sealing of the monument (in this case mostly removed during the 1869 and 1960–1 excavations and further tidied away when the monument was 'restored' in 1961).

Photograph: © Adam Stanford.

longer, duration, and a mortuary ritual focused on maintaining the bodily remains intact rather than the earlier practice of separating flesh and bone, and then disaggregating the separate elements of the skeleton, which were often reinterred elsewhere.

As we saw earlier in this chapter, it was not uncommon for individual barrows to have a complex developmental history, with significant changes

being registered in the form of the structure, or even its wholesale replacement. In the case of the five sites subject to the first detailed Bayesian
chronological studies, the mound at Ascott appears to have been enlarged
less than fifty-five years after its initial construction, while Hazleton was
constructed as a single, if perhaps protracted, episode. The chambers and
mound at West Kennet probably represented a single event of building, but
kinks observed in the side ditches may indicate that the tail of the mound
was an addition to an initially smaller tumulus containing the chambers,
resulting in a truly colossal structure. At Fussell's Lodge the wooden mortuary structure was in use, and enlarged, over a period of more than a century
before the massive mound was raised over the 'bone repository', bringing its
use to an end. The similar wooden chamber at Wayland's Smithy was in use
for a much shorter period before it was sealed beneath a small earthen
mound. Around a century after this first chamber was built a more dramatic
change took place: an entirely new structure was built over and encapsulated the earlier mound, on a monumental scale. Not only was this structure
at Wayland's Smithy massive and built with a stone kerb defining its edges
in a huge trapezoidal shape, but a façade comprising massive individual sarsen stones was built to create a forecourt with, as its central focus, a stone-
lined and walled passage that extended into the new mound to give access
to a whole group of chambers radiating from it (Fig. 3.11).

The chambers were themselves lined and roofed by massive stones in a
closely similar way to those at West Kennet and other 'chambered tombs',
and they then became the receptacles for the interment of a further series
of mortuary deposits. While the earlier burials were placed largely intact upon
a 'pavement' of flat stones within the first barrow, where they slowly collapsed
and became intermingled, the bones placed in the stone-lined chambers at
the subsequent, more massive Wayland's Smithy barrow would have been
accessible despite temporary blockings. The term 'repository' is therefore all
the more apt for this later structure (Fig. 3.12). One question that inevitably
arises from appreciation of this sequence and complexity is how typical it
was of the hundreds of other known sites of long barrows not only in
southern but also in western and northern Britain. As yet, unfortunately,
there are too few sets of dates to be able to create detailed chronologies of
the kind already mentioned: but it is clear that in time some fascinating
patterns of co-occurrence and development are likely to emerge to amplify
further this key aspect of Neolithic history.

Fig. 3.11 The full façade of Wayland's Smithy chambered tomb, in snow

The multi-phase construction of the Wayland's Smithy long barrow is far from evident from what appears to be a unitary structure when viewed today. The monument is located only 300 m to the south of the north-facing scarp overlooking the Vale of the White Horse, Oxfordshire (formerly Berkshire). Its dramatic façade of upright sarsen stones faces southwards onto the Ridgeway some 50 m away. This presumed ancient long-distance track links Overton Hill near Avebury to the Thames at Goring and extends north-eastwards along the Chiltern scarp towards Cambridgeshire.
Photograph: February 2010, © Adam Stanford (website: http://www.aerial-cam.co.uk/).

The greater diversity of barrows that began to be created in western and northern Britain after around 3700 BCE often formed distinctive regional groups. It has been argued that some simple passage tombs, distinguished by a box-like chamber of stone uprights accessed by a short, walled passage in a small round cairn, may be earlier than this, even perhaps dating to the fifth millennium BCE. However, there is at present little unambiguous evidence for this. We have seen that the example at Broadsands in Devon dates to the thirty-eighth century BCE, and that the new evidence from Carrowmore suggests a similar or slightly later date. Nonetheless, a case has

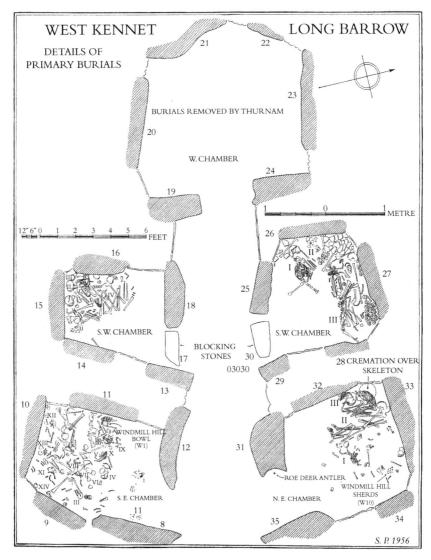

Fig. 3.12 Plan of the chambers at West Kennet long barrow

The sequence of building of the sarsen-enclosed structures at the east end of the West Kennet monument includes the late blocking of the façade, thus inhibiting direct access to the chambers. This did not prevent the insertion of subsidiary material into the mound, however, including during the Beaker period.

Plan: reproduced from the publication of the excavation by Stuart Piggott (HMSO).

been made that the excavated cremations and their accompanying antler pins may post-date the construction of the tombs, and that earlier deposits may have been removed, leaving no trace. Recent radiocarbon analysis from the passage tomb of Baltinglass Hill in Co. Wicklow has produced one result of 3946–3715 cal BCE from a calcined human cranial fragment, but others that fit more comfortably in the thirty-seventh century. The single, anomalously early date might result from the introduction of curated bone into the tomb, or might simply be inaccurate, placing the site temporally alongside the new dates for Carrowmore. A more radical view has it that many of the Carrowmore monuments are not passage tombs at all (but simple dolmens that were later architecturally elaborated), that Broadsands is too ruinous for its affinities to be realistically assessed, and that the earliest passage tombs in Britain and Ireland are actually the Maes Howe-style monuments of Orkney, such as Quanterness. The Baltinglass results perhaps argue against this perspective. We have already noted that long cairns in Ireland and western Scotland began to be built in appreciable numbers in the thirty-seventh century BCE, but there may have been earlier outliers within this overall pattern. An example might be the recently excavated 'Clyde' cairn at Blasthill on Kintyre, which was possibly built at an early point in this sequence.

The builders of most of these groups of barrows ultimately took their inspiration, and borrowed particular constructional devices, from the Continent, especially western and northern France. However, this does not mean that they had always seen the precursor monuments for themselves: the stylistic connections are generally imprecise, and architectural elements from different sources (potentially including southern Scandinavia and the North European Plain) were seemingly mixed together and elaborated upon. Meanwhile, the distinctive 'portal dolmens' of Wales, Ireland, and Cornwall have no precise Continental parallels at all (Fig. 3.13). These consist of a massive capstone raised on a series of supporting uprights, including an arrangement of three stones that *might* have mimicked a doorway. The effect of this would have been that the chamber was closed, so that continued access to any mortuary deposit was presumably not a priority. Indeed, it may be that the *display* of the capstone was the principal objective in constructing the monument, and that the incorporation of human remains may have been a secondary issue. This could be compared with the pairs of earthfast upright posts that we have seen were often incorporated into timber mortuary structures, but that might initially have been more significant as a conspicuous arrangement of massive timbers. Portal dolmens apparently had small or vestigial mounds or cairns, so that the large capstone would probably always have been visible. While all the barrows that included large stones in their make-up may have contained the remains of the dead (although

Fig. 3.13 Pentre Ifan portal dolmen, Nevern, Pembrokeshire

Pentre Ifan is regarded as a 'classic' portal dolmen, a class of monument that has a mostly westerly distribution in southern Britain (see also Fig. 3.14). Such structures, with a frequently massive capstone balanced upon three or more monoliths, have until recently been presumed primary burial chambers once covered over with (long) cairns of stones. However, in 2014 Vicki Cummings and Colin Richards proposed instead that the capstones were dug out from their natural (glacially determined) former resting places during the Neolithic period, and were raised in situ (witness large pits observed through excavations at some sites). In this case, the primary purpose was to mark a location by the dramatic device of having the massive capstone appear to 'float free' from the ground—an image vividly conveyed in this photograph.

Photograph: September 2013, © Adam Stanford (website: http://www.aerial-cam.co.uk/).

this cannot be demonstrated in many areas with acidic soils, where bones have not survived), making a visual impact on the landscape sometimes appears to have been of equal or greater importance (Fig. 3.14).

As for the date of the appearance of this distinctive form of megalithic structure, there remain uncertainties. At Dyffryn Ardudwy in Gwynedd, for example, a small pit containing the sherds of four carinated bowls was found immediately in front of the portal stones of such a structure, suggesting an early beginning, perhaps as early as 3800–3700 BCE. This impression is reinforced by the fact that the structure was later incorporated into a long cairn that featured the piling up of stones around and perhaps over the original dolmen. If typical, this would imply a date early in the Neolithic for portal dolmens, but the radiocarbon evidence presently remains equivocal. Dates on human remains from the Poulnabrone dolmen in western Ireland

Fig. 3.14 St Lythans portal dolmen, near Barry, south Wales

The 'portal' of portal dolmens refers to the creation of a kind of stone doorway within the monoliths supporting the capstone. The location of the megalithic structure shown in this highly evocative photograph at the centre of a slightly later, larger, stone-built and kerbed long barrow at St Lythans was demonstrated in a recent test-excavation project directed by Ffion Reynolds. This suggests that even if the origin of the dolmen here was the same as has been suggested by Cummings and Richards for Pentre Ifan in Pembrokeshire (Fig. 3.13) or Lanyon Quoit in west Cornwall, it was nonetheless (like several others) subsequently encased within a long cairn.

Photograph: November 2011, © Adam Stanford (website: http://www.aerial-cam.co.uk/).

are also early, but their relationship to the chamber is unclear. In the meantime, if we are to judge from the existing available radiocarbon dates, many of these dolmens may date instead to the mid fourth millennium BCE.

An appreciable proportion of these monuments underwent multi-phase construction like that at Dyffryn Ardudwy (Fig. 3.15). That is to say, an initial structure that may have been relatively diminutive had a series of additional bodies of cairn material added to it. In some cases this simply rendered the site much more massive, but in others the addition of a tail, or

Fig. 3.15 Dyffryn Ardudwy, Merioneth, Wales: chambers within a long cairn

This view is uphill and eastwards along the long axis of the Dyffryn Ardudwy cairn located on the westwards, sea-facing slopes of Moelfre hill in coastal mid Wales. The small primary east-facing portal dolmen is visible in the foreground. This was encapsulated within an oval cairn with a splayed east-facing forecourt, within which had been dug a pit that was found to contain large rim-sherds of carinated bowl vessels, standing upright amidst the infilling stones. The larger stone-capped chamber to the east was subsequently constructed apparently integrally with the large trapezoidal stone cairn. It is assumed that the stones of this cairn once entirely covered over the then-inaccessible chambers.

Photograph: February 2008, © Adam Stanford (website: http://www.aerial-cam.co.uk/).

long cairn, gave it a distinct orientation within the landscape. It may be that this practice was simply a matter of growing communities being able progressively to render up greater amounts of labour to honour their ancestral dead. But equally, it may instead signal a shift of priorities, towards the creation of a more visible imprint on the land, and a new specification of the conditions under which the living could approach and experience the resting places of ancestral remains.

Creating enclosures and delimiting space within a circle or curve

The increasingly common creation of barrows featuring large stones in the west of Britain coincided with the introduction of a new kind of monument, initially in the south-east of England. Causewayed enclosures are so termed because they feature one or more (mostly) concentrically ordered rings of interrupted ditches, ranging between 100 and 600 metres in diameter (Fig. 3.16).

Some of these rings form complete circles or oval-shaped enclosures; some sites feature multiple, sometimes linked rings; and others form arcs of ditch that cut off promontories or are sited next to rivers or steep scarps. Around eighty of these sites have been recognized in southern Britain,

Fig. 3.16 Knap Hill, Devizes, Wiltshire, viewed from the west
The banks of the causewayed enclosure that overlooks the Vale of Pewsey on the promontory of Knap Hill are some of the most pronounced to have survived anywhere.
Photograph: © Julian Thomas.

although less than half have featured excavation by modern standards, and many have not been examined at all. Although the sausage-shaped segments of ditch may be associated with a bank or palisade, and the bank may be continuous, this is not a means of construction that in any sense maximizes the defensive potential of any of the sites in question. Ditched enclosures developed on the Continent, in earlier stages of the European Neolithic. Small enclosures were a feature of the later decades of the *Linearbandkeramik* villages of Germany and Belgium, while larger sites developed during the later fifth millennium BCE. Enclosures with interrupted ditches, banks, and palisades were a feature of Chasséen and Michelsberg communities in Germany, northern France, and the Low Countries. Examples very similar to the British ones are found in the Rhine valley and the Pas-de-Calais. Yet from the earliest, the British enclosures were associated with styles of pottery and stone tools that had developed in the insular context (and coincided also with the emergence of the decorated ceramic styles discussed already). They rarely contain any kind of internal structure other than groups of pits, and their use has been a topic of debate for many years.

In the *Gathering Time* study, some twenty-seven among the seventy-four sites recognized as causewayed enclosures (by the period of data collection between 2006 and 2009) were found to be amenable to detailed chronological evaluation. One of the most significant facts underlined by the study was that nearly all the earliest-dated enclosures occur in south-eastern England. Moreover, the earliest dates, going back to around 3750 BCE, have been obtained for sites overlooking the coastal plain of Sussex and located on and around the Thames Estuary. If this chronology is an accurate representation of reality, it is difficult to avoid the conclusion that it was in precisely those areas that were in a position to maintain close contact with the Continent that this innovation of enclosure was first developed. Given the increasing contrasts in material culture that by this time existed between the Continent and Britain, it is likely that the idea of enclosure may have travelled with individuals rather than representing a mass migration as such, and in these terms causewayed-enclosure creation may have involved a deliberately adoptive process.

Clues as to the role of causewayed enclosures in the Neolithic period in Britain were identified early on in their archaeological investigation. One of the first British sites to be examined was Windmill Hill near Avebury in Wiltshire, excavated by Alexander Keiller in 1925–9. The results were eventually published by Isobel Smith four decades later, and on the basis of the large quantities of non-local pottery and stone axes recovered from the ditches, she proposed that the enclosures had served as meeting places and marketing-centres for dispersed populations. More recent excavations at the same site conducted by Alasdair Whittle and Joshua Pollard have demonstrated that very large numbers of animal bones, predominantly cattle, had been deposited in the ditches. This would suggest that the collective consumption of meat in appreciable quantities, arguably during feasting events, also occurred at some of these locations. At a number of sites it has been inferred that the cattle remains represent only a fragment of very large, mobile herds, predominantly either young adult females, or older cows culled when they were beyond milking age.

At another extensively investigated site, on Hambledon Hill in Dorset, two separate enclosures and two long barrows were enclosed within a massive system of outwork banks and ditches covering a series of interconnected chalk spurs (Fig. 3.17).

This complex developed piecemeal, over a period of time, beginning at 3680–3630 cal BCE, with activity on the hilltop continuing over a period of 310–70 years in total. The larger, main enclosure was one of the earliest elements, and contained numerous pits filled with deer antler, pottery fragments, sandstone rubbers, and stone axes, while its ditches held appreciable quantities of human bone. These included skulls that had clearly been placed on the base of the ditch. One possibility is that the enclosure had been used as a 'cemetery', where the dead were exposed to the elements, with fragments of bodies entering the ditch as a consequence of the activities of carrion eaters. However, in some cases the remains had apparently been deliberately placed, while the presence of marks caused by scraping the flesh from bones with stone tools indicates that corpses were sometimes actively 'processed' rather than simply left to decay (see Chapter 4 for further discussion of mortuary practice at Hambledon Hill).

Isotopic analysis of these bones has shown that the people concerned had enjoyed a greater diversity of diets than would be represented amongst the burials in any single tomb or barrow of equivalent date. The implication is that the people concerned belonged to a number of different communities, and came from a relatively wide geographical area. The second enclosure, on the Stepleton spur, had been constructed a few decades after the main site and may have been sporadically occupied rather than used for ceremonial activity. The system of cross-ditches and outworks became progressively more elaborate, and it is implied that this activity was a response to a growing

Fig. 3.17 Hambledon Hill: the main causewayed enclosure from the north

This view is southwards from the southern ramparts of the Iron Age hillfort towards the north- and west-facing line of ditch and bank segments of the main causewayed enclosure (visible running leftwards from where the horses are grazing at right in this view). The Neolithic enclosures were excavated by a team led by Roger Mercer four decades ago due to severe plough-damage affecting the hilltop. A series of trenches and area-excavations were opened by Mercer and his team, and the evidence for human remains retrieved from the ditches of the main enclosure led him to describe it as having 'reeked' of decaying flesh in the mid fourth millennium BCE. English Heritage supported the excavation, and its publication by Mercer and Frances Healy was a model example of how much information could be extracted using modern analyses of the remains from a chalkland site such as this one.

Photograph: June 2017, © Keith Ray.

threat of violence. Two episodes of aggression appear to have taken place in the mid fourth millennium BCE. In the first, the inner Stepleton outwork had been burned, shortly after its construction, and a mature adult male was found on the base of the ditch. Eighty metres away, a young man had been buried with a mass of burnt material. Perhaps a century later, the body of a young man who had died by arrowshot entered the ditch of the outer Stepleton outwork, while another was found on top of the rubble fill of the inner Stepleton outwork ditch. Broadly contemporary with these two violent deaths was the articulated upper body of a woman, found in the ditch of the Stepleton enclosure, which was now largely silted.

Similar traces of burning and the shooting of large numbers of arrows were found at the enclosure on Crickley Hill in Gloucestershire, which stands out from the scarp overlooking the Severn Valley near Cheltenham. The early dates for the Ascott and Hazleton barrows nearby are complemented by slightly later dates for the earliest of the arcs of ditch that cut

across the promontory at Crickley. This location had already seen human activity in the form of a series of small, circular stake-built structures, which may represent a Mesolithic occupation, and a group of small pits enclosing an irregular eight-metre long oval, referred to as the 'Banana barrow'. The outer and inner causewayed ditch circuits of modest size were dug around 3660–3610 BCE, and these had been deliberately backfilled and re-dug on numerous occasions. Only toward the end of the use of the site had a much more substantial, continuous, and defensive ditch been dug, in the period between 3565 and 3535 BCE, complemented by a stone rampart. The palisade at the back of this rampart had been burned, probably sometime after 3490–3450 cal BCE, and numerous leaf-shaped arrow points were distributed along its length, as well as being concentrated in the entrances through the defences. Structures within the enclosure appear to have been burned at much the same time, and this episode may have brought activity on the hilltop to an end.

There is considerable variation in the period over which individual enclosures remained in use. Some may have been abandoned shortly after construction, but the enclosures on Hambledon Hill and Crickley Hill demonstrate that others endured for many generations. Where this is the case, enclosures developed complex biographies, in which structural alterations and changes in the character of activity would presumably have been matched by changes in meaning. The Hambledon and Crickley enclosures

both became notably more defensive in character in time, but this was by
no means a universal pattern. However, similar developments may also be
demonstrated by the enclosure set around a prominent rocky granite hilltop
'tor' at Carn Brea near Redruth in Cornwall, and at the causewayed enclosure (also apparently set alight) on the inland hill-promontory at Hembury,
north-east of Exeter in Devon.

The pattern noted at Crickley Hill, of causewayed enclosure ditches
being repeatedly re-dug, sometimes after deliberate backfilling, is one that
has been reported at numerous other sites. If the significance of enclosing
an area with a discontinuous ditch is that it was primarily a means of defining a particular space as special, and appropriate for specific kinds of activity,
this recutting would serve to renew and reiterate that status. In some cases,
it might have been the means of re-establishing the temporary conditions
required for gatherings, feasts, and inter-community negotiations or
exchanges. A particularly spectacular example was discovered at Briar Hill
near Northampton, where meticulous excavation and recording revealed an
enormously complex series of recutting events (Fig. 3.18).

At Etton in the Cambridgeshire fens, a small, single-ring causewayed
enclosure had been utilized for the best part of four centuries, although the
density of finds in the ditches was modest by comparison to Hambledon or
Windmill Hill. Having been subject to seasonal freshwater flooding, the site
was waterlogged, and organic material had survived in the ditches. The
eastern arc of ditches had been backfilled shortly after it was first dug, but it
was recut on numerous occasions. There were many examples of carefully
placed deposits. These included a complete bowl on a birch-bark mat,
an intact axe-haft, and a bundle of cattle bones, as well as a series of animal
skulls. At Etton, there appears to have been a close relationship between the
practice of recutting and the placement of objects in the ditch segments.

There seems to have been considerable variation in the activities that
took place at different causewayed enclosures. In the Neolithic enclosure
that underlies the massive Iron Age hillfort at Maiden Castle in Dorset,
it appears that flint axes were being finished, ready for use. By contrast, at
Etton some of the Langdale stone axes represented had been deliberately
smashed in the ditches. While the creation of interrupted ditch circuits
transformed the status of the enclosed space, it nonetheless maintained its
accessibility (although see Chapter 6 for a reading of the reason for segmentation that focuses instead upon a potential lineage identity and descent
dimension to the practice). The transitory or temporary character of some

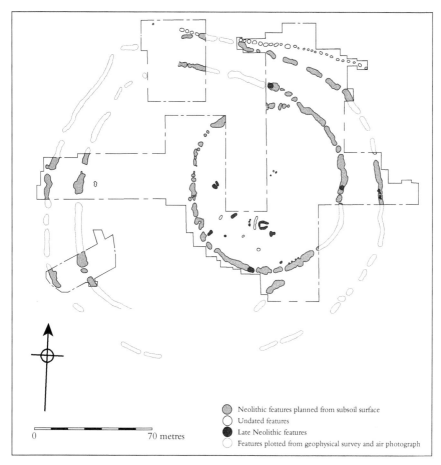

Fig. 3.18 Briar Hill causewayed enclosure, Northampton: plan

The multiple circuits of the Briar Hill enclosure and the juxtaposition of its elements illustrate well just how complex the developmental history of a site such as this could be. The clear sequence of recutting of the ditches added to this complexity, although the original early dating of the site has been revised in the light of Bayesian analysis undertaken as part of the Gathering Time *project.*

Plan: redrawn by Julian Thomas from an original published by Helen Bamford.

of these sites (at least initially) that were repeatedly brought into being, and then 'decommissioned', implies that their use was sporadic and episodic, perhaps seasonal, as Stuart Piggott once argued. People, animals, and artefacts all came to these enclosures from elsewhere, often from great distances, and in each case significant events in their personal histories took place within the bounded space of the site. Artefacts were created, destroyed, and displayed, cattle were slaughtered, the recently dead were 'processed' in various ways, and food was consumed in large quantities.

It is reasonable to assume that other, less tangible transitions and transformations might also have taken place at causewayed enclosures: marriages
arranged and celebrated, alliances negotiated, liaisons and friendships
established, exchanges of valuable items conducted, disputes settled. All of
this makes a great deal of sense in the context of the kind of society that was
emerging in the second quarter of the fourth millennium BCE: increasingly
competitive and violent, less reliant on cultivation, more focused on the
accumulation of herds and fine artefacts, more mobile and dispersed, more
unequal. The establishment of temporarily occupied, politically neutral
spaces where different groups could come together at particular times of
year created the conditions under which the recurrent enmities of the time
could be set aside, and the important business of exchanging goods, information, and marriage partners could be carried out. They could perhaps
have been perceived as places of armed truce, but in some cases they may
gradually have become associated with the activities of powerful social fac-
tions that were emerging at this time, or disputed and fought over by rival
communities (Fig. 3.19).

The *Gathering Time* studies of Alasdair Whittle, Frances Healy, and Alex
Bayliss sketched out a chronological narrative of changing patterns of use
and development of these enclosures on a region-by-region basis, at least
where numbers of them have been investigated in southern and eastern
Britain, and where, especially within those regions, their sequences have
begun to be closely dated. For example, by combining a variety of estimates of effort expended in digging the ditches of causewayed enclosures
with the dating of different circuits of these enclosures, a fascinating picture has emerged of how and where most effort was put into their construction. Broadly, it looks as if the proportion of ditch length dug, mapped
against the passage of time, rose rapidly from the second quarter of the
thirty-seventh century BCE, then fell markedly from around 3625 cal BCE,
reaching its lowest point at about 3575 cal BCE. Construction activity had
then picked up somewhat by 3450 cal BCE. The early 'peak' of construction
was apparently mostly a south coast and Thames-side/Cotswolds phenomenon, with the 'end' of the peak coinciding with the creation of enclosures
in eastern and south-western England. Such a broad-brush portrait, of
course, masks many complexities, and some of the detail concerns the timing of the digging of multiple circuits of ditches where these occurred,
episodes of recutting of ditches, and the relative timing of construction of
'pairs' of sites.

Fig. 3.19 Dorstone Hill causewayed enclosure under excavation

The causewayed enclosure at Dorstone Hill in south-west Herefordshire used to be thought to be represented by the long mounds that have now been shown to have been raised over the remains of a series of deliberately burned early halls here. The causewayed enclosure now known to have been created on the site was discovered only in 2016 by geophysical survey. This was sited further up the hill to the south of the long mounds, and excavation in the summer of 2017 shown here demonstrated that the original causewayed ditches were succeeded within a few years, probably also in the mid fourth millennium, by a timber palisade set in a near-continuous trench cut through the earlier segments.

Photograph: Adam Stanford; project directed by Julian Thomas and Keith Ray.

We have seen that the length of time that such sites were in use also varied, and that several seem to have been short-term projects that began and ended within a single generation. The tempo of use is also an important consideration, and here the *Gathering Time* team introduced further innovation into their calculations. Estimates were made from known lengths of ditch from which quantified amounts of early 'Neolithic Bowl' pottery and struck flint or chert pieces were recovered, and comparisons were made between sites. This indicated that some of the shortest-lived enclosures such as Abingdon by the Thames and Maiden Castle near Dorchester in Dorset also featured the greatest intensities of deposition of artefacts in their ditch-segments. At some sites such as Hambledon Hill, at Windmill Hill, and at Etton, the initial digging of the ditches was accompanied by relatively few artefact deposits, while the later fills of the same ditches were often relatively artefact-rich.

Causewayed and related enclosures had a total primary (that is, Early Neolithic) use-span of between 400 and 450 years, but again, their falling out of use was neither gradual nor unimodal. There was a period of little more than fifty years either side of 3500 BCE when over 30 per cent of the total went out of use. By approximately 3400 BCE, however, the number falling out of use, compared to the (by then) total number of sites, had reduced rapidly to less than 25 per cent, largely owing to the commissioning of new sites or the creation of new circuits, or the recutting of previously dug segments. This number of 'decommissionings' arose again to nearly 30 per cent of the then total by 3300 BCE. However, the increase in abandonments thereafter was so sharp that the number of newly redundant sites had reduced to not much more than 10 per cent by 3250 BCE, before they had all ceased being used, at least in terms of their initial purposes, by not long after 3200 BCE.

The complexity of development and use of some causewayed enclosures should occasion no surprise, given the multiple circuits and multiple indications of recutting of ditch segments indicated at many sites. Windmill Hill near Avebury was mentioned earlier, and the recent close dating programme revealed not only that previous ideas about the sequence of construction of the rings of ditch-segments (and banks) there were correct, but it also established the actual duration of the periods involved. So the inner circuit is now thought most likely to be the first to have been created, its segments having been dug in the period 3670–3645 cal BCE. The outer circuit was probably created marginally later (though it could have been started while the 'final' segments of the inner were still being cut), sometime between 3670 and 3635 cal BCE. And meanwhile the middle circuit appears likely to have been created a little later, having been dug sometime between 3640 and 3615 cal BCE. The whole 'edifice' was therefore very probably completed in less than seventy-five years, and could easily have been built within an individual (short) lifetime of between twenty and fifty-five years. The complex history of the filling and recutting of the segments was such that activity continued sporadically at the site for a period of 350 years or so, concluding around 3350 BCE. However, it is thought that this 'ending' really represented a change of use, and some later fourth-millennium deposits, though less common, could still involve substantial amounts of material.

Delimiting space in a linear way

The advent of causewayed enclosures in Kent and Sussex broadly coincided with the emergence of a very different monumental tradition in the lowlands of Scotland. 'Cursus' monuments are much less well dated than the enclosures, owing in part to radiocarbon samples that have been dominated by wood charcoal, which may produce less accurate results than bone or antler. They had certainly developed by the thirty-seventh century BCE, but may date back into the thirty-eighth. The earliest cursus monuments were elongated rectilinear enclosures composed of numerous free-standing timber uprights or small pits, and therefore defined by a permeable boundary comparable with the causewayed enclosures. They range in size between the sixty-five-metre long example at Douglasmuir in Angus, and the six-hundred-metre Milton of Guthrie cursus, also in Angus. The post-defined examples have been found to have often contained internal divisions, and sometimes very large post-holes or pits were set within the enclosed space. This organization of space invites comparison with the timber halls discussed earlier, and it is arguable that entering a timber cursus would have been redolent of being inside a very large, if roofless, building (Fig. 3.20).

Moreover, like the wooden halls and a variety of other timber structures of the period, it seems that many of these early cursus monuments of northern Britain had been deliberately destroyed by fire. At Holm Farm in Dumfries and Galloway, for example, such a post-defined monument had apparently been burned and rebuilt on a number of different occasions, with the result that some individual post-holes contained the charred stumps of a number of different uprights. Unlike the causewayed enclosures, cursus monuments have few close parallels on the European continent, and it is fairly clear that they developed entirely in the insular context. It is arguable that they evoke the ideas of the house, the household, and the collective history and identity of the domestic group on a massive scale, and it is also evident that they must have been used in an entirely different way from the

Fig. 3.20 Dunragit cursus excavation

The arc of post-holes defining the terminal of the Early Neolithic post-defined cursus crosses this trench, excavated in the summer of 2001. The post-holes become deeper and wider towards the terminal, suggesting that the timber uprights rose up and became more substantial towards the end of the monument. The post-hole fills were dark and heavily charcoal-stained, and the gravel of their edges often intensely scorched, indicating that the timbers had burned in situ.

Photograph: 2001, © Julian Thomas.

enclosures. The linear interior of the cursus hints at procession and a sequential ordering of events, while the nested rings of an enclosure are more suited to the containment of gatherings within a privileged space. While, as we have seen, the quantities of pottery, animal bone, and flint found at causewayed enclosures are often very great, post-defined cursus monuments produce only modest numbers of finds. This is in part a result of the contrast between ditches (which may be left open for a period) and post-holes (which are quickly sealed once the post has been inserted) as potential 'traps' for objects. But it also arguably reflects another aspect of the contrast between the ways in which these structures were used. The profligate consumption of food and destruction of artefacts were not characteristics of cursus monuments.

It is open to question whether these two different orderings of space could simply be identified with two distinct 'liturgical' traditions or systems of belief. These structures are unlikely to have been used for activities that can be narrowly defined in terms of 'religion', while metaphysical beliefs may not have been consistent or coherent across time and space in such pre-literate societies. Nonetheless, the two kinds of architecture will have facilitated entirely different kinds of presence, performance, and practice. In general terms, then, it is possible that they represented competing forms of organization of social practices and interaction, and their geographical manifestation and sequence of appearance may shed some light on this. Causewayed enclosures spread rapidly from the south-east as far as Cornwall, Wales, and the English Midlands, and while there are small numbers of examples in Ireland and Cumbria, they are conspicuous by their scarcity in Yorkshire. Meanwhile, pit- and post-defined cursus monuments were concentrated in southern Scotland, so that the two traditions did not initially overlap spatially. However, towards the middle of the fourth millennium BCE the character of cursus monuments began to change fundamentally. Pit and post structures ceased being built and at the same time new forms of parallel-sided structures began to appear. These featured continuous ditches surrounding linear spaces, with either squared or curved terminals. This process of change is demonstrated very strikingly at the site of Holywood North near Dumfries, where a post-defined monument was enclosed within a ditched cursus that was more than two hundred metres long (Fig. 3.21).

While ditched cursus often have breaks in the ditches along their sides, they rarely have any means of access at their ends. It follows that it could be

Fig. 3.21 Holywood North cursus, Dumfriesshire

This aerial photograph shows in plan the northern end of the Holywood post-defined and ditched cursus monument, the first construction of which was dated to 3800–3650 cal BCE. Cropmark evidence indicates that the southern end of the cursus had a subtly different alignment to the northern half, and that it was aligned directly upon the square-ended ditched Holywood South cursus, the northern end of which (occupied by a ring-ditch) was excavated during the same project.

Photograph: © Julian Thomas.

argued they are not self-evidently ideal for use as ceremonial routeways. One explanation that has been put forward for this state of affairs is that rather than defining a space down which participants could have processed, ditched cursus monuments were built to enclose an existing pathway and render it inaccessible. The former processional space was, in this perspective, perhaps sanctified, reserved for spirits and ancestors, or even cursed. As such, these may not have been spaces for the living to move within, but instead to venerate or fear. Ditched cursus are much more widely distributed across Britain than the pit and post versions, with major concentrations in the Thames Valley, and in parts of East Anglia, Yorkshire, the Welsh borders and the Midlands. There is a tendency for them to occur on the flat expanses of river valleys. This may simply be because these areas afforded the space necessary for massive linear constructions, but it has also been conjectured that some kind of affinity was being asserted between the cursus and the river. They may, for instance, have been connected in some way with mortuary practices focused on rivers, a suggestion supported by the discovery of rather later Neolithic human remains in a logjam in a former channel of the River Trent at Langford Lowfields in Nottinghamshire. Alternatively, Kenneth Brophy has suggested that cursus may have been understood as equivalents of flowing rivers, embodying ideas of time, linear movement, and mortality. Cursus monuments also often incorporate and link together existing monuments, such as long barrows, ring-ditches, and mortuary enclosures. They are, moreover, sometimes much larger than the earlier post-defined structures: the Greater Stonehenge Cursus is nearly three kilometres long, while the Dorset Cursus on Cranborne Chase extends for a massive ten kilometres.

Despite their sometimes colossal size and the enormous quantities of labour that must have been invested in constructing them, cursus monuments rarely have any internal features, and their ditches contain few if any finds. The Greater Stonehenge Cursus was unusual in this respect, in that the ditch deposits at the western terminal near Fargo Plantation contained numerous clusters of flint-knapping waste. But the character of this working was enigmatic: entire nodules had been flaked until little remained, with few artefacts being produced. It is conceivable that in this context it was the act of knapping itself that was important, rather than the manufacture of any particular object (see Chapter 4 for further discussion). The two cursus monuments in the Stonehenge area, the Greater and Lesser Cursus, are both dated to slightly later than the nearby causewayed enclosure, Robin Hood's Ball. In the Thames Valley, numerous cursus are again a century or two later than the causewayed enclosures scattered across the gravel terraces. So in some areas, causewayed enclosures and cursus monuments are closely juxtaposed, even if their construction was not precisely contemporary. However, it is entirely possible that particular people would have experienced the activities conducted at both kinds of structure within their lifetimes. Significantly, at Fornham All Saints in Suffolk, a large cursus runs directly across two intersecting causewayed enclosures. A similar relationship was observed between the cursus and causewayed enclosure at Etton, while as we have already seen, at Maiden Castle in Dorset a bank barrow was found to have cut across and involved the levelling of the bank and ditch of the enclosure. Bank barrows and cursus monuments are closely related: indeed, the Cleaven Dyke in Perthshire and the Stanwell Cursus at Heathrow were each effectively a bank barrow contained within a cursus ditch. So given that in several cases it is clear that cursus monuments slighted the earthworks of causewayed enclosures, it seems probable that the practice of creating cursus monuments represented the eclipse of one form of order and way of structuring activity in the landscape, and the emergence of another.

What, therefore, exactly were cursus monuments, if they were not simply meeting places that in some way were equivalent to causewayed enclosures? The near-absence of associated finds would appear to question the parallel with causewayed enclosures anyway, given that the latter seldom feature few finds (although some, like the Mavesyn Ridware and Alrewas enclosures in the Trent valley do seem to have been almost devoid of material). Archaeologists are surely right to have noted that the linear character of cursus enables 'landscape statements' to be made, whether restricting or directing passage across the land, linking the locations of former monuments, or pointing to features on hillsides that they were oriented towards. We would argue that we should not necessarily focus so much upon the 'monumentality' of these constructions, however, whether in timber or as earthworks, as if that monumentality requires an explanation of ritual or functional importance in its own right. Cursus are perhaps best seen as indicative or mnemonic devices acting dramatically and emphatically within a historicized landscape. Adopting this view, we would accept and extend the argument that Jonathan Last has made that cursus were perhaps developed as a way of ensuring that the idea of a journey or passage became a key metaphor for the societies in question. This metaphor was made manifest in material form, whether the transit was along, or across, a river valley or other significant landscape. As such, the act of constructing the cursus, especially in view of its referencing of past monumental features (frequently long barrows, but also the causewayed enclosures of the then-recent past), was a means of integrating key concepts involving movement and connection (and even the very performance of acts of referencing), in a vivid way. It was the act of creation of a cursus monument that in these terms was important, and not necessarily what subsequently went on within or around it in terms of (for instance) assembly, exchange, or ritual action. That said, once each cursus was in place, it did apparently act as a node within particularly ritually and, one might add, historically charged places in the landscape.

As we have observed already, causewayed enclosures fell out of use during the third quarter of the fourth millennium BCE, and it is arguable that in some sense cursus monuments supplanted or superseded them. While there is little evidence for activity *within* cursus, they seem to have 'attracted' subsequent structures and deposits, including ring-ditches, single grave burials, timber circles, henge monuments, and pits containing fine artefacts. This development probably does not indicate one population replacing another, but might just possibly be seen as the eclipse of a largely Continentally inspired set of practices by an alternative that had been generated in Britain. As we have noted, this contrast may not have been as specific as that between two religions or ideological systems, but it may indicate differing ways of organizing or articulating communities. And interestingly, the proliferation of ditched cursus monuments throughout much of the British mainland coincided with a series of other fundamental changes.

Cultural diversities and elaborations

From around 3400 BCE onwards, the decoration of ceramic vessels used in Britain began to become appreciably more ornate. The shouldered bowls that had been sparsely ornamented during the Earlier Neolithic now became the core of a new style of pottery, known as Peterborough Ware. Rims became heavier, sometimes amounting to a collar, below which there was often a groove or cavetto zone. Decoration expanded to cover much of the outer surface of the vessel (sometimes expanding into the interior as well), and was usually composed of multiple impressions forming horizontal bands. These were executed using fingertips and fingernails, twisted cord 'maggots', and the articular ends of bird bones. In a path-breaking doctoral thesis completed in 1956, Isobel Smith suggested that the development of Peterborough Wares involved a sequence of three styles—Ebbsfleet, Mortlake, and Fengate—in which decoration became progressively more florid and expansive, rims were transformed into collars, and the rounded bases inherited from the Early Neolithic were eventually replaced by flat pedestal bases. There are also differences between the fabrics and finishing techniques of the different substyles that have been recognized. However, as radiocarbon dates began to emerge for deposits associated with pottery in these styles it became clear that there was a good deal of chronological overlap in their manufacture and use. Moreover, as the variability in the different styles has become clearer, and the contexts of deposition have become better understood, it has been recognized as being likely that these different substyles were used in slightly different ways. All three styles of pottery often occur deposited in pits, but Ebbsfleet Ware is especially common in cause-wayed enclosures and round barrows, Mortlake Ware in open sites, rivers, and megalithic tombs, and Fengate Ware also in causewayed enclosures. As Vincent Ard and Timothy Darvill have recently reaffirmed, Peterborough Wares often seem to have been used in locations that were associated with the past: at overgrown and decrepit monuments. This apparent referencing or veneration of places and ancestors many generations old gives the impression that as the British Neolithic had reached maturity, society had become increasingly backward-looking, a tendency that would only be reversed at the turn of the third millennium. The precise significance of the enhancement of decoration on pottery is hard to explain, although ethnographic examples suggest that it may be connected with heightened concern over interpersonal transactions involving the preparation and consumption of food and drink. It is possible, then, that the development of Peterborough Wares has something to tell us about increasingly fraught, or contested, relationships between people of different statuses, ranks, or genders.

If increasingly elaborate ceramics were connected with a need to define boundaries or mark out identities in the casual encounters and activities of everyday life, this harmonizes with a more general growth in the diversity and elaboration of material things in the later part of the fourth millennium BCE. A variety of new kinds of portable artefact was created at this time. These included jet belt sliders that were dress fittings suggestive of the emergence of new and more elaborate ways of presenting oneself in public. The skills of grinding and polishing flint were employed to create distinctive new kinds of knife and axe, including the flaked and partially polished axes and adzes of Duggleby and Seamer type. The leaf-shaped flint arrowheads of the Earlier Neolithic were replaced by new, chisel-shaped styles. And maceheads of stone began to be manufactured again, complementing the existing polished stone axes. None of these objects would have been more efficient or helpful in carrying out everyday tasks. All of them were visually arresting, and each would have been very clearly associated with a particular person, worn or carried in social interaction. These items may or may not indicate that social differentiation or ranking had increased by the thirty-fourth century BCE, but they certainly suggest that roles and identities were in need of clarification or qualification. British communities may have become more unequal, or there may simply have been a proliferation of statuses and offices in an increasingly diverse and fragmented social world. If the period of the causewayed enclosures was one of more frenetic social interaction, growing competition, and enhanced conflict, its aftermath was perhaps an interlude in which order was reasserted, often by looking back to established traditions and places with ancestral associations.

The descent and diversification of traditions

It is highly salient that many of the new kinds of artefact, suited as they were to display and the expression of personal identity, have been recovered from graves. The practice of burying a single person, crouched in a grave beneath a small round mound, and accompanied by a number of distinctive artefacts, did not represent a sudden and radical break with convention. All the elements of this way of treating the dead already had a long history. Single grave burials had been performed since the start of the Neolithic (as we have seen with the example from Yabsley Street), while round mounds containing multiple bodies had been constructed in a number of regions, notably eastern Yorkshire. Furthermore, the single graves of the later fourth millennium often explicitly drew on existing practices, suggesting continuity with the past. For example, at Barrow Hills, Radley in Oxfordshire, two crouched burials were found in a grave beneath a small long barrow adjacent to the Abingdon causewayed enclosure. But the inhumations dated to the later fourth millennium, and were accompanied by a set of striking artefacts. At Whitegrounds near Burythorpe in Yorkshire, a single male burial with a polished axe and a jet slider was inserted into an existing mound that already contained an Early Neolithic linear mortuary structure (see Chapter 4 for more extensive discussion of these two sites). And at Four Crosses in Powys, the first in a series of burials interred in a round mound over a protracted period was deposited within a two-post structure that harked back to Early Neolithic prototypes.

These Middle Neolithic burials were not distinguished by standardized forms of body treatment or artefact sets, as would be the case with the Beaker graves a millennium later (see Chapter 5). But they do stand out from the long barrow and long cairn mortuary practices that we have already discussed. If the latter had involved the accumulation of a group of 'founding ancestors' over a generation or two, from whom an extensive community reckoned their descent, there was now an emphasis on the death and celebration of particular, singular persons. The implication is that new and more exclusive lines of kinship and inheritance were being established in the later fourth millennium, enabling people to identify themselves in relation to a specific, and perhaps relatively recent, ancestor. These tendencies are most spectacularly exhibited at the site of Duggleby Howe on the Wolds of East Yorkshire, where a massive round mound grew up through a series of stages of deposition and construction, associated with a group of burials introduced sequentially over a period of at least half a millennium. The earliest of these burials had been deposited in the thirty-sixth or thirty-fifth century BCE, before mound construction had begun, in a deep shaft grave. At the base of the shaft a mature adult male had been laid out, possibly in a wooden coffin, with a pottery bowl in the local Towthorpe style and several flints, including three serrated flakes and two cores. Higher in the same pit was the body of another man, aged about 60, with the skull of another person at his feet, who had apparently died from severe blows to the head. This skull lacked a lower jaw, and had probably been buried in a defleshed state, so the possibility is that it did not represent a burial as such, but a war trophy, an heirloom, or part of an ancestor, retrieved from elsewhere. A little higher in the shaft was the body of a 4-year-old child, and at the top was another man aged about 60, with a macehead worked from red deer antler and a lozenge-shaped arrowhead in front of his chest, and a flint axe with a finely polished blade beside his knees. This body had been buried two or three centuries after the first, demonstrating that the location was one that people had retuned to sporad-ically in order to bury the dead over a lengthy period even before the mound was raised. The positioning of these bodies in the shaft reveals an intention to create connections between people who lived at different times, so that the burial place embodied the lines of descent passing through the generations. The presence of the separate skull and the antler macehead, which was apparently already a century old when deposited, add to this sense of sequential funerary events as a kind of historical narrative.

The sense of continuity in the use of a specific location was enhanced by the addition of a second, shallower grave beside the shaft, perhaps some time shortly after 3000 BCE, and thus more than two centuries after the final burial that the latter contained. The tightly contracted body in the base of this grave was another adult man, with a bone pin, beaver teeth, boar's tusk blades, and a chisel-shaped arrowhead. These objects significantly prefigure the items that would be found with cremated burials at various sites during the first half of the third millennium. Another body, of a man who may have been as old as 70, was laid out on the land surface between the two graves, had a very fine polished flint knife, and had been placed there perhaps a century later (Fig. 3.22).

This was the last burial before the circular barrow began to be raised over the two graves. The first element of this was a low mound of earth and clay, and four children were buried in this and the layer of chalky grit or fine rubble above it, possibly overlapping with a progressive change in mortuary activity toward the deposition of cremated human remains. The burnt bones of fifty-three people were eventually inserted into the mound, three of them with bone pins similar to that found with the body in the shallower grave. A clay capping and coarse chalk rubble eventually completed the mound. There is no indication of any abrupt cultural change between the two different forms of funerary activity. So although there was a shift towards what might have represented a more spectacular form of funerary activity, with cremation events that might have been witnessed by large numbers of people, the principal emphasis at Duggleby Howe appears to have been on continuity, expressed through the protracted use of a single location. These dead were buried sporadically, with prolonged gaps in the sequence, rather than in an abbreviated episode. This implies the repeated restatement of the importance of a particular genealogical line through time. The recurring presence of quite elderly men amongst the burials at Duggleby suggests that it may have been household or lineage heads that were being afforded this distinctive form of treatment in death, although this may have reflected their position in kin relations as much as their personal authority. Finally, in the twenty-fourth century BCE, a massive ditch about 370 metres in diameter was built encircling the mound, and it is likely that the final chalk rubble capping of the barrow represented the up-cast from this feature. It is open to conjecture whether this ditch was intended to enhance the importance of the mound, or to sever it from the surrounding landscape.

Although much later in date, the ditch surrounding Duggleby Howe continued another trend that began in the final centuries of the fourth millennium: the development of circular enclosures, some of which contained earlier features, and which were often associated with the dead. A good example is at Monkton Up Wimborne in north Dorset, where a ring of substantial pits surrounded a much larger central pit, from within which a circular shaft descended to a depth of seven metres. In a secluded location on the opposite edge of the large pit was a grave, which contained the remains of an adult woman and three children, only one of whom appeared

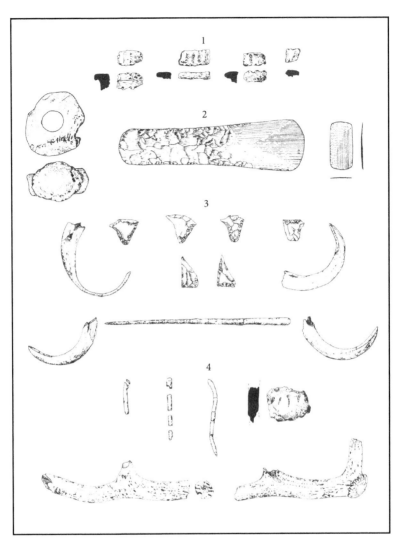

Fig. 3.22 Objects from a series of burials at Duggleby Howe, Yorkshire Wolds

These objects were found accompanying some among a complex sequence of burials beneath the estimated 5,000 tons of chalk making up the round mound located near the head of the Gypsy Race valley, dug into by John Mortimer in 1890. The sherds at the top (1) are fragments of a crushed 'Towthorpe Bowl' (a local variant of developed carinated bowls), found together with flint flakes and two cores next to an elderly male burial. This burial, recently dated to the thirty-sixth or thirty-fifth century BCE, had been placed in a wooden coffin at the base of a shaft cut nearly three metres deep into the chalk. The man was not local, and may have lived much of his younger life either in western Scotland or Cornwall. Indeed, a curiosity of the Duggleby burials is that none of them was local to the area. Higher up the shaft were the bones of a 60-year-old man, those of an adolescent who had suffered trauma to his head from a blow by a blunt instrument, and the body of a 4-year-old child. The Middle Neolithic edge-polished flint adze (2) and the polished and perforated crown antler macehead to its left in the drawing were found with another elderly male burial that had been inserted near the top of the shaft some 200–300 years after the primary burial. The macehead was separately dated in the recent radiocarbon dating programme and was shown to have already been 100 or more years old when buried with this corpse. The group of objects (3) was found accompanying the burial of another 60-year-old man inserted between 150 and 350 years later still, in a pit dug next to, but carefully avoiding, the original shaft. The bone pin was placed behind this person's back, with six Late Neolithic transverse flint arrowheads, beaver incisors, boar's tusks, and worked flint flakes placed around the body. A 70-year-old male was then inserted face down into the top of both pit and shaft, with the thin, highly polished opaque flint knife (to the right of the adze in this drawing) carefully placed in front of his face. Only after this burial had been made was a small mound raised over the burials, and this was made massive in the very same period in the later third millennium, when mounds such as Silbury Hill in Wiltshire were also being hugely enlarged.

Drawing: Mark Edmonds, reprinted from Richard Bradley and Mark Edmonds, *Interpreting the Axe Trade* (Cambridge University Press, 1993).

to be closely related to her. Strontium isotope values from the tooth enamel of the four people demonstrated that they had moved on at least one occasion to and from an area with a more radiogenic subsoil than the Wessex chalk, probably the Mendip Hills. The burials were radiocarbon-dated to around 3300 BCE, and their diet had apparently been exceptionally rich in dairy foods. This is an interesting result, given that, as we have seen, the evidence for the use of domesticated cereals had declined appreciably in southern England by this time. However, it may be that the animal-based diet reflects the mobile way of life of only a segment of society, following herds across the country. A further remarkable discovery from Monkton Up Wimborne was a large block of chalk found at the base of the shaft, which bore pecked linear designs similar to those found on the stones of passage tombs in Ireland and western Britain.

The Monkton Up Wimborne decorated block provides a link with another circular enclosure of the late fourth millennium, at Flagstones House on the edge of Dorchester in Dorset. The Flagstones site had an interrupted ditch similar to a causewayed enclosure of earlier date, although it formed a rough circle about 100 metres in diameter. As we will see later in this book, this feature links the Flagstones enclosure to the early phases of activity at Stonehenge. A series of infant burials were identified in the ditch segments, some of them covered by large sarsen stones. In four places around the enclosure circuit, engraved pictograms were found in the chalk surface of the side of the ditch. The designs included parallel lines, a chequerboard motif, concentric circles, and nested arcs. As at Monkton Up Wimborne, the obvious comparison is with the Irish passage-tomb tradition, which was reaching its zenith at this time. The Monkton and Flagstones 'art' provides a tenuous indication that new, longer-distance contacts around the coasts of Britain and Ireland were starting to form by about 3300 BCE.

We have seen that the passage tombs of Ireland were probably in existence by the thirty-seventh century BCE, and that the largest and most complex examples in the Boyne Valley probably date to the later part of the fourth millennium. Passage-tomb architecture is distinctive amongst megalithic monuments, with chambers lodged inside often circular mounds accessed by long stone passages. This style of construction originated in western France and Iberia, spreading gradually to Ireland, north Wales, northern Scotland, and eventually Scandinavia. Yet while there are distinctive elements shared between regions, there are also local variations in the ways that passage tombs were constructed and used. Thus in Ireland predominantly cremated human remains were deposited in the chambers, sometimes in distinctive stone basins, but in the Orkney Islands the Maes Howe style passage tombs were used for successive inhumation. Passage tombs in Ireland are associated with a style of decorated pottery called Carrowkeel Ware, but this is not present on the Continent, or in Wales or Scotland. One shared element apparently peculiar to passage tombs is the presence of decorative motifs on the stones of passage, of chamber, and sometimes also on those of a surrounding kerb. While the art of the Iberian passage tombs includes painted designs, that of Brittany and Ireland is principally pecked or incised onto the surfaces of the stones, and incision is more common in the Orcadian tombs. Some of the Breton motifs are figurative (of animals, axes, crooks, and bows), but those in Britain and Ireland are predominantly geometric and non-representational, composed of elements including zigzags, nested arcs, concentric circles, parallel lines, lozenges, and triangles. However, this does not mean that they are without meaning. Detailed analysis by Guillaume Robin has demonstrated that particular combinations of motifs are more likely to occur in distinct locations within the Irish passage tombs, including portals and the backs of chambers. While it would be quite misleading to cast the decoration of passage tombs as anything approaching 'writing', the carvings nonetheless appear to have drawn attention to the stages of the process of entering the monument, and moving down the passage toward the chamber area.

By comparison to the chambered long cairns of the earlier fourth millennium BCE, the encounter with the inner space of passage tombs was a more richly sensory experience. The long passage, which could often not be negotiated in an upright position, was clearly differentiated from the chamber, and separated the mortuary deposit from the outside world. As a result, the chamber was often a dark and secluded space. In some cases the passage had an alignment on a particular celestial event: the interior of the tomb is illuminated by the midwinter sunset and sunrise respectively at Maes Howe in Orkney and Newgrange in Ireland. In other words, particular conditions were being created under which it was appropriate to experience the chamber and the remains that it contained. The simple implication of the effort expended on elaborating the experience of entering these tombs is that they were intended to be occupied repeatedly, over a long period of time. While the funerary deposits in the earlier megalithic tombs had often accumulated in less than half a century, those in passage tombs were usually more extensive, and had been deposited over a longer period. At Knowth, the cremated remains of more than a hundred people had been interred over several centuries, while at the Mound of the Hostages at Tara there were over three hundred burnt and unburnt burials. Similarly, at Quanterness in Orkney, bodies may have been deposited in a fleshed state and subsequently reorganized over a period in excess of 400 years. So although the total number of bodies in these tombs is often large, they may have been introduced relatively infrequently: just a few in any decade. It is worth comparing Duggleby Howe with the passage tombs, for in both cases the deceased were slowly added to a monument that was undoubtedly associated with the unfolding history of a specific social group. This monument did not celebrate a group of collective ancestors in the relatively distant past, but embodied a specific line of descent, traced from past to present. With the emergence of developed passage tombs and single grave burials, the relationship between the living and the dead had begun to shift, apparently decisively.

FOUR

Social being and cultural practices

Chapter frontispiece: 'Tree with a Long Memory'

This image is a detail from the eponymous original wood-engraving made on a section through a box-tree, the growth-rings of which are echoed in the concentric lines that also provide the 'landscape' within which the depicted features (including Stonehenge and the Chanctonbury Ring, Sussex) are situated. Rather than making a specific reference, this image stands as a metaphor for the Neolithic landscape itself, and for its history as 'recorded' within the tree-ring sequence for Britain that now reliably stretches back, for oak trees at least, beyond the beginning of the Neolithic period.

Wood-engraving: Hilary Paynter (website: http://www.hilarypaynter.com).

Human societies are held together by relationships, conventions, traditions, institutions, and tacit understandings. These things are intangible, and while humans themselves are reproduced as corporeal beings, their societies are sustained by practical activities that continually recreate knowledge, customs, and interpersonal bonds. Just as a language would ultimately disappear if it ceased to be used as a means of communication, so the rules and routines of social life are maintained only if they are practised. The corollary of this is that societies are not fixed and bounded entities as much as arrangements that are continually coming into existence, works (if you like) that are never completed. But material things are also in flux, constantly ripening, maturing, being made, being used consecutively in different ways through their 'lifespans', eroding and decaying: so that the social and substantial worlds are as one in being in an unending state of becoming. Nonetheless, objects often have the capacity to endure longer than habits, rules, or affiliations. They continue to exist independently of human beings and their actions. As a result, old artefacts and places occupied in the past can serve to give structure to current practices and transactions, providing cues and prompts, or reminding us of past events and appropriate modes of conduct.

Hunter-gatherers have generally lived a way of life that involves making continual reference to natural features and landmarks. Certain distinctive cliffs, hills, islands, trees, and lakes have represented places to return to, or at which to arrange meetings or encounter game. As such they will have been places of periodic resort, and were incorporated into collective history and mythology. Meanwhile, other places acquired a meaning simply because specific people camped there, or met there, or died there. During the Mesolithic in Britain, some locations seem to have been persistently returned to over very long periods of time. One example is the site at North Park Farm, Bletchingley in Surrey, which appears to have been visited sporadically over hundreds of years, although the structural evidence for this at the site was sparse, being limited to a group of fireplaces. Similarly, the middens composed of marine shells and other materials found in coastal areas, particularly in the west of Scotland, were locations that people reoccupied at intervals and used for a variety of activities, including the manufacture of tools from animal bones and the processing of human remains. The way that these places gradually became established as focal points in the landscape would have lent a degree of consistency and predictability to the rhythms of everyday life.

All of this changed subtly with the start of the Neolithic. The material world that people inhabited abruptly began to contain more artefacts and more structures crafted by people. While hunter-gatherers had minimized the material equipment that they carried with them in order to facilitate mobility, Neolithic people had new kinds of object that enabled them to organize their activities in newly distinctive ways, or to express their relationships and identities anew. The first use of pottery meant that foods both old and new could be stored, cooked, and served in novel ways, while the possession of polished stone axes exchanged over long distances were an immediately recognizable indication of a person's status. Equally, timber halls, long mounds, and, later on, causewayed enclosures provided new settings that gave a distinctly novel structure to encounters, tasks, and observances, while features such as the timbered linear Sweet Track in the Somerset Levels defined patterns of movement through the landscape, even if temporarily, and even though in some cases these routes may already have existed more informally before they were marked in this manner. In a variety of different ways, these new artefacts and a more architectural punctuation of space reduced the need for lengthy deliberation in social life, potentially rendering more of people's activities habitual and unconsidered. Where actions and transactions are repeated while reducing the need for explicit consideration, social relationships can acquire a greater degree of stability. There could be less fissioning of groups prompted by the vicissitudes of the movements of game or year-on-year variation in the availability of wild foods. People did not necessarily need to debate and evaluate their every move, and the richer world of crafted things that the Neolithic offered would have had the effect of entrenching patterns of practical activity that may have contributed to a comparative fixity of social arrangements.

Hunter-gatherers often have had a way of life that combines fluidity and flexibility of living arrangements with extensive networks of mutual aid and support. Bands of people have congregated and then split up seasonally or according to circumstance, and have had to share whatever they possess to ensure mutual survival. But with the adoption of domesticated plants and animals came the possibility of creating distinct and bounded social groups who had collective ownership over herds, seed corn, and land, but whose use of those resources was (or could be) exclusive to those groups. Such a changed relationship to the means of subsistence was the product of a novel investment in those resources, in terms for instance of the management of herds, or the forethought required to plant and the need to protect those crops. And these people had to have made the investment in time and energy and seed-stock to sow them in the first place. The owners of these resources are the 'invested lineages' that we have already mentioned. We should not simply assume that it was the availability of new resources that created a shift to a more structured social order: rather, such a social order is equally likely to have been a prerequisite for a *subsequent* shift to herding and cultivation.

To look at the same issue from a different perspective, we can note that archaeologists often presume that the elaborate material culture of the Neolithic was effectively a set of luxuries that was made possible by the more productive economy offered by farming. The reverse may in fact be the case: the more channelled, extended, and formalized social practices of the Neolithic provided the necessary stability and definition for an ever-increasing dependence on domesticates. As we have seen, John Robb has perceptively argued that while it would have been relatively easy for hunter-gatherers to become entangled in this new world of pots, axes, tombs, houses, and gardens, it would have been much harder for them to extricate themselves. This, again, was presumably also a matter of having made the novel investment in breeding, stock-management, sowing, watering, and harvesting (for example), which became difficult to abandon without a palpable measure of loss. For this reason, few communities ever reverted to a Mesolithic way of life, and the tendency was for the Neolithic lifestyle to proliferate over time.

The Neolithic communities of Britain were pre-literate, and were non-state societies. They obviously lacked the institutions that sustain order in the modern world: government, legal systems, education, armed forces, finance, and the media. In their absence, social relationships and shared knowledge had to be continuously maintained through the performance of traditional practices, anchored in the material world. While acts and ideas are continually emerging, their habitual reiteration may render them as routine and conventional, and this process was facilitated in Neolithic times by the creation of a durable framework of artefacts and structures, which guided and constrained everyday activities. Neolithic groups were 'traditional societies', in the sense that understandings of the world and ways of doing things were passed down from one generation to the next, and, as we will see in Chapter 6, the consequence of this was that past generations remained a powerful presence among the living. Cultural memory, shared history, and collective ancestry maintained potent connections with the past.

Many of the practices that we will discuss in this chapter contributed to the stabilization of social life. For instance, herds of cattle had a temporality (in other words a series of inbuilt relationships to elapsing time and cyclical events) and a momentum of their own, and as such maintaining the herd lent a necessary stability to each human group that tended them. But as we shall see, the roles of kinship and descent in this self-sustaining of the Neolithic world were of critical importance.

Working and extracting flint

At various places in this book we will imply that the contemporary Western conception of matter as inert, inanimate, and passive is unlikely to have obtained during the Neolithic. Ethnographers have observed that in many societies, substances and materials are conventionally understood as being imbued with forces, and with potential capacities, often being viewed as having a dynamic role to play in the workings of the human social world. Inevitably, chipped stone technology remained of fundamental importance during what we term the 'New Stone Age', but it may be unwise to consider it in purely mechanistic terms. Working flint and other rocks which upon striking produce a conchoidal fracture requires the application of force to detach removals (waste flakes) from a surface. This activity demands an engagement that is intensely physical and reactive, and in which the artisan continually turns the block of stone over in their hands, identifying the right place and angle from which to strike it. Almost certainly, this activity would not have been perceived in terms of the imposition of an abstract and preconceived template onto the material, as has sometimes been assumed by archaeologists. Rather, ethnographic testimony gathered among the Australian First Peoples, for example, suggests that it is likely that it was the immanent potential of the stone, hitherto locked within a 'raw' flint nodule or stone block, that was being released through the striking action, setting free the flint or stone blade or axe, or the flint or chert scraper or knife that was perceived to be slumbering in the nodule or block.

If the knapping of flint and the working of stone involved more than the routine stamping of form onto matter, the interaction with the protean forces embodied in these materials is likely to have been seen as a powerful event in itself. An indication of this may be represented by the 'nests' of flint flakes sometimes found in the ditches of earthen long barrows and cursus monuments (see Chapter 4). The explanations that have been offered vary from the possibility that the base of a ditch offered a comfortable place to work flint, sheltered from the elements, to the notion that nodules encountered during ditch-digging may have been 'tested' to ascertain their utility for tool-making. However, in some cases the flint nodule had been knapped until nothing remained beside the mass of flakes, with few tools, or even none at all, having been produced. During an excavation of the western terminal of the Greater Stonehenge Cursus conducted by one of the authors in 2007, numerous groups of flint flakes were encountered throughout the primary silting of the ditch. This demonstrated that the knapping had taken place over a period of months or years, and not solely at the time of ditch-digging. We suggest that in these circumstances, as much as the production of tools, the act of knapping can be identified as a process that released the potency of the material into its environs, thereby contributing to the creation of the monument's distinctive identity or efficacy. Alternatively, or perhaps complementarily, the expenditure of the potential of a flint nodule that might otherwise be used to form 'useful' artefacts could have represented in its own right a dedicatory act, a gift to the gods, spirits of place, or ancestors. This was perhaps either to appease the disturbance of opening up the ground, or to give thanks for the successful execution of the project of building the structure or monument.

One of the most notable developments in the working of stone during the Neolithic was the appearance of flint mines with deep central shafts and, wherever seams of prime-quality flint nodules (known as floor-stone) were encountered, radial galleries. These were neither a feature of the Mesolithic, nor of the earliest Neolithic in north-west Europe, but are first observed in the Low Countries, southern Scandinavia, and the Upper Vistula at around the same time as the beginning of the Neolithic in Britain, or a little earlier. Such is the scale of investment in digging shafts down through ten metres or more of chalk to encounter tabular flint, that mining has routinely been seen as evidence for the beginnings of an industry in the contemporary sense. This characterization is almost certainly misleading, implying as it does the mass production of utilitarian commodities. Throughout the Mesolithic, flint had been acquired from surface exposures on beaches, in river gravels, and on the clay-with-flints, often accessing high-quality raw material for items such as 'tranchet' axes (with a transverse rather than symmetrical blade). As described in Chapters 2 and 3, shortly after 4000 BCE deep flint mines began to be dug in the area of the South Downs immediately to the north of modern Worthing in Sussex. Like the other near-contemporary European sites, the mines occurring at intervals close to the crests of these hills at Cissbury, Harrow Hill, Blackpatch, and Church Hill, Findon, appear to have been concerned primarily with the manufacture of roughed-out and polished flint axes. While the modern geochemical sourcing of flint remains in its infancy, there are indications from macroscopic inspection of the glassy cryptocrystalline silex core of struck flakes that axes with a milky opaque matrix from Sussex were widely distributed in Britain during the earlier part of the Neolithic. So the earliest flint mines in Britain were primarily concerned with the manufacture of a rather special kind of arte-fact, and their status as amongst the very earliest Neolithic sites in the area suggests that the first digging of these mines was intimately connected with the beginning of the process of Neolithization in Britain. The practice of flint-mining was undoubtedly introduced from the Continent, but certain details suggest that distinctive elements were immediately added. Most markedly, this involved the use of red deer antlers as the main extractive tools, in contrast to the use of stone tools in Belgium, as we have seen.

As we noted in the Introduction to this book, alongside the houses at Skara Brae and the chambered interiors of some long mounds, flint mines offer us the rare opportunity to come close to a personal 'three-dimensional' experiencing of the Neolithic in Britain. They represent a remarkable form of architecture, which served to structure both the process of extraction and the interpersonal relationships of those involved. In common with other aspects of the Neolithic material world, flint mines contained and regulated human activity, channelling movement and establishing habitual ways of working. As Mark Edmonds has observed, flint mines are composed of two distinct elements. The broad, circular shaft was essentially a large open pit, dug collectively by a group of people, some levering out the chalk with antler-picks, others dragging the spoil to the surface and dumping it. The galleries that radiated out from the base of this pit, and from which the flint was removed, were so narrow as to only admit one person at a time. So much was this the case that some would have been too tight for a male adult to enter. In this sense, the space of the mine embodied the relationship between the labour of individual people (of diverse ages and genders) and that of the community, while at the same time possibly serving to 'map out' social distinctions. Different stages in the production process were spatially segregated, with blocks of flint being removed from the galleries and the base of the shaft, but being flaked into preforms or roughouts on the surface surrounding the pit. The final grinding and polishing of axes appears to have taken place elsewhere, and this reflects the position of the mines in the wider landscape.

Anne Teather has pointed out that flint mines created their own kind of inaccessibility beyond the physical: descent into the earth, like climbing up to remote rock locations, took the 'extractors' into realms that were both physically removed and dangerous. She has, moreover, noted that the range of depositional practices within the shafts and galleries are in some ways comparable to the complexities of deposition in causewayed enclosures, and similarly the mining shafts and galleries are wholly constructed spaces: they were in effect monuments in their own right. In view of their relative remoteness from the world of everyday activity, the manifest dangers of their excavation and the extraction of flint nodules, and their very character as humanly created places, it is hardly surprising that among the debris are highly structured deposits, scratched markings on walls, and a considerable number of 'decorated' detached blocks and both shaped and scored chalk items. It is difficult to avoid the impression that many such items and markings were left as offerings to unseen, fundamental forces, or were apotropaic (that is, having the power to avert evil influences) in character. As such, the flint mines served both as source and as shrine.

The Sussex flint mines would have been conspicuous features in the landscape, surrounded as they would have been by glistening white spoil tips and replete with carpets of flaking debris glinting in the play of sunlight and shadow. While these mining sites were often positioned on false crests that would have been visible from the coastal plain and the sea beyond, they may have been less obvious from further inland. There is only modest evidence for occupation in the immediate environs of the mines, and it is probable that they were relatively distant from areas of settlement, being visited and worked in the summer months. These were special places, set apart from much of the rest of daily life, where special objects were brought into being in a new and different way. As distinct from other forms of lithic procurement, this involved entering into the earth, a growing preoccupation as the Neolithic progressed. While the various depositional practices that we have previously discussed involved placing things into the ground, Alasdair Whittle has argued that flint axes might have been construed as 'gifts from the earth', reiterating the possibility that the land itself was seen as a living entity with which people enjoyed reciprocal relations. In similar vein, Miles Russell has suggested that entering a flint mine would have constituted a rite of passage, encountering a place of metaphysical as well as physical peril. Visitors would return to their communities in a changed state, so that the mines represented places of transformation in which the identities of both axes and people were created.

The character of flint mines as special, and perhaps marginal, places is reflected in the materials that were deposited in them. There are several burials in the Sussex mines, and interestingly some of them are of women, which contradicts any simple assumption that the extraction of flint would have been an exclusively male activity. The use of mines for burial implies that their use may have been monopolized by particular kin-groups, who asserted their proprietorship in this way. Cattle remains are also present, such as the two ox skulls in Tindall's pit at Cissbury. Upon their abandonment, the mines were often backfilled, and this was sometimes undertaken with some formality. There are often layers of flakes or nodules in the backfill, as if it mattered that they were returned to a former, inviolate state. Indeed, in some cases the deposits that had been quarried from the shaft had been returned in reverse order, replicating an envisaged former order.

In the Late Neolithic, the pattern of special rather than everyday objects being produced at the flint mines in Sussex and Wiltshire was continued and developed at Grimes Graves near Thetford in Norfolk (Fig. 4.1).

This was the largest flint mine complex in Britain, with four or five hundred shafts, although only a fraction of these would ever have been open at a given time. Only small numbers of flint axes were produced at Grimes Graves, and the emphasis was now firmly placed upon the production of more specialized items: discoidal and plano-convex knives, oblique arrowheads, and fine flint daggers. Like the axes from the Sussex mines, the artefacts from Grimes Graves are likely to have been made for exchange, sometimes over considerable distances. Indeed, rather little of the flint extracted from the mines has been discovered in the immediate vicinity. It is perhaps significant that the working of these mines strongly coincided with the main period of production of Grooved Ware pottery, itself connected with the establishment of new networks of long-distance contact between several among the different regions in Britain. Grooved Ware is present at Grimes Graves, sometimes occurring in the context of carefully arranged deposits. At the base of one of the shafts, for example, sherds from internally decorated Grooved Ware bowls were found associated with an organic deposit placed on the surface of a platform of chalk blocks. As with the Sussex axes, it is to be presumed that the value of the knives, arrowheads, and daggers created at Grimes Graves derived from the location and manner of their manufacture.

Fig. 4.1 The 'floor-stone' galleries at Pit 1, Grimes Graves

Between 450 and 600 mining shafts were dug at the place long known as 'Grimes Graves' during the period from 2600 to 2400 BCE within an area of more than 30 hectares. They were up to 14 m (46 ft) deep and were as much as 12 m (39 ft) broad at their tops. Their Neolithic excavators dug down to, and through, an upper band of naturally occurring flint nodules known as 'top-stone', and then through another band termed 'wall-stone', before the floor-stone (preferred for its flawless, durable, and easily worked character) was reached. Here, as many as eight radiating galleries were then dug to retrieve the flint. Some 2,000 tonnes of chalk were removed from each shaft to reach the floor-stone. An average of 140 red deer antler-picks were recovered from where they had been left by the miners at each of the four shafts excavated in the 1970s. Nearly all the antlers used were cast (that is, naturally shed rather than taken from dead animals), suggesting that the deer were actively managed and protected to 'harvest' their shed antlers, rather than just hunted for food.

Grimes Graves flint mines stamp design, illustration by Rebecca Strickson and photograph by Rolph Gobits, taken with the kind permission of English Heritage © Royal Mail Group Limited 2017.

The evidence of rather formal and symbolically charged actions conducted in the mines indicates that here, too, this process was hedged about with ritual.

From feasting to deposition

In this chapter we are drawing attention to some of the practical engagements that made and remade Neolithic societies, many of them mediated through the manufacture, use, consumption, and discard of material things.

Some of these activities were more or less constant throughout the period, while others were transformed in fundamental ways. One of the more conspicuous areas of human conduct throughout the Neolithic is the sharing of food amongst groups of people, which often amounted to feasting. Given the abundance of debris that has been identified from events of large-scale consumption, this was presumably to an extent performative, and involved the assembly of groups of people to share food in ways that maintained or enhanced social bonds, sometimes also developing patterns of prestige, obligation, and indebtedness in the process. This is achieved because the significance was in the killing, not just the eating, of animals (sometimes in a formalized manner, for instance as sacrifices) and the conspicuous consumption, in which much of the food provided might be deliberately wasted. Attending a feast engages people through the sensory experience of taste and satiated hunger, but also through witnessing the spectacle or the formalities involved, and affirming the social relationships that are reinforced in the process. Archaeology has sometimes tended to concentrate on the most distinct and spectacular forms of feasting, which can readily be identified through their material correlates. But in reality there is a continuum between the shared domestic meal and the sumptuous feast that seals an alliance between large social groups, or celebrates an important birth, marriage, or funeral. Moreover, the latter may acquire its efficacy by being understood as a more elaborate version of the former. That is, participants may come to feel a sense of mutual attachment similar to that experienced by immediate kinsfolk.

The scale and context of feasting activities in Neolithic Britain seem to have varied considerably. Runnymede Bridge, in Surrey, a site with extensive recurrent settlement during the middle of the fourth millennium BCE, produced an assemblage of animal bones that indicated that joints of beef had been roasted over open fires, but that the bones and scraps of meat had subsequently been boiled in pottery vessels for soups or stews. Such was the quantity of meat involved that, in the absence of salting, storage, or elaborate distribution mechanisms linking dispersed communities, any slaughter of cattle would only have taken place when an appreciable number of people had gathered together. An adult cow produces in the order of 300 kg of meat and offal. The slaughter of numbers of these animals attested from ethnography implies communal meals consumed by at least dozens and possibly hundreds of people, with more informal consumption taking place on subsequent days. Recent analysis of animal remains from pits on the

Rudston Wold in East Yorkshire indicates a similar pattern of feasting on a moderate scale, concentrated in the winter months, during the Late Neolithic.

However, a more variable pattern of consumption is represented elsewhere. For instance, at the large settlement that preceded the construction of the henge monument at Durrington Walls in Wiltshire (see Chapter 5), animal bones from house floors and from pits associated with the abandonment of buildings showed that within or around these buildings meals had been shared by relatively small groups of people. These meals had occurred throughout the year, and many of the bones came from mature pigs in their second year of life. In sharp contrast, the remains from two large middens seemed to have been derived from much larger feasts held at midwinter, at which younger pigs had been roasted. Lipid residues from the Grooved Ware pottery from these middens showed that most of the vessels concerned had contained pork fats, whereas pots found in the vicinity of the large southern timber circle had held mostly dairy fats. It is possible to conclude from this pronounced difference that a distinct group of people, gathered in a focal area of the site, may have consumed particular foodstuffs in a distinctive way. This could represent an example of what Michael Dietler has referred to as a 'diacritical feast', in which the specifics of who eats what, and sometimes how, can serve to acknowledge and enhance social differences.

Another example of feasting on a grand scale in a distinctive way, apparently involving yet more overt display, came from the Beaker-era Barrow 1 at Irthingborough in Northamptonshire. Here, the skulls of 185 cattle had been incorporated into the limestone cairn of the round mound. These were prime young animals that had been butchered and stripped of their flesh some time before deposition. The meat from at least thirty-five of these animals had been consumed in the immediate vicinity of the barrow, and it is estimated that this much beef would have been enough to feed roughly a thousand participants. It is therefore possible that the barrow deposit as a whole could represent the bringing together of the remains of several such feasts during extensive mortuary feasting rituals within this part of the Nene valley, culminating in the deposition event marking the 'topping out' of the barrow, in much the same way that many of today's building completions are celebrated. This Irthingborough extravaganza may, of course, be atypical, but it does provide us with a glimpse of the potential extent of funerary events at the very end of the Neolithic period, marking the passing of particularly important individuals, or groups of such people. In the context of rather later pre-Classical Greek culture it would be possible to conceive of such an event as the aftermath of a serious martial encounter.

There is an obvious link here between events of consumption and episodes of deposition, in that one is often the outcome of the other. The deliberate placement of artefacts, human and animal remains, and other substances including charcoal and midden-material in pits, in ditches, and in the chambers of barrows was a pervasive theme throughout the Neolithic. While these materials are to some extent mundane, they may nonetheless have been understood as potent or polluting (or, paradoxically, both), owing to their status as the residues of either everyday, or more special, human activities. Hearth ash, for instance, is virtually ubiquitous in Neolithic pits, potentially having connoted both the role of the fireplace as the focus of the household and the importance of fire in the preparation (and transformation) of food. Although in later periods of prehistory pits were dug as storage facilities, particularly for grain, and only used as receptacles for rubbish when they were no longer needed for this primary purpose, Neolithic pits were dug deliberately to receive these kinds of specific deposit. Their edges are generally sharply defined, indicating that at the point of refilling they were freshly dug and therefore not yet weathered. They rarely give any impression of having been used for any other activity. Furthermore, they are usually of neither an appropriate size nor shape for use as a cereal store.

There are two aspects that differentiate the contents of these pits—selectivity and arrangement—and both contribute to an impression of increasing formality, and a more rigidly structured series of acts as time progressed. Generally speaking, pits from the earlier part of the Neolithic period contain deposited material that gives the impression of having been scooped up from a midden or occupation surface, and any objects contained within the soil and ash are disordered and confused. An exception is the site of Roughridge Hill in north Wiltshire, where groups of items including pottery fragments, stone tools, bone pins, and animal bones had been placed around the pit edges. But the more common pattern is described by Amelia Pannett amongst a series of pit groups in Carmarthenshire, the earliest of which contain jumbled masses of material that might easily have derived from domestic activity, while later Neolithic examples included fragments of human bone and stone tools that had deliberately been broken. In Ireland, Jessica Smyth has described a similar situation, with unusual artefacts and concentrations of human bone being progressively added to a standard pit assemblage of charcoal, flint, pottery, and burnt hazelnut shells from the later part of the fourth millennium BCE. On the Isle of Man, Timothy Darvill has identified a variant of this pattern, where the random scatters of Early Neolithic pits were replaced by more spatially structured arrangements which sometimes included Ronaldsway jars buried up to their necks, and human remains.

This tendency toward greater structure and complexity in pit contents reached a peak with the appearance of Grooved Ware pottery. Joshua Pollard has described as 'sculpted' the bowl-like forms of Grooved Ware pits, which sometimes contain sherds of pottery that have been arranged to form distinct surfaces within the pit fill. They can also often contain objects that are distinctive, or have been conspicuously placed, such as the group of flint scrapers that had been piled one on top of another at Over Site 3 in Cambridgeshire. Another good example is the large circular slate plaque engraved with a chequerboard pattern recovered from a Grooved Ware pit inside a causewayed enclosure of earlier date near Truro in Cornwall. At Firtree Field on Down Farm in north Dorset, sixteen Late Neolithic pits containing Grooved Ware were found in two distinct clusters (Fig. 4.2).

The northern group was associated with a series of three-metre diameter arcs of stake-holes, probably indicating a former occupation site. Yet the southern group was positioned closer to the nearby Dorset Cursus, and contained the richest and most complex material. The kinds of items placed in these pits included boars' tusks, an ox skull, red deer antlers, and a slab of pottery laid decorated side up. These materials were placed on the bases of the pits, and were evidently intended to be viewed, at least for a short period of time. Such arrangements may have been intended to be witnessed openly, by an entire community, or they could have been committed to memory by a restricted group officiating at what may have amounted to a form of ceremony. Equally, they could have been undertaken as part of an ongoing dialogue with the unseen: spirits, natural forces, 'gods', or ancestors. It is important to recognize that any one of these three possibilities could have produced the same outcome, and that some acts of dedication would have combined elements of any of the three. While the implication of this is that pit deposition might sometimes have constituted a kind of 'ritual', we would emphasize that this does not mean that it was set apart from everyday life. If the materials employed were often the remnants of unexceptional activities, their deposition might constitute a more reflective moment woven into the commonplace, as when people of faith today either cross themselves when

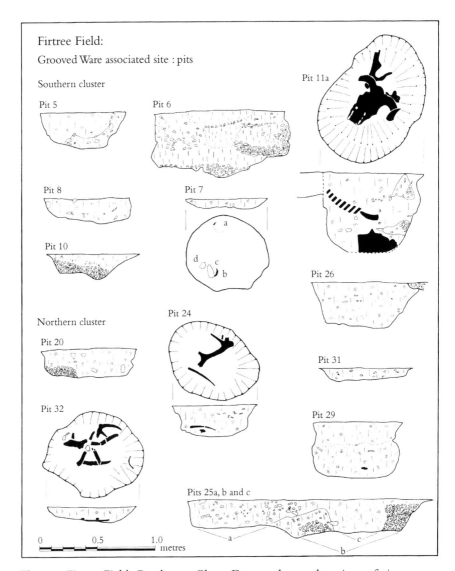

Firtree Field:

Grooved Ware associated site : pits

Southern cluster

Pit 5

Pit 6

Pit 11a

Pit 8

Pit 7

Pit 10

Pit 26

Northern cluster

Pit 24

Pit 20

Pit 31

Pit 32

Pit 29

Pits 25a, b and c

0   0.5   1.0   metres

Fig. 4.2 Firtree Field, Cranborne Chase, Dorset: plans and sections of pits

The Late Neolithic pits excavated by Martin Green at Firtree Field close to the Dorset Cursus produced a rich assemblage of items, including an ox skull, boars' tusks, red deer antlers, a stone axe, and numerous sherds of Grooved Ware.

Plan: from J. Barrett, R. Bradley, and M. Green, *Landscape, Monuments and Society* (1991), © Cambridge University Press.

passing a wayside shrine, or unroll a prayer mat in their place of work, or offer a benediction before a meal.

Deposits in and near monuments, often in ditches or post-holes, should not be understood as categorically different from those in pits, although they may have served to embed the potency of materials and substances in specific places. From the later fourth millennium onwards, it is significant that deposits were often made after structures of one kind or another had gone out of use. Grooved Ware pits were sometimes dug close to the remains of the timber halls of the earliest Neolithic, including White Horse Stone and Parc Bryn Cegin, as well as the rather later unroofed timber structure at Littleour in Perthshire, whose form arguably mimics that of a hall. At Durrington Walls in Wiltshire, more pits containing Grooved Ware were cut into the floors of the Late Neolithic houses when they went out of use, as part of the abandonment process. This echoes the way that pits were dug during or after episodes of habitation on more ephemeral occupation sites throughout the Neolithic. Similarly, pits filled with Grooved Ware and animal bones were dug into the tops of the rotted-out uprights of the great southern timber circle at Durrington. This could be compared with the elaborate deposits placed into the ragged craters left behind after the withdrawal of massive posts from the Dunragit palisaded enclosure in Galloway. This was part of the process of decommissioning, but it was also a means of committing the past to memory, and perhaps a way of reinforcing the connection between monuments and houses, for both were treated in the same way at the end of their use-life. There is also reason to suspect that some of the large monuments of the third millennium BCE drew their power from being understood as the collective 'houses' of large groups of people, as we will see in Chapter 5.

However, just as substances and artefacts were placed in pits that served to mark or secure the memory of places where human activity had occurred, sometimes pit deposits seem to have anticipated or conditioned the later use of a location. The large Early Neolithic pit at Coneybury, which we have already discussed, was first discovered because it lay close to the Coneybury Hill henge monument. Other monuments that had been preceded by pits include the henges at Balfarg in Fife and the Pict's Knowe near Dumfries, the Middle Neolithic enclosure of Flagstones House in Dorset, the stone circles of Machrie Moor on Arran, and the Holywood South cursus, also near Dumfries. Although pits can hardly have left a substantial physical trace in the landscape, it seems highly likely that the accumulated histories of particular localities were intimately known, and remembered for very long periods. Indeed, this knowledge of places, and of who had done what and where, is likely to have been fundamental to how Neolithic people became familiar with the land and found their way around. This might be seen as a means of anchoring people into a sense of their rights to the inhabitation and use of particular places, particularly where occupation was sporadic and episodic rather than continuous.

Mesolithic people certainly showed an interest in the world below the earth's surface, making use of caves and sometimes digging pits. Indeed, developer-funded archaeology in eastern Scotland has recently revealed that Mesolithic pits may be much more common than has often been assumed, especially in the later fifth millennium BCE. A significant proportion of these pits contain no artefacts, and their date is only revealed if a radio-carbon determination is undertaken. So pit digging is another practice that spans the Mesolithic–Neolithic transition, and there are sites such as Girvan Warehouse 37, where Mesolithic pits were re-dug in the Early Neolithic and sherds of carinated bowl pottery introduced. However, having said that, it has become clear from the by now numerous archaeological excavations of often quite considerable tracts of landscape that from the start of the Neolithic the proliferation of crafted objects and built structures was matched by an exponential growth of interventions into the earth. Pits that received deposits were only one aspect of this development, alongside the ditches of enclosures and long barrows, the post-holes of timber structures of various kinds, flint-mine shafts, and the insertion of cultural materials into the open-ings left by the root-boles of toppled trees and natural shafts such as those at Fir Tree Field in Dorset, Cannon Hill in Berkshire, and Eaton Heath in Norfolk. Similarly, Jessica Smyth has drawn attention to the deposition of items including axes and arrowheads into the beam-slots of Early Neolithic buildings in Ireland. In this way, while Neolithic people extracted materials from the earth (clay for potting, flint for knapping, daub for building, quar-ried stones for structures or to stand upright, chalk used for carved objects and for the fabric of monuments), they also replaced them with other things. In a world in which substances from, and features of, the landscape may have been understood as being animate and imbued with force and poten-tial, it is conceivable that these actions were seen in terms of reciprocity with the earth itself, as a means of making reparation for opening up wounds in the land, as we have already argued in the case of flint mines.

Placement of artefacts in a pit generally represented the end of their use-life, but other forms of deposition might have provided a more temporary resting place. The gathering together of a variety of different organic and inorganic materials in mounds or spreads of 'rubbish' as middens can be identified as a means of storing value, potency, and potential, sometimes for later retrieval. In this respect, such middening represents a variation on the theme of *accumulation* that more widely characterizes the Neolithic, and is also seen in the amassing of herds of cattle, or the gathering up of human remains and placing them in the chambers of long mounds. Flint cores, axe fragments, pottery vessels and animal bones were placed in middens, from where they might potentially be recovered at a later time. Middens represented an important element of British landscapes from the start of the Neolithic, although it is arguable that they shared some features with the shell-middens of the Mesolithic, which we have already mentioned. In the area excavated in advance of the creation of Eton Rowing Course by the River Thames near Windsor in Berkshire, a series of large middens built up in existing hollows in the ground from the thirty-ninth century BCE. While these deposits were not accompanied by significant structural evidence, they appear to have accumulated as a consequence of cyclical or recurrent occupation beside the river. Here the middens themselves may have served as enduring markers of commitment to a particular location.

Throughout the period, objects occur in Neolithic contexts that seem to have been conserved for appreciable periods before their final deposition. In Chapter 6 we shall discuss the cattle and deer bones from the ditch of Stonehenge, which were already more than a century old when they were deposited. In the Firtree Field pits mentioned above, three pieces of Peterborough Ware were found amongst an assemblage that was otherwise dominated by Grooved Ware. All are recognizable rim sherds, parts of vessels that unambiguously represent a different ceramic tradition. Although it is probable that the Grooved Ware and Peterborough Ware traditions overlapped chronologically to a limited extent, the most likely explanation for the co-occurrence of such contrasting styles of pottery is that the Peterborough Ware fragments were already ancient, and had been retrieved from a midden with the intention of redepositing them. A similar phenomenon was recognized at Horton in Berkshire, where organic residues on a large fragment from a Peterborough bowl produced a radiocarbon date centuries earlier than charcoal from the Grooved Ware pit from which it was recovered.

As we shall see in Chapter 6, this particular practice was by no means an isolated one.

Ann Woodward has acutely observed that some of the graves of the Beaker period contained fragments from pots that were apparently much older than the principal vessel that accompanied the burial. Her view is that special pots, particularly those that had been used in feasts and other important events, or that had belonged to significant persons, might have been secured in middens for generations before being used as funerary goods, thus bringing with them a tangible trace of collective history. Other objects, too, seem to have been retained for long periods and deployed in mortuary contexts during the final stages of the Neolithic. At Raunds Barrow 1 in Northamptonshire a pig tusk placed in the primary grave was centuries older than the burial, while an archer's wrist-guard found nearby had been refashioned from a stone axe of Cumbrian origin, which may have been as much as a millennium old when desposited. We will have more to say about these practices of 'curation' and their relationship to history and memory in Chapter 6.

Dwelling

At several points throughout this book we have referred to the burying of various items in pits, more and less formally. Among reasonable questions to ask are: what relationship did pits have to the places where people were living? And, if people occupied living structures other than the timber halls identified at the beginning of the period and the cellular houses known at the end, what form did such buildings take? One potential difficulty that is raised by a focus on practices and activities in the past is that it can lead us to think of human life as composed of a series of bursts of action, during which the archaeological evidence that survives into the present is created. In between, past people fade from our concern somewhat, apparently no longer doing anything significant. One answer to this is to complement our interest in *cultural practices* with the issue of *dwelling* or *inhabitation*. By this we mean that humans are constantly involved with their world, attentive to what is going on, responding as required, in a rolling dialogue with other people, animals, and things. Their plans and projects are always maturing and being carried forward, at once informed by their past and projected into the future. So rather than thinking about separate episodes of *doing* being scattered about the landscape, we should consider instead the way that the course of life draws these happenings together in the continuous flow of human conduct.

How then might this perspective affect the way that we understand pits, middens, and buildings? To begin with, there are many deposits that derive from the debris of living—in particular from the preparation and consumption of food, and from the working of various materials in the course of making, using, and repairing things. We know, of course, that the sites of some long barrows were initially marked by the formation of middens, and how these middens comprised mounds or spreads of such debris. Middens have also been found on the margins of stream-channels, where they could, as at Runnymede Bridge by the Thames in Surrey and Eton Rowing Lake near Windsor in Berkshire, have been very extensive and in use repeatedly. There may have been to some degree, and at certain times and places, an overlap between the occurrence of middens and pits, and some but by no means all pits were places where 'midden-debris' could be disposed of (instead of being used to help form middens). The messiness involved in the placing of material in these various ways should not surprise us; nor should it be expected that Neolithic places were tidy in any modern sense (although the interior of some structures was clearly regularly swept clean). Two things that we do need to try to explain, however, are why the contents of pits differed in any one location, and to some extent between them; and what the relationship was between middens, pits, and 'dwellings'.

Some recent investigations have gone a long way in helping us to address these issues. As was discussed in Chapter 3, at Kingsmead Quarry, Horton in Berkshire, a number of timber halls or houses have been identified, dating to the thirty-eighth century BCE (Fig. 4.3).

Some generations later, a cluster of pits was created close by, whose rectilinear arrangement seemed to echo that of one of the buildings. The pits are suggestive of temporary occupation, and at Wellington Quarry in Herefordshire it has been suggested that the activities represented in pit contents are indicative of a stay of two or three months at a time. But neither houses nor pit locations need have been inhabited year-round, although both might have fulfilled the role of tethering and channelling human lives. At Kilverstone in Norfolk, meticulous analysis by Duncan Garrow, Emma Beadsmoore, and Mark Knight has illuminated the formation of the contents of 226 Earlier Neolithic pits, which formed a series of discrete clusters (Fig. 4.4). Both burned and unburned sherds of pottery that could nonetheless be refitted with each other were found to have been buried in

Fig. 4.3 A Neolithic house at Kingsmead Quarry, Horton, Berkshire

During the course of a fifteen-year programme of 'strip, map, and record' archaeological investigation at Kingsmead Quarry just to the west of Heathrow Airport, a total of four Early Neolithic houses have been revealed and carefully examined. Dated to around 3750 BCE, the sites of the rectangular houses have produced burnt flint, animal bones, flint tools (especially leaf-shaped arrowheads), flint-knapping debris, charred plant remains, cereal grains, and hazelnut shells, along with grinding stones and in one case a flake from a polished stone axe from Great Langdale in the Lake District.

Photograph: © Wessex Archaeology, courtesy of Alistair Barclay.

Fig. 4.4 Neolithic pit-group at Kilverstone, Thetford, Norfolk

The photograph shows pit cluster K at the centre of Area E at Kilverstone, prior to their excavation and viewed from the east (scale is 1 m long). This was one of eighteen clusters of pits in Area E (with ten such clusters in area A), with the overall activity dated to the period 3650–3350 cal BCE. The pits produced quantities of flaked flint and pieces of broken pottery. Careful post-excavation study and the fitting together ('re-fitting') of flakes struck from the same flint core and pieces from the same pots showed a complex pattern of distribution between the different pits across the site, the discrete patterning of the pits in clusters nonetheless suggesting 'repeated and persistent' but not continuous occupation, with the scale and duration of these episodes varying widely. The finds, which included charred cereal grains, indicate that cultivation took place close to the site, probably in woodland clearings.

Photograph: © and courtesy of Duncan Garrow.

different pits. The fact that they had also been affected by differential degrees of abrasion indicates that they had been subject to a range of different processes between breakage and deposition. Along with food debris and flintworking residues, they formed part of the gathered-up mess from what was a perhaps a seasonal settlement. This gradual accumulation of residues was punctuated by the digging and filling of more pits. Although the refitting exercise conducted by the archaeologists showed that there was material from the same items located in different pits within the same groups, the contents of the *groups* of pits overall were found to have been mutually exclusive. In turn this suggests that each set of pits related to the activities of a distinct group of people, possibly those who occupied the ephemeral structures implied by the layout of each cluster, just as at Horton. The overwhelming impression was of repeated returns to a particular location, over a period of possibly fifty to a hundred years, by a community composed of a number of distinct segments, or households.

In a subsequent analysis of assemblages from the Etton causewayed enclosure in Cambridgeshire (already introduced in Chapter 3), Garrow, Beadsmoore, and Knight went on to demonstrate that the deposition of material in the ditch segments was organized in an entirely different way from that in the Kilverstone pits. While fragments of pottery and flint exhibited conjoins that linked only pits within a given cluster at Kilverstone, the refits at Etton spread across the entire enclosure. It follows that the spatial character of activity was quite different in the two sites, and to a degree (by extension) the two kinds of site. Furthermore, while deposition at Kilverstone was more intensive, taking place energetically over a short span of time, that at Etton may have been more sporadic in nature, with perhaps shorter episodes of occupation dispersed over a much longer period of time. While Kilverstone produced greater quantities of flint, Etton revealed more pottery, perhaps demonstrating a greater preoccupation with consumption at the enclosure, rather than the manufacture and maintenance of tools. These contrasts are highly instructive, but it is important to remember that both sites represent merely facets of the way in which a landscape as a whole was inhabited by Neolithic communities.

Herding and hunting

The advent of the Neolithic changed the relationship between people and animals. While Mesolithic people had no doubt often decisive encounters with deer, aurochs, pig, and other species in the course of hunting and tracking, these creatures were unlikely to have been viewed as 'property', even when they were killed and their meat distributed within a community. Domestication is a biological process in which human beings come to influence the conditions under which animals reproduce. But equally importantly, it is a social process in which the relationships between people and the creatures they raise become more continuous and more thoroughly interwoven, and the notion of investment in stock management inevitably leads to the development of proprietary attitudes. Such cohabitation also brought about a transformation in two other dimensions of food acquisition. On the one hand, the ongoing practices of hunting during the Neolithic were likely to have become focused in a different way as a supplement to, rather than a mainstay of, subsistence. While hunting would always have been to some extent a recreational and a 'testing' activity for its participants, the group-composition of game animals taken to supplement the diet or provide specialized foods for more limited consumption would have differed subtly from previously, and may have been seen to pertain to 'ancestral' relations and practices. On the other hand, herders have to feed and water their animals, move them between pastures, control their breeding, wean them, milk them, and keep them safe from pests and predators. All this requires people to accommodate the rhythm and tempo of their lives to those of their livestock much more closely than following the seasonal habits and movements of game, or the appearance of naturally growing forage foods. The attachment of a human community to a herd of animals that represents a collective investment tends to have a more strongly routinizing effect, both through the coordination of everyday practice demanded, and by limiting social fission or fragmentation. In Chapter 6 we will discuss further the particular connection between cattle herds and human kinship, and the ways in which history and descent were embodied in livestock.

The groups of animal bones found during archaeological excavations of Neolithic sites in Britain were dominated throughout the period by the bones of domesticated species. However, one recurrent exception to this is the very large numbers of red deer antlers found in flint mines, and in the ditches and post-holes of long barrows, causewayed enclosures, cursus monuments, and henges. These antlers, with all but the brow tine removed, were used as picks for levering chalk and stone from the ground. In the 1967 excavations at the great henge of Durrington Walls in Wiltshire, a group of fifty-seven such antler-picks was found dumped on the base of the ditch terminal immediately to the south of the southern timber circle. A further staggering 354 picks were recovered from the post-holes of the circle itself, prompting the suggestion that they had been deliberately abandoned because their use elsewhere would have been considered inappropriate. The great majority of these antlers had been shed, rather than taken from deer that had been slain, but the abundance of antlers at these sites provides an interesting contrast with the relative paucity of deer bones from most Neolithic contexts, and particularly those identified with domestic occupation.

One exception is the large pit known as the 'Anomaly' excavated on Coneybury Hill, south-east of Stonehenge, dated to the later thirty-eighth century BCE, and already discussed in Chapter 2. This pit contained the remains of ten bovines, two red deer, one pig, and several roe deer, which had all presumably been butchered nearby. While the roe deer had apparently been eaten on site, the meat of the cattle and red deer had been taken away for consumption elsewhere. The Coneybury Anomaly assemblage suggests an important social episode such as a feast, but why had so much food been removed? It may be that part of the answer lies in a degree of cultural ambivalence over the killing and butchering of deer. The event at Coneybury had clearly taken place at a remove from some other location, to which the choicest of the meat had been taken. This same ambivalence has been identified by Niall Sharples at a number of sites in Late Neolithic Orkney, at which red deer had been killed or consumed outwith settlements, where deer bones are rarely found at all. At the Point of Buckquoy, an isolated midden was found, containing numerous bones of red deer. At the Bay of Skaill, a butchery site was excavated, with the remains of four deer and a number of flint knives that had been used to remove the meat from the carcasses. Finally, at the settlement of the Links of Noltland, fifteen red deer had been slaughtered in a single episode and dumped in a heap, before being left to rot. The animals were deposited beside a wall retaining a midden deposit, distinct from the settlement area. They were predominantly females, and all but one had been laid on their left-hand sides.

Seemingly, red deer (and perhaps wild animals in general) were routinely consumed by British Neolithic people, but dealings with them were kept separate from dwelling areas. Their bones may, therefore, be underrepresented at some occupation sites. Two possible interpretations suggest themselves. First, although it is very unlikely that the modern distinction between 'culture' and 'nature' was consciously applied by people in the Neolithic period, it is possible that animals that had been fully incorporated into human society could be brought near to dwellings, but that creatures that were encountered only intermittently, and that were connected with the forest and the wild, had to be kept at arm's length. Alternatively, it may be that deer in particular retained an association with an increasingly mythic pre-Neolithic past. As a particularly important animal that had been hunted during the Mesolithic period, deer might have been displaced as a primary food source while at the same time their meat became more highly prized. As such, this meat may have been consumed in more particularly ritualized and exclusive, even perhaps semi-clandestine, circumstances, following which their antlers were collected and used for digging, but abandoned in their place of use. Equally, animals that rarely came together in groups, and that inhabited the forest or other remote places, such as the aurochs (or wild cattle), may have been hunted under special circumstances with attendant inhibitions. Their bones occur in a trophy-like manner in Neolithic sites, mostly as individual finds and apparently not as the debris from feasting.

Harm

Vicki Cummings and Oliver Harris have proposed recently that following the transition from the Mesolithic to the Neolithic, the practice of hunting continued, but it came to be focused on people as well as animals. While the burial record for the Mesolithic is such as to inhibit comparisons, there is little doubt that Neolithic societies in both Britain and Europe engaged in some level of violence. The earliest Neolithic societies of central Europe, known collectively as the *Linearbandkeramik*, are associated with a number of massacre sites. These include the Talheim 'death pit' near Heilbronn in Germany, containing what may potentially have been the entire population of a small settlement, many of whom had been dispatched by blows to the head from stone axes. While the Mesolithic should certainly not be construed as a period of idyllic peace, it does seem that one of the innovations of the Neolithic was likely to have been an increase in interpersonal conflict. Rick Schulting and Michael Wysocki have described thirty-one instances of healed and unhealed cranial trauma from a sample of 350 skulls from funerary monuments in Britain. This would not in itself represent a high level of injuries, but when post-cranial and soft-tissue wounds, and in particular projectile impacts, are added, it is enough to suggest that violence was a significant factor in Neolithic life in Britain. Other indications of aggression include the evidence for attack at the enclosure sites of Crickley Hill in Gloucestershire and Hambledon Hill in Dorset, in the form of extensive burning, dense concentration of flint arrowheads, and in the latter case a body in the ditch with an arrowhead in its chest cavity. Similar indications of conflict are evident at the Cornish tor enclosures (rocky hilltops enhanced with walls made from piled stones) of Carn Brea and Helman Tor, where large numbers of leaf-shaped flint arrowheads have been found, that appear to have been shot towards and into entranceways, as if the latter places had been under ferocious attack.

Moderate but continuous levels of violence, or endemic conflict, are often a feature of pre-state societies. For social anthropologists, these can be understood as cases of 'negative reciprocity', the darker counterpart of exchange, feasting, and gift-giving. Whom one fights against, and whom one fights alongside, can have considerable consequences for the reinforcement or dissolution of social relationships. Indeed, the main purpose of creating alliances between communities may be to facilitate aggression against other groups. Joining a war band or a raiding party is often an obligation imposed on those who find themselves in a position of indebtedness, while deaths that happen during conflict may need to be compensated by the payment of blood-price. Yet while these structural aspects of warfare are fundamental, it is also important to point out that violence is both an embodied activity and, to some extent, a performance. In many pre-industrial societies fighting provides a context for display, in which reputations are built and maturity or adulthood is achieved. Some Neolithic artefacts such as bows and arrows, hafted flint and stone axes, and, in the Beaker phase, flint daggers had the capacity to link aggression with personal identity. Not all such items had to have been used in anger, but it is nonetheless probable that the achievement of personal repute in the Neolithic was often connected with martial prowess. The evidence for archery in particular provides some important clues regarding the changing character of violence during the period. In the Mesolithic, arrows were made using multiple microliths inserted into a wooden shaft and held in place with resin and twine. One small flint might form a point, but numerous others would make up rows of fearsome-looking barbs. In the woodlands of the mature postglacial period, such weapons were well suited to hunting deer and pigs. In a context where such animals might emerge from the undergrowth and be visible only momentarily, a well-aimed arrow might not kill outright, but would lodge in the creature's flesh, causing an aggravated wound that would drip a trail of blood that could be followed as it tired. The leaf-shaped arrowheads of the Early Neolithic, however, were quite different in character, comprising as they did a single blade-like point, best suited to piercing. These arrows were more readily used against human beings, in the changed circumstances of the fourth millennium. With the formation of more closely bounded communities that maintained more exclusive control over resources, conflict between social groups might be expected to have increased. Most pertinently, cattle now constituted a form of mobile wealth that could increase a person's social standing in manifold ways. While the causes and forms of conflict during this period may have been numerous, we would reiterate that cattle-raiding is likely to have featured prominently amongst them.

By the later part of the millennium, the character of arrowheads had changed yet again, first to a preponderance of chisel-shaped (so-called *petit tranchet*-derivative) forms, and then to lopsided oblique types, often with a hollow (concave-curving) base and sometimes with delicate ripple flaking on the dorsal surface. These arrows would have been less aerodynamically efficient than the leaf-shaped ones, and in the case of the oblique styles, less suited to killing an opponent outright. However, the deployment of such projectiles in close combat would have had the potential to cause spectacular and bloody wounds, severing ankle tendons (for example) and disabling opponents, causing them to retire from the immediate engagement. Descriptions of historically attested and comparatively recent warfare in various parts of the world suggest that in some cases it is preferable to incapacitate than to kill an opponent, where the latter might result in reprisals and revenge killings. One possibility, therefore, as pointed out by Edmonds and Thomas as long ago as 1984, is that during the Middle and Late Neolithic the nature of conflict became more ritualized and constrained by convention, and more concerned with performance and display than with the wholesale slaughter of enemies. Another indication that archery was not entirely utilitarian in character during the Late Neolithic is provided by the animal bone assemblage from Durrington Walls. Here, many of the domestic pigs had been killed with arrows, rather than simply having been slaughtered by poleaxing or having had their throats cut. The implication is that pig-killing involved a degree of arranged spectacle, with animals perhaps having been allowed to run free within a reserved space before being shot, performatively, as a combination of sport and ceremonial, or as part of the initiation rites concerning the passage of young people into adulthood.

Communicating with pots?

One of the considerable 'laboratory science' advances that has had an immense impact on Neolithic studies in recent years has been in the study of residues that have long been noted adhering especially to the insides of pottery sherds. More than this, the fatty substances (known as lipids) that have been absorbed into the very fabric of such often open-pored vessels as a result of cooking, storage, or processing of food have left a chemical trace that can be identified by a variety of techniques. One such, involving compound-specific stable carbon isotope analysis, has enabled the identification of meat and dairy products (especially milk) from Neolithic sherds, such that the consumption of milk and secondary dairy products (such as butter, cheese, and ghee) is now well attested (with all its implications for the tolerance—or otherwise—of lactose among the relevant populations).

Yet while new possibilities are opening up for the scientific study of residues in Neolithic ceramics in Britain, the significance of their design and decoration continues to be a topic of some debate. In this respect the study of Neolithic pottery in Britain and Ireland contrasts a little with that on the continental mainland of Europe. In the Scandinavian *Trechterbekercultuur* (TRB), the central European *Linearbandkeramik* (LBK) or the west French Middle Neolithic, finely grained internal sequences of typological development have been gradually refined and employed as a proxy means of dating. The British material has largely proved resistant to such an approach, while British archaeologists have often shown greater enthusiasm for independent, scientific forms of dating than their Continental counterparts. Pottery was one of the most distinctive innovations of the Neolithic, and while Mesolithic communities in some parts of northern and eastern Europe made and used ceramics, this was not the case in Britain. Pottery was therefore a radically new container technology, which introduced new possibilities for mixing, cooking, storing, and serving food and drink: a new 'culinary alchemy', which would potentially have changed the experiences of eating and drinking by creating unfamiliar flavours. It is also a highly plastic medium that offers the opportunity to create a great diversity of material forms. Pottery vessels can vary in size and shape, in surface finish, and in decoration, while the technological choices involved in achieving these outcomes can be quite extensive. Pots can engage the onlooker visually, and they can also offer haptic experiences of surface texture, while their shapes and sizes oblige people to engage with them in specific ways. Some of the variation in ceramic form can be put down to practical requirements: to withstand thermal shock, to contain different quantities of different materials, to serve different numbers of people, or to stand on different surfaces. But to some extent, pots of quite varied appearance may be equally fit for purpose, and their distinctive character cannot be explained exclusively in functional terms. In particular, we need to ask why distinct 'traditions' of pottery developed and were maintained for long periods during the Neolithic, and why they sometimes came to be replaced by others, occasionally within quite short periods of time. When the potential for creating distinctive pots is so great, why did people continue to replicate the same styles?

For the archaeologists of the interwar period this was a straightforward question to answer, since it was assumed that members of particular communities automatically inherited the 'norms' (or conventional ways of making and doing things) that had been developed by their group, and simply reproduced them without deliberation (see Chapter 6 for further discussion of this point). However, once we recognize that people make explicit choices in manufacturing and decorating objects, this view is undermined. Artisans always have the option of doing things differently, and one consequence of this is that their products can potentially carry some form of message, even if this is often quite mundane. This means that the different styles of pottery manufactured during the Neolithic did not simply reflect the ethnic or cultural identities of their makers: in some cases they may have conveyed information at a number of different levels, to different potential audiences. Some of these messages may have been quite vague and unspecific, as today when our choice of clothing or jewellery makes a statement about ourselves that may be only vaguely formulated. But in specific contexts, the use of particular pottery vessels may have carried connotations that were absolutely unambiguous.

This may be the case with the first pottery employed in Britain, the carinated bowl tradition, which was generally not decorated, but was nonetheless highly distinctive. It is notable that the very earliest of these assemblages, identified with the first Neolithic activity in the south and east of England, were relatively uniform in character, dominated by upright, bipartite vessels with simple rims, in fine, thin-walled fabrics with smooth surfaces. These were small groups of pots, often used for hospitality and the sharing of food at funerals, gatherings, and feasts. Their form had been selected from more extensive suites of vessel types in use in north-east France and the Low Countries (and slightly later from north-west France), and this suggests that the message they carried was not only one of adherence to a new set of social conventions, but also of connectedness to distant, prestigious, and powerful communities. Later forms of the carinated bowl tradition had surfaces that were ripple-burnished, and a few were sparingly decorated with incised lines. Subsequently, pots came to be used in more mundane activities, assemblages became larger, and their fabrics became coarser and thicker. A wider range of vessel forms was employed, generally drawn from Continental prototypes, but not always from the same sources. Furthermore, when incised, stabbed, and impressed decoration began to be more extensively applied to pottery from shortly before 3700 BCE, the pattern of 'mixing and matching' that we have identified in other aspects of culture came into play: decorative motifs that would not have been out of place in northern Europe were applied to vessels of north-west French affinity, for instance. As discussed in Chapter 3, these Decorated Bowls formed distinctive regional groupings, but the boundaries between these were not strongly defined, while decoration was preferentially applied to particular forms of vessels (notably, but not exclusively, shouldered bowls) (Fig. 4.5). This may indicate that any message that the pots conveyed was related less to regional identity than to the activities or contexts in which pots were employed, or the specific people who made and used them.

The emergence of Peterborough Wares and Scottish Impressed Wares in the thirty-fourth century BCE might be seen as a continuation and intensification of this Decorated Ware tradition, and the imperatives that gave rise to it. The shouldered bowl was transformed into something more densely sensual, with thick fabrics from which the large flint or quartz grits visibly

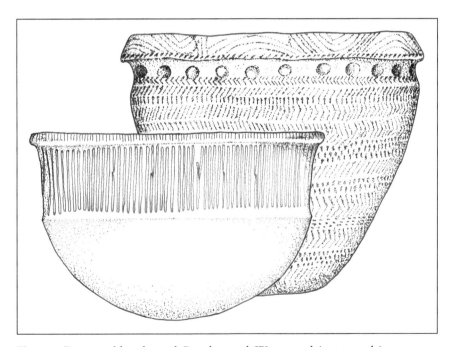

Fig. 4.5 Decorated bowl vessel, Peterborough Ware vessel (not to scale)
These two styles of pottery were current in the middle and later centuries of the fourth millennium BCE, respectively. The Decorated bowl vessel (left foreground) is drawn from a vessel found at Windmill Hill causewayed enclosure (rim diameter 36 cm), while behind it is a drawing of a pot, the sherds of which were retrieved from a pit at Westbourne, West Sussex (rim diameter 22.9 cm).
Drawing: Tim Hoverd.

protruded, and increasingly heavy, florid rims. A wider range of media was used to create multiple impressions over a greater area of the surface of the vessel, and these were more readily recognizable as the imprints of human extremities, bird bones, and natural fibres. If pottery can serve as a means of expression, the message was now more emphatic, and less easy to ignore (or perhaps it was merely identifiable at a greater distance). As we suggested in Chapter 3, this might mean that the interactions and transactions in which pottery was employed had become more vexed, and required greater protection or clarification. Yet unlike the Early Neolithic decorated pottery, the different substyles of Peterborough Ware were less obviously regional in character (although Yorkshire and Scottish variants were more geographically specific), and overlapped spatially. Ebbsfleet, Mortlake, and Fengate Wares were apparently in use alongside each other, and it may be that they were each favoured by different social groups within a locality, or were the prerogative of different groups of potters, or were reserved for specific segments within a community (based upon kin relations, age, gender, or status), or employed in different ranges of practices. The latter may be hinted at by the contextual variation in their occurrence.

Grooved Ware, from the end of the fourth millennium BCE onwards, marked both a change in the form of pottery from round-based bowls to tubs and buckets, and in the character of decoration (Fig. 4.6).

Unlike the earlier ceramic styles, Grooved Ware deployed motifs that had already enjoyed an existence in another context, in passage-tomb art. Grooved Ware thus served as a carrier for images that might also migrate onto carved chalk objects, stone plaques, carved stone balls, and maceheads. Not all of these necessarily occurred in the same places, or were used in the same practices, as Grooved Ware. Where Peterborough Ware bore the physical imprints of human bodies, animals, and plants, these were rarely shared with other media. The designs on Grooved Ware were generally more abstract, but also more obviously composed and geometric: chevrons, zigzags, lozenges, triangles, concentric circles, and spirals. They were truly symbolic, rather than indexical, so that if they represented anything in particular (or several things) they did so in an arbitrary and conventional way (although in some cases the skeuomorphic representation of basketry may have been intended: see 'The art of transformation in skeuomorphic practices', below). They established connections between separate contexts and locations, so that Grooved Ware constituted one element of a suite of material forms that introduced the same set of symbols or concepts into a range of different interactions. The same might be said for Beaker pottery, which was more

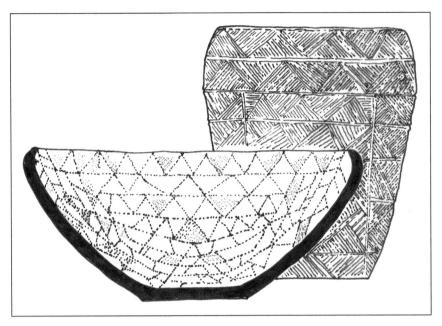

Fig. 4.6 Two Grooved Ware vessels (not to scale)

Grooved Ware features a number of different forms and styles of pot and their decoration. Among the commonest forms are broad open bowls with highly elaborate incised decoration (left, bowl from Grimes Graves, rim diameter 26.1 cm), and upright, tall, straight-sided, and flat-bottomed urn-shaped pots, often with vertical cordons and panels infilled with cross-hatching, as shown at right (behind the bowl, a 'Durrington' style vessel, rim diameter 14.7 cm, excavated from the 'type-site' itself in the late 1960s). The panels simulating a woven effect on the Durrington vessel may be skeuomorphic of basketry or leatherwork, while the irregular pattern of linked triangles on the Grimes Graves bowl may be skeuomorphic of netting: and this may also explain why the pattern was placed around the inside of the vessel, as if the 'net' was viewed from above.

Drawing: Tim Hoverd.

obviously intrusive in the British context. Beakers were often densely decorated, but given the presently unresolved issue of who the users of Beakers might have been, it remains an open question whether this was principally ornamental or whether Beakers could be 'read' by some or all of those who encountered them.

Timberworld

The 'Maerdy Oak' post discussed in Chapter 2, and the pine posts mentioned there and elsewhere in this book, indicate clearly that Mesolithic people in Britain had the capacity to create substantial structures in timber, albeit that the larger posts were likely to have been free-standing and not always erected as part of structures. It is only in the Neolithic, however, that a more extensive suite of practices involving the use of wood in various ways becomes well attested. As is particularly evident in the case of the Sweet Track in the Somerset Levels, it is both the scale and the skill of such works, and their deployment from as early as the opening centuries of the fourth millennium, that impresses even the casual observer. Moreover, as will be noted in Chapter 6, the very acts of clearance in both the late Mesolithic and the earlier years (at least) of the Neolithic often involved the marking of the place formerly occupied by the boles of the removed trees with deposits either of mixed midden material or more carefully selected groups of objects.

While, therefore, wood from trees was probably never regarded simply as timber, it was nonetheless the case that, from an early stage and at various points throughout the Neolithic period, whole tree trunks were cut and inserted upright into the ground, often along with poles cut from branches or from coppice stems that were used to create smaller or ancillary structures. We know about such usages from the survival of the holes dug to receive these normally vertically set timbers, and from the rotted or burned posts that in many places have been found to have survived within them. We have noted already that many such timbers in the Early Neolithic were parts of structures such as rectangular houses and halls that were likely to have been roofed over, but that from even before the middle of the fourth millennium BCE others were part of free-standing settings of posts. In Scotland, these latter comprised post-defined, parallel-sided monuments that approximated to what were later built in southern Britain as ditched cursus monuments, while throughout mainland Britain they occurred as retaining structures, façades, and forecourts for long barrows. In the period from the later years of the fourth millennium BCE, timber settings of upright posts occurred as part of palisades defining oval areas sometimes enclosing many hectares, or as simple circles of such posts with or without accompanying enclosing ditches and banks. More rarely, they occurred as concentric circles of posts such as the Northern and Southern Circles at Durrington Walls, and the nearby Woodhenge in Wiltshire, or more recently established by geophysical survey among the stone circles at Stanton Drew on the edge of the Mendip Hills in Somerset (Fig. 4.7).

The discovery of timber monuments, not only as precursors of stone structures and in areas especially of northern and western Britain where stone was abundant, tends to counter the notion that timber was only used for building such structures where stone was unavailable. Indeed, current understanding of the ubiquity and diversity of timber-built structures across the whole span of the Neolithic demands more inclusive explanations for

Fig. 4.7 Durrington timber circle reconstruction

The reconstruction shown here was made during the filming of a Time Team *special programme focusing upon the work of the Stonehenge Riverside Project at Durrington Walls and nearby sites. It is a replica of the Southern Circle at Durrington, one of two large rings of concentric uprights contained within the massive henge earthwork, located at the end of an avenue connecting it to the River Avon.*

Photograph: © Julian Thomas.

the frequency with which the mostly oak trees concerned were cut and removed for erection as upright elements of complex architectural arrangements. In a survey of the variety of these kinds of timber structures in Scotland, Kirsty Millican has recently proposed that there was a major shift in timber building at around 3300 BCE, with the linear or rectilinear character of the Early Neolithic timber monuments replaced thereafter substantially by circular or curvilinear forms (though straight and rectilinear settings did sometimes continue to form elements of the later complexes concerned). This shift was reflected also in a change in the manner in which these sites were decommissioned. Before 3300 BCE they were often burned down to bring about their termination, but afterwards this practice is much less common and the timbers of the structures appear to have been left to decay. The fact that this shift correlates with other changes in material culture and social practices at the time strengthens the impression that this was part of a wider reordering of cultural links.

The question remains as to why such structures with monumental timber elements were built in the first place. One idea that has been popular among archaeologists, such as Gordon Noble, working in northern Britain is that they represented a kind of domestication or absorption of the forest within the social world of humans. This view certainly has its attractions, particularly when considered in reference to the proximity of many such structures to areas of woodland, or even their creation within clearings. The cutting and raising of so much timber clearly involved transformations, both to the landscape (Dan Charman and Ben Gearey showed over twenty years ago, for example, that one whole flank of Rough Tor on Bodmin Moor was clear-felled in a single fourth-millennium episode) and in the process of converting trees to timber. Beyond this, however, the construction of these buildings and settings arguably harnessed the scale and density of living, growing trees into particular projects that ordered them within a very human appreciation of order, creating specific effects of perspective, movement, concealment, and auditory cues. As such, they represented a transformational choreography of woodland and a three-dimensional arena for the renegotiation of social relations.

Trails of the axes: from procurement to exchange

Stone axeheads are among the most ubiquitous of the objects that permeated the world of Neolithic Britain, and they have long fascinated archaeologists by their variability as well as their abundance (Fig. 4.8).

It is nearly impossible to produce accurate numbers of the axeheads that have been found, but in Ireland a 1990s study coordinated by Gabriel Cooney and Stephen Mandal produced a database of more than 20,000.[1] This was a substantial increase from previous estimates, and unless Ireland is massively different from Britain, similar increases might be expected from future systematic studies in Scotland (previously estimated as 4,000), and Wales and west-central England (a 1980s database comprised only 2,200 axeheads). And these are simply the known (that is, reported) discoveries of complete axeheads. If the recorded numbers are even as much as 50 per cent of the total past production (probably a considerable underestimate), it can be appreciated that the number of whole axeheads that found their way into the ground would have been double the recorded number, and then if the

1. It should be noted, however, that just under half this number had no provenance because their place of discovery was unknown or doubtful. Such totalling of numbers has only been possible in Ireland due to the centralized structure of museums north and south of the border.

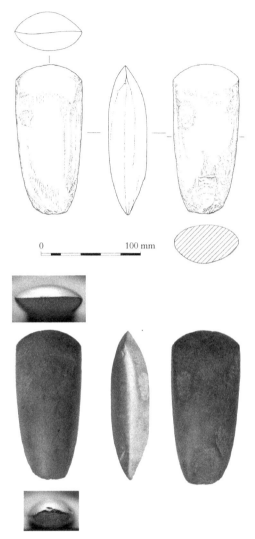

Fig. 4.8 'Group VI' (Langdale) axe from Wellington Quarry, Herefordshire

This fine example of an axe from the central Cumbrian quarries was found by a machine operator at the site before formal excavations began in the early 1990s. Several clusters and isolated examples of both Early and (Peterborough Ware associated) Middle Neolithic pits have been found here, in a valley-bottom close to former meandering stream channels of the River Lugg. A series of Middle Neolithic hearths was also found at the site, in one instance with two carefully laid in the same location but separated from one another stratigraphically by what appear to be deliberate spreads of gravel. The hearths were located in places apparently purposely segregated from the areas nearby where the pits were being dug.

Drawing and photograph: Laura Templeton, © Worcestershire County Council (courtesy of Robin Jackson).

fragments found were to be 'translated' into former whole axes, this could lead to a further doubling.

Despite these uncertainties over the totals involved, one thing that can be noted is that their distribution is uneven geographically. So, for example, around 34 per cent of the 1990s Irish total came from County Antrim in the extreme north-east of the island. This is perhaps not surprising given that the main sources of porcellanite stone were quarries at Tievebulliagh and on Rathlin Island, and that two-thirds of the closely studied 1,300 or so porcellanite axes were roughouts (shaped but not polished examples). Moreover, Antrim was also the only Irish source-location for flint axes. A significant proportion of the Irish axes (3,000 or so from a sample of 13,569 whose lithology was analysed) were nonetheless made from sandstones and mudstones unlikely to have travelled far from their place of manufacture.

While studies of the quarrying locations and practices have produced many insights about the organization of production, the matter of distribution deserves equal notice. It used to be thought, for example, that it was specifically larger axes that were the main items that travelled long distances, as gifts or at least not simply as 'functional' items for cutting down trees (the assumed main purpose of axes). However, the Irish study showed that the Group VI Langdale axes found in Antrim varied between the more massive end of variation (over 30 cm in length) to the smallest (indeed miniature) examples. Most of these Langdale axes had been retrieved from bogs (through hand-cutting of peat) or from rivers, and again this offers clues as to the fact that it was probably the deposition of such items rather than their use that was most important to their 'consumers'.

Throughout Britain those axeheads that travelled furthest from any of the major source-locations of quarried stone appeared more exotic, often in types of green, blue-green, or grey-blue stone (from Langdale in the English Lake District, from west Cornwall, or from the northern coastal area of Snowdonia, for example) that perhaps echoed some of the qualities of the jadeitite axes from the Italian Alps. The largest concentrations of Group VI Langdale axes, for example, are those recorded in eastern Yorkshire and in East Anglia, while there is a marked concentration of 'Cornish' greenstone axes around the Thames Estuary. Moreover, the Langdale axes in Yorkshire were most often polished all over their surface, in contrast to more locally sourced flint axes that were almost always polished only near their blade-edge. Within Ireland, Antrim was found to have been in receipt of the highest numbers of Langdale axeheads, as well as of those made in gabbroic stone presumed to have come from western Cornwall, and probably also of those produced in coastal Pembrokeshire. Such correlations could be taken to imply that there was indeed an 'axe trade' between the different centres of production of the more eye-catching forms of axehead, but what is most likely is that this was more about the acquisition of prestige than the workings of a market.

As we hope to have shown in respect to other Neolithic material, it is sometimes the apparent anomalies among the patterns of form and distribution that may provide the most interesting insights into former cultural practice. In respect to stone axeheads, two examples that one of us has previously discussed are the occurrence of axes in groups and the existence of perforated examples. In each case, we have to consider first the assumptions made about them in the past. Groups of *bronze* axeheads from later prehistoric times found together in the past were automatically considered to be founders' hoards, not least because they appeared to contain items that could be regarded as scrap metal. That reprocessing of metal partly determined what was assembled in these groupings of items is undoubtedly the case, but in early studies there was too little attention paid to the context of deposition (for instance in watery places, in remote places, by rock outcrops, and so on) which would have inhibited retrieval if that had been the original intention—which it almost certainly was not. Such considerations then influenced the way that stone axeheads found in groups were interpreted for the Neolithic period, and so these groups are often described as 'hoards'—items cached together for later retrieval, depending upon the vagaries of fortune.

However, while this logic might obtain for market economies, it seems likely that for much of prehistory the 'transactions' involved, if not associated with either competitive gift-giving or the conspicuous competitive destruction of accumulated 'wealth', were more between the living and the dead, or between corporeal living persons and the unseen world of spirits, ancestors, or gods. What is noticeable among some of the larger of such groupings of axeheads is the apparently deliberate selection of different sizes and forms. In some groups brought together, axeheads of different sizes and forms are present in pairs, for example. While this could be said to reflect 'stocks' of different-sized axes for different purposes, such claims are difficult to sustain where the axeheads concerned could not have been used (because they were too fragile and easily shattered) for prosaic tasks such as woodworking. It seems, rather, that symmetries in the collections themselves were of more importance: they may, for instance, have formed a representation of the extent of virtuosity in production.

As for the perforated examples, the fact that a number of them had evidence of prior use-wear has led to the suggestion that the drilling of holes for suspension was carried out so that they could be used suspended as items of personal ornament considerably after their practical utility had ended. This interpretation is another example of modern assumptions about use-value, and also surmises that the only reason for such perforation was to facilitate personal adornment. Studies of historically recent Melanesian exchange practices suggest, however, that the items concerned could have been suspended as parts of *composite* artefacts created specifically to sustain exchange networks, with organic as well as inorganic components constituting the 'assembled' artefact.

The art of transformation in skeuomorphic practices

The reproduction of an object in a familiar form but in an alternative substance was never an accidental outcome of an unrelated process, or an otherwise unanticipated act. Indeed, while decoration (and for that matter all artistic expression) can be dismissed as simply the workings of the creative imagination, or a play on the forms of different kinds of object, it is more difficult to sustain such a view when both the form and the context of an object have been transposed. The most pervasive such reference, arguably, is to be found in the surface decoration and sometimes also bodily form of pottery. This is most noticeable in bag-shaped pots with lines of indented or impressed decoration made by the repeated application of fingernails or 'maggots' of cord, and is most pronounced in the case of the classic Mortlake bowl of the Peterborough tradition of the late fourth to early third millennium. Here the out-turned rim, the cavetto-style, inwardly moulded neck, and high shoulder itself serve to accentuate the bag-shape and other conventions of basketry, while at the same time facilitating the suspension of such pots within houses or other roofed structures (see Fig. 4.5). We should anticipate that the coexistence and possible co-use of pots and baskets would have served to signal the unity of the social realm within which they existed, whether this was domestic, or gendered, or otherwise.

Other pots were decorated (and particularly on their bases) by actual woven fabric, such as the circular-weave mat impressed onto the base of a Grooved Ware pot found at Barnhouse on the mainland of Orkney (see Chapter 5). The more upright, tub-like forms of many larger of the Grooved Ware vessels provided a context in which the domains of woven objects and formed clay in Late Neolithic Britain might be mutually referenced and related. This is nowhere more evident than in the Durrington Walls-style vessels, the upright surfaces of which were often covered with panels separated by vertical grooves. The panels were then often covered by square or elongated smaller rectilinear areas of narrow grooving set at angles to one another. This closely approximates the warp and weft of fabric and has the effect of enhancing the richness of the surface texture of the vessels concerned (see Figures 4.6 and 7.4).

Particularly in central southern England, numerous chalk items have been found that are in some way representational. These include incised plaques that demonstrate an affinity with the decoration found carved into the chalk walls of ditches, pits, or shafts. Others were carefully carved and fully depictive phalli. Other items again represent skeuomorphs of objects more familiar in other materials. In this way, chalk 'cups' and 'spoons' that were scarcely functional also featured in the chalk-carving repertoire. Among the more celebrated examples of such artefacts are two miniature chalk axe-heads retrieved from two post-holes in the outer rings of the six concentric rings of posts at Woodhenge (Fig. 4.9). Given that these were presumably placed in these holes when the structure was first raised (or after the posts had rotted out), their survival is itself remarkable.

The co-presence of the presumed dedicatory burial of a 3-year-old child near the centre of the circle could mean that these were 'toys' somehow associated with that very young person (though in this case it would perhaps be strange not to have buried them with the infant). Alternatively, they were late deposits associated with the decommissioning of the structure. A more prosaic explanation might be that there were no stone axes to hand when the decommissioning took place, so the necessary dedicatory examples were rustled up as substitutes. But in neither case is the explanation for their presence satisfactory, although in the latter case it is notable that stone and flint axes were scarce at the nearby Durrington Walls henge. Instead, they surely speak to the pervasiveness of the axe, and were created as skeuomorphs in order to disrupt normal expectations. As symbolic axes they were perhaps redolent of vegetation clearance and the taming of the wild as part

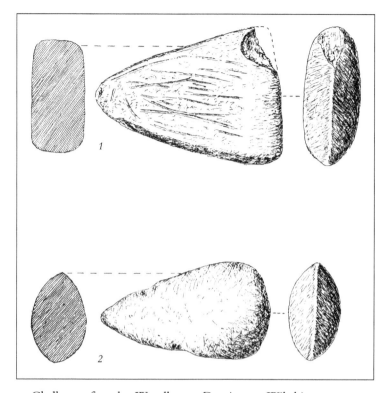

Fig. 4.9 Chalk axes found at Woodhenge, Durrington, Wiltshire

One each of these two representations, or models, of stone axeheads rendered in chalk were found separately in two different post-holes of the two outer rings of the concentric-ring timber post structure at Woodhenge, immediately to the south of Durrington Walls.

From: M. Cunnington, *Woodhenge: A Description of the Site as Revealed by Excavations* (George Simpson & Co., 1929).

of an agricultural revolution as the traditional view has suggested, or of the long-distance exchange relations that the axes were a principal medium for.

That this was not either a unique occurrence or only a Late Neolithic referencing is demonstrated by the fact that several such miniature chalk axes have been found during the excavation of flint mines. One thing that such miniaturization of objects itself can achieve is the infiltration and permeation of the aspects of life and social relations that the items habitually connote into a wider range of locations and situations than they might normally access. When the item concerned brings into play the range of connotations that something as powerfully evocative as the axehead no doubt was in Neolithic societies across Europe, its potency was undoubtedly potentially the greater.

Nor are the chalk versions the only skeuomorphic treatments of axes. When a wooden model of a hafted axe was found at the Turbary site beside the wooden Sweet Track in Somerset, it was dubbed not an axe but a 'tomahawk' by the excavators, and regarded unproblematically as a child's toy. This is not surprising given that all the deposits made by the side of the Track and discovered during the 1970s excavations were interpreted prosaically, despite the sometimes curious circumstances and in some cases the precious nature of the items concerned. Clive Bond challenged these explanations in an article in which he focused upon the liminal nature of the Track and its surroundings, and the apparently non-casual character of the deposits of items. In this light, although the 'child's toy' interpretation of the hafted axe model is not entirely implausible, its potential metaphorical referencing of real axes may be a local equivalent of the replacement of real axes by chalk ones at Woodhenge (Fig. 4.10).

Dealings with the dead: histories of the body

One of the most pervasive kinds of transformation evident to anyone studying the remains of ancient communities in any part of the world is that from life into death. All peoples have had to confront this, and the impact it had upon the social relations that had been shaped to a lesser or greater degree by the departed individuals. It is a truism that funerary rites and processes have served in many times and places to make the loss more bearable for the surviving kin and community, and to mediate the spiritual and social disruptions caused by the absence of the deceased. These were universally harder transitions to manage, the more abrupt, unanticipated, or violent the deaths concerned.

The apparent contrasts between the British Neolithic and the Mesolithic that preceded it are particularly pronounced in respect to the archaeological visibility of the dead. Aside from the fragmentary bones discovered in the shell middens of Oronsay, human remains are rarely encountered dating to the period between 5000 and 4000 BCE, and Chantal Conneller has suggested that during this time bodies may routinely have been broken down and dispersed across the landscape following exposure and decomposition. Conneller speculates that the disarticulation of human cadavers in the Mesolithic may have been in part achieved by scavenging animals, which

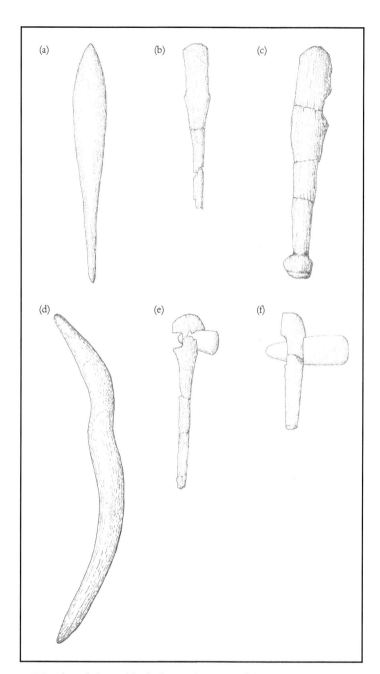

Fig. 4.10 Wooden clubs and hafted axes (not to scale)

The fact of interpersonal conflict in the British Neolithic has been demonstrated by the circumstance of arrowheads embedded within neck vertebrae, ribs, and body cavities, and the evidence of impacts upon and fractures in skulls. Meanwhile, concentrations of arrowheads by the entrances to causewayed and tor enclosures suggest co-ordinated attacks. The wooden clubs drawn here, from Chelsea (c, 64 cm length) and from Ehenside Tarn in Cumbria (a, 64.8 cm; b, 46.4 cm), and what appears to be a throwing-stick also from Ehenside Tarn (d, 90.4 cm), represent just the kind of weapon that could have been used to inflict the cranial traumas, while the two hafted axes from the Isle of Lewis (48.7 cm length) and from Ehenside (32 cm length) might just as easily have been used as weapons as axes for cutting and shaping wood.

Drawing: Tim Hoverd.

Fig. 4.11 Penywyrlod chambered long cairn, Talgarth, Breconshire

This photograph shows one of the north-facing side-chambers (Lateral Chamber NE 1) initially excavated by H. N. Savory in 1972, and recently re-excavated by Bill and Jenny Britnell. The view is looking out north-eastwards towards the Wye Valley. It shows in the foreground the shattered stumps of the walling slabs of the inner (SW) compartment and beyond this the site of the outer (NE) compartment. Beyond this again the upright slabs mark the inner face of the inner revetment wall.

Photograph: Keith Ray, July 2016, with thanks to W. J. and J. Britnell and Clwyd-Powys Archaeological Trust.

might also have dragged body parts away from places of excarnation. If so, this suggests a kind of symmetry between humans and the creatures of the forest: the former acquired sustenance from deer, pigs, and aurochs, and later provided food for wolves, foxes, bears, corvids, and raptors. Yet in the earlier part of the Neolithic disarticulation was still practised, and the contrast lies between the dispersal and the accumulation of remains, in mortuary facilities of one kind or another. However, while funerary structures ranging from long barrows and cairns to megalithic dolmens are a conspicuous aspect of Neolithic archaeology, Richard Atkinson pointed out long ago that only a small number of the Neolithic dead were disposed of in ways that have left any discernible trace. So as we noted in Chapter 3, it is conceivable that the majority of the deceased were treated in much the same way as their Mesolithic predecessors: suspended in trees, exposed on platforms, consumed by animals, or immersed in rivers. This is not to suggest, however, that the remaining few are uninformative, however atypical they may be. In contrast to a modern world in which our contact with death is carefully managed and somewhat sanitized, Neolithic people often engaged with the dead in ways that were (for us) surprisingly physical and direct. Moreover, these practices demonstrably changed through the period, arguably alerting us to shifting preoccupations within contemporary society. In this section, we will build on the discussion of funerary monuments in Chapter 3 and anticipate the narrative of Chapter 5, to focus in more detail on the changing ways in which human bodies were manipulated and deposited after death.

At one time, it was widely believed that the chambered tombs and timber chambers of the Earlier Neolithic were 'ossuaries', into which human remains were placed following a period of exposure, and once reduced to dry bones. This would explain both their disarticulated condition, and the variable state of weathering in which bones were sometimes found. However, a series of painstaking recent excavations have contested this view, and have provided much more detailed post-mortem 'histories' for the dead. Notable amongst these is the Hazleton long cairn in Gloucestershire, investigated by Alan Saville, in which two stone chambers deep within the linear monument were accessed by narrow passages opening onto opposed sides of the structure. A total of twenty-one adults and perhaps as many as nineteen younger people had been deposited in this tomb, and it appeared that all had been introduced in a fleshed condition and allowed to decay before body parts had begun to be moved and disaggregated. Some of this movement may have taken place before all the flesh and ligaments had entirely rotted away. This displacement of bones may have simply been an expedient way of making space for more bodies, but in practice a certain amount of deliberate reorganization had taken place, with skulls and longbones carefully arranged. The character of mortuary activity at Hazleton was fortuitously clarified by the collapse of some of the uprights in the outer northern passage, some time after human remains had begun to build up in the chamber. The deposits found in the northern entrance therefore represented a truncated sample of the overall sequence of activity within the monument. In the entrance area beyond the collapse and blockage lay the articulated remains of an adult man. Below his right elbow lay a large flint core, and at his left hand a quartzite hammerstone (Fig. 4.12).

This body lay on top of the lower part of the skeleton of another man, and the disarticulated remains of a third man and two younger people. All the deposition inside the chambers took place over no more than two or

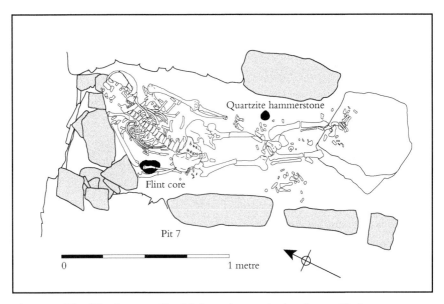

Fig. 4.12 The 'flint-knapper' burial from the north chamber at Hazleton

The burial of a young to middle-aged male was placed feet-first into the northern chamber at Hazleton close to the end of the use of that receptacle for burials in the long barrow on the Cotswolds west of the modern-day settlement of Eastleach. This drawing shows the skeleton and, highlighted, the hammerstone placed in or near the left hand and the flint nodule/core placed within the crook of the right elbow.

Plan: redrawn by Julian Thomas from an original plan published by Alan Saville.

three generations, starting in the period between 3695 and 3650 BCE, and ending by the 3620s.

Several points are suggested by the information from Hazleton. First, the entire mortuary process was conducted within the tomb, which is better identified as a 'place of transformation' intended to contain the potentially dangerous and volatile transition from fleshed corpse to clean bone, rather than an ossuary. For many societies, death is a gradual rather than abrupt change of state, and the person's spirit has not left their body until the flesh has fully decayed. Similarly, the breaking of the skeleton down into its component elements, and their reorganization within the tomb, can serve as a means by which the person's singular identity gradually recedes into the collective community of the unnamed dead. Significantly, only the man in the northern entrance at Hazleton was associated with any grave goods, and the occurrence of other objects inside the chambers of long cairns of the Cotswolds and south Wales may suggest that the dead were sometimes accompanied by personal items, only to be separated from them as their bodies were reduced to separate bones. The implication is that the close relationship between a person and an object was dissolved as they ceased to be a whole and integral body, and were transformed into a different kind of being.

In both chambers at Hazleton an unusually high proportion of the dead were affected by a variation of the kneecap called a vastus notch. This may be an indication that the people making up the burial population were related by kinship. By implication, these people may have all come from a single, closely interconnected community. This possibility is further supported by nitrogen isotope values from the bones, which indicate that they shared an exceedingly homogeneous diet, rich in meat or animal products. If the mortuary deposits accumulated over a period of perhaps fifty years or less, we might consider them to have constituted the founding generation of a particular local group, as proposed in Chapter 3. Although interment took place over a relatively short period of time, the tomb clearly retained its importance, for animal remains representing either joints of meat of complete carcasses continued to be placed inside the monument for three centuries or so, presumably as offerings of some kind.

It may be helpful to compare the remains at Hazleton with the situation at Whitwell in Derbyshire, where, as we saw in Chapter 3, a small round cairn was eventually enclosed within a larger trapezoidal monument. Before either structure was built a linear, boxlike stone and timber chamber had

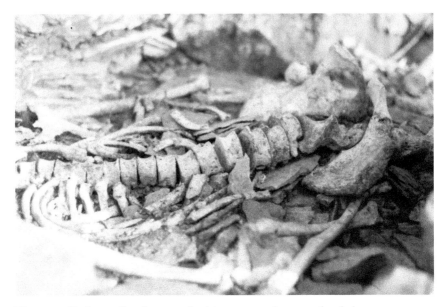

Fig. 4.13 Hazleton flint-knapper, looking eastwards across the skeleton

This photograph was taken by Julian Thomas during the Hazleton North excavation, specifically across the body of the 'flint-knapper' to show the flint core in the foreground and the hammerstone in the background, with the spine of the deceased exactly midway between these artefacts (and therefore most clearly in focus). The photograph demonstrates vividly the immediacy of the decease and reinforces one's sense of the non-randomness of the placement of knapping-tool and raw material.

Photograph: 1981 © Julian Thomas.

been constructed, with a massive wooden upright at either end. Inside this box, as at Hazleton, complete and at least partially articulated bodies began to be deposited in the period 3790–3710 BCE, for a duration of thirty to eighty years. Four adults and a child were interred in this time, becoming gradually disarticulated. Eventually the large posts were withdrawn, and around 3700–3660 BCE the mortuary structure was incorporated into the large trapezoidal cairn, accessed by means of a stone passage. A layer of stone paving was laid over the existing burials, and a new set of bodies began to accumulate over the next few decades (Fig. 4.14).

This time, the cadavers again became disarticulated, but the movement of individual bones down the axis of the chamber was more marked, indicating a more determined process of reorganization. A similar sequence can be recognized at Whitegrounds, near Burythorpe in Yorkshire, where the chamber area represented a narrow slot defined by drystone walling inside a small oval cairn, closed off by a removable plug of rubble. The primary

Fig. 4.14 The arrangement of bodies on the Whitwell cairn pavement

The primary phase of activity at the Whitwell trapezoidal cairn involved the laying of a linear pavement of stones upon which were placed the remains of four adults and one child. This event occurred sometime between 3780 and 3720 cal BCE. This mortuary structure was then covered over by a small oval cairn before the much larger stone-built trapezoidal barrow encapsulated this earlier monument. At this point another six bodies were placed above the primary mortuary deposit. Photograph: © and courtesy of Blaise Vyner.

burials probably dated to around 3700 BCE. The remains of five people were scattered in the bottom of this confined passage, intermixed with sherds of carinated bowl pottery. Three partially articulated skeletons were concentrated in the far end of the burial area: an adult man and woman, and a younger person. All had their heads removed post-mortem, and these had been gathered together in a 'nest' of skulls.

The use of Early Neolithic barrows and cairns as contexts in which fleshed bodies were slowly transformed into dry bones, and then reordered within the chamber, is very widespread. Often, as we have seen, skulls and perhaps longbones were treated with care or even reverence, but the remainder of the postcranial skeleton was often afforded less consideration. Sometimes, too, skulls and longbones may have been removed from these contexts and continued in circulation amongst the living. However, this pattern is not universal. At Parc le Breos Cwm in south Wales, flesh-bound bodies had apparently been laid out in the passage leading in through the front of a long cairn, in the manner already discussed. But in the four small chambers at the end of the passage, the human remains were much more fragmented, and had been subject to attack by dogs or foxes when soft tissue had still been on the bones. These body parts had seemingly been collected and deposited in the tomb after a protracted period of exposure, during which they had been accessible to scavenging animals. This is comparable with the evidence from Giant's Hills 2 long barrow in Lincolnshire, which had contained a similar linear mortuary structure to that at Whitwell: a timber box with a large upright post at either end. Inside this structure, the mortuary deposit took the form of a compact mass of bone representing the partial remains of three or four people. These had been subject to varying degrees of weathering, as well as gnawing by rodents and carnivores. The tight grouping of these remains indicated that they must have been deposited in a single act, perhaps within a bag or sack. Again, these were undoubtedly fragments that had undergone the process of defleshing in some other location, and by implication the relationship between the monument and the remains that it contained was different from that at Hazleton, Whitegrounds, or Whitwell. Rather than being a place where the dead were transformed, it is arguable that a structure such as Giant's Hills required human body parts drawn from elsewhere in order to achieve some form of legitimacy or authenticity. This may also have been the case at the Fussell's Lodge long barrow in Wiltshire, where some of the bones in the timber chamber were apparently 'ancestral' remains brought to the site already defleshed, but complete bodies were subsequently introduced. Chris Fowler has argued that some caves in various parts of Britain were used for successive burials in ways that are comparable with these tombs and barrows. However, these deposits rarely exhibit the same evidence for extensive manipulation and reorganization. If these dead were not physically engaged with, and 'helped' in the process of leaving the world, it may be that they were different in kind, and perhaps shunned or excluded.

Long mounds and megalithic tombs were not the only contexts in which the dead were deposited and processed during the earlier part of the Neolithic. At many causewayed enclosures human remains occur, whether as isolated burials (often of children) or as skeletal parts in ditch deposits. Far the most spectacular example is the causewayed enclosure complex at Hambledon Hill in Dorset, where the bones of around seventy-five people were encountered in excavations conducted by Roger Mercer during the 1970s and 1980s, and presumably many more remain unexcavated. Only five of these represented formal burials in distinct graves cut into ditch fills or on the Stepleton spur of the hilltop. Six other bodies were articulated, but not all were complete. One body identified in a ditch segment in the Stepleton enclosure consisted only of the upper half of an adult skeleton, for instance, while the pelvis and femurs of a young man were found in the main enclosure ditch. The complete skeleton of another young man was found sprawled in the ditch of the Stepleton enclosure, and a leaf-shaped arrowhead was recovered from his chest area. It was conjectured that this person had been shot during the hostile activity that was also represented by a collapse of burnt daub into the ditch. However, careful analysis by Jacqueline McKinley demonstrated that the body had sustained defleshing cuts on the radius and three ribs. Similarly, the articulated skeleton of a further young man encountered in the ditch of the main enclosure had been extensively gnawed by scavengers, but the flesh had been stripped from his upper legs using stone tools. McKinley suggests that these bodies might have been rolled into the ditches following partial processing. This does not mean that they did not die in a violent altercation on the hilltop, but it does imply that they had been subject to significant post-mortem manipulation, rather than being left where they fell.

The majority of the remains from Hambledon Hill were completely disarticulated, and in general they were more weathered than the animal bones from the same site, demonstrating that they had been subject to more extensive exposure and circulation rather than prompt burial. The kinds of cut-mark identified on the Stepleton body had also affected the remains of another twenty-two persons, and had largely resulted from the cutting of muscle attachments and the stripping (or 'filleting') of tissue. This activity was not related to cannibalism, for none of the bones had been chopped or broken to extract marrow. What is remarkable, though, is that the activity was piecemeal rather than systematic, and bodies were sometimes temporarily buried in shallow graves or beneath flint cairns, in various states of decomposition. Temporary burial may have served to shelter bodies from animal scavenging, but some bones had been gnawed, and it is probable that many others had been carried off. Some bones may have been dragged into the ditches by animals, others may have rolled there, and others again may have been placed by human action, alongside other items. There was certainly a preponderance of skull and longbone fragments in ditch contexts, which may indicate a degree of selectivity. Fifteen complete skulls were found in the ditches, eight of them clearly having been positioned on the ditch bottom as formal deposits. Three of these had mandibles attached, indicating that they had been placed as severed, partially fleshed heads.

Altogether, the evidence from Hambledon implies a set of mortuary activities that are comparable with those found in Early Neolithic tombs and barrows: bodies of the recently deceased were brought to a special architectural context, and allowed to gradually decay, with the help of sporadic interventions from people and animals, followed by selection and deposition. Particular attention was paid to skulls, which might have been understood as especially potent and imbued with ancestral force. In a sense the causewayed enclosure was being treated like a massive tomb, although one in which other activities ranging from feasting to gift-giving also took place. The stable-isotopic evidence that people with different diets, probably from different social groups and locations (contrasting with the results from Hazleton just discussed), congregated at Hambledon lends a greater significance to this treatment of the dead. We have argued that the comparatively short bursts of deposition at some tombs and barrows are indicative of new communities being brought into being through the creation of a group of founding ancestors to whom the living group could claim filiation. At Hambledon, it seems that a much larger social entity was being engineered, by creating a location that physically embodied the transformation of the dead of multiple kin groups.

In the later part of the fourth millennium BCE, mortuary practices began to change, as the passages of long cairns were progressively blocked up, and building of long mounds ceased. From the start of the Neolithic, people had occasionally been simply deposited in graves and pits, as we have seen in the case of the Yabsley Street burial. However, from the thirty-fifth century BCE onwards, burials under small round mounds or within ring-ditches began to become more common, sometimes associated with distinctive grave goods, as discussed in Chapter 3 with particular reference to Duggleby Howe. One such burial, of a man in his late twenties, was introduced into the top of the Whitegrounds cairn described above, which had now been remodelled as a large round barrow with a stone kerb. Behind his back were a slider, or belt fitting, of worked jet, and a finely polished flint axe, and in a pit beneath his body were a calf's jaw and a pig's humerus. Another good example of such a 'single grave burial' (or in this case, double) was excavated in a distinctive monument located close to the Abingdon causewayed enclosure in Oxfordshire, at Barrow Hills, Radley. This was a small oval or rectangular mound (effectively a very late manifestation of the long barrow tradition) surrounded by two concentric ditches that had been dug in a series of episodes, and that contained deposits of pottery, flint, red deer antler, and human skull fragments. In a small oval grave on the axis of the barrow were the crouched skeletons of a man and a woman, both probably in their late twenties, with their heads pointing in opposite directions and their legs overlapping. The man had been buried with a jet slider and a leaf-shaped arrowhead, and the woman with a polished flint blade. They had clearly been interred at the same time, probably in the thirty-fourth or thirty-third century BCE. While their burial with these fine objects is striking, it is perhaps not a huge departure from the Hazleton 'flint knapper' with his core and hammerstone. What is arguably more significant is that there was no extended period of decay and rearrangement, in which death could be managed and negotiated over a lengthy interval. Instead, the removal of a person from society was marked by a single event: the digging and filling of a grave, presumably observed by a body of witnesses or celebrants, and the raising of a mound to commemorate the deceased. Some archaeologists have argued that the development of the single grave rite can be identified with the emergence of 'the individual' in the modern Western sense. This is perhaps improbable, in that individuality is strongly connected with notions of agency, autonomy, and free will that developed during the sixteenth to eighteenth centuries CE. A more modest proposal is that Neolithic people always understood themselves to be embedded in a tangle of relationships with others, but that the character of these relationships altered somewhat toward the end of the fourth millennium BCE. If the multiple mortuary practices of the Earlier Neolithic were concerned with the formation of a collectivity of founding ancestors, to whom all community members could equally claim relatedness, the new emphasis on the death and burial of specific persons reveals a growing preoccupation with particular lines of *descent*. That is, some members of a living group were increasingly able to invoke prestigious connections with the past, thereby enhancing their own authority and standing in the present.

Single grave burials were not numerous, nor did they represent the only means of coping with the dead in the later fourth millennium. At Banbury Lane, on the edge of Northampton, a large pit was dug into the innermost of three concentric ditches of a pre-existing circular enclosure twenty-three metres in diameter (Fig. 4.15).

A mass of 7,500 human bones was deposited in this pit as a single event, dated to 3360–3100 BCE. Intriguingly, these bones have depleted levels of

Fig. 4.15 Ossuary pit at Banbury Lane, Northampton

At Banbury Lane south-west of Northampton, a triple-ditched circular enclosure was found to have had the narrow entranceway through the inner circuit blocked by the insertion of an elongated pit filled with the disarticulated bones of up to 130 people. The burial event was dated to 3360–3100 cal BCE, but besides the interment of the remains of so many people, this was no ordinary deposit. Most of the bones present were from limbs, and while there were many skull fragments present, the rarity of vertebrae and ribs, and the absence of the bones of hands or feet, together with the torsion lesions around the limb-joints, suggest the defleshing of corpses elsewhere and the deliberate disarticulation and then gathering together of selected bones for reburial.

Photograph: courtesy of Andy Chapman, and © Northamptonshire Archaeology.

carbon isotopes, which might have been a consequence of either starvation or disease, hinting that the burial population may have died over a relatively short period of time as a result of a famine or epidemic. At least 130 people were represented, most of them adults, but the bones seem to have been selected from a much larger assemblage. Femurs and skull fragments were especially common, while the small bones of the hands and feet were missing. This would suggest that the material had been collected following excarnation, but there was also extensive evidence for manipulation of the bones. They had been chopped with stone tools and battered with blunt instruments, ligaments had been severed, and joints had been gouged apart. In contrast with the more limited and partial defleshing at Hambledon Hill, this was a brutal kind of dismemberment, a form of violence enacted on the bodies of a large number of people who may have perished in a traumatic incident.

Not far from Banbury Lane, at Milton Ham, the cremated remains of two people were found in small pits, dated to 3340–3040 BCE. We have noted that cremation had been a minor theme throughout the fourth millennium, particularly in the north of Britain, and at some tombs such as Hazleton North and West Kennet small quantities of burnt human bones have been identified amongst the disarticulated skeletons in the chambers. One explanation that has been proposed for this is that people who died when they were far from their birthplace may have been cremated as an expedient way of returning their remains to their community. However, the Milton Ham burials may have been an early manifestation of a more general turn away from inhumation and toward the burning of the dead from around 3000 BCE onwards. As we will see in Chapter 5, there is no suggestion that this change in practice is indicative of the arrival of 'new people' at this time, and there is some continuity in the places where the dead were interred and the artefacts that were deposited with them. At sites including Stonehenge, Duggleby Howe, Forteviot, and Dorchester on Thames, cremated remains began to accumulate in 'cemeteries', often in places that had already acquired some significance. For example, the cremated bones of an adult woman were deposited into the socket of a wooden upright that had been withdrawn at the timber enclosure at Dunragit in Galloway. While this stress on continuity with the past (and the apparent reuse of monuments that were in some cases already old when deposition took place) is important, with cremation we should perhaps pay more attention to the event of burning itself. In the earlier fourth millennium, mortuary activity had emphasized the gradual transformation of cadavers into skeletal material, through the removal or decay of soft tissue. With the single grave burials the focus had shifted to the moment of burial, and the embedding of a specific deceased person in collective memory through the creation of an enduring memorial monument, as a physical mnemonic. Cremation achieved both of these things simultaneously. Burning a body on a pyre rapidly transformed it into a stable residue of charred bones and ashes, while at the same time constituting a spectacular event that could be witnessed by an audience. As Kenneth Brophy and Gordon Noble have recently emphasized, this would have involved observing the body undergoing rapid and shocking changes, as the flesh and viscera burned off to reveal the bones. Such a dramatic, memorable, and even cathartic experience might have enhanced the collective solidarity of the onlookers, while indelibly marking the pyre location, affecting the way in which it might be used in future.

In the first half of the third millennium BCE, most of the dead that we can identify archaeologically were cremated. The few exceptions tend to be children, and this echoes a more general tendency for the very young to be treated differently in death throughout the Neolithic. As we have seen, three of five formal burials at Hambledon Hill were of children, and articulated child burials occurred at other enclosures such as Flagstones in Dorset and Windmill Hill in Wiltshire. It is common in many societies for children to be seen as anomalous, whether as lives unlived or as creatures who have not yet acquired fully human characteristics. Toward the middle of the third millennium BCE, cremation burial was abruptly replaced by a return to single grave inhumation, now associated with the Beaker package of grave goods. The Middle Neolithic single grave assemblages had been diverse, with axes, arrowheads, maceheads, boars' tusks, flint knives, belt fittings, and pots all being placed with the dead in seemingly random combinations. With Beaker burial there is a greater sense of standardization or rule-governed conduct, with the Beaker vessel itself being especially ubiquitous. The re-emergence of single grave burial was one element of a more extensive set of changes, which we shall consider at greater length in Chapter 5.

FIVE

Narratives for the third millennium

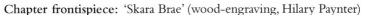

Chapter frontispiece: 'Skara Brae' (wood-engraving, Hilary Paynter)

This engraving shows the Bay of Skaill in the background and the passage leading into House 1 in the foreground. The artist wrote in Full Circle *(Woodend, 2010), 55, that the remains of the ancient settlement disappeared 'when a sand-storm buried and preserved the dwellings. A more recent storm blew away some of the sand again and revealed a hint of what was waiting to be excavated. The site is now vulnerable to the encroaching sea and gradual erosion.'*

Engraving: 1991, © Hilary Paynter (website: http://www.hilarypaynter.com).

By the later part of the third millennium BCE, Britain had become connected to mainland Europe by the so-called 'Beaker network'. This appears to have involved the circulation of people, materials, and cultural innovations over trans-continental distances. Most tellingly, it included direct evidence for cross-Channel contact and the movement of individual people into Britain who had lived much or most of their lives in continental Europe. However, the evidence for such contact during the previous few centuries is very much sparser. If, as it seems reasonable to infer, developed passage tombs were ultimately an Atlantic European phenomenon that was adopted in idiosyncratic ways in Ireland, Scotland, and finally Scandinavia during the course of the fourth millennium, routine interactions with the Continent are less easy to identify thereafter. In marked contrast with this, the period after 3000 BCE saw the emergence of a range of new interregional connections *within* Britain and Ireland. These have been less consistently recognized, as they conflict with the traditional narrative in which populations in central and south-west Asia engaged in periodic wholesale migration northward and westward. Such a narrative of external stimulus to change is less secure in this period because we now realize that the social and cultural changes that overtook Britain in the earlier third millennium originated predominantly in the northern and western parts of these islands.

Orkney house societies

Some of the most significant innovations of the third millennium throughout Britain were ultimately generated in the Orkney archipelago and its immediate sphere of contact (Fig. 5.1).

While aspects of the unique developments that took place in the Orkneys can be attributed to connections with Ireland and the Western Isles, these contributed to the emergence of a distinctive social formation that was at once highly competitive and spectacularly creative. By the start of the third millennium, Orkney had become a crucible of social and cultural change, but developments in the islands arguably began to diverge from those on the mainland soon after the Neolithic began, perhaps during the thirty-seventh century BCE. While in southern Britain in particular, the accumulation of large herds of cattle took on great importance for societies that retained a fair degree of residential mobility, Orcadian communities enjoyed a more obviously sedentary way of life throughout the Neolithic in which the

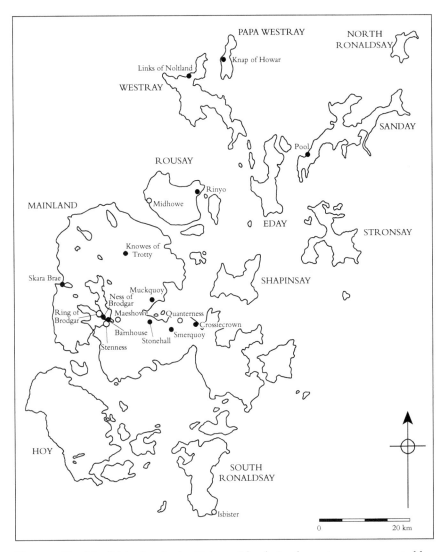

Fig. 5.1 Key Neolithic sites in the Orkney Islands (settlements are represented by closed circles, other sites by open circles).
Map: 2017, © Julian Thomas.

house became, and remained, the focus of social life. Large deposits of carbonized cereals recently discovered at Ha'Breck, Varm Dale, and Wideford Hill provide an indication of the enduring importance of cultivation in the Orkneys, with less evidence for a decline in the contribution made by domesticated plants from the later fourth millennium. The most dramatic material manifestation of this cultural distinctiveness was the emergence

on the islands of a concentration of Neolithic villages unparalleled elsewhere in Britain. The earliest Neolithic settlements in the Orkneys, such
as Wideford Hill, Green, Smerquoy, and Ha'Breck, date to the period
between 3600 and 3300 BCE. Architecturally, they comprised dispersed
groups of timber buildings, circular or sub-rectangular in plan, and with a
central scoop hearth that was sometimes surrounded by four substantial
posts—the latter presumably supporting the roof. These dwellings generally
seem to have been quite short-lived, with little evidence for maintenance or
rebuilding, so that residence was still somewhat unstable and shifting over
the medium term.

Fractionally later, perhaps by 3500 BCE, stone- and earth-built elongated
mounds known as 'stalled cairns' began to be constructed, among other
things as repositories for the remains of the dead and fixed points within
a landscape of more fluctuating activity (Fig. 5.2).

The core of these distinctive structures comprised a series of stone compartments divided from each other by upright slabs arranged on either side
of a central passage, and generally housing 'benches' or horizontal stones.
The compartments have often been found to have been used as store-houses
for the bones of dead people. Although these are generally few in number,
the deliberate arrangement of skulls and longbones suggests that, as with the
chambered cairns of much of western Britain, these tombs were used for
the decomposition and subsequent disarticulation of fleshed cadavers. While
it is often the case that tombs for the dead are modelled after the dwellings
of the living, in Orkney the opposite appears to have been the case. For
by around 3400 BCE, the wooden buildings began to be complemented by
stone structures that took their architectural inspiration from the stalled cairns,
and might indeed be described as 'stalled houses'. Examples at Smerquoy,
Stonehall Meadow, and the Knap of Howar were distinguished by sub-
rectangular inner spaces with faced walls, from which pairs of upright slabs
projected, dividing up the internal area of the house.

As Colin Richards has argued, this demonstrates both a new commitment
to living in specific places over the long term, and a desire to emphasize
continuity with the past by introducing reminders of the dead into domestic life. Both these tendencies point to the increasing durability of the house
itself and the household community. While some of these buildings appear
initially to have been isolated in the landscape, the ensuing development
was unequivocally towards the formation of progressively more tightly
nucleated villages. A first step in this direction took the form of the 'pairing'

Fig. 5.2 The Midhowe 'stalled cairn', Rousay, Orkney

The elongated, oval Midhowe chambered cairn stands close to the southern shore of the Isle of Rousay overlooking the Eynhallow sound and facing the northern shore of Orkney Mainland. The cairn has a single entrance and a single central passage 23.6 metres long, on either side of which are a series of twelve compartments divided by single stone slabs (and sometimes with shelves against the wall at the rear), giving the impression of 'stalls' in a barn. A larger terminal compartment was, like the passage and side chambers, once roofed over by stone slabs (now covered by a modern artificial fibre 'dome'). The bones of at least twenty-five people were found when the tomb was first opened, some in a crouched position on the shelves. The bones of cows, sheep, skua, cormorant, buzzard, fish-eagle, gannet, and carrion crow were also found, together with the bones of bream and wrasse.

Photograph: Lawrence Jones, Wikimedia Creative Commons.

of houses, either side-by-side or end-on-end, at the Knap of Howar, Green, Howe, and the Knowes of Trotty, creating larger enclosed spaces.

Owing to its remarkable state of preservation and early exploration, the most famous Neolithic housing site in Orkney is Skara Brae, located on Skaill Bay in the north-western corner of the Orkney Mainland (Fig. 5.4).

However, the site at Barnhouse, located just over ten kilometres south, next to the Stones of Stenness on the southern isthmus that separates the lochs of Harray and Stenness, provides at present the best-documented series of early structures. Here, a group of free-standing sub-circular stone houses dating to the thirty-second century BCE onwards were clustered around an open central area that was likely to have been used for communal activities. By the time that Barnhouse was occupied, some significant

Fig. 5.3 Smerquoy house, Orkney Mainland

Smerquoy is located at the foot of Wideford Hill, overlooking the Bay of Firth on the northern side of Orkney Mainland. This house takes its architectural cues from the stalled cairns of Orkney, and, together with buildings at the Knowes of Trotty, Stonehall, Ha'Breck, Green, and the Knap of Howar, represents an example of the stone structures that replaced the earliest, timber buildings on the islands around 3400 BCE.

Photograph: © Adam Stanford (website: http://www.aerial-cam.co.uk/).

developments had taken place. Passage-tomb architecture, manifested in sites such as Maes Howe and Quanterness, had been introduced, probably from Ireland and the Western Isles. The construction of these monuments involved creating a series of concentric 'skins' of masonry and other materials around a central chamber, and this was to influence both the development of domestic architecture in Orkney and the formation of new monumental traditions, notably henges. Further, Grooved Ware pottery had started to be made, emerging alongside the round-based Unstan bowls that had hitherto been in use, and was the only ceramic tradition represented at Barnhouse. As we mentioned in Chapter 4 and will pursue further in this chapter, Grooved Ware employed decorative motifs drawn from the Irish passage-tomb tradition, mixing them with Orcadian potting skills. In both cases, elements borrowed from distant regions contributed to the creation of something quite specific to the insular context. Each of the Barnhouse buildings had a central box hearth with rectangular stone-lined recumbent

Fig. 5.4 The Bay of Skaill and Skara Brae, Orkney Mainland

Skara Brae and the Bay of Skaill are located some 3 km to the north-west of the Ring of Brodgar (itself just 300 m to the north of the Ness of Brodgar) and the Loch of Stenness. This view looking north over the houses and settlement at Skara Brae (with House 1 at rear centre) mirrors both the main frontispiece to this book, and the frontispiece to this chapter. What it additionally shows, however, is the wider shape and setting of the Skara Brae settlement set among the dunes, and in particular in relation to the sandy Bay of Skaill itself.

Photograph: August 2012, © Adam Stanford (website: http://www.aerial-cam.co.uk/).

'beds' (presumably when in use containing heather- or bracken-filled pail-lasses) to right and left of the entrance, and a stone 'dresser' placed so as to face the doorway. The term 'dresser' was attached many years ago to these otherwise mysterious shelved fixed items of furniture, on analogy with recent historic Scottish practice. This interpretation of their role has been restated in recent years because it has been proposed that the visual prom-inence of these facilities would have rendered them suitable as open display-cabinets for treasured items (such as carved stone balls, polished maceheads, and ground stone objects that might constitute heirlooms) that in some way were important to the identity and projected values of the household.

This four-square organization of interior space around a boxed central hearth is understood as the 'classic' internal arrangement for houses in Later Neolithic Orkney, and arguably elaborated on the internal structure of the earlier houses. Some of the houses at Barnhouse were repeatedly rebuilt on the same site, while the hearthstones were often reused in new buildings, underlining the importance of the fireplace as the physical and conceptual focus of the household. However, the site is also distinguished by the emer-gence there of the phenomenon of 'big houses', which are not only larger but also structurally distinct from the other buildings.

The first of these was House 2, an elongated structure containing two separate hearths, and with a dual-cruciform interior in which a series of alcoves were defined by four corner buttresses. This arrangement is reminis-cent of some of the passage tombs of Orkney, and it may not be coincidental that there was a cavity beneath the floor containing what appeared to be the remains of a burial. Increasingly, the living and the dead were being brought together in the same spaces. It was evident from bone and other debris that the eastern part of this interior space, nearer the entrance, had been used for food preparation and dining, while the more secluded western part featured detritus indicative of stone tool manufacture. The later big house at Barnhouse, Structure 8, was a massive square building surrounded by a clay platform that in turn was bounded by a stone wall, manifesting the tendency toward multiple concentric boundaries. This building contained a series of hearths, and again combined elements of house and tomb architec-ture. Within this huge structure, food was being cooked and eaten on a larger scale than elsewhere on the site, and this suggests that it was a venue for communal meals or feasts. However, Structure 8 was as much a monument as a house, and was constructed over the remains of other buildings at a time when the settlement was in decline.

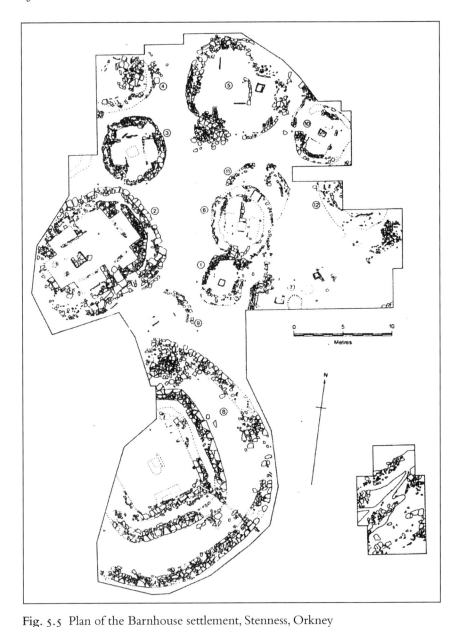

Fig. 5.5 Plan of the Barnhouse settlement, Stenness, Orkney

The Barnhouse settlement was found and excavated by Colin Richards in the late 1980s, having previously been regarded simply as a ploughed field south of the Stones of Stenness. His excavations revealed both a complexity of settlement history, and the phenomenon of the 'big house' as a communal focus within Orkney Neolithic 'villages'.

Plan: © Colin Richards and Cambridge University Press.

At Skara Brae, small free-standing buildings like those at Barnhouse were eventually replaced by a structure in which the houses were not only more substantial but were also joined together, embedded within a mass of midden material seemingly representing the rotted-down debris of past occupation. But at the same time, the individual dwellings were rigorously segregated from each other by walling and sillstones in the passages. There is a suggestion that this change in the character of occupation followed a period in which activity slackened somewhat in some areas of Orkney, coinciding with the change from Grooved Ware that was decorated with incised lines to new styles with applied decoration. The tendency of settlements to become large conglomerate mounds was complemented at sites such as Muckquoy and Rinyo by containment within walls or ditches, completing the trend toward nucleation and consolidation. Yet although the trend was for settlements to become more tightly knit over time, there are also indications that the separate households retained their independence, and competed against each other, jealously retaining fine artefacts and hosting feasts as a form of rivalry.

The most remarkable among the Neolithic settlements in the Orkneys, however, is the recently discovered site that lies on the Ness of Brodgar, the northern isthmus that separates the lochs of Harray and Stenness in south Mainland. In this prominent location it is therefore also bracketed between the two celebrated ditched henge monuments containing massive upstanding stone circles: the Stones of Stenness to the south and the Ring of Brodgar to the north. It is, moreover, less than a kilometre away from Barnhouse. The beginnings of activity at the Ness of Brodgar are presently mysterious, as there are plainly earlier structures beneath the Late Neolithic buildings that have been investigated to date, which explain the subsidence that has affected these. Earlier stone houses that have been glimpsed so far are internally divided by upright slabs, rather than the pairs of opposed stone piers that characterize the buildings that, revealed by excavation, stand to roof height in places today. Activity at the site probably began before 3000 BCE, perhaps much earlier. Similarly, the timing of the end of occupation is not certain, although it may be as late as 2300 BCE. It is evident, however, that the intensity of activity varied considerably, and may it be that the site was actually abandoned for a period around 2700 BCE, in a development comparable to Skara Brae. The Ness was certainly a massive complex, extending over 250 metres by 100 metres, and contained within a colossal stone wall.

Fig. 5.6 Ness of Brodgar, Orkney Mainland: general view looking north

Like Barnhouse, the presence of this extraordinary settlement located on the northern isthmus of land that divides the Loch of Harray (on the right of this photograph) from the Loch of Stenness (to the left) was until a decade ago almost entirely unsuspected. In an already very 'busy' landscape, the discovery of another major complex, and moreover one that represents massive communal gathering and living together in the Middle and Late Neolithic, has transformed our understanding of the organization of Orkney during the centuries concerned. The Ring of Brodgar (Fig. 5.8) can just be made out on a rise further up the isthmus in the middle distance.

Photograph: Scott Pike, courtesy of Nick Card.

Among the most astonishing things about this unique site is that in its later phases it was composed entirely of at least seven of the 'big houses' that are found singly or in pairs at other settlements. These take the form of embellished versions of the characteristic Late Neolithic house, elongated or extended in design. Moreover, these structures were architecturally very diverse, with idiosyncratic combinations of internal partitions and buttresses. Like the big houses at other sites, these buildings contained concentrations of special objects, which might conceivably have been identified with the histories of particular kin groups. Equally, the Grooved Ware pottery found there was more varied than any ceramic assemblage retrieved from any other Orcadian site. One implication of this may be that, rather than having been occupied by a single community, the Ness of Brodgar was set apart as a special place of assembly in a special location, used as a gathering point or ceremonial focus for disparate groups drawn from a wider area. In such a location, the stone enclosure wall would have served not so much as a defensive structure as a means of symbolically removing the activities that took place there from the realm of the everyday.

Yet paradoxically, although the houses are bigger than elsewhere, and occupation may not have been continuous throughout the year, there is plenty of evidence for everyday activities having taken place at the Ness of Brodgar. Pottery was made here, and flint and ground stone were worked nearby, with the evidence for different crafts being concentrated in different buildings. As at Skara Brae, a huge quantity of midden material has been found in and around the site, providing an indirect indication of the intensity of occupation. Indeed, a mound of midden material seventy metres across and four metres high was positioned immediately to the south of the walled area, offering tangible evidence of the longevity of the settlement. This may have built up over an abandoned chambered tomb. The buildings at the Ness of Brodgar are unusual also in that as well as scratched decoration on the walls, traces of coloured pigment have been recorded covering parts of the walls, and numbers of stone roofing 'slates' have also been recovered from among the debris. While all these houses are massive, and the excavator, Nick Card, has conjectured that they might best be described as 'temples', one stands out as particularly huge. This is Structure 10, which appears to represent an even larger equivalent of Structure 8 at Barnhouse. Like that building, Structure 10 combined aspects of the architecture of houses and tombs, most notably the rather small cruciform inner chamber, which invites comparison with the passage tomb of Maes Howe, located 1.4 kilometres to the east. Yet while this enclosed space contained a freestanding 'dresser', its walls were not finely dressed like those of the Maes Howe chamber. It was instead the *exterior* of Structure 10 that was much more imposing, contained within an outer wall which enclosed a paved passage. When excavated, this passage revealed a huge deposit of cattle bones, in which the hind limbs of the animals predominated. It appears that a massive feast, the debris from which was strewn about the outer part of the structure, marked the termination of activity in the building, and perhaps at the site.

At the Ness of Brodgar, therefore, the 'basic model' of the cellular house was elaborated to provide enclosed spaces that were used for a variety of domestic and non-domestic activities (Fig. 5.7). Indeed, as Colin Richards has pointed out, there appears to have been a degree of equivalence between a series of different architectural forms in Later Neolithic Orkney: houses, tombs, henge enclosures and 'temples', halls, or shrines. This blurring of categories is most obvious in the case of the circle-henge of the Stones of Stenness, whose ditch and ring of stone uprights contained a massive, centrally placed box hearth. It may simply be that this was a location at which communal meals could be taken by large groups of people. But another possibility is that this had been a 'big house', whose remains were now contained within a series of concentric boundaries. As we will see below (under 'Henging, mounding, and the dead') this provides an important clue to understanding the development of henge monuments.

According to Richards, the efflorescence of Neolithic Orkney from the end of the fourth millennium BCE can be understood in terms of the

Fig. 5.7 Ness of Brodgar house (Structure 12) under excavation

Structure 12 at the Ness of Brodgar, shown here, was a massive stone structure with a box hearth on either side of a double-cruciform plan roofed space. The multiple recesses in the walls invite comparison with the architecture of contemporary passage tombs.

Photograph: Hugo Anderson-Whymark.

paradoxical development of a society characterized by volatile and competitive household groups, who nonetheless constantly needed to signal social cohesion and collective identity. 'Houses' asserted their origins and continuity through domestic architecture, the transmission of heirlooms, and relations with the dead. But at a higher level, communities became more nucleated and built massive corporate monuments in the course of the earlier third millennium BCE. The clearest example of this was the Ring of Brodgar henge, whose upright stones had been dragged from a variety of different locations, representing the unity of disparate social groups (Fig. 5.8).

Fig. 5.8 The Ring of Brodgar

The massive henge-like monument known as the 'Ring of Brodgar' has two opposing entrances and a large 3-m deep ditch, but apparently no surrounding bank. The circumference of the outer side of the 9-m-wide ditch is some 380 m, and along the outer edge of the space enclosed within the ditch is a circle of originally up to sixty massive stones. At 104 m diameter, this is the third largest stone circle in Britain, and the relation of stones to ditch with entrance gaps across the ditch echoes the smaller henge at Arbor Low in the Derbyshire Peak District (where the stones are nonetheless prone), and the yet more massive henge at Avebury.

Photograph: November 2011, © Adam Stanford (website: http://www.aerial-cam.co.uk/).

Packed together in the competitive pressure cooker of the Neolithic Orkneys, these rival 'house societies' created a series of architectural and artefactual innovations whose subsequent dispersal would be of decisive importance to Later Neolithic Britain.

The Grooved Ware phenomenon

The pottery that was made and used at all of these Orcadian 'village' sites from Barnhouse onwards was Grooved Ware, a pot-making and -using tradition that stands out as being quite unlike any other in Neolithic Britain. And more: Grooved Ware has no obvious parallels in continental Europe either. In particular, while the carinated bowl, plain-and-decorated bowl, and Peterborough series were all composed of round-based vessels, Grooved Ware pots were predominantly flat-based tubs and buckets. It is very likely that Grooved Ware developed in Orkney in the first instance, and indeed at the sites of Pool on Sanday and Crossiecrown on the Orkney Mainland there are sequences in which Grooved Ware directly replaced the plain round-based Early Neolithic pottery and decorated Unstan bowls. It has been suggested that this stylistic shift is related to changes in the use of pottery vessels that were perhaps increasingly displayed on just those flat stone surfaces so prominent within the houses.

In the Orkneys, the earliest Grooved Ware is characterized by incised decoration comparable to that employed on the broad collars of Unstan Ware pots, while on later vessels more elaborate plastic decoration was present. A recent re-evaluation of the dating of the chambered tomb of Quanterness has indicated that Grooved Ware was in use at that site by 3200 BCE. Perhaps the most remarkable aspect of Grooved Ware, however, is that although it developed out of the ceramic traditions of northern Scotland, the decorative motifs employed on the pots were clearly derived from the passage-tomb 'art' of Ireland. It is germane here, therefore, to note that it has been argued that the passage tombs of Ireland increased in scale and complexity from 3600 BCE onwards, reaching a climax between 3300 and 3000 BCE. At around this time, the abstract decoration on the stones of passage, chamber, and kerb changed from what has been characterized as a haphazard scratched or picked 'depictive' style to a more carefully arranged and more plastic sculptural form. The particular designs that were seemingly adopted for use on Grooved Ware (meanders, chevrons, triangles, zigzags, lozenges, and lattices)

Fig. 5.9 Location of third–millennium sites
Map: 2017, © Julian Thomas.

belong to the period of overlap between these two styles. We observed in
Chapter 3 that the spatial distribution of these motifs within the tombs was
clearly grouped and therefore probably purposive. It follows, therefore, that
there may well have been a particular significance residing in this formerly
stone-focused symbol-system that was being transferred to the pottery.
Moreover, as we pointed out in Chaper 4, elements of this suite of symbols
were also carved onto a range of other portable artefacts, including carved
stone balls, stone and antler maceheads, and plaques of stone and chalk. This
implies that whatever connotations the designs carried, they were being
introduced into a wider range of contexts. Some of the stones within the
tombs in Orkney were also decorated with a combination of incised linear
motifs and pecked curvilinear forms. But the walls of the houses had only
the linear designs, and these were the ones that were also found on Grooved
Ware. One way of interpreting this distinction is to suggest that the pottery
bore images that were appropriate for the houses of the living, not those of
the dead. Moreover, with their flat bases and vertical cordons, it has been
proposed that some Grooved Ware pots evoked the architecture of circular
houses and timber circles. This implied connection between Grooved Ware
and the house or household is echoed in the results of petrological analysis
of the crushed rock used as temper, conducted by Andrew Jones. This
showed that each dwelling at Barnhouse had its own distinctive 'recipe' for
placing rock inclusions in the fabric of its Grooved Ware vessels, suggesting
in turn that each household maintained its own time-honoured traditions
of practice and ways of asserting its identity as a distinct descent group. Yet
the inclusions were hidden beneath the surface treatment of the vessels, and
decoration of the pots was highly standardized throughout the settlement,
expressing the developing tension between the household and the greater
community.

After having been used principally in Orkney for two centuries or so,
Grooved Ware began to be adopted in much of Britain and Ireland in the
two centuries after 3000 BCE. There are indications that the Orkney Islands
were increasingly involved in long-distance contacts from this time onwards:
flint from the Scottish mainland, pitchstone from the Isle of Arran, and
volcanic tuff from Cumbria all occur on early third-millennium sites.
This expansion broadly coincided with the development of new forms of
monumental architecture, including the circles of upright timber posts at
Temple Wood in Kilmartin Glen, Argyll, and at Machrie Moor on the Isle
of Arran. In Ireland, similar circles of pits and posts are sometimes found

near to the passage tombs that were now beginning to go out of use, as at Newgrange, Knowth, and Ballynahatty. As Grooved Ware was introduced to different regions, distinctive variations of form and decoration began to appear. Notably, on the British mainland small tubs with raised horizontal bands that converge in knots form a Woodlands style, while much larger, slightly concave, bucket-shaped vessels with vertical applied or incised cordons are characteristic of the Durrington Walls style. The production of much larger pots in the south of England than had originally been used in Orkney was complemented by a change in the way that these vessels were being used. Analysis of the residues from Grooved Ware in Orkney indicates that they were often employed to contain milk or cattle meat. Yet in the south of England, there was a much more emphatic focus on pig fats. Although pigs cannot be milked, and provide no other products aside from leather, they are very well suited to the sporadic provision of large quantities of meat. Pigs have large litters of young, which mature relatively quickly, so that herds can be repeatedly culled and bred up to strength again. The capacity rapidly to generate large quantities of fat-rich food for collective consumption was an important element of a new social pattern that was beginning to develop at the start of the third millennium BCE.

The symbolic encapsulation of the house

In Orkney, then, there was a degree of overlap between houses and other structures intended primarily for funerary or ceremonial activity, and over time the houses themselves became more substantial and elaborate, along the way incorporating the remains of the dead in some cases. At some point during this sequence, houses of a design closely similar to those in Orkney began to appear elsewhere in Britain and Ireland, and it is reasonable to suppose that the adoption of this building style was part of the same process that led to the insular dispersal of Grooved Ware pottery. Like the earlier houses in Orkney, these presumed domestic buildings were mostly light structures of wattle and daub construction attached to a wooden frame, but some like those at Durrington Walls appear to have had dressers and beds made of wood. Sometimes, as with the two buildings discovered on a hillside at Trelystan in Powys, they contained stone box hearths. In other cases, as at Wyke Down in Dorset, the stake-hole ring of the outer wall surrounded four sturdier roof posts. Both of these arrangements constitute a square within a circle, a pattern that is so recurrent that arguably it came to embody the very concept of the house and household in Later Neolithic Britain. At other sites, the square-in-circle format manifested itself on a larger scale: at Greenbogs in Aberdeenshire, for instance, the structures concerned may have been large roofed buildings. However, examples at Machrie Moor on Arran, Knowth in Ireland, Durrington Walls northern circle, and Durrington 68 (both in Wiltshire), were more likely to have been open and unroofed. Here, four large free-standing posts were enclosed within a fence or a ring of lesser uprights. These open constructions might be referred to as 'shrines', with the central posts taking on an enhanced role as the symbolic focus of the whole. Joshua Pollard has argued convincingly that in some cases what began as ordinary settlements became progressively sanctified, emerging as ceremonial monuments. A case in point is the henge monument at Coneybury Hill near Stonehenge, in which a large, fenced, four-post structure stood amidst the traces of an episode of domestic occupation, and was later enclosed within a substantial penannular bank and ditch. In other cases, buildings that may have been domestic in character were incorporated into much later monuments. The two small houses at Trelystan, mentioned already, were sealed beneath an Early Bronze Age round barrow, while a sub-rectangular stake structure associated with pits that contained Grooved Ware sherds at Raigmore near Inverness was identified underneath a Clava-style passage tomb of probable Early Bronze Age date. As in Orkney, then, the house provided a spatial archetype that could be elaborated or appropriated in a variety of different ways (Fig. 5.10).

A singularly massive variation on the theme of wooden post architecture was represented by the so-called 'palisaded enclosures' that were built from around 2800 BCE onwards, if not earlier. These were often sub-circular or oval in plan, were composed of rings of contiguous or evenly spaced upright timbers, and generally extended to 200–400 metres in diameter, although the colossal example at Hindwell measured about 800 by 525 metres. Several palisaded enclosures are found in Scotland, and a group of sites cluster together at Hindwell and Walton in the Walton Basin of Powys. Since these timber-built monuments are not visible in the modern landscape, they have generally been identified only in the past few decades (often through the means of aerial photography), and this has begun to redress the balance of Neolithic studies toward these so-called peripheral areas, as discussed in Chapter 1. The Scottish enclosures seem all to date to a horizon between

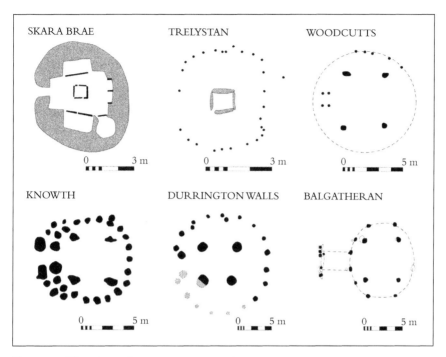

Fig. 5.10 The plans of structures associated with Grooved Ware across Britain

Some common organizational principles can be seen to have been shared by broadly contemporary house structures across Britain in the early third millennium BCE. The central hearth structures at Skara Brae and other Neolithic Orkney houses are paralleled by those from Trelystan on the flank of the Long Mountain in the middle Severn Valley in Powys, Wales, and now by the houses at Durrington Walls and at Marden in the Vale of Pewsey, Wiltshire. The four-post structures at Woodcutts on Cranborne Chase on the Dorset/Wiltshire border are closely similar to those found at Knowth and at Balgatheran (near Drogheda) in the Boyne Valley in Ireland, and also now several that have recently been found in north-eastern Scotland.

Plans: from Richard Bradley, *The Prehistory of Britain and Ireland* (2007) © Cambridge University Press.

2800 and 2500 BCE, potentially placing them quite early in the sequence. Moreover, it positions them in broad contemporaneity with comparable palisaded enclosures in Denmark and Sweden. In both areas, the emergence of a new suite of large enclosed sites coincided with the creation of new networks of interregional contact, which circulated objects and practices over wide areas (the Battle Axe complex and the Grooved Ware complex, respectively). This might arguably have created new conditions in which places where large numbers of people could gather were required. If the Scottish enclosures were constructed shortly after Grooved Ware began to be dispersed across the British mainland from north to south, it is not surprising that radiocarbon dates for enclosures further south, at Hindwell, Marne Barracks, Catterick, Mount Pleasant, Dorset, and Greyhound Yard, Dorchester, all fall in the later third millennium BCE or later.

However, some recent developments place the north-to-south narrative for palisaded enclosures in question. First, a new analysis by Alex Bayliss and colleagues has placed the accepted dating of the two large palisaded enclosures at West Kennet near Avebury in north Wiltshire in dispute. Their argument is that at the time of excavation it was not recognized that the enclosures were associated with a rather later Grooved Ware settlement (which might represent the 'worker's camp' for the construction of nearby Silbury Hill), and that the samples strictly associated with the palisade structures indicate a construction date of around 3300 BCE. Secondly, Alasdair Whittle pointed out some while ago that the two dates for the construction of the palisade at Mount Pleasant may have come from material that tumbled into the voids left behind by the timber uprights when they rotted out, and thus are much later than the actual time of construction. It is therefore conceivable that the palisade slot and the internal post circle (Site IV) together constituted a timber phase of the monument, which preceded the digging of the henge ditch, and whose date has yet to be satisfactorily determined. It follows that the notion of an enclosed space defined by contiguous or spaced wooden posts may have been one that developed in various parts of Britain in the centuries around 3000 BCE, in response to similar forces or needs. We have seen already that early cursus monuments used earth-fast timbers to delineate an area, while palisade slots were employed at causewayed enclosures at Orsett (Essex), Haddenham (Cambridgeshire), and Crickley Hill (Gloucestershire). In a sense, 'walls' of wood already formed part of the architectural vocabulary of Neolithic Britain.

Some palisaded enclosures, such as West Kennet and Ballynahatty near Belfast, were associated with smaller structures, whether post circles or smaller palisaded monuments. This would seem to confirm their connection to the broader array of Late Neolithic architecture, including square-in-circle structures. Some of the large palisaded monuments, including Hindwell, Marne Barracks, and Enclosure 1 at West Kennet, were composed of two concentric post rings. That at Blackshouse Burn in Lanarkshire later had a stone bank added, filling in the space between the two post circles. At Dunragit in Galloway, there were three rings of uprights, the outermost of which was quite irregular in plan (Fig. 5.11).

These rings were probably not all contemporary: at any given time, the structure would have consisted of a very large ring of free-standing posts, surrounded by a more continuous fence. In this respect, Dunragit was similar to many of the smaller Late Neolithic timber monuments, in having an internal structure contained within a perimeter, which served as a focus for attention and deposition. Like many of the timber enclosures in Scotland and Wales, Dunragit had a narrow avenue-like entrance (sometimes described as a 'gunsight' passage), which was aligned on the large prehistoric mound 400 metres away at Droughduil. Indeed, massive mounds or barrows are often found in close proximity to palisaded enclosures, and their roles may have been in some way complementary. From the start of the third millennium onwards, monuments of various kinds increasingly formed integrated 'complexes' that encompassed entire landscapes, composed of structures of different kinds which nevertheless appear to have been mutually related. Indeed, it is notable that palisaded enclosures were often constructed in landscapes that had already accumulated other monuments: the Womaston causewayed enclosure and Hindwell and Walton Green cursus in the case of the Walton Basin enclosures; further cursus monuments at Dunragit and Marne Barracks. Cremation burials were present at Foreteviot and Dunragit, while Grooved Ware has been found at Dunragit, Greyhound Yard, and the West Kennet enclosures. These associations again suggest that palisaded enclosures formed part of the suite of cultural innovations that were adopted across Britain around 3000 BCE.

One novel way of integrating this evidence interpretively is to argue that the house or household had re-emerged as a powerful organizing principle at the start of the third millennium, and that structures occupied by a group of people (or dedicated to their collective ancestors) were playing a renewed role in binding them together as communities. The period between 3000 and 2300 BCE saw the appearance of a series of regional monument complexes, which included structures built on a scale that had not previously been attempted. Most notably, these include the edifices at Avebury, Silbury Hill, Durrington Walls, and Stonehenge, and it seems likely that these feats of construction were made possible by the development of new means of social integration, in which collectivities of people reasserted an understanding of themselves as 'households'. This may have been particularly important on the British mainland, where subsistence activities were heavily focused on livestock, and groups of people may not have been co-resident

Fig. 5.11 A night-time gathering at Dunragit

What is envisaged in this vivid reconstruction by the archaeologist-artist Aaron Watson is the scene overlooking a huge gathering for feasting and exchanges at the complex of free-standing timber structures (including a double concentric ring of large posts interspersed with smaller ones), and the massive Droughduil mound, at Dunragit, Galloway, one night sometime in the summer of one of the years of the twenty-eighth century BCE.

Reconstruction image: Aaron Watson.

throughout the year. The development of the Ness of Brodgar complex in the very different circumstances of Orkney provides an interesting parallel trajectory: a concentration of Great Houses within a single enclosure rather than a monument fashioned after the house. In this way, alternative physical manifestations of the house ranged between small dwellings and massive timber circles or palisaded enclosures, and in some cases these were juxtaposed. At Wyke Down, for example, small circular houses occurred alongside two modestly sized henge monuments with segmented ditches, while inside the western part of the massive henge enclosure at Durrington Walls in Wiltshire two or more houses were each enclosed within a palisade surrounded by a bank and ditch (Fig. 5.12). These western enclosures could profitably be compared to the house-inside-a-henge at Stenness, and identified as a further example of the principle of concentric enclosing rings, ultimately attributable to the passage-tomb tradition. Whether these structures should be identified as the dwellings of important people, or as cult houses or ancestor houses, as some prehistorians have proposed, remains an open question.

A further aspect of the embellishment of the house concerns the role of pits, which we discussed in Chapter 4. At the eastern entrance of the Durrington Walls henge in Wiltshire, excavations by the Stonehenge Riverside Project in 2004–7 revealed numerous stake-built houses with central hearths in rectangular floors. The material for the chalk plaster on the wattle walls of these buildings had been scooped from a series of borrow-pits surrounding them, while the decommissioning of many of the houses after their use was marked by the digging of a substantial pit through the floor, into which occupation debris including animal bones and pottery was placed. So in this instance the life history of the house, from building to destruction, was played out between episodes of pit digging. We have seen in Chapter 4 that the practices of structured deposition in pits became markedly more complex with the introduction of Grooved Ware, alongside, in many cases, the careful placing of fine artefacts and near-complete pottery vessels in an ashy matrix redolent of the hearth and the house. So it appears that activities that commemorated and materially memorialized episodes of domestic dwelling were made more complex and spectacular at a time when the house itself was taking on a greater social importance. And as we have seen, some of the more monumental structures that were derived from the architecture of the house were *treated like houses* for depositional purposes. Thus at the massive southern timber circle at Durrington Walls, the decay and collapse of the upright timbers were followed by the digging

Fig. 5.12 One of the Western Enclosures at Durrington Walls

This image represents one of a series of small enclosed buildings located inside the western part of the huge henge monument at Durrington Walls in Wiltshire. Other small houses dating to the middle of the third millennium BCE were clustered together at what would become the eastern entrance of the enclosure, around the avenue that linked the southern timber circle to the River Avon, but these structures were arranged about the natural amphitheatre overlooking these features. Each small house had a central hearth, and was surrounded by both a palisade and a henge ditch (which may have been later in date). This example also had a façade of colossal posts, which may have supported wooden lintels. It is open to conjecture whether these were the dwellings of important people, shrines, or lineage houses.
Reconstruction image: Aaron Watson.

of a series of pits into the tops of the post-holes, into which pottery sherds, animal bones, and other materials were deliberately placed. This might be described as an 'architecture of memory', commemorating a building whose physical embodiment had now wasted away.

Timber circles and palisaded enclosures were, in these circumstances, effectively massive houses. Meanwhile, although Grooved Ware vessels in southern Britain were often very large, they had been connected in the first instance with the preparation and sharing of food in the domestic context. We have seen that their flat bases implied use within a house, and their shape possibly evoked the house. Pit-deposition introduced a physical reminder of the life cycle of the house into the landscape, while another aspect of domestic life that was amplified and dramatized was the consumption of collective meals. At Durrington Walls, pigs had apparently been shot with arrows before being barbecued over open fires, generating colossal quantities of bone debris. Pig bones and porcine fat residues on pottery are common on Grooved Ware sites in southern Britain. In Orkney, more modest feasting appears to have taken place at the household level. In the south, the scale increased appreciably, as the sharing of huge quantities of food arguably became a means of achieving social cohesion, as well as potentially constituting a form of competition between regional communities or exceptionally powerful people. Taken together, the evidence suggests that from 3000 BCE onwards a social order was created that relied at least to some degree upon display, drama, and spectacle. Collective identity was 'acted out' through processions, pilgrimages, feasts, funerals, and the construction of increasingly massive monuments, to which people who may have been dispersed over very large areas would have claimed affiliation. Through public performances of shared belonging, new, more extensively networked, and in some cases much larger, social entities were created and sustained in an otherwise highly unstable world. Paradoxically, however, being dependent for their social dynamic upon periodic gatherings and episodes of consumption rather than the rhythms of everyday life, these more closely networked political entities may nonetheless have rendered themselves both more volatile and also shorter-lived.

Henging, mounding, and the dead

The expenditure of colossal amounts of labour in the construction of earth and stone monuments may nevertheless not be a reliable indicator simply of the scale and complexity of communities in the way that has sometimes been suggested. It may, rather, reflect an intention to bring into being qualitatively different social bonds and structures. Construction can in such circumstances constitute a form of display or theatre, which also brings new architectural spaces into being that, once established, can host subsequent performances of other kinds. These points are especially pertinent in discussing *henges*, a new kind of monument that developed during the earlier third millennium BCE (Fig. 5.13).

The term 'henge' is something of a misnomer, originally used by T. D. Kendrick to describe a disparate variety of prehistoric sanctuaries or religious sites, while referring specifically to the trilithon stone arrangements (or 'hinges') at Stonehenge. Over time the word has come to distinguish a group of Later Neolithic and Early Bronze Age circular or oval enclosures, generally defined by a ditch with a bank positioned on its outer

Fig. 5.13 'Church Henge', Knowlton, Dorset

This site is typical of henges featuring a ditch surrounded by an earthen bank and with a single entrance or (as in this case) two opposing entrances, belonging to the early centuries of the third millennium BCE. This view from the south also features the eponymous medieval church placed centrally within the henge enclosure, but subsequently abandoned. Church Henge is one of a series of seemingly broadly contemporary circular enclosures and hengiform monuments within a few metres of one another here at Knowlton that have been levelled over the centuries in this area of gentle slopes on the southern flank of Cranborne Chase north of Wimborne Minster.

Photograph: September 2013, © Adam Stanford (website: http://www.aerial-cam.co.uk/).

side. These range in size from small hengiforms (which can enclose an area less than ten metres in diameter) to the massive embanked enclosures of Wessex (Avebury, Marden, Mount Pleasant, and Durrington Walls), which are up to half a kilometre in extent.

Henges can contain a range of internal features, including both timber and stone circles, four-post structures, and 'coves' (or rectilinear settings of upright stones). These enclosures, reversing as they do the normal defensive pattern of a bank within a ditch, have long been understood as separating out by a ditch a central reserved space, with further significant 'exclusion' from outside view being provided by the high enclosing bank, which might nonetheless have sometimes served as a place of vantage for an audience. However, two recent insights have transformed this received and perhaps obvious understanding of these structures. First, in discussing the much later 'royal sites' of Iron Age Ireland, which may have some general structural affinity with henges, Richard Warner has suggested that a monument with an internal ditch and external bank is likely to represent a means of enclosing and containing powerful alien forces: the 'Otherworld'. This point is best considered in relation to other developments towards the end of the fourth millennium. We have noted already that the architecture of passage tombs differed from that of earlier funerary monuments in being composed of a series of 'rings' of different materials, surrounding a central chamber. In Ireland the outermost of these rings was generally a kerb of large, sometimes decorated, stones. But in the Hebrides, passage tombs such as Dun Bharpa (Barra) were contained within a 'peristalith', which amounted to a circle of upright stones. Indeed, at Calanais on the Isle of Lewis, the most elaborate and well known of the stone circles (locally known as Tursachan) actually contained a small passage tomb. Colin Richards and Vicki Cummings have suggested that the isolation of the peristalith as an architectural unit gave rise to the emergence of stone circles as a distinct kind of monument around 3000 BCE (Fig. 5.14). More generally, we argue that this emphasis on 'wrapping' and containment can be placed alongside the enhancement of decoration on pottery in the Peterborough Ware tradition to indicate a growing cultural anxiety over the control of potent and volatile influences, both material and immaterial. This same imperative to create boundaries around problematic entities lay behind the creation of henge monuments.

Secondly, Alex Gibson has observed that in many cases the structures enclosed by henges appear to be earlier in date than the bank and ditch. For example, at Arminghall (Norfolk), North Mains (Perthshire), and Balfarg (Fife), timber circles predated the ditches that surrounded them, while at Dyffryn Lane (Powys) and perhaps also Arbor Low (Derbyshire), stone circles were contained within later henge enclosures. In other words, 'henging' was a means of placing a boundary around some existing entity, thereby controlling or restricting its efficacy and influence, or affording it a greater sanctity by severing it from the profane world. Even where a henge contains no detectable structure, it is possible to argue that it was built to encircle and control or neutralize the site of an important or inauspicious event. 'Henge'

Fig. 5.14 Castlerigg stone circle near Keswick, Cumbria

Three 'Group VI' Cumbrian polished stone axes were found during early investigations at Castlerigg, indicating (along with its morphology) a Late Neolithic origin for the structure. The 'circle' of originally forty-two stones (now thirty-eight) is somewhat more egg-shaped in plan than fully circular, with a diameter of around 30 m. The stones themselves vary in height from 1 m to 2.3 m. The circle has an entrance on the northern side, and an 'outlier' stone to the west-south-west in common with other third-millennium stone circles. An unusual feature is a rectangular setting of stones against the inside of the eastern arc of stones, which is reminiscent of some stone circles on the Isle of Man. The view here is from the north-west.

Photograph: 2016, © Julian Thomas.

is therefore as much a verb as a noun. As Kenneth Brophy and Gordon Noble have maintained, henging represented one aspect of a suite of practices that sought to manage places and materials that were understood as imbued with unstable vital forces, or tainted by malevolent residual ancestral or spiritual presences. The prophylactic or restorative practices concerned possibly also included deposition in pits, the gathering of materials in middens, and the throwing up of mounds over structures and occupation sites, hence in practice sealing them over. An example of the latter is the pile of stony material containing Grooved Ware sherds and burnt animal bone raised over a sub-rectangular timber structure contained within the early henge at Balfarg Riding School in Fife. Here, the excavator originally suggested that the wooden construction might have served as a platform for the exposure of the dead, although it may equally have represented a shrine whose form evoked an ancestral dwelling place.

The beginnings of henge monuments are poorly understood. Certainly, towards the end of the fourth millennium BCE, circular earthworks of

various kinds were being used to enclose significant areas, often associated with the dead. In Chapter 3 we discussed the two sites of Monkton Up Wimborne and Flagstones House in Dorset, both of which had discontinuous perimeters and contained burials, predominantly of children (Fig. 5.15).

It seems that human remains were one of the difficult influences that increasingly needed to be controlled, and indeed we can identify the beginnings of this trajectory in the blocking of the entrances of long cairns, and the digging of enclosing ditches around earthen long mounds in the mid fourth millennium. The use of circular or oval ditches as a means of containment can also be recognized in the development of small pit- and post-circles and penannular ring-ditches, like those that clustered around the cursus at Dorchester on Thames in Oxfordshire, dating to the period 3500–2900 BCE. Numerous deposits of cremated human bone had been introduced to these structures, and in some cases it may be that they had been created as repositories for this material, which might itself have been understood as singularly powerful or polluting. A comparable site was investigated at Sarn-y-bryn-caled in Powys, again in close proximity to a cursus monument. Here a C-shaped ring-ditch with a pair of upright posts flanking its entrance causeway contained a group of four cremation burials. The earliest of these was dug directly into the base of the ditch terminal, while the other three were cut from higher in the ditch fill, following a redigging of the ditch associated with sherds of Peterborough Ware and radiocarbon dates falling into the interval 3000–2700 BCE.

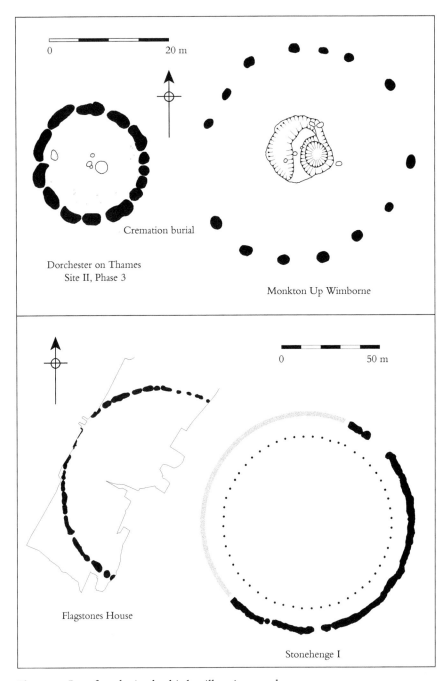

Fig. 5.15 Late fourth-/early third-millennium enclosures

The appearance of henge monuments around 3000 BCE was prefigured by diverse monuments which enclosed or 'reserved' spaces in different ways. The Dorchester on Thames example was one of a group of small ring-ditches and pit circles constructed in the vicinity of an earlier cursus monument, and used for the deposition of cremated human remains. Monkton Up Wimborne, Flagstones, and the first monument at Stonehenge also have associations with the dead, but none can be identified as 'true' henges.

Plans: drawn by Julian Thomas, from various sources.

The appearance of henge monuments therefore seems to have involved a process of convergence, with diverse enclosed sites gradually trending toward greater homogeneity of form. The passage-tomb-derived practice of enclosing a space within multiple concentric boundaries probably had a role in this development, reaching its most evolved form in the double-ditched henges of Yorkshire, such as the Thornborough Circles. Some apparently early henges lack the classic external bank, including Stonehenge I and Balfarg Riding School, which both probably date to around 3000 BCE. Henge A at Llandygai in north Wales had a broad, shallow ditch and an internal bank, and contained at least one cremation burial in a pit. The burnt bones produced a date of 3200–3100 BCE, and the henge ditch 3330–3020 BCE. Immediately outside the single entrance of the enclosure, a pit circle comparable with those at Dorchester on Thames contained the cremated remains of a further six people, and gave similar dates to the ditch. The Stones of Stenness, discussed earlier, was also relatively early, probably built in 2940–2900 BCE, although structurally it more closely approximates to the 'classic' henge than these other 'formative' sites. Interestingly, the construction of Stenness surrounding the remains of a possible big house was contemporary with the digging of a ditch surrounding the nearby passage tomb of Maes Howe (Fig. 5.16).

At the later end of the henge-building tradition, the construction of archetypal henge monuments with external banks appears to have continued into the Early Bronze Age in Scotland, as demonstrated by recent investigations at Pullyhour in Caithness, Broomend of Crichie in Aberdeenshire, and the Pict's Knowe near Dumfries. At Broomend, the henge enclosure was constructed surrounding a deep shaft grave containing two Beaker-era burials. Richard Bradley explains that the bank and ditch served to screen the mortuary structure from the outside world, but an avenue of posts prescribed a pattern of movement through the henge and past the grave. Bradley argues that while some Late Neolithic henges had been used for feasting and gathering by the living, these very late henges primarily represented the settings for elaborate funerals. This may also have been the case at the Pict's Knowe, which had been built enclosing a small sand island in an area of saltmarsh. This island had previously been used for occupation in the earliest Neolithic, and a small oval mound had been built there, flanked by large timber uprights. This was later obscured by a layer of levelling material contiguous with the henge bank, but its position appears to have determined the location and orientation of the enclosure's entrance (Fig. 5.17). The central area of the henge had been disrupted by rabbit burrowing, but

Fig. 5.16 Maes Howe passage tomb, Orkney, from the south-west

Maes Howe is the best known among the passage tombs of Orkney, a local variation on a form of funerary architecture found in Iberia, France, Ireland, Wales, Scotland, and Scandinavia. The view here shows the entrance to the passage, which is oriented south-westwards. In the December days leading up to the winter solstice, the last rays of the setting sun cast beams of light along the slab-lined passage to momentarily illuminate the darkness of the main chamber. The care taken to create this alignment and effect indicates the importance given to this key transition point in the annual calendar, and the wish for its significant light to penetrate the recesses occupied by the bones of the ancestors.

Photograph: © Adam Stanford (website: http://www.aerial-cam.co.uk/).

produced fragments of Collared Urn pottery and human bone, suggesting that the bank and ditch had enclosed an Early Bronze Age burial.

The oval mound beneath the Pict's Knowe can be placed alongside the timber building at Balfarg Riding School and the Stenness house as examples of earlier structures that had been incorporated into henges. This recurrent relationship of henge-construction to the process of enfolding and segregation of traces of past activity suggests that henges embodied and incorporated the collective, or summative, histories of Later Neolithic communities. At the same time, both Jan Harding and Colin Richards have conjectured that henges maintained an intimate relationship with their surrounding landscapes, with their entrances aligned in parallel with rivers, and their banks and ditches mimicking the immediate topography in microcosm. This is characteristic of a change in the nature of monumentality in Later Neolithic

Fig. 5.17 The henge ditch at Pict's Knowe, Dumfriesshire

The Pict's Knowe, near Dumfries (Dumfries and Galloway, Scotland) is an example of a 'late' henge monument, with a substantial ditch and bank surrounding a small sand island that would have broken the surface of a saltmarsh in prehistory. The photograph shows an advanced stage in the excavation of the southern terminal of the east entrance to the henge. Little prehistoric evidence was recovered from the ditch, but it contained a dense deposit of waterlogged wood of Iron Age date, demonstrating the importance that these sites often retained into later prehistory.
Photograph: © Julian Thomas.

Britain. Rather than existing as isolated entities, the monument complexes that we have already mentioned increasingly encompassed entire earthly and more abstract 'landscapes': land and water, earth and sky, past and present. Most of the palisaded enclosure complexes of Scotland, for instance, were located to command networks of natural routeways: rivers, valleys, and coastal strips.

The very large henge monument at Avebury in north Wiltshire originally had a ditch that was more than ten metres deep, cutting through the chalk to the greensand beneath, so that at times it would have contained standing water (Fig. 5.18).

This great henge was eventually physically connected up to the stone circle that stood on Overton Hill 2.3 kilometres to the south-east. By this time this stone circle, which, thanks to the observations and speculations of

Fig. 5.18 Avebury: painting of the south-western arc of stones
This highly evocative winter view looking southwards takes in the renowned beeches at the southern entrance to the henge. This latter is the point where the Avenue, extending north-westwards from the Sanctuary on Overton Hill next to the A4, reaches Avebury.
Painting: 1996, © Anna Dillon (website: http://www.annadillon.com).

the early antiquaries, has long been known as 'The Sanctuary', had replaced a circular timber structure. The connection between the massive henge and the much smaller stone circle was achieved by constructing the West Kennet Avenue, a broad sinuous 'path' bordered by two long parallel lines of upright sarsen stones. Roughly 600 metres from the southern entrance of the henge, the avenue stones pass through what has been described as an 'occupation site', containing Peterborough Ware, Grooved Ware, and Beaker pottery. One possibility is that this represented one of the large Neolithic middens found in the Avebury region, a repository of cultural material including sherds of several traditions of pottery which had accumulated over a considerable period, and which the path of the avenue had been designed to incorporate.

A second sinuous parallel line of stones, the Beckhampton Avenue, ran instead south-westwards from the Avebury henge, right across a slightly earlier ditched enclosure, to terminate 1.5 kilometres away at the Longstones, a box-like setting of upright stones. If these Avenues were designed to facilitate procession along their length, participants would have been able to view Silbury Hill, the West Kennet long barrow, the West Kennet palisaded enclosures and the Beckhampton long barrow at various points along these specially demarcated routes.[1] Whether this viewing was an integral part of their purpose or not, the effect of the creation of the Avenues, continuing the tradition of building parallel-sided, long, linear monuments into the third millennium, was to integrate structures and deposits that had built up through a more or less haphazard historical process into a single overarching pattern. Arguably, this could be seen as a more elaborate way of encapsulating the shared history of a community within a single structure, here in the form of a spatial narrative, in which different structures were revealed sequentially. The logic of containment or wrapping was also expressed at Avebury: the two inner stone circles, both encircled by the outer circle as well as the henge bank and ditch, each surrounded a unique stone structure at its centre (Fig. 5.19).

The Southern Inner Circle was built surrounding the Obelisk, the tallest single stone in the Avebury complex, and the enigmatic Z feature, a linear setting of smaller stones. Recent geophysical survey conducted by Mark Gillings, Joshua Pollard, and colleagues suggests that these settings actually constituted a square-in-circle arrangement rendered in stone, comparable to the timber structures discussed in this chapter, with the Obelisk at its centre. By contrast, the Northern Inner Circle surrounded the Cove, a box-like setting of three (or perhaps four) massive sarsen stones, redolent of the chamber of a megalithic tomb. Recent investigations have hinted that these stones may represent one of the earliest elements of the Avebury monument, possibly dating to the late fourth millennium BCE. If so, they may sit alongside a possible timber circle and a small ditched enclosure (potentially an oval barrow) as features that were deliberately incorporated into the Late Neolithic complex.

---

1. We have attempted to convey this landscape connectivity with several images in the book: see the frontispiece to Chapter 1; Figure 5.25 (this chapter); Figure 6.1; and the frontispiece to the Conclusion.

Fig. 5.19 Avebury from the east: aerial view

Just as with the Stonehenge area, the region surrounding Avebury at the headwaters of the River Kennet in north Wiltshire saw the development of an elaborate complex of large monuments during the Later Neolithic, which encompassed an entire landscape. In the case of Avebury, the two avenues of upright sarsen stones leading eastwards to the Sanctuary on Overton Hill and westwards to the Beckhampton 'cove' provided the medium through which this spatial integration was achieved. This photograph shows the main features of the monument including the circle of massive stones, the deep ditch and surrounding bank, the four entrances at approximately the cardinal directions, and the remains of the Northern Inner Circle (right) and Southern Inner Circle (left) visible in the central space. The partially reconstructed (Overton) Avenue can just be discerned approaching the southern entrance at left.

Photograph: © Adam Stanford (website: http://www.aerial-cam.co.uk/).

At the Duggleby Howe mound in East Yorkshire, described in Chapter 3, the inhumation burials gave way to cremations as the sequence progressed and the barrow continued to grow in size through the addition of layers of chalk and clay. This change appears to have taken place during the first two centuries of the third millennium BCE. Meanwhile, amongst the passage tombs of Ireland, cremation was the normal funerary rite throughout the second half of the fourth millennium. In this connection a very significant site is Kiltierney Deerpark in County Fermanagh, a cremation cemetery at which both the Carrowkeel Ware often found in passage tombs and Grooved

Ware were found. So here in Ireland, groups of cremation burials had begun to be deposited in contexts other than chambered tombs. As with Grooved Ware itself, with palisaded enclosures and with square-in-circle buildings, the progressive accumulation of cremated remains in places that may have been set aside to contain them was seemingly part of a new way of structuring human communities in the earlier third millennium. This apparently related complex of novel practices seemingly emerged from contemporary interactions across the Irish Sea and the North Atlantic. As described in Chapter 4, between 3000 and 2500 BCE cremated human remains dominate the mortuary record of the British mainland, and inhumations are very scarce indeed. Aside from Duggleby Howe, groups of Later Neolithic cremations are known from small circular enclosures and ring-ditches at Barford in Warwickshire, West Stow in Suffolk, and Imperial College sports ground at Harlington near Heathrow. But the best-known group of Later Neolithic cremation burials was the one located at Stonehenge (Fig. 5.20).

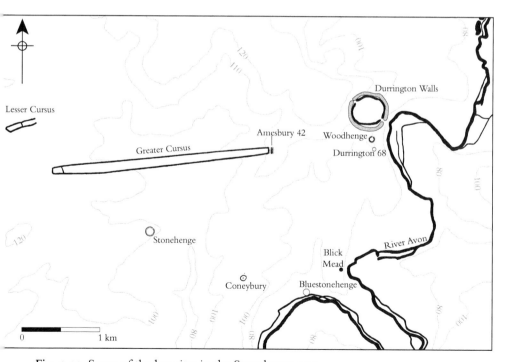

Fig. 5.20 Some of the key sites in the Stonehenge area
Map: © Julian Thomas, after an original by Joshua Pollard.

Stonehenge

Many of the themes that distinguished the first half of the third millennium BCE are well exemplified by the development of Stonehenge and its immediate environment.

As Mike Allen has recently argued, some of the chalk uplands of Wessex, and particularly Salisbury Plain, may not have been covered by dense, unbroken forest after the end of the last Ice Age. Instead, a patchwork of open woodland, scrub, and grassland may have prevailed, which might have encouraged the local aggregation of wild ungulates, including deer and aurochs. These circumstances may explain the longevity of the Mesolithic site at Blick Mead near the River Avon to the east of Stonehenge, which we described in Chapter 2. In this comparatively open landscape, the periodic gathering of large numbers of Mesolithic people for the purpose of collective hunting may have been complemented by ceremonial or spiritual pursuits that ultimately established the conditions for the construction of Stonehenge. Excavations on the much later ditched Avenue that connects Stonehenge with the River Avon have demonstrated that at the western extremity of its course this feature both encloses, and follows the orientation of, a series of periglacial fissures which are fortuitously aligned toward the midsummer sunrise and midsummer sunset. Before the Stonehenge Avenue banks and ditches were constructed, these fissures would have shown up as variations in the vegetation. So the location at the end of this formation, where the sun rose and set along corrugations in the earth's surface at significant times of year, and which would later be chosen as the site of Stonehenge, may already have been perceived as a special, and even magical, place during the Mesolithic. This much is implied by the alignment of pine posts set in massive sockets that was constructed very close by during the eighth millennium BCE.

The earliest activity at Stonehenge itself took place around 3000 BCE. This included the digging of a segmented circular enclosure ditch with an internal bank. Immediately inside this perimeter a ring of fifty-six flat-bottomed circular pits was dug (known as the Aubrey holes, after John Aubrey who first observed them as shallow depressions on the surface). While many accounts maintain that these pit features had held timber uprights (or that they had contained nothing at all), the re-excavation of Aubrey Hole 7 in 2008 revealed traces of the characteristic crushing of the chalk on the sides and base of the pit, which demonstrates unequivocally that it had once served as the socket for a stone monolith. It has long been argued that the smaller bluestones of Stonehenge (a mixture of rhyolites, dolerites, and tuffs from the Preseli hills in west Wales and sandstones from other sources) may have arrived at the site long before the larger sarsen stones that make up the sarsen circle and the five great trilithons at the centre of the monument. The sockets of some of these sarsens appear to have intersected with two concentric rings of features (known as the 'Q' and 'R' holes), which had apparently held the bluestones at some point. This was thought to prove that a double bluestone circle had predated the arrangements of sarsens. However, recent excavations in the central area of Stonehenge by Timothy Darvill and Geoffrey Wainwright have revealed that many of the sarsen sockets had been partially re-dug and expanded in later times, so that the relationship with the Q and R holes may actually be spurious. It now seems probable that the bluestones were initially located in the Aubrey holes, and that the bluestone circle was later, and integral to a configuration that also included the sarsens.

Stonehenge may therefore have initially taken the form of a bluestone monolith circle eighty-six metres in diameter, surrounded by a bank and ditch. From the beginning, this monument was used for funerary purposes, and many of the Aubrey holes contained cremation burials, presumably inserted alongside the bluestones. Further deposits of cremated bone were introduced to the bank and ditch, often later in date and smaller in quantity than those in the Aubrey holes. Altogether, it is estimated that the cremation cemetery at Stonehenge may have contained the burnt remains of between 150 and 240 people, buried between 3000 and 2400 BCE, although perhaps not at a constant rate. Women and men were equally likely to be represented, but children were less numerous. At a rate of one burial every three or four years, it is clear that not all members of a community would have been interred here, and some criteria must have existed to decide which of the deceased would have been afforded this privilege. The possibilities are numerous. One is that these early dead at Stonehenge were members of an elite group of some kind. It is also conceivable that they were ritual specialists or members of a specific kin group. A further alternative is that they represent the cremated remains of people brought from many different and possibly far-flung communities to be buried together here, over time. If this were the case, Stonehenge might be compared with the Ring of Brodgar as a physical embodiment of the alliance between disparate social groups. At least one of the cremation burials, from Aubrey Hole 32, has produced a radiocarbon date which is rather earlier than the digging of the Stonehenge ditch. This may mean that the bluestone circle initially (briefly) stood in isolation, only later to be encircled by the ditch, confirming the view that henges were a means of enclosing places that had already acquired importance, or were in need of containment. Alternatively, it may mean that the remains of this person had been 'curated' for a period of time, and then only subsequently interred in the hole concerned.

If Stonehenge had originally comprised fifty-six bluestones, there were apparently rather more in later iterations of the monument, eventually forming the bluestone oval and outer bluestone circle. Some of these were probably added from 'Bluestonehenge', a recently discovered circle that was made up of around twenty-one uprights. This stone circle had been raised at West Amesbury, where the Stonehenge Avenue meets the River Avon (Fig. 5.21).

'Bluestonehenge' had eventually also been enclosed within a henge ditch, after the stones had been pulled from their sockets. Their imprints, preserved in the damp chalk of the site, revealed the distinctive pillar-like form of the bluestones. However, even before arriving on Salisbury Plain, it is possible that the bluestones had already had a complicated history. The geologists Richard Bevins and Rob Ixer have produced geochemical evidence suggesting that the spotted dolerite from Stonehenge originated at the outcrop of Carn Goedog in Preseli (see Fig. 2.3). Mike Parker Pearson and colleagues have recently examined this site where ready-formed squared pillars of stone could be prised from the mass of vertically bedded rock. This team have also excavated a quarry at Craig Rhosyfelin, located in the deeply incised valley of the Brynberian stream only three kilometres away. Here they have demonstrated that the rhyolite rock-face was exploited during the Neolithic period for the extraction of tabular stones. Parker Pearson has speculated that the stones may originally have been quarried to construct one or more monuments in the Nevern Valley, before these were demolished and the stones carried overland to Wiltshire.

The repeated relocation of the bluestones, and their movement over very long distances, recall the reuse of decorated stones in Irish passage tombs, discussed in Chapter 3, and the incorporation of fragments from broken standing stones into passage tombs in Brittany. Evidently, the bluestones represented more than just a source of suitable building material: their appearance and the known history of their extraction and use, and the effort

Fig. 5.21 Stonehenge and the Stonehenge Avenue, from the north-east

This view looking south-westwards over the excavation trench dug across the Avenue close to Stonehenge as part of the Stonehenge Riverside Project shows the natural geological striations that were enhanced by the communities that came together to build Stonehenge. They were therefore used to create the parallel-ditched feature known for centuries now as 'The Avenue' linking the River Avon (and what we now know to have been the site of 'Bluestonehenge') with Stonehenge.

Photograph: © Adam Stanford (website: http://www.aerial-cam.co.uk/).

involved in their removal, would all have contributed to the respect or even awe with which they would have been regarded. Darvill and Wainwright have proposed that the stones were brought to Salisbury Plain because of their perceived healing powers. This thesis was argued on the grounds that there are numerous examples of skeletal trauma amongst prehistoric burials in the immediate vicinity of Stonehenge, and that in *The History of the Kings of Britain* of 1136, Geoffrey of Monmouth relates that the philosopher-magician Merlin advocated the removal from Ireland of a stone circle endowed with curative properties. This correlation is perhaps open to question, but the interpretation has the merit of reinforcing the idea that the special colours and textures of the Preseli stones imbued them with their own power, efficacy, and even animacy, rather than simply constituting attractive but inert matter. The idea that prehistoric communities perceived stone as a vibrant substance that embodied metaphysical forces and was capable of causing effects in the world is actually quite compatible with Parker Pearson's view of Stonehenge as having been principally concerned with managing the forces of death and ancestry.

The large sarsen stones that make up the trilithons and the great lintelled circle probably arrived at Stonehenge during the twenty-sixth or twenty-fifth century BCE (that is, sometime between 2600 and 2400 BCE). Sarsens are boulders of silicified sandstone rock that are found scattered across the chalk landscape of Salisbury Plain, but such massive examples as those used at Stonehenge are likely to have been brought instead from the Marlborough Downs, some twenty kilometres to the north, at the centre of which stands Avebury. During the eighteenth century William Stukeley described a group of stones of appropriate size at Clatford, but these have since vanished, presumably broken up for building purposes. The construction of the distinctive sarsen settings at Stonehenge, together with the creation of the double bluestone circle, coincided with the principal period of activity at Durrington Walls. This place, located some three kilometres to the north-east of Stonehenge, is the largest of all Britain's henge monuments. It is nearly 500 metres in diameter, and encloses the head of a dry valley facing downhill eastwards towards the River Avon, and forming a natural amphitheatre (Fig. 5.22). But as with other henges, the enormous bank and ditch post-dates the most intensive activity on the site.

The settlement of small houses at the eastern entrance of the henge actually runs under the bank. Taken together with further occupation traces in other parts of the enclosure, this constituted a very large-scale occupation of the site indeed. The houses clustered around a broad 'track' made up of closely packed flint cobbles between two chalk banks, which led from the bank of the River Avon up to the large Southern Circle of timber uprights. Thus both Stonehenge and the Southern Circle, which share some architectural similarities, would eventually have been linked to the river by another kind of 'avenue', and might arguably constitute the two ends of a single passage of movement. Moreover, the two structures have complementary solstitial alignments, suggesting that there may have been particular times of year when it was appropriate for people (or, as Parker Pearson has suggested, the spirits of the dead) to pass from one to the other. The area later enclosed by the henge also contained the Northern Circle with its four huge central posts, and the western enclosures mentioned above, small buildings inside penannular ditches and palisades, arranged around the head of the valley.

Immediately to the south of Durrington Walls stood another large timber circle known as Woodhenge, which was, like The Sanctuary near Avebury, later replaced by a stone setting.

But at Woodhenge the stone circle was enclosed within its own henge ditch; and again nearby there were at least two substantial four-post timber structures (Fig. 5.23). So during the twenty-fifth century BC the Durrington Walls area contained numerous shrines, ceremonial buildings, and dwelling structures, and at times it must have been occupied by very significant numbers of people. The large-scale feasting mentioned earlier appears to have taken place principally at midwinter, and both cattle and pigs were brought to the settlement from elsewhere for consumption. Although many of the pigs at Durrington were quite young, the isotopic analysis of the teeth of both species indicates that only a minority of the animals had spent their lives on the Wessex chalk, and some had come from as far away as the south-west peninsula, or from Wales, or even from Cumbria and Scotland. It follows that people must also have walked these great distances, in some cases the same distances as travelled by the bluestones. Yet the radiocarbon evidence from Durrington Walls tells us that the entire sequence of activity was compressed into a period of less than fifty years. It is hard to escape the conclusion that the short-lived concentration of people, animals, and materials into this area represented a concerted political project, and that this project involved the mobilization of the labour necessary to construct the sarsen settings at Stonehenge.

Rather than seeing this undertaking as an end in itself, the precursor of the festivals that people feel drawn to recreate today, we should understand the creation of the sarsen monument as a means of drawing different groups into a greater community, perhaps thereby securing an overarching spiritual or political hegemony. This kind of unification 'project' could possibly also have been responsible for the construction of Silbury Hill, near to the existing henge at Avebury. Although Jim Leary and colleagues

Fig. 5.22 Durrington Walls from the south, next to Woodhenge

The view here is looking north across the suspended dry valley that became the site of the Durrington Walls henge-enclosure site close to the modern military encampment at Larkhill. The huge earthen embankment raised to define the perimeter of the henge-enclosure is visible in the background, curving around the head of the combe that descends steeply eastward down towards the River Avon. Woodhenge is just a few metres behind the photographer.

Photograph: June 2017, © Keith Ray.

have now demonstrated that this mound is only one of a series of such massive Late Neolithic conical monuments with a distribution concentrated around the chalk downs of the Avebury and Amesbury areas of Wiltshire, Silbury Hill remains the largest of the series (and is still the biggest artificial mound in Europe). It was built shortly after Stonehenge, in the twenty-fourth century BCE, and by that time the social order that had been created through resurrecting the ideas of house and household was facing quite new challenges.

Dye in the blood: the appearance of Beakers in Late Neolithic Britain

The closing centuries of the fourth millennium BCE have been termed the 'Beaker' age, and have often been classified as part of the 'Early Bronze Age' because of the appearance of a certain number of metal objects along with

these distinctive forms of pot, and the reappearance of a rite of burial that mainly involved the interment of a single, flexed body (Fig. 5.24).

More recently, debate has turned upon whether the period from around 2500 BCE can instead be defined as a British 'Chalcolithic', or 'Copper Age', in line with similar classifications in use in mainland Europe. In response, it has been pointed out that individual copper objects could in principle have found their way into Britain from at least the beginning of the third millennium BCE, and that also the numbers of such metal objects involved are very small: they do not represent a wholesale technological change. What is significant is that Beakers, as their name indicates, are a distinctive form of pottery with an upright, broadly tubular form that, on the one hand, does not have a direct equivalent from earlier periods and, on the other, had a near-contemporary pan-European presence. This is in marked contrast to the Grooved Ware vessels discussed earlier in this chapter that were an entirely British and Irish phenomenon. However, at least in the earliest centuries of the manufacture and use of Beakers in Britain, they were made and used alongside, that is contemporaneously with, Grooved Ware vessels. Moreover, although the two forms of pottery rarely occur together in the same contexts, Beakers, or more usually *pieces* of former Beaker vessels, are found time and again placed within Neolithic monuments of earlier date, especially in southern Britain.

Fig. 5.23 Woodhenge from the north: aerial view

Woodhenge is typical of henges featuring a ditch surrounded by an earthen bank (ditch now infilled and bank levelled) and with a single entrance, but is unusual (though with a parallel at 'Site IV' within the massive henge at Mount Pleasant to the east of Dorchester in Dorset) in having had the entire interior space filled by a series of concentric rings of upright timber posts (the positions of which are now marked by low cylindrical concrete markers). This view shows the massive Durrington Walls henge enclosure in the background, located immediately to the north of the Woodhenge circle.

Photograph: 2006, © Adam Stanford (website: http://www.aerial-cam.co.uk/).

While we can be sure that Beakers mark a horizon shared with, and an influence received from, continental Europe, it has proved difficult to argue on *purely archaeological* grounds that they represent a wholesale migration of people from the Continent to Britain. Two forms of evidence suggest that individuals did make the journey from Europe to Britain, however, and the incidence of this evidence is potentially very revealing of the multiplicity and diverse nature of the contacts concerned.

The first form of evidence is direct, and derives from the analysis of the skeletons of people interred in Beaker graves. The most striking instance of

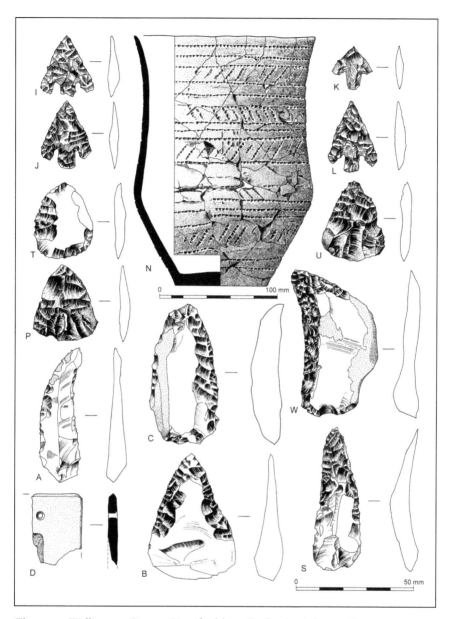

Fig. 5.24 Wellington Quarry, Herefordshire: Beaker burial assemblage

This drawing illustrates twelve of the sixteen flint implements (four barbed and tanged arrowheads, three arrowhead blanks, three flint knives, two triangular points, and four flint flakes) that were found accompanying the mostly decayed-away flexed burial laid in an oval grave-pit at Wellington Quarry. The flint objects were found placed around the corpse, together with the traces of a copper knife, a stone perforated wrist-guard fragment, and the Beaker pot placed at the feet of the body in the south-eastern extremity of the grave-pit. The Beaker is of the fine 'zone decorated' type with Iberian affinities and dates to around 2350–2200 BCE.

Drawing: Steve Rigby, © Worcestershire County Council (courtesy of Robin Jackson).

this so far known is the Amesbury Archer, buried not far from Stonehenge in the highly standardized flexed or crouched Beaker burial mode in an oval-shaped pit. Something that is striking about this burial, apart from the fact that the male individual may have been crippled by the loss of a patella (kneecap), is that when he was buried (sometime between 2470 and 2280 BCE) he was accompanied by a wide variety and great number of grave-gifts that included no fewer than five Beaker pots, fifteen fine barbed and tanged flint arrowheads, two edge-flaked flint knives, two stone wrist-guards or archery bracers, three copper daggers made of metal from two different sources, four boar's tusks, a 'cushion stone' of a type thought to have been used to work copper and gold, and two gold personal ornaments (basket-shaped earrings or hair-tresses). This is one of the most elaborate Beaker-associated grave assemblages found anywhere in Europe. Strontium analysis of his teeth enamel demonstrated that he was likely to have grown up in southern Germany or the Swiss Alps. Whether the status accorded to this individual was enjoyed in his lifetime or idealized at the point of enactment of his mortuary rites, he had clearly been accepted within the Salisbury Avon valley community after ranging a great distance from his homeland. It has been suggested that he was a craft or ritual specialist, perhaps (as a metalworker) having both these roles simultaneously. The correlation between metal items, metalworking tools, and elaborate burials is found widely in contemporary Europe, indicating that such people were held in high esteem. Nonetheless, although the Amesbury Archer burial is unusual for its richness and exoticism, the theatricality of the placement of grave-goods within an individual tomb is common to many Beaker graves.

The second form of evidence is the formal and decorative similarity between individual Beaker vessels found in Britain and other such vessels from Continental locations. An example is the AOC-LC (All-over Cord impressed Low Carinated) vessel from Newmill, Perthshire. This has a striking formal and decorative resemblance to a very few individual pots (of Dutch 2IIc style) from the Netherlands, including those found at Barger-Oosterveld (Emmen), at Soesterberg, Barrow 3 (Amersfoort), and at Aalten (Drenthe). This implies close links featuring individuals who have migrated from, or the presence of people who had visited, the Low Countries. Although made from local clays, the closeness in style evident in the Newmill and Dutch vessels makes it highly likely that the potter concerned made two pots at an interval of only a few months in widely separate locations and using local clays in both instances, and that in effect they replicated one another. This suggests that the networks of exchange that were developing at this time included the exchange of marriage partners and shifts in residence that cemented these contacts.

This does not automatically mean that such contacts between Britain and the near Continent were a novelty at this time, but rather that the pan-European nature of the making and using of Beakers made such linkages *visible*. The relatively rapid appearance of the Beaker phenomenon, and the close similarities of some aspects of practice (and in particular the eponymous vessels) across a wide area including the Netherlands, Germany, Belgium, (especially northern) France, Brittany, northern Italy, Spain and Portugal, Britain, and Ireland, has been explained in a number of ways apart from 'migration'. The variety of local practices that occurred in all these places indicates basic continuity of occupation and peopling, but it has been suggested that, rather, the use of Beakers became so widespread because it represented adherence to a cult, or suite of related ritual practices, or an ethos of prestige display. Furthermore, the large-scale isotopic study of Beaker burials across Britain has demonstrated that although an appreciable number of them had been interred in locations remote from their places of birth, there was no sudden 'arrival' of Beaker folk at the beginning of the period. Instead, there was a pattern of more or less consistent mobility on the part of a significant minority of individuals and small groups throughout the period between 2400 and 1500 BCE. Yet most of these had travelled far shorter distances than the Amesbury Archer, and it may occasion no surprise in the light of the discussions in the middle part of this chapter that a number of those buried in the Stonehenge area appear to have been brought up in western Wales.

Into this interpretive 'mix' there has recently been cast a bombshell: the claim based upon genetic studies that the Beaker phenomenon in Britain (and uniquely so in Europe) resulted in the near-total replacement of the indigenous, Neolithic population of Britain by the middle of the Bronze Age. This claim has arisen from an entirely different kind of study that has involved looking at the ancient DNA preserved in partial form in the bones of people who had lived in the fourth, third, and second millennia, and comparing it with modern populations. The study concerned, reported in 2017 in an article authored by an international team of 110 scientists and archaeologists, involved the analysis of DNA extracted from 170 prehistoric individuals across Europe, matched against a sample of 2,572 present-day individuals. Among the most interesting results of this study, in which a group of 100 Beaker-associated individuals was central to the 170 prehistoric people whose aDNA was tested, was the discovery that there was very limited genetic affinity between Iberian and central European Beaker-complex people. As a consequence it was concluded in the study that migration could be discounted as a significant factor in the spread of Beaker use and practices into and within Spain and Portugal.

However, in marked contrast to the Iberian situation, migration was understood as a result of this genetic study to have had an important role in the dissemination of the Beaker complex to, and within, Britain. The data from eighty newly analysed samples from prehistoric people in Britain dated to between 3900 BCE and 1200 BCE showed that British Neolithic farmers were closely similar genetically to contemporary populations in continental Europe, and in particular to Neolithic Iberians (see Chapter 2). But from the Beaker period onwards, this pattern changed to a much closer affinity to people of Steppe ancestry eastwards from central Europe: and it is this group that are claimed to have influenced the population genetics of most of north-central continental Europe. This mirrors the strong stylistic affinities evident in the material culture, and particularly the Beaker pots found in Britain, with the lower Rhine region that we have already alluded to. However, the genetic links with this region were found in the study to have been particularly strong, with fourteen of the nineteen individuals concerned having an especially close 'match' with populations (ancient and modern) from the area around Oostwoud (in Noord-Holland in the Netherlands). The most remarkable conclusion of the study, however, results from the investigation of the later (that is, 'post-Beaker') Early Bronze Age and Middle Bronze Age samples, from which the claim arose that the Beaker migrants and their descendants effected a 90 per cent replacement of Britain's Neolithic gene pool within a few hundred years.

If we are not yet entirely ready to tear up our observations from the preceding pages of this chapter concerning the Beaker phenomenon in Britain, it is to a large degree owing to the caveats acknowledged by the authors of the article concerned. Several concern the science around making comparisons between relatively few and fragmentary ancient DNA samples and modern populations. The biggest concerns that have already been voiced by archaeologists are nonetheless about the sampling biases inbuilt into the study. To begin with, the sample of British Beaker-associated skeletons was limited to nineteen individuals. Within these there was a strong imbalance between the 'Beaker' bodies sampled from eastern Britain (several) and western Britain (a handful). This is despite the strong indications of a western maritime element that may have linked western Britain and Ireland to populations in Iberia. Moreover, the samples are inevitably biased towards inhumations, for which the bones have survived sufficiently well preserved to enable aDNA to be extracted. And yet both during and after the 'Beaker period', cremations accounted for a considerable, if statistically uncertain, proportion of the population. So if the rite of cremation became a practice that was used to differentiate indigenous from migrant communities, the contribution of the former to the overall population would be systematically underestimated: and this would be a bias affecting the later samples as well as the earlier. Furthermore, both cremation burials and inhumations together only represent a small minority of the contemporary population who were treated preferentially in death. As is the case throughout the Neolithic, the great bulk of the people who lived and died during this period have not left tangible remains that are accessible to us. Those who were buried with Beaker vessels might easily constitute an elite of Continental origin who had imposed themselves on an indigenous population who are archaeologically invisible.

These concerns should not be taken to detract from the intrinsic interest and importance of aspects of the study, although the claim for what is in effect population replacement remains to be substantiated by future investigations. Whatever eventual further research produces, there can surely be no doubt that Beakers became a must-have kind of object, and their association in sites in both Scotland and England as containers with meadowsweet and other sweeteners, and their cup-like form, have led to the suggestion that the cultic practice concerned involved the consumption of quantities of intoxicating beverages (Fig. 5.25).

Appealing though this interpretation is (especially to a generation of British archaeologists habituated to the personal consumption of sometimes prodigious quantities of real ale), given that the size-trend for Beakers is much smaller than the bucket-like Grooved Ware, it does not necessarily explain the ubiquity of Beaker vessels in a variety of contexts. At least equally likely is the possibility that it is bound up instead with the emergence of a category of people of special repute, probably as metalworkers and ritual specialists, who in some cases were connected with cult practices including performative archery. The perhaps deliberately emphasized exoticism of such individuals, and the practices they were associated with, may therefore have been emulated by very many individuals and their kin

Fig. 5.25 Selection of Beaker pots found in Wales

The seven Beakers illustrated here are from sites in Bridgend, from Carmarthenshire, and from Glamorgan, Denbighshire, and Powys, and they are all now in the collections of N.M.W. The pots mostly accompanied burials in stone cists, some with other grave goods, some alone. They range in height from 16 to 20 cm, and in date from c.2400 to 2150 BCE (the handled Beaker at right, from Cwm Du in Breconshire, is probably the latest in date).

Composite photographic image: © Amgueddfa Cymru—National Museum Wales.

through the possession and use of these distinctive vessels in what was nonetheless a wide variety of places and circumstances. In other words, simple emulation and prestige-association, rather than adherence to a particular religious or cultic practice, may have been the mechanism by which the practice of Beaker-using spread so rapidly.

Despite this variation in the context and location of use, there is a sense in which the Beaker burial rite was both standardized and stereotypical. The body posture, the presence of the Beaker vessel in a specific location in the grave, and the addition of other items from a rather restricted repertoire indicate adherence to a widely accepted way of representing a person in death. In some cases, the identity that was being constructed in the funerary performance was clearly at variance with reality. Some of those who were buried with archery equipment possessed infirmities that would have precluded them from ever using a bow. More generally, the emphasis on warlike paraphernalia (battleaxes, metal and flint daggers, arrowheads, and wrist-guards) conflicts with the rather limited incidence of skeletal trauma amongst these burials. Apparently there was appreciably less interpersonal violence in the Beaker era than in the Early Neolithic period. Fascinatingly, it has now been demonstrated that the 'round' skull shape that was once seen as an indication that the 'Beaker folk' were a distinct racial group is more likely to be the result of deliberate cranial deformation in infancy. Seemingly, both in life and death, considerable importance was now being attached to personal appearance, as a means of securing one's recognition as a person of importance.

Both single crouched burials in pits with grave-gifts and small round barrows were a feature of insular British funerary practice in the later fourth millennium. Equally, massive round mounds at Marlborough, Knowlton, Droughduil, and the Conquer Barrow at Mount Pleasant, Dorset, formed part of the suite of Late Neolithic monumental architecture, alongside henges, palisaded enclosures, and timber circles (Fig. 5.26).

These mounds might easily have inspired a return to funerary mound building on a smaller scale. Yet as we have seen, from 3000 BCE onwards most of the funerary deposits identified in Britain are cremations, and the size of most round barrows was, relatively speaking, rather modest. Conversely, in both Corded Ware and Beaker times in areas such as the Lower Rhine, flexed burials with accompanying pots are found both in isolated pit-graves and beneath small round mounds. It is therefore possible to cast British Beaker mortuary practices as either a deliberate throwback to long-established traditions, or something new and intrusive. The impression of a continuing link to local ritual practices from the Neolithic is reinforced by the evidence for the reopening of some pits, the removal of some bones, and the insertion of bones from elsewhere (the Amesbury Archer, for instance, had a rib removed at some point subsequent to his burial). And yet there were significant changes in practice, as with the emergence in Britain of the placing of wooden chambers, or coffins, as containers for the body in the burial pit, a phenomenon well attested across Europe. Beakers are a frequent accompaniment to these burials, but not in all cases, and from around 2300 BCE cremated bone was often placed into graves otherwise containing inhumations.

Although the Beaker rite of crouched inhumation and orchestrated funerary display including flint knives, barbed and tanged flint arrowheads, and stone 'wrist-bracers' was a novelty widely evident in Britain from around 2400 BCE, contemporary burials occurred in other forms and places, including in monuments that had last been used up to a millennium earlier,

Fig. 5.26 Droughduil mound, Galloway, under excavation

Droughuil, on the edge of the extensive dune system of Luce Sands beside Luce Bay in Galloway, is a large tumulus that had formerly been identified as a medieval motte, or castle mound. However, the avenue of timbers making up one of the entrances of the Dunragit palisaded enclosure, 400 metres to the north, was aligned precisely on the mound. Excavation in 2002 demonstrated that the sides of the structure were stepped, and optically stimulated luminescence dating (OSL) (which identifies the period of time since grains of quartz and feldspar had last been exposed to sunlight) on the base of the mound gave a date of approximately 2520 BCE. This indicates that the mound was indeed an element of the Late Neolithic monument complex, comparable to the much larger Silbury Hill in Wiltshire.
Photograph: 2002, © Julian Thomas.

such as causewayed enclosures and long barrows. Meanwhile there were numerous cases of insertion of pieces of Beaker pottery and characteristic flintwork in pits and midden-spreads in such places. The frequency of occurrence of such referencing of earlier monuments is such as to render unlikely the notion that this was a deliberate attempt to legitimate incoming groups by identifying with or appropriating these earlier remains. Rather, it suggests that there were manifest and continuing links between the people who were burying their dead at this time, and their ancestral communities.

What, then, do Beakers tell us about the 'ending' of the Neolithic in Britain? To whatever extent migration was a factor in the changes observable for the later third millennium BCE, Beakers do mark the beginning of a significant change in the nature of the communities and their activities from that time onwards. This represented to some degree a break with earlier traditions, with the ending of some long-established practices, and especially the Grooved Ware-associated creation of major monument complexes. However, there was also a renewed emphasis on some other well-attested practices and the amplification of certain trends. So while the particular kinds of gathering and feasting associated with the making and breaking of Grooved Ware appear to have faded away in this period, Beaker pots were often smashed and their pieces placed in (for example) the re-dug tops of causewayed enclosure ditches, as well as isolated pits. Changes in farming practice seem also to have been taking place in at least some parts of Britain at this time, such that while the attachment to cattle and feasting associated with the accumulation of herds continued unabated in some areas, there appears to have been renewed interest in cereal cultivation, and hints of the emergence of fixed plots farmed on short rotations.

This perhaps quite localized 'stabilization' of arable cultivation was mirrored in the forms of inhabitation represented by buildings, again drawing upon but amplifying earlier traditions of practice. So it is that roundhouses comparable in size to the buildings found at Neolithic sites such as Trelystan close to the English–Welsh border in Powys around the turn of the third millennium BCE begin to appear in greater numbers towards the close of that millennium, this time associated with Beaker pottery. Moreover, other practices attested in the Neolithic, such as the heating of stones in a fire and their immediate transfer to large containers of water to heat it for cooking (with a resulting accumulation of shattered burnt stones), or for the processing of fibres to create fabrics, become more common and more widespread at just this time. The focus upon such practices presages changes to a whole suite of activities that we tend to think of as being associated with the Bronze Age, not least the development of barrow cemeteries that differ markedly from the repositories of the remains of (some of) the ancestral dead that characterize the Neolithic. Often these barrows comprise a sequence that includes an originating inhumation burial, later covered over by a mound, followed by the later insertion of subsequent 'mortuary' deposits (most often of cremated bone) that reference that primary burial, or the mound itself. In very many cases, that originating burial comprised an inhumation featuring the 'Beaker' rite of a flexed corpse accompanied by the eponymous vessel. The cumulative addition of more barrows, and further subsequent burial deposits, nonetheless presents another aspect of continuity. The continuing theme is the emphasis upon descent and lineage, and its marking, or mapping, monumentally. The overriding impression across both fourth and third millennia is that there remained a concern with the charting of inheritance, and through that, the tracing of a lineal history: and it is this creation and sustaining of history that the next chapter will focus upon.

SIX

Kinship, history, and descent

Chapter frontispiece: 'Cows and Daisies' (wood-engraving, Hilary Paynter)

Cattle were an extremely important resource in Neolithic Britain, and the wood-engraver's image here captures the essence of black cattle happily at graze in rich meadows.

Engraving: 1964, © Hilary Paynter (website: http://www.hilarypaynter.com).

For traditional societies, by which we mean those peoples whose worlds are permeated by kin relations and obligations, and among whom past societies such as those of Neolithic Britain are mostly to be counted, the most precious inheritance is knowledge. Inherited knowledge is of many kinds, the most overt of which is instrumental knowledge—how to make a rope from fibre, where to look for and how to utilize medicinal plants, and so on. Alongside this, however, is a plurality of less obvious but equally fundamental *knowledges* that include kinds of behavioural knowledge (in the sense of customs and prohibitions, for example), forms of discursive awareness (how to negotiate the social world; what to recall and recount as story and history), and understandings of esoteric beliefs and their concomitant 'necessary' actions. Collective cultural and customary knowledge, then, is a resource that makes possible the sustaining and renewal of human social relationships through time.

There is a modern tendency to see history as a progression of tableaux, or a montage of scenes, a cavalcade; or, as we noted in Chapter 1, an ascent through measurable social evolutionary stages from relative cultural simplicity towards a present of multilayered complexity. In the modern world, history is expressed in the form of narratives that have been standardized and systematically ordered, and published in a diversity of media, as well as being contested by alternative perspectives in print and online. This contrasts with the way that knowledge and tradition are conveyed in societies that lack written literature, which generally takes the form of oral transmission. However, they are also expressed and fixed (however fleetingly) and transformed through the use of material items and material culture, including the built environment. For such societies, history may take the form of a shared memory of significant events, but these are always experienced and mediated through the filters of social relationships of dominance and subordination, and of kinship. This latter is composed of the shifting elements of genealogy, lineage, and descent, although any or all of these may be fictional in character, and open to a degree of manipulation.

The challenge in writing the history of un-historicized peoples (that is, people whose history has not been written for them, or has indeed been written over their heads), and particularly those in remote time, is to try to approach the substance of their social reproduction in a tangible way. As we have already suggested, the writing of Neolithic history in Britain involves an identification and exploration of forms of practice attested from the artefacts and residues that were created by those temporally distant people.

Fig. 6.1 Silbury Hill, Wiltshire, with Windmill Hill in the distance

This photograph shows not only the remarkable conical mound built on the very end of a northwards-trending promontory intersected by the A4 Bath Road, but also the Neolithic time-depth that is traceable in this landscape. Beyond Late Neolithic Silbury Hill and to the right, on the hill on the horizon, for example, is the site of the causewayed enclosure at Windmill Hill (marked also from this angle by two prominent Bronze Age round barrows). These two sites differ not only in their material manifestation (one a series of concentric rings of ditches and low banks, the other a prominent and tall flat-topped mound), but also by the fact that they are separated in time by up to 800 years.
Photograph: June 2015, © Keith Ray.

In this chapter, the aim is to distil some understanding of the dynamics of social interrelations from an appreciation of particularity and difference in cultural practices through time: sometimes in one location, and sometimes through a comparison of events and processes at more than one place. The aim is also to see how the passing of time was historicized by the Neolithic people whose remains we encounter.

Beginning with trees: encapsulating a hunting and gathering past

We have identified a central paradox of the century or so either side of 4000 BCE (which continued to be important until at least 3800), that we can recognize continuity in some Mesolithic traditions and practices at a time when major transformations were also taking place, affecting the same communities. This is seen principally in the reuse (and perhaps veneration) of ancestral places, sometimes selected for the building of specialized structures, as well as in the continued practice of hunting and the collection of wild foodstuffs. Red deer continue to make an appearance in the deposits formed by Neolithic communities: yes, occasionally as foodstuffs, but also as another among those kinds of animal whose bones, in some circumstances (but not as frequently as those of cattle), could be appropriate to bury along with those of people, and also in particular whose shed antlers appear to have been the preferred tool for prising out lumps of the earth, chalk, and rock in the digging of pits and ditches. Moreover, the resource of hazelnuts was harvested, as formerly in 'hunting and collecting' times: but in the Neolithic, as we have already noted, these nuts became, in their charred form, a substance that recurs time and again in contexts that suggest that their presence was a requirement for the formation of the residues concerned rather than an incidental result of otherwise prosaic practical activity.

The opportunities associated with living in an environment in which forests continued to exist, but that had in many places already by 4000 BCE taken on a park-like open or scrubby aspect, have recently attracted some comment. Mike Allen and Julie Gardiner have noted, for example (based upon studies including analysis of tree pollen, surviving ancient land snail shells, and preserved ancient soils), that a pattern of human exploitation of a mosaic of vegetation and tree cover emerged in the later Mesolithic in some of the chalklands of southern Britain that continued to be frequented in the Neolithic. Within this mosaic were some locations where quite extensive grasslands opened up alongside tracts of woodland, such that the interface between them would have encouraged the growth of hazel and of the berry-bearing plants of the woodland margins. This in turn would have attracted herd animals, providing perfect browsing conditions, and there would have been an incentive therefore for people to congregate in these areas. Meanwhile, elsewhere, such as in the East Anglian fenland, continuities have been observed from the Late Mesolithic to the Early Neolithic in the use of tree-throw holes both as repositories for possibly midden-derived material and as locations (marked also by post- and stake-holes) for temporary periodic dwelling.

Early to mid fourth-millennium structures such as long barrows and causewayed enclosures were in some places created in new clearings from mature woodland. One way to regard this is to see this process as a deliberate placing of such structures in areas that were marginal to settlement, and as the 'domestication' of wilder or more remote areas. However, although in some regions causewayed enclosures were constructed peripherally in relation to concentrations of other kinds of monument (Hambledon Hill, on the edge of the chalk upland of Cranborne Chase, being a case in point), they were not always created in woodland clearings. Others were built within regenerated woodland, or in the scrubland margins of extensive areas of woodland, or, apparently, in areas such as the north Wiltshire downs and Salisbury Plain, places that featured long-established grazed grassland.

The Sweet Track: histories in and between *place*

Careful dendrochronological study of selected oak and ash timbers (those which featured the best-preserved sapwood) from five of the six excavated trenches dug along the course of the Sweet Track in the Somerset Levels has revealed that the Track was built either late in 3807 BCE or sometime during 3806 BCE, and was in use for only around ten years (Fig. 6.2).

The 'Track' is in fact a raised walkway of narrow oak planks placed end to end, supported by a cross-work of rods and poles in other species of wood, and extending for nearly two kilometres northwards from the Polden Hills to Westhay island across the reed and sedge marsh. It is conceivable that the clearance of the trees attested around this time on the Poldens and along the length of Westhay island, as well as the coppicing of the hazel also used in the construction of the walkway, were Early Neolithic innovations locally. Yet there were disturbances of the local vegetation in the decades and centuries preceding this and there have been unequivocally Mesolithic flints found in those same places where the trees were cleared.

The building of the raised walkway evidently resulted from the wish or the need to cross the marshlands between areas of drier ground. It has been estimated experimentally that once the major timber components had been cut and stored, ten people could have carried the timber for its construction along its course, and have built it in place within a week. Whether or not this was the case, it was in part the narrowness of the track that enabled it to be built relatively quickly. Yet even so its 1.8-km-long course was estimated to have contained over 4,000 metres of planks, 2,000 metres of heavy rails, and 6,000 roundwood or split pegs and at the least this attests to a high degree of organization of people and coordination of efforts. Moreover, its short span of use nonetheless featured enough traffic in both directions (and passing with difficulty) that an appreciable number

Fig. 6.2 The Sweet Track: as excavated (left) and reconstruction

Several lengths of the Sweet Track were revealed and investigated in a series of research excavations directed by John and Bryony Coles in the early 1970s. In this illustration, a drawing of the excavated timber trackway is on the left, and a drawing of a reconstruction of the track as built is on the right. The oak planks that provided the level upper walkway were around 3 m in length, and the crossed pairs or groups of thin wooden pegs that cradled the planks at regular intervals were a mix of oak, ash, poplar, hazel, dogwood, and elm. Long thin 'fixing' rails up to 4 m in length had been set underneath the trackway first, to stabilize the marsh.

Drawing: Tim Hoverd.

of items were dropped and lost. The patterns and character of loss (in soft marshy ground that soon converted to peat, thus preserving organic remains) provide rare glimpses of the ebb and flow of activity in different parts of the landscape. Mixed and relatively dense woodland characterized the southern end of the trackway, and it was in the southern one-third of its course that all the wooden bows and the leaf-shaped flint arrowheads found during the archaeological excavations of the 1970s were encountered (some arrow-heads with fragments of the hazel-rod shafts still adhering to them).

Although it may be the case that the ubiquitous presence of dung-beetles indicates that cattle were driven along (or rather alongside) the walkway, it is also evident that it was a focus for deposition (accidental or otherwise) involving whole bowls, axes, flint arrowheads, and a number of wooden artefacts. It is, however, the presence of another, slightly earlier, timber trackway, the Pole Track, whose remains were disrupted and displaced, and then partly incorporated into the later walkway, that indicates the likelihood of a continuity of practice here from before such loss of the Early Neolithic items. The Pole Track followed a course immediately adjacent to, parallel with, and partially under the course of the Sweet Track, and its timbers have been dated to only some thirty years earlier, around 3838 BCE. Its excavators suggested that this stratigraphically earlier work was in fact an access structure that enabled the Sweet Track to be built, and that the difference in dates of the wood indicates merely that the timber used for it had been stored in preparation for the 'main' construction event. This seems to us to be inherently unlikely, however. Rather, it indicates that the need or desire to reach an otherwise not easily accessible location from the higher ground to the south (when the marshland waters rose in winter, the trackway became impassable) was one that spanned generations of people. This suggests in turn that rather than being entirely an innovation, both trackways were replicating and reproducing an access-route of some historical time-depth. Time-depth is marked also in the growing and harvesting of the wood used in construction of the Sweet Track, since the hazel was clearly coppiced, and the hazel pole tree-ring evidence indicates that the trees concerned were in existence up to (or had been growing from boles as long ago as) twenty-five years before the trackway was built. Moreover, the oak had come from two different areas of woodland: at the northern end of the trackway, large mature oaks had been cut down to produce the planks, while at the southern end, the oaks were young.

As such, as well as solving the practical problem of crossing marshy ground from one dry place to another, the Sweet Track can be understood as referencing in a dramatic way a historicity of action in place, and perhaps the continuing importance of access not simply to grazing but also to the resources, both vegetative and game, that the seasonally inundated Levels environment had from time immemorial afforded. And yet surely it was a lot of effort to expend to build such an extensive track simply to access the western end of Westhay island from the Polden Hills to the south. Is it possible, rather, that it was a time-honoured place to access for superordinate reasons? The excavators argued for the prosaic in the interpretation of their finds, but we find it difficult to envisage what practical reason would have induced people to carry along such a narrow and difficult raised walkway a pot full of porridge with its wooden spurtle intact, or indeed to transport several other fine thin-walled vessels (some of which had been painted in different colours and were found intact), two unused axeheads from exotic sources, or, for that matter, a model (assumed toy) wooden axe or 'tomahawk' (see 'The art of transformation in skeuomorphic practices' in Chapter 4), and then curiously to have dropped all these items closely beside, and sometimes actually tucked underneath, the track. What we can envisage instead here is the need to access an otherwise remote location that may indeed have served immemorially as a hunting station (though the bows and arrows were all found at the landward end), or newly created summer grazing grounds, but that also had a special place in the hearts and minds of those people who were prepared to go to such lengths to reach that place through the swampy morasses. The trackway was made necessary by a climatic change that led to a phase of increasing inundation of what we now think of as the peat-filled Levels: but what the Pole and the Sweet tracks indicate is that there was an overriding reason that caused them, for a brief period of a few decades until access by this means was rendered impossible, to create a humanly constructed facility to continue to visit a place that had an inherited importance, probably from millennia before. In this way, the significance of an honoured (potentially even Mesolithic) past was encapsulated in a task that may have not taken a huge amount of time to execute, but that involved the deployment of considerable forethought, effort, and resource to achieve.

'In the kinship of cows' revisited

In 2003 we, the authors of this book, published an account of why we thought that cattle in particular were of pre-eminent social and cultural importance to at least some societies in southern Britain during the Earlier Neolithic period. The evidence that had led us to this conclusion included the way that the remains of cattle had been deposited in a variety of 'structured' ways, had been placed alongside the bones of humans, and in some cases had been treated as equivalents for humans. For example, it is now evident that the so-called 'head and hooves' associated with the burial deposit at the Fussell's Lodge long barrow actually consisted of two separate deposits. The skull of an ox had been placed at the eastern end of the mortuary structure, while the foot bones from on top of the flint cairn that covered this structure were apparently later in date, and may have formed part of a hide draped over the cairn. Here, the deposition of cattle remains together with humans was evidently a *recurrent* practice. By contrast, at the Amesbury 42 long barrow near the Greater Stonehenge Cursus, the antiquary John Thurnam reported a deposit of cattle bones that appeared to substitute for any human burials. We went on to pose a variety of questions about the occurrence of cattle bones in particular contexts, and we noted how in some cases the cattle bones had seemingly been curated over extended periods of time, up to a century or more. We envisaged cattle as representing an important resource to Neolithic people, a form of wealth as well as sustenance that was mobile and managed, and that could be employed as gifts, as feasts, or to acquire followers. The destinies of animals and their herders were intertwined through the transmitted knowledge of breeding and rearing. But the bones of cattle were also a resource, as by analogy with recent historic cattle-herding peoples, the blood-stock and lineage of animals are a matter of the greatest possible interest. Moreover, the composition of a herd represents a physical reminder of relationships and transactions between people. Cattle herds are therefore a repository of collective history, and the bones of the animals from these herds a tangible trace of this history.

Where the bones of past individual cows had been retained for long periods, they might constitute a resource of memory, and especially a mnemonic of past cattle populations, in a way that paralleled the retention and apparent circulation of some of the bones of dead humans as representative of the ancestral remains of past human communities. In a sense, the storing and circulation of the bones of humans and cattle reinforced each other: the herds with their own patterns of (bred) descent reflected the ancestral human individuals and communities (with their own associated patterns of familial descent) that had kept and bred them. This close relationship between people and animals might simply have been reflected in the careful burial of cattle bones, but it was made more conspicuous by their placement alongside human corpses. Further, it was the curation of cattle bones over long periods that demonstrates that this activity was related to descent.

The precise radiocarbon dating of cattle bone is infrequent, so the presence of individual curated cow bones in the Neolithic has rarely been recognized. It is for this reason (the rarity of dating of individual cattle bones) that it is specifically at Stonehenge that the deliberate placing of two 'ancestral' cattle jaws dated to the fourth millennium in the primary ditch at the first Stonehenge monument (that had nonetheless demonstrably been dug at the end of the fourth millennium) has been demonstrated. The importance of understanding the dating and phasing of a key context at such an important site meant that the cattle bones found in that context were dated: not primarily through interest in the cattle, but simply that their bones provided suitable material for obtaining chronological information. But having dated those bones, and having demonstrated that they were far older than the context in which they had been placed (which also yielded 'younger' dates on other material), the curatorial genie was let out of the bottle, so to speak. So there was deliberate retention and re-deposition of ancient cattle bones, even if the 'curation' concerned was among other debris within middens. In this connection it is perhaps significant that the ox skull from Fussell's Lodge is noted as having been 'very soiled', and had therefore perhaps been exhumed or brought from elsewhere before deposition.

Such demonstrable curatorial practice, and perhaps also the scratched markings on cattle bones from the ditches of the Fen-edge enclosure at Etton near Peterborough, or the three carefully laid out ox skulls beneath the Beckhampton Road long barrow near Avebury, recorded more than the keeping and breeding of those animals, however. It may also have evoked the series of transactions (alliances, marriages, funerals, gifts, and barter) and events (feasts, raids, and shifts of residence) that had given rise to the particular composition of stock represented by those cattle remains. The power of the metaphorical connection—'cattle bones represent herds and record kinship relations over time'—resides in the degree to which both cattle and people were seen to share a traceable (in the sense of avowed and acknowledged) kinship and a shared, even corporate, history.

In the Stonehenge area, Sarah Viner and colleagues have carried out strontium isotope analysis study of the tooth enamel of thirteen Late Neolithic cattle teeth from jawbones recently excavated at Durrington Walls. This indicates at least the possibility that cattle herds were brought together on Salisbury Plain from some distance away, given that eleven of the teeth were from cattle raised beyond the chalklands of southern Britain, even from as far afield as Cumbria and the Scottish Highlands. Pigs were also brought to the site for consumption, but the available evidence suggests that 70 per cent of these came from within a distance of two days' walk. That a bigger percentage of the cattle were brought from further away perhaps indicates the importance of an assembly of herds of different origin. This would have provided a context for the display of animals, and for the cementing of alliances and the sustaining of relationships between different groups, as well as for conducting the exchanges that facilitated the tracing of bloodstock through social relations extending over considerable spans of distance and time.

Times and lives: some clues concerning Neolithic concepts of time

That Neolithic people experienced the passing of time is undoubted, at the very least through diurnal and seasonal rhythms and the passage of the life cycle through birth, childhood, coming of age, reproduction, and death.

Fig. 6.3 Loughcrew Neolithic cairns and the view across the Vale of Meath

The cairn cemetery located on a hilltop west of Kells overlooking the Vale of Meath to the north-west of Dublin is one of the most impressive cemeteries of Neolithic circular kerbed and passage cairns anywhere in Ireland (or beyond). The stones of both the passages and the chambers of some of the larger cairns were favoured locations for the creation of rock-art featuring designs with affinities with earlier structures on the western Atlantic fringes of continental Europe and contemporary parallels in the Boyne valley passage tombs nearby and further afield on Anglesey in north Wales.

Photograph: © Adam Stanford (website: http://www.aerial-cam.co.uk/).

Much writing about the Neolithic, especially in Britain, has been devoted to pondering why certain features of chambered tombs, for example, are oriented and built in such a way that, at sunrise or sunset at key seasonal junctures such as midsummer and midwinter, shafts of light penetrate into the furthest recesses.

Ideas of rebirth and even spiritual resurrection may have been behind such considerable efforts to produce the desired effects. Much less attention has been paid, however, to a related question that is ostensibly equally unanswerable. That is, did Neolithic people in Britain possess or develop any *theories* about time? While there can be no certain answers to this question, we should perhaps not simply ignore the clues that may be present.

One such clue that has been noted often as a remarkable presence, but has rarely been commented upon further in terms of its potential significance, is the placement of a slab-like Jurassic limestone monolith containing much of a large fossil ammonite in a prominent position in the façade of the chambered tomb at Stoney Littleton just to the south of Bath in Somerset (Fig. 6.4).

The long barrow is some thirty metres long and is unusual in that it occupies sloping ground above the Wellow Brook that flows north-eastwards to join the River Avon some five kilometres away. The passage is unusually elongated, and it is likely that the seven 'transepted' chambers each had numbers of skeletal parts deposited within them in the manner that the West Kennet barrow did (Figure 3.12). Two aspects of this stone placement and barrow-arrangement merit special mention. The first is that the forecourt of the tomb not only occupies the break of slope, such that it is the only part of the barrow that is prominent when approached from the east; and that the barrow is so oriented south-eastwards that the early morning sunlight at certain times of the year falls directly upon it. The second aspect is that the 'half' of the ammonite within the stone actually forms the southern jamb of the entrance. This arrangement can hardly be considered accidental, and the ammonite itself in this way would have 'greeted' the deceased as their remains were inserted into the barrow. It is, of course, impossible to know what this signified, but it seems at least possible that the spiral fossil was given such prominence as a metaphor both for the passage of time and for the eternal cycle of death and rebirth.[1]

It could, of course, be claimed that this was a one-off expression of such possible ideas, and that the featuring of spiral patterns in Later Neolithic

1. Note the Aveline's Hole double-burial ammonites here: see the reference in the Bibiographical commentary.

Fig. 6.4 Stoney Littleton long barrow, Wellow, Somerset: forecourt

The 30-m-long Stoney Littleton long barrow is located on the south side of the Wellow Brook to the south of Bath and to the north-east of the Mendip Hills. It occupies an unusual position sited facing up the slope above the stream, with its façade and forecourt on the crest of the slope facing southwards. Beyond the centre of the deeply in-turned dry-stone walled façade a 13-m-long passage provides access to seven chambers, three on each side and one at the end. The fossil ammonite can be seen at lower left centre, just above ground level. It was excavated in the early years of the nineteenth century and restored in 1858 by Thomas Joliffe: by inscriptions built into the fabric of the tomb.

Photograph: © Adam Stanford (website: http://www.aerial-cam.co.uk/).

passage tombs was merely a consequence of decorative play. However, Anne Teather has recently highlighted another example, this time involving the *representation* of what looks like a fossil ammonite rendered upon a chalk block. This object was discovered at The Trundle causewayed enclosure on the South Downs near Goodwood north of Chichester in 1931 by an excavation team led by Cecil Curwen. It was found at the base of the ditch of the innermost circuit, along with a chalk cup, another perforated chalk block, a number of other smaller blocks, and a mass of charcoal. The inner circuit is thought to be the first to have been dug, and the dates obtained are among the earliest for causewayed enclosures anywhere in Britain. The block itself, measuring thirty centimetres across, took the form of a C-shape with a broad semi-circular central void created by smoothly hollowing out the chalk. Around the upper lip of this void was a raised band, beyond which radiated a series of striations made with a sharp flint tool. These lines were carefully etched only five centimetres in length, and were arranged in batches of four or five striations each, set in such a way as to imitate the whorls of an ammonite.

The metaphors literally embedded within these 'ammonite' features may have been mirrored, if not in terms of exactly similar references, in other practices of placement. Here it may be instructive to return to the suggested metaphorical placement of the 'grave goods' of a hammer stone and knapped flint nodule or core possibly in the hands (or arm-crook in the case of the core) of the so-called 'flint-knapper' burial that had been laid in the north chamber of the completely excavated Hazleton long barrow in the Cotswolds, discussed in Chapter 4. This could indeed have referenced the adult male concerned as a particularly skilful knapper of flints in life, or it could have made a more general reference to the art and practice of flint-knapping. It might also have been that the decision to include the pieces was reflective of the point at which that person died: in 'mid-knap', so to speak (without trying to make light of the circumstance). However, another twist to the metaphors embedded within the act of knapping may also have been referenced here, in a particular way reflecting the passage of time and life. This is because the core concerned comprised not a completely, nor even nearly completely, knapped nodule. Rather, it was half-knapped: and this may have been expressive of the idea that the knapping of a flint nodule was like the living of a life. The adult male was not young, but neither was he senescent. Could it not be therefore that what was being connoted by this particular selection of a core and arrangement of the objects concerned was the passage of a life only half-lived and a decease that was premature?

Identity and descent implicated in the placing of pottery

In Chapter 4 we noted that the ceramic vessels of Neolithic Britain were not created randomly, but that their manufacture and surface embellishment appear to form a series of stylistic 'traditions'. These styles find expression, for example, in different pre-firing pot-building techniques, ways of incorporating fluxing agents such as crushed rock fragments, the creation of a range of related shapes and forms, the incorporation of particular treatments such as burnishing of surfaces or the eversion (that is, out-turning) of rims, and the use of particular devices or patterns of decoration. Archaeologists have long observed that these traditions of manufacture tend to have a characteristic life cycle, of appearance, reproduction, elaboration, and decline. In the era before the introduction of chronometric dating, much effort was put into the relative ordering and temporal sequencing of styles, as a means of establishing a chronological framework for prehistoric times. While in the case of the British Neolithic the results of these procedures were less finely grained than in other periods and regions, different pot styles were also believed to provide clues to the identity of the different groups of people who made and used them, in terms of isolable 'cultures'. The decline of this culture-historical way of differentiating communities of people from the formal characteristics of their artefacts transformed discussions of the 'style' of material things within archaeology. Increasingly, the sharing of decorative motifs or manufacturing techniques was identified as reflecting the extent to which different social groups had been engaged in interaction, while the stylistic idiosyncrasies of individual objects were attributed to ways in which people conveyed information about their personal identities.

While the habitual replication of pottery forms and decoration is no longer automatically seen as indicative of bounded cultural identities in the past, it does nonetheless provide us with clues concerning how the practices through which pots were made, distributed, used, and discarded were maintained over time. Of these, it is necessarily the discard or disposal of pottery that is most often represented in the form of residues encountered by archaeologists. For the most part, broken pots have been recognized as a diagnostic indicator of deposits that might be defined as 'rubbish', whether these are pits, dumps, or middens. As we saw in Chapter 4, these perceptions have been altered to some degree by the explicit consideration of structured or intentional deposition. It is now generally acknowledged that the kinds and quantities of objects placed in various contexts were sometimes subject to a degree of selection, and that in some cases choices were made regarding *the way in which* items should be deposited. So the arrangement of sherds from broken vessels in such a way as to appear to be lining the early fourth-millennium BCE Coneybury pit near Stonehenge, for example, appears far from random. While entire vessels were only rarely deposited in pits or the segments of causewayed enclosure ditches, the fragments that were selected

for deposition were frequently those that were most diagnostic of a particular style of pot (rims, carination, decorated portions). The relationship
between the deposited sherd and the entire pot was clearly significant, and
the former might be said to be representative of the latter. As we saw in the
case of Kilverstone in Chapter 4, the distribution of conjoining potsherds
between different pits within a single site has sometimes been charted
systematically. Parts of pots were separated and recombined, and this process
arguably had a deeper significance. For the histories of manufacture and use
of individual pots, and the associations of specific types of pots, were introduced into these depositional contexts, perhaps becoming fused together
there. Such practices were 'knowledgeable', without necessarily always
entering the realm of explicit and conscious awareness, as already noted.

The way in which styles of decoration have been deployed on pots and
reproduced over time has sometimes been identified as an example of
'information redundancy': important for the maintenance and reproduction
of the style, but possessing little intrinsic significance. If you were to ask (as
many an ethnographer has) a traditional potter why he or she decorates a
pot in a particular way, the answer would probably consist of reasons such as
'custom' or the aesthetic pleasure of producing 'a good pot'. However, the
pots that were produced during the mature stages of the British Neolithic
often suggest that style was being manipulated in quite deliberate ways. It
appears that particular stylistic devices were recognized as specifically and
self-consciously expressive of a known and celebrated tradition that carried
into the present not only 'memory' but also connotation, from past practice.
The emergence of novel forms of pottery may indicate the proliferation of
new contexts for the use and display of ceramics, over and above the routine
patterns of production, circulation, and discard. One example is the relatively rapid elaboration, including sometimes profuse surface decoration, of
several kinds of pot among the repertoire of mid fourth-millennium BCE
plain bowl and bag-shaped forms, and their association with the deposition
of other items, and human and animal bones, within a novel form of monument, the causewayed enclosure.

In the past, archaeologists have been attached to the idea that one style of
pottery has ultimately been replaced by another that has become more
'fashionable'. A more interesting variant of this argument is the suggestion
that specific kinds of pot acquired a high status or prestige when they
were newly introduced, but that this was gradually eroded, allowing them
to be superseded by innovating styles over time. However, the *re-placing* of

pots (or sherds thereof) from an 'earlier' tradition in the same contexts as later styles appears to have been a practice that occurred widely in the third millennium. This is most notably the case with the co-occurrence of Peterborough Ware and Grooved Ware. The highly structured and elaborated character of some such practices has been traced and investigated closely in modern studies at particular sites and locations, and this will be discussed at greater length below, in the discussion of deliberate curation.

The creation, incorporation, and embodiment of the 'House'

The idea that the corporate expression of family, kinship, and descent can and should be marked by the metaphor of the 'House' is one that has a long lineage in European history, being made explicit in literary works in Greece from at least the fifth century BCE. Arguably, its origins can be traced back to the first Neolithic longhouses of continental Europe, and in Britain to the founding halls that have already been discussed at length in this book. Both the formation of 'house societies' in the centuries immediately following 4000 BCE, and the later deliberate mixing of the bones of various people drawn from different places together in the ditches of causewayed enclosures, may have represented acts of consolidation and incorporation into wider alliances and corporate identities. The former in particular deserves some further consideration. The *house* may only sporadically and unevenly have manifested itself as a communally occupied dwelling in Neolithic Britain, and just as often expressed itself in the form of a major funerary (or other) monument. Houses in this sense are social entities distinguished by an identity that endures through time, and a set of objects and activities that are passed down between the generations. 'Houses' in this sense have much in common with 'families', as corporate descent groups that trace their origin back to a founding ancestor, who may be entirely mythological.

   In the case of causewayed enclosures, archaeologists have long pondered why it is that while there are instances where mid fourth-millennium enclosures have continuous ditches with only one or two entrances, by far the majority of such enclosures comprise one or more concentric circuits of *discontinuous* lengths of ditch, separated by undug gaps, or 'causeways'. The digging and filling of these ditch segments exhibit both distinctiveness and similarities, and different degrees of structuredness of deposition. Some of the more intensively investigated among these sites reveal contrasts in the character of activity between the two sides of the ditch circuit, as at Etton, and there are other, more subtle ways in which the character of deposition appears to draw attention to distinctions between different parts of the enclosure. In some cases the density of pottery and flint may vary between the different rings of ditch segments, while particularly rich concentrations of finds may be clustered at the butt-ends of ditches, as with the group of skull fragments, an axe butt, and traces of burning identified at Haddenham in Cambridgeshire.

Different patterns and sequences of representation and deposition characterize the different causewayed enclosure sites so far investigated: no two sites are identical. Indeed, in the relatively rare instances where two such sites have coexisted in adjacent locations, the differences have sometimes been profound, with the main and Stepleton enclosures at Hambledon Hill offering a case in point. One more detailed example will have to suffice here. At Kingsborough Manor on the Isle of Sheppey, two causewayed enclosures were found to have been in use across almost exactly the same spans of time in the mid fourth millennium BCE. They had been built on either side of the crest of a ridge and were sited barely fifty metres apart. While one enclosure overlooked the Thames Estuary northwards, the other faced the Swale southwards, and the Medway valley beyond. The latter was an area in which there were many contemporary arenas of activity including long barrows, other enclosure sites, and places where pits and other features were concentrated, while the former comprised wide marshy estuarine wilds. The busyness of the southern landscape appeared to be reflected in the multiple gatherings of people that had taken place at the south-facing enclosure, such gatherings being represented by the casual burial of debris from feasting events including quantities of broken pottery and exotic items. In contrast, the north-facing site possessed only small deposits of material that had been extremely carefully placed, so indicating that infrequent, intimate events had taken place there.

And yet all such sites involved the demarcation of (mostly circular or oval) areas contained within circuits of discontinuous ditches. Time and again the ditches have produced indications of having been rapidly back-filled, sometimes episodically, and sometimes with repeated recutting of the segments at subsequent points in time. The depositional emphasis that we have noted on the ends of lengths of ditch suggests that 'opposing' terminals could be envisaged as points of contrast with the 'next' segment, and this tends to support the idea that the physical segmentation of the ditches might reflect the social segmentation of different kin groups.

While this does not necessarily imply the deliberate mapping of lineage history at such sites, it does suggest some kin-based segregation of activity. The combination of the periodic drawing together of groups of people and their differentiation from one another in the same setting sits comfortably with the idea that among the purposes of such enclosures were exchange, and the working out of familial relations between groups potentially occupying very broad but not necessarily contiguous living-space territories. The inclusion of human remains in some of these segmented ditch lengths, and the elaboration of contemporary pottery with sometimes profuse surface scoring and decoration, may represent further expression of this kind of social and familial distinction. The frequency of such deposition of human remains at some sites, as at the main enclosure at Hambledon Hill, has even led to the suggestion that they were primarily places of exposure of corpses prior to bone collection and circulation. Of more interest, however, in the light of the above discussion, is the placing of both whole human skulls and whole inverted pots at intervals along the base of some excavated enclosure segments not only at Hambledon Hill, but also at Etton in the Cambridgeshire fenlands, in a manner that suggests that each could stand proxy for the other (pot::skull), perhaps as 'vessels for (in the sense of representing or connoting) the ancestors'.

Nor were causewayed enclosures necessarily the only manifestation of the lived practice of collective representation of a fundamentally socially segmented world. Both stone circles and (perhaps slightly later on in British prehistory) stone rows can be read in terms of the assembly (albeit potentially in very different ways) of ancestral presences that stood proxy for the foundation and descent of different lineages within contemporary social formations. This is not necessarily, either, only a matter of ethnographic analogy. To Mike Parker Pearson's Madagascan colleague, Ramilsonina, it was blindingly obvious that the stones of Stonehenge must have represented the ancestors of the builders of that monument in some way. This was a visceral reaction from someone whose particular Malagasy heritage, with its close involvement in raising stone memorials as part of elaborate funerary rituals, predisposed him to 'reading' British prehistoric monuments in this particular way. While this provoked interesting insights into past practice on the part of Parker Pearson, it should not necessarily be regarded as the only way to make the particular arrangement of stones at Stonehenge intelligible.

Colin Richards may have moved us some way towards a more closely situated understanding of the context of multiply sourced creation of such monuments by his observations concerning both quarries and stone circles in Orkney. He has suggested that the complex lithology of stone circles such as that at Brodgar is attributable to the fact that several communities each 'contributed' a stone from a quarry in their home territory and brought it and erected it in place where different clans or lineages had assembled for fairs and festivals, to conduct exchanges, give gifts, and arrange alliances (see Chapter 5). The nature of the circle is such that different stones can also 'point' in different directions, perhaps towards the source-areas of each of the individual stones. This might also explain why so often each stone in a circle appears to be so deliberately individual: the stones could represent, both in their own right and as a grouping assembled in one place, at one and the same time a coming together and a representation of the individual character of each of the contributing and (perhaps albeit temporarily) cooperating groups. Indeed, Richards sees this bringing of a stone gift from each group in competitive terms: a kind of Highland Games where each group brought along and put down their own marker and symbolic competitor. This may also place Stonehenge, interpretively, in a new light: the deliberate organisation of the stones brought from more than one location (bearing in mind the sandstones as well as rhyolite, dolerite, and sarsens there) into a uniform template could have been a metaphor for societal unification that stood in deliberate contradiction to the 'polyglot' circles elsewhere. And perhaps the ultimate symbolic expression of such a superordinate bond was the permanent physical linking together of the sarsens by lintel-stones.[2] It may be this single factor that explains why Stonehenge is unique and still has a strongly resonant impact upon visitors even today.

The communication and 'seeding' of history in stone

In Chapter 4 we described a variety of social practices that gave form and texture to the lived worlds of the Neolithic. But some of the same materials that we discussed there also have aspects that are pertinent to the issues of

2. It has been suggested by Alex Gibson and others that timber circles may have been linked together by lintels, but even if this was the case, it is the connection of *stones* in this way that is unarguably unique to Stonehenge.

time, history, and inheritance. It is for that reason that a brief return to discuss axes of flint and stone is instructive. While we have dealt with the transport and dissemination of axes, we will now turn to their deposition and destruction, the final phases of their individual life histories. In the past two decades, archaeologists have increasingly made use of the notion of 'object biographies' as a means of drawing together the production, distribution, and consumption of artefacts, which had hitherto often been subject to entirely separate analyses. These personal histories of things can be both distinctive and diverse, since items can have extremely varied degrees and forms of interaction with people (comprising different degrees of knowledge and skill, and different forms of use), and can also have experiential lives of their own, involving decay, corrosion, and wear, sometimes occasioning repair and maintenance on the part of their owners and users. In the case of Neolithic Britain, a number of authorities have recounted the possible 'lives' of axeheads, since often these have not only travelled considerable distances from their places of extraction, but also were clearly highly prized objects, whose ownership reflected or contributed to the roles, statuses, and identities of people. The different stages in this progress would generally have involved quarrying from the living rock and 'roughing out' to create the basic axe shape, followed by the grinding, honing, and polishing of their surfaces, their transportation and circulation sometimes over considerable distances, their reworking (and sometimes their deliberate fragmentation), and finally their deposition in a variety of different kinds of place.

The jadeitite axehead found beside the Sweet Track, and therefore dated to 3806 BCE (at least as far as its deposit, accidentally or otherwise, in that location is concerned), is a case in point. On typological grounds in reference to morphologically similar jadeitite axes found in Brittany, this axe was manufactured in the period 4500–4200 BCE and could have been brought to Britain at any time subsequently. The fineness of this axehead, which showed no sign of having ever been hafted or used, could have been the main reason why it had been kept intact (and just possibly it could have been curated by the 'Mesolithic' precursors of the trackway-builders), eventually to be given to the waters at this particular place and time.

The other of the two 'unused' axeheads found next to the Track was yet more interesting in terms of its location. This axehead was made, it would seem, from flint being mined during much the same period on the Sussex Downs. Its blade was partly polished, and it also had no indications of ever having been hafted or used: it was, in other words, in perfect condition. But most telling was a find made just four metres away, on the other side of the Track. This was of a rectangular twenty-centimetre length of oak stem, the centre of which had been hollowed out to create a deep rectangular recess. The impression is that this oak object therefore formed the main element of a lidded box. It just so happens that the pristine flint axe fits snugly into the recess in the wooden 'tray', raising the possibility that the latter was the lower part of a wooden box, and that when the box was opened deliberately, or dropped accidentally, the axe flew out from its secure place to be 'swallowed' by the nearby silts. In turn, it hints also that a normal means of transportation of fine axes was either boxed or wrapped (the jadeitite axehead could equally, by analogy with Netherlands examples where the wrapping has been inferred from wear traces, been transported carefully enveloped in fabric).

A common phenomenon of the Neolithic in Britain, then, is the casual loss, and quite probably also the deliberate placing, of complete (and frequently unused) stone axes in the landscape, in watery places, in long mounds, in the ditches of causewayed enclosures, and so on. While we cannot distinguish between the purpose of deposition for the vast majority of accidental discoveries of such whole axes, their distribution across the landscape is not necessarily random, and an association with water is frequent enough to consider the possibility that they were deliberately placed, in the same way that in later centuries bronze objects were similarly so placed. As valuable items, there may have been a 'dedicatory' aspect to such deposition (as also where they occur in primary contexts, for instance in causewayed enclosure ditches, as at Etton in Cambridgeshire). However, given that many such axes exhibit no indication of ever having been used, and that they occur as chance finds also in areas that may have been wooded, another explanation is possible. This is that, rather than always having been casual losses while their owners were out in the woods cutting trees or stems, or woodworking, they were deliberately placed in those same woodlands, as offerings. Given their ubiquity, might they even be regarded as having represented a 'seeding' of the land with a potent symbol of clearance and human intervention in the landscape?

For the past century or so, the study of stone axes has focused upon these complete or nearly complete examples. However, by far the most common excavated examples of such axes have been quite small fragments representing the deliberate flaking or fragmentation of whole axeheads, and these have often been carefully (rather than randomly) placed with other items, including other carefully selected fragmented items, such as pottery sherds, in such locations as pits and the ditches of causewayed enclosures. While this process of deliberate destruction has been widely remarked upon, reasoned explanations of why the practice took place are harder to find.

The consequences of this axe-shattering practice have been so remarkable at some sites as to receive special mention. Whole finely worked axeheads from the mountain quarries at Graig Lwyd had, for example, been brought to the nearby site at Parc Bryn Cegin, Llandygai, near Bangor in north Wales, where a number of fourth-millennium Early Neolithic rectangular buildings had stood. Flakes were cut out of the surface of these stone objects to exfoliate their surfaces and, together with a burnt butt-end fragment of another axe in the same material, had been carefully buried in pits and other places at the site, over the whole course of the Neolithic period. One of the pits containing Grooved Ware pottery as well as axe exfoliation flakes at the site had been placed carefully overlapping the site of one of the timber houses built several hundred years earlier, and a similar pit and contents were found in exactly the same relation to such a house at the adjacent site at Llandygai close to two Late Neolithic henges. This apparent commemoration of an early site is something we shall return to shortly, but for the moment it is the character and duration of the practice of, in various ways, slicing up and scattering the debris of Neolithic axes that is of interest here.

John Llewelyn Williams and Jane Kenney have suggested that 'woefully vandalistic destruction', 'orgies of smashing in bucolic merriment', and 'the potlach [sic] phenomenon of the west coast of North America' could equally well explain the break-up and deposition of the Graig Lwyd axes at Parc Bryn Cegin. They concluded that, given how many axes were treated in this way at the site, 'there is no doubting the sanctity of the fragmented debitage to the Neolithic supplicants' there.[3] Meanwhile, at two Later Neolithic settlement sites at Rothley, on the River Soar in Leicestershire, axes were similarly destroyed, in similar ways. At Temple Grange, near a circular posthole defined house, a large Charnwood-type stone axe had been found in a

---

3. The language used by these authors is instructive, and is important in terms of what we described in the Introduction concerning 'encounters with the Neolithic' achieved through excavation. This can not only be vivid but also somewhat 'shocking', as with this axe-smashing episode in north Wales. Similar experiences have been conveyed in reference to some of the more intensively studied sites discussed in this book. For example, Francis Pryor described his amazement at first encountering the debris of woodworking at Etton, and even more notably Roger Mercer was struck forcefully by his realization that warfare had produced dire consequences for individual people at the Stepleton enclosure on Hambledon Hill.

pit along with flaked fragments from its polished surface, while fragments of the same axe had also been found sixty metres away. In the larger of two pits at Rothley Lodge Farm nearby, another two Charnwood-type polished stone axeheads had been deliberately exfoliated in just the same way, and were buried along with 'thousands' of sherds from broken-up, highly decorated Grooved Ware pots, more than twenty-five flint scrapers and waste-flakes, and a miniature stone plaque incised with a face-like design. The smaller pit featured deliberate deposits of a single Grooved Ware vessel, an elongated, squared stone rubbing or polishing stone, a spherical clay ball, and many burnt bones. A flint axe also found in this pit had been deliberately burnt to the point where it had exploded and shattered into hundreds of pieces.

Is it possible to suggest, given the ubiquity of the suite of practices involved, a wider explanation for this deliberate fragmentation of objects redolent of long-distance connections between communities? We have already noted that, especially as the Neolithic progressed, it seems that the place of extraction of rock to be used for the manufacture of stone axes acquired, or accumulated, some special significance and that the remoteness and 'topographical difficulty' of such places seemed to imbue the process of acquisition (and therefore by association the axeheads themselves) with a certain mystique and importance. Moreover, the selection and treatment of individual pieces of flint or rock seems to have become integral to this process of the promotion of items from the prosaic to the profound. In some cases, for example, what might otherwise have been seen as flaws (such as fossils embedded within flint nodules) were highlighted rather than disguised in the roughing-out and polishing of individual axeheads. So why did some of these objects have their surfaces deliberately flaked off, while others were smashed up into pieces, or burnt and disintegrated? One explanation for a similar breaking and burning of axeheads at the Etton causewayed enclosure was ventured by Mark Edmonds in the mono-graph publication of the site. He wrote: 'It may be that these artefacts were harnessed, broken and/or burnt within important rites of passage . . . [and] collected on the completion of certain rites and deposited with some deliberation. Placed in the earth and in association with other cultural materials, their presence may have helped to sustain the associations of the site and a sense of continuity for specific social groups.' In this way, local Neolithic 'history' would have included a memory of such events and their significance.

Alternatively, the axeheads may have been regarded as having stored up ritual power or magic, or ancestral benefaction. In such circumstances it would not necessarily have been seen as destructive to break the items up, but rather it would have been regarded as a means of distributing their power more widely, enabling them to somehow release their embodied energy and to transmit whatever values they were seen to embody, across both space and time. We could compare this with the flint nodules that had been knapped entirely away in the ditches of certain monumental structures, as noted in Chapter 4. This is not entirely different from the way that the relics of holy people were distributed in medieval Europe, and could indeed have been the equivalent in stone of the rendering down and circulating of the remains of the dead in Neolithic Britain (see Chapter 4, and the next section here). The temporal character of these actions is of critical importance. While whole axes might be lost, or exchanged, or deliberately deposited in pits or watery places, the distribution of axe fragments could be envisaged as a wider 'seeding' of pieces of objects that had acquired associations with the past. This would focus all the associations and links to people, to events, and to journeying that they—literally—embodied into series of dedicatory acts undertaken at intervals (reflected at Parc Bryn Cegin and elsewhere in a series of pits) that created a history of such deposition at an ancestral location.

Curation of remains from the past in the Neolithic

Had we been writing this book two decades ago, it is entirely possible that the kinds of materials and contexts that we have been addressing in this chapter would not have been connected to the kin relations and patterns of descent of past communities. These issues would more likely have been considered exclusively in relation to the remains of 'the ancestors' themselves. These, of course, have most frequently been encountered in the excavation of long barrows and chambered tombs, and also increasingly in the ditches of causewayed enclosures. In Chapters 3 and 4 we discussed at some length the treatment of the dead, ranging from excarnation, defleshing, and dismemberment to cremation and the burial of complete bodies accompanied by grave goods, in facilities ranging from tombs and barrows to pits and enclosures, while acknowledging that this diverse evidence may represent only a small sample of the total.

A clear theme that has emerged is that the retention and subsequent placing of the bones of people and animals is a recurring, if far from universal,
practice identified at numerous Neolithic sites. There is an obvious parallel
with the way that fragments of pottery and other items (including bones)
appear to have been stored in middens, constituting a cultural resource that
might be expended or manipulated much later, by deposition in an appropriate context. While to some extent the chambers of long barrows and chambered tombs might be identified as ossuaries or repositories for human
remains, we have also argued that they were containers of transformation, in
which the volatile cadavers of the recently dead achieved the stable condition
of clean, dry, ancestral bones. In this way they took on a form in which they
might be reorganized, and perhaps selected for removal and further circulation or deposition elsewhere. We might say that both middens and tombs
amounted to accumulations of potential and power, in each case attributable
to the past, and specifically the collective histories of particular communities.

We have already noted the curated cattle mandibles placed in the ditch
at Stonehenge. But archaeologists are increasingly identifying the retention
of a variety of objects over what were often lengthy periods of time in
Neolithic Britain. For instance, Anne Teather has recently drawn attention
to a process that she described as 'cultural reclamation', in which already
ancient bones and other items were appropriated in order to manufacture
links with a mythic, and quite possibly fictional, past. It is possible that the
presence of engraved stone plaques, like the one that we have just noted
from Rothley Lodge Farm in Leicestershire, alerts us to particularly important deposits associated with Late Neolithic Grooved Ware. Another similar
pit at King's Stanley in the Vale of Gloucester potentially represents a very
dramatic example of curation. Here, fragments of Grooved Ware were found
at either end of the base of a pit filled with a single-event deposit dated to
the late third millennium BCE. Flint and animal bone, and many lumps of
limestone, were found scattered throughout the pit: but at its centre at a
slightly higher level, in effect enfolded within the Grooved Ware vessel
pieces, were found burnt hazelnuts, a miniature limestone plaque incised all
over with groups of parallel scored lines, and, especially significantly, most of
the sherds from a whole Mortlake-style bowl that belonged to a tradition of
pot-making that had ceased at least 400 years before its deposition here.
Instrumental or functional explanations for such ordering of residues simply
fail to capture the complexity of meaningful reference instanced here. While
we cannot hope to access the significance of the thought and traditions of

cultural practice that went into the digging and filling of this pit, we can identify the fact of structuring, the incorporation of old pots with new (and the mapping of the past that this doubtless involved), as well as the surely purposeful inclusion of a strikingly symbolic and perhaps deliberately miniaturized artefact (the scored stone, with its at least possible connotative reference to binding or packaging up).

Patterns of commemoration: burning and marking

One of the arguments for continuity in the occupation of the land of Britain throughout much of prehistory concerns the endurance of practices that can be demonstrated or inferred to have taken place repeatedly in the same location. We have already dwelt at length on instances of this phenomenon at either end of our period, at around 4000 BCE and at the time of the introduction of Beaker pottery. Sometimes these continuities can range over enormous temporal spans, as with the lower Wye Valley caves at which practices of careful human burial are attested repeatedly, at intervals, across a span extending from the end of the last Ice Age 12,000 years ago through to the sixth century CE. This continuity can perhaps be explained through simple attachment to place, or by a suite of beliefs concerning entry to an 'other-world' beyond life, through the portals of cave entrances (Fig. 6.5).

However, we suggest that during the Neolithic the themes of durability, stability, and continuity took on a new and greater significance. The cre-ation of social entities that were not so liable to fragmentation as those of the preceding Mesolithic period, and who had exclusive access to shared resources, was a precondition for a way of life that involved a significant role for the herding of animals and/or the cultivation of crops. Thus we have argued throughout this book that an important innovation of the period was the emergence of 'invested lineages', by which we mean corporate social groups held together by the presumed sharing of blood and ancestry, and often by at least temporary co-residence. The 'investment' to which the term refers is the communal ownership of the means of production, as well as dwelling structures and ceremonial monuments, and presumably also less tangible goods such as names, titles, rituals, songs, and dances. In addition, it seems probable that these groups will have *invested* their collective efforts in the production of a common history, which served both to bind the com-munity together and as a basis for the exclusion of others. For Neolithic

Fig. 6.5 Gop Cave and cairn, Trelawnyd near Prestatyn, from below

The drama of the south-facing complex on the upper slopes of Gop Hill in north Flintshire, overlooking the Vale of Clwyd and the north Wales coast from the east, cannot easily be conveyed in photographs. The cave, which is in a low horizontal fissure, may have been occupied in the later Upper Palaeolithic and the Mesolithic periods. However, it also featured a cemetery and a small group of pots from the Early Neolithic, which lends substance to the idea that the Gop Cairn sited on the brow of the hill above it is also in origin a Neolithic structure.

Photograph: courtesy of Howard Williams.

societies, the creation of history was partly achieved through the collective labour involved in bringing buildings and monuments into being, and partly through the manufacture, circulation, giving, and use of portable artefacts such as fine pots and polished axes. It was also produced in the ebb and flow of meetings and partings, fission and fusion occasioned by the periodic assembly of people, animals, and things at places such as causewayed enclosures. Finally, history will have been created, renewed, and sometimes selectively transformed through practices that drew the past into the present, through commemoration, remembering, and forgetting.

This emphasis on commemoration is graphically attested at individual sites where the memory of the significance of an event can echo down the centuries within the Neolithic and beyond, into the Early Bronze Age period. One example that we have already raised is the construction of halls and houses, and in some cases the deliberate burning, burying, and other decommissioning events associated with their demise. Three frames of temporal duration were involved in the burning down of a house and its subsequent ruin and memorialization. The first was the immediate act of setting and tending the fire that destroyed the building. This was immediate in its temporal frame and presumably relatively brief, if dramatic, in its temporal duration. The vividness of the act, and to some degree its extravagance, was what would have imprinted the memory of the event upon the witnesses, and may well have given rise to oral traditions committing it to shared remembrance. At sites such as Dorstone Hill in Herefordshire and Warren Field, Crathes, on Deeside in north-east Scotland, it may well have been the case that the burnt building remained as a shell, with the stumps of its principal upright timbers visible for some years. This duration would have been equivalent to the length of time of individual lives, and memories attached to the ruin would have spanned several generations. In many cases the ruins were subsequently in some way 'encapsulated' within a larger structure that monumentalized the place, and fixed the memory of the events there into what might be described as a 'legendary' frame of temporal awareness. These patterns applied also to the stone houses of the Orkney Islands, which were often abandoned with some ceremony, as in the case of the cattle and sheep skulls placed on the floor, and rich deposits of cultural material in the filling of parts of the Grobust building at the Links of Noltland on Westray.[4] Some Orkney houses were also monumentalized after their use, as we have seen.

Our investigations in recent years at Dorstone Hill have recorded events that serve to bring together a number of the strands of history, practice, and descent that we have introduced in this chapter. Three early hall-like buildings were each memorialized by burning and encapsulation within funerary long mounds, but the easternmost of these in turn also contained a primary linear mortuary structure, which was itself commemorated in a series of ways. After this chamber had been dismantled, its position had been marked by the digging of a U-shaped ditch surrounding it on three sides, the spoil from which was thrown up to create a small mound that sealed its traces,

---

4. The Neolithic settlement of the Links of Noltland on the island of Westray is located in an area of sand dunes behind Grobust Bay, and was originally excavated by David Clarke of the National Museum of Scotland between 1978 and 1981. These investigations revealed a building containing dense occupation residues, including materials apparently connected with the closure of the site. More recent work, since 2007, has exposed further buildings, a Bronze Age settlement, and two Neolithic figurines.

Fig. 6.6 Dorstone Hill, Herefordshire: mortuary structure

Seen from the air, the trough-like mortuary structure at the western end of the easternmost of three long mounds on Dorstone Hill in Herefordshire is bracketed between two large post-holes, and enclosed with a U-shaped ditch. The up-cast from this ditch formed a small mound that was later incorporated into the larger barrow, which sealed the burnt remains of a timber building.

Photograph: © Adam Stanford (website: http://www.aerial-cam.co.uk/).

and which was only later bonded to the larger barrow covering the burnt debris of the building (Fig. 6.6).

Some while into the natural silting process, this ditch was then strewn with an organic deposit that, along with what was possibly rotted midden material, contained a great quantity of highly fragmented, cremated human bone. This might conceivably have been removed from the chamber itself. The bone was then sealed beneath a mass of stone thrown into the ditch, which at some later point was cut through by a stone–lined cist, which may potentially have held a further burial. It was probably at least two centuries after the raising of the mound that a further commemoration of the chamber site took place, in a quite remarkable way. A small drum-shaped pit was inserted, shaft-like, in the later fourth millennium, into the top of the mound. Into the base of this pit was placed a polished flint axe with a fine blade (and which contained in its flint matrix a highly visible fossil), along

Fig. 6.7 Dorstone bifacially worked flint knife

This fine flint artefact was one of a group of objects deposited in a small, cylindrical pit dug beside the mortuary structure beneath the eastern mound at Dorstone Hill. Some of the waste flakes from the manufacture of this item were also recovered from the pit, indicating that it had been made not long before it was buried.

Photograph: © Adam Stanford (website: http://www.aerial-cam.co.uk/).

with other flints, while a polished stone axe recovered from an adjacent modern drain is also likely to have originally been held within this pit. The flints comprised a large, thin, leaf-shaped, bifacially worked knife, together with some at least of the flake debris from its final dressing (Fig. 6.7).

Meanwhile, a series of very large pits had been cut through the main mound. Each was dug down as far as the intensely burnt daub and timber of the building, and no further, and each was lined with large slabs of stone, before fragments of cremated bone of humans and cattle were deposited.

These circumstances reveal a series of ways in which a single location had come to embody collective history and enduring links with the past. The timber mortuary structure and its enclosing ditch had been located in proximity to a wooden building that had been conspicuously destroyed by fire, and both were eventually covered by a unified mound that served to memorialize them in a massively material fashion. But the key features of both structures, and the histories they embodied, were apparently recalled in some detail, and sporadically commemorated in a series of acts of veneration. The small cylindrical pit had been carefully inserted close by the mortuary structure, and contained two axes that must have been brought to the site from some distance. But the presence of the knife and the flakes from its manufacture are perhaps more significant, for they demonstrate that the object was made then and there, with the sole intention of gifting it. Both the creation of the object and its placement therefore formed parts of a performance whose intention was to bring the dead back to mind. Similarly, the digging of the larger pits in the main mound reveals that a knowledge of the burnt hall had been sustained, and the materials that were placed into them were quite deliberately being positioned in juxtaposition to the brightly coloured building debris that their excavation revealed. Finally, like the drum-shaped pit, the cist had been dug with an appreciation of the position of the mortuary structure, with the aim of establishing a spatial relationship between a newly deceased person and a location of ancestral presence. In each case these intimate relationships between new deposits and the tangible vestiges of the past demonstrate how history was being produced and refined through a series of discontinuous acts that repeatedly asserted continuities with an original founding community. This pattern is by no means unique to Dorstone Hill, and throughout this book we have drawn attention to particular locations that developed through time to become the repositories of collective memory, as the bodies of the recently deceased and potent objects were placed in relation to structures and deposits that were now old but still recalled in some detail. Good examples would include the sequence of graves, burials, and episodes of mound construction at Duggleby Howe, and the many reconfigurations of Stonehenge.

Making and recording history through practice

The discerning reader may well be thinking that the present chapter has involved not only a reprise, but also to a large extent a repetition, of much that was introduced and discussed at some length in our chapter on 'social being and cultural practices'. Rather, we would suggest, it has involved an abstraction of, and a concentration upon, the specifically historical dimensions of such practices. The reason why peoples are seen to be 'without history', whether in the past or the present, is that, for traditional peoples, tradition and history are elided. Historical consciousness for such people may not hold the precision that a chronological, recorded, calendrical realization of history demands of Western-influenced societies today. But it is far from the case that such societies lived 'outside history'. While this may be immanent in the residues that archaeologists encounter and investigate, it is hard to articulate closely. What we have been highlighting here are the practices that have embodied both continuity and change through the two millennia concerned, and the recording of these practices today is just beginning to enable us to write 'history' in both a narrative and explicatory sense. However, it is the evidence for curation, and for what we have termed the strategic deployment of artefacts and residues, which enables us to appreciate that history was a living, as well as a lived, experience in the fourth and third millennia BCE. As recorded in the descent of practices focused upon particular events and particular times, or extended through repetition and allusion over longer spans of time, history registered via descent and tradition itself was in a number ways a self-conscious practice and a renewable and revitalizing resource for the people of Neolithic Britain.

Conclusion
A lived Neolithic

Closing frontispiece: 'Silbury Hill from the Sanctuary' (painting, Anna Dillon)

Anna Dillon's painting perfectly captures the sense of Silbury Hill as 'a hill among hills' that is nonetheless by its artificially consistent profile set entirely apart from those hills. It remains the largest-known humanly created earthen mound in Europe, but, despite a fuller appreciation of how it was built in several phases, its exact purpose remains a mystery. Research by Jim Leary and others in recent years has indicated that the similar mound in the grounds of Marlborough School just down the Kennet valley to the east was also raised during the Neolithic, and several other mounds both locally in Wiltshire (for instance near Warminster) and beyond were broadly approximate. The fact that Silbury is one, albeit the largest, of a particular type of Late Neolithic monument has led us to suggest that they were in some respects the equivalent of henges.

Painting: 2010, © Anna Dillon (website: http://www.annadillon.com).

Experiencing the Neolithic in the present

Why is the Neolithic period in Britain of continuing importance today? For one thing, as we observed in the Introduction to this book, places like Stonehenge, Avebury, and the components of the Heart of Neolithic Orkney World Heritage Site such as Skara Brae, the Stones of Stenness, and the Ness of Brodgar provide an enduring fascination for a wide public, and therefore attract visitors from around the world (Fig. 7.1) (even if they don't arrive presidentially, as Obama did).

Confronted with these spectacular but enigmatic remains, it is inevitable that visitors will find themselves looking, and often struggling, for explanations that meet their expectations of the real world. Most obviously, they want to know who made these things, and why. Beyond this, many visitors also want to identify where these people came from, what mattered to them most in their lives, and, perhaps most important of all, how they are connected to those of us inhabiting 'their' space, however much it has changed, today. But an equally important issue is that the way we view the Neolithic can have important ramifications for our understanding of the contemporary world, and how it came into being. For example, the adoption of farming appears to have been an escalating process from which British societies have been unable to extricate themselves, and that has led to environmental degradation and other modern ills. But it has also been a process that has shaped our perception of the landscape, and of what is 'natural' in our environment. And while the majority of us live a metropolitan way of life in contemporary Britain, our everyday language nonetheless remains full of reference to the land and its working.

The popular answers to the 'whys' of the Neolithic of Britain have been legion, ranging from the pre-industrial folk stories making intelligible the chambered mounds as giant's graves or fairy caves, to antiquarian invocations of Merlin or the Druids, and more recent suggestions of priestly astronomers. Equally, as we saw in Chapter 1, each generation of academic archaeologists has brought new conceptual resources to bear on Neolithic Britain, and has come up with novel interpretations. It is, we contend, no coincidence that each new school of archaeological thought invariably finds itself addressing this particular set of evidence (for Neolithic Britain), for the same reason that the 'person in the street' is drawn to ponder the significance of a standing stone or a stone circle when they come upon them by chance in the landscape.

Fig. 7.1 Stonehenge from the west, in summer-evening sunlight
Photograph: © Julian Thomas.

The British Neolithic presents us with the rich material traces of a remote and in many respects a 'lost' world, with no shred of a written record to explain them. Even the decorative media of the period are predominantly abstract, and resist straightforward readings. Yet it is abundantly clear that these tangible things signal a set of long-lost experiences and understandings that were formed in conditions very unlike our own.

The preceding Mesolithic period would undoubtedly seem just as alien and puzzling to a modern sensibility, and quite possibly more so. But that lost age of bands of hunters and gatherers does not impose itself upon us visually, demanding our attention in the way that Silbury Hill or the Calanais stones do (Fig. 7.2, Stones of Stenness).

It is not too far-fetched to say that the landscapes that we now inhabit actually began to acquire aspects of their present texture during the Neolithic. Later periods, from at least the arrival of the Romans onwards, already have a 'history', in the sense that writers of the time (whether Julius Caesar or the Venerable Bede) have sketched out a narrative for us, which we can choose to build upon or contest, but not ignore entirely. The Neolithic presents us with no such received outline, and yet we have been at pains in this book to stress that this does not mean that it is a period without history. We have tried to draw the reader's attention to a paradox: on the one hand, Neolithic

history was different from our own, wholly enveloped as it was in relationships of kinship and descent, in practices and traditions, in inherited knowledge and stories, in herds of animals, in stone axes and pottery vessels, in middens and cultivation plots, in the bones of people and cattle, and in monuments of stone and earth that were, and remain, unique to it, and that would no doubt sometimes seem bizarre to our twenty-first-century sensibilities. But at one and the same time, in seeking to grapple with this kind of history and shape it into a written narrative, we unavoidably transform it into the kind of history with which we are familiar. One of the ways in which we have tried to resist this latter process has been to focus throughout on the notion of *experience*.

Our writing of the Neolithic is informed by our own experiences of artefacts and archaeological sites in the present. These encounters are not identical with those of past people, because our expectations and assumptions are inevitably those of modern Westerners and we bring a different cultural inheritance to bear on the material. Nonetheless, if we approach these remains with an awareness of the customs and practices, and the inherited resources of knowledge and wisdom of recent pre-industrial peoples, although the monuments and artefacts are shards and fragments of an existence different from our own, our understandings of them have the potential to challenge and dislodge at least some of these preconceptions.

Fig. 7.2 Scale and silhouette at the Stones of Stenness, Orkney

The Stones of Stenness, like the nearby Ring of Brodgar, have elements indicative of a place in the henge-building tradition. However, the discovery of a box-like structure at its centre indicates a role for the monument also as a symbolic transformation of the domestic forms of the Orkney Neolithic household into the realms of the superordinate, the godlike, and the universal. The vertical scale of the monument is difficult to comprehend, until a skilfully composed photograph (such as this one is) reveals something of its proportions set against people visiting the site.

Photograph: © Adam Stanford (website: http://www.aerial-cam.co.uk/).

Nor is the stock of traces of that Neolithic past a given: a further paradox is that while no new remains of the Neolithic can be created, any more than can be for any time in the past including the twentieth century, fresh discoveries are made virtually every day. One of the reasons why the Neolithic is able to surprise us, year on year, therefore, is because new and unfamiliar material is constantly coming to light through excavation. The Neolithic is anything but a closed book, and the evidence available for study has mushroomed over the past few decades. This is significant for two reasons. First, in the absence of a written history, and provided we do not overly predetermine the framework of interpretation for what we find, material things are not simply illustrative of our understanding of the past, but substantially frame, and continually also disrupt, that understanding. Any archaeological narrative is woven out of the residues left behind by human communities, but this is *exclusively* so only in the 'prehistoric' era. Secondly, we have drawn attention to the quite particular importance of new kinds of, and more numerous, objects to people living in the centuries we denote 'Neolithic'. These items, we would assert, were far more than the symptoms or products of human existence or particular ways of gaining a living. When we talk about arch-aeological 'evidence', we generally mean that potsherds or flint tools *point towards* some faintly glimpsed and subtly intangible past reality that we can never directly encounter. The crucial point here is that in the Neolithic these kinds of object and material forms were *integral to* that reality. As a way of life, the Neolithic was sustained by things just as much as by language, and articulated through things perhaps even to a greater extent than through language. Artefacts and architecture provided the framework within which social life was conducted, the settings in which interaction took place, and the media through which tasks were performed, but they did not exist as a static constant. Not only were they continually being modified throughout their periods of use, they also stood or were used within landscapes that were marked by continual movement. Archaeologists are increasingly aware of the scale and frequency of contacts and linkages between regions, dem-onstrated by the widespread dispersal of artefacts, images, and species, from stone axes to patterns of lozenges and nested arcs to the Orkney vole.[1] So as well as recognizing that landscapes and places were in continual flux, there has been much debate over the possibility of pilgrimages and processions to, and between, focal places. We would add that the networks involved would have had two critical roles. First, they would have served as a means of extending kin relations over space, thereby reinvigorating lines of descent. And second, these were no doubt the primary 'vehicle' for the transmission and acceptance of new customs, ideas, and practices.

People and things

It has been conventional to define the Neolithic as the period during which agriculture began. So, routinely, archaeologists and others have accepted without question the dictum that *the Neolithic was caused by farming*. As such,

---

1. The Orkney vole (*Microtus arvalis orcadensis*) is a rodent found in Orkney, but not elsewhere in Britain, which apparently arrived in the islands around 3200 BCE, possibly from Belgium. Another indication of far-flung contacts has recently come from DNA analysis of red deer in the Outer Hebrides and Orkneys, which suggests that they were introduced during the Neolithic, not from the Scottish mainland, but from an unknown source further afield.

living in villages, using pottery vessels, making a wider range of stone tools, treating the dead in elaborate ways, and constructing imposing field monuments were all held to be consequences of domesticating plants and animals. We have argued, on the contrary, that it is important to reverse this logic if we are to gain an understanding of the profoundly social character of 'becoming Neolithic'. Hunting and gathering people have (and have had) robust and successful ways of existing, which have often survived with little perceptible change for millennia. These ways of living have often depended upon minimal social differentiation, the limitation of personal possessions to what can be carried, the maintenance of extensive networks of kin, the existence of trusted allies across considerable distances, and the sharing of whatever one has, particularly food. These arrangements are highly effective in securing the survival of mobile, small-scale societies. However, when people start to invest their labour in resources that will be consumed at a later time, and that need continual care and management, this way of life meets its limitations. This changed suite of practices includes, of course, the domestication of plants and animals, but also the species-specific 'cultivation' (that is, the active and defended management) of wild plants such as hazel, acorns, and berry-bearing plants. It also involves the use of technology such as fish weirs, animal traps, and fishing boats, and the storage and mass processing of sometimes large quantities of foodstuffs. These developments can only occur when groups can assert collective ownership over resources, excluding others from sharing them.

The emergence of more deliberately bounded communities, more able to exercise collective ownership, was therefore one important aspect of the Neolithic as a social entity. Another was the way that social relationships were rendered more durable by marking investment in those relationships through multiplying the material things that bonded people together. In recent years this has been described by some archaeologists and anthropologists as an 'enmeshment' or an 'entanglement' from which it became ever harder for communities and individuals to break free. In this way, a Neolithic *society* was not just composed of people: it was made up of human beings together with non-human entities, including both artefacts and animals. Paradoxically, this made Neolithic societies better insulated from natural shocks but more vulnerable to the consequences of the kinds of community tensions that an increase of continual living together creates.

As we have been at pains to demonstrate, Neolithic communities possessed a sense of collective identity and continuity through time that rested not only on kinship with, and descent from, other persons, but also a collective investment in herds of animals, the circulation and inheritance of fine artefacts, the shared use of ceremonial spaces, the veneration of the bones of ancestors and their stock, and the acknowledgement of shared traditions and modes of conduct. In other words, the 'Neolithic history' that we have been discussing throughout this book was actually the precondition for a way of life involving the herding of animals and the cultivation of cereals. This kind of history, vested as it was in material things and the bodies of humans and animals, was continually renewed through performance, habit, and experience. To reiterate the point: the 'evidence' that we as archaeologists experience in the present was both the outcome of, and integral to, the very particular way that social life was experienced and sustained during the Neolithic.

Neolithic Britain and the wider world

The Neolithic has long been identified as a major horizon of change in the Old World, in which the shift from food collection to food production paved the way for a sedentary way of life, greater accumulations of population, craft specialization, and ultimately urbanism and the state, leading in turn to capitalism, industrialization, and modern democracy. Displacing the foundations of this narrative slightly, as we have attempted to do, has interesting consequences. Some of the presumed marginal aspects of Neolithic life are revealed as having had a greater causal role to play than has often been supposed. We have argued that the Neolithic represented a new formation of relationships between people, animals, and things, linked together historically. Adopting this formulation, there are considerable rewards to be gained from an 'immersion' in a Neolithic world. For the henges, stone circles, and chambered tombs that we can experience today are revealed as media through which social relationships were constructed and maintained, rather than ostentatious 'optional extras' that demonstrated the success of past societies in generating a surplus from an essentially unchanging set of economic activities.

As a collection of often large offshore islands, Britain has, since the loss of the land bridge to continental Europe, always been distinctive. And yet there is also a shared inheritance stemming from the two principal geographical directions of Continental linkage. One concerns what is still sometimes termed the 'Atlantic Arc'. Two decades ago, Andrew Sherratt

Fig. 7.3 The Rollright Stones, Oxfordshire, at twilight

The Rollright Stones are enigmatic, and it has been suggested on more than one occasion that the close proximity of the stones to one another suggests, that this circle is the product more of the workings of the antiquarian imagination than of Neolithic people. In fact, the Rollright Stones are just part of a larger complex of cairns, standing stones, and other structures (including a portal dolmen, the evocatively named 'Whispering Knights' stones) that occupied a prominent ridge right on the border between the later counties of Oxfordshire and Warwickshire.

Photograph: © Adam Stanford (website: http://www.aerial-cam.co.uk/).

drew attention to the particularity of the far north-west fringes of Europe (Britain, Ireland, and Armorica—that is, Brittany and Normandy), where monument building achieved extremes of scale and complexity not seen anywhere else on the Continent (Fig. 7.3).

While the earlier third millennium BCE saw the emergence of what are termed by archaeologists the Corded Ware and Globular Amphora complexes in central Europe, distinguished by the burial of flexed bodies with accompanying ceramic vessels in grave-pits, this development was delayed until the Beaker period in the north and west. Here, megalithic constructions developed toward 'complexes' such as those of the Carnac alignments of the Gulf of Morbihan in southern Brittany, the Calanais circles of the Isle of Lewis in the Outer Hebrides, and the passage-tomb cemeteries of the Boyne valley north of Dublin in Ireland. These complexes not only feature elaborate major monuments that required quite unprecedented quantities of labour for their construction, but also encompass entire landscapes. Rather than dismiss these assemblies as mere window dressing, we would prefer to identify them as characteristic of a distinct kind of Neolithic world, in which community, identity, and authority were constructed in specific ways. In other words, they distinguish a particular historical experience that was quite remote from our own.

The transformation of social worlds

We have discussed change as a constant, and sometimes an accelerated, factor in the history of Neolithic Britain, but we have perhaps directed less immediate attention to the concept of 'transformation'. This is in part owing to our reluctance to cast the advent of the Neolithic as the only significant transformation that occurred in the 1600–1800 years or so in question. It is likely that there were, in terms of rates of change and their social causes and consequences, several historical junctures that could be described as transformational in the centuries concerned. However, we must be careful to distinguish between the incremental changes that can generally be identified whenever we chart a society's development over time, and more fundamental shifts in the way that life is structured and ordered. Change is constant and continuous, even where it can barely be perceived. Transformation, however, is contingent (that is, it emerges out of locally specific circumstances, which may depend of the workings of chance, or the unintended consequences and unrecognized conditions of people's actions), is episodic (not necessarily happening all at once, but often featuring a 'chain reaction' or a tipping point at which the alteration of circumstances becomes perceptible), and is often profound in terms of both its immediate and long-term consequences. When we speak of the transformation of social worlds, then, we mean that at certain points during the British Neolithic the fundamental terms under which social life was conducted shifted in categorical ways.

The beginning of the Neolithic would certainly qualify as such a transformation, but we would argue that the wholesale reorganization of community life associated with the Grooved Ware complex could be regarded as a development of comparable significance. At this point, existing media of social life (houses, the consumption of food, pottery vessels, depositional practice) were embellished and increased in scope in order to enable a step-change in the scale and reach of social relationships. Such a development qualifies as transformational in that it permeated a series of aspects of life, whose individual alteration was arguably mutually amplifying. The mobilization of labour to create new ceremonial centres, the emergence of new means of feeding huge gatherings of people, and the proliferation of architectural forms based on the cellular house together facilitated the production of new forms of collective identity. This is turn was the precondition for the construction of Stonehenge and Avebury, which might, quite reasonably, be identified as the apogee of the cultural possibilities that had been established during the British Neolithic.

Rewriting—and always learning more about— the Neolithic of Britain

We shall conclude this book by returning to the issue with which we began, especially in Chapter 1, which is the problem of writing about the Neolithic in Britain with an understanding fully in mind that not only did it *have* a history, but that we need to be aware that one of our primary aims in writing that history is to re-establish more closely both the pace and the 'texture' of its unfolding. At various places in the book we have drawn attention to the more precise chronological resolution that has recently had a revolutionary effect on Neolithic archaeology. This has self-evidently been of great benefit, but it brings with it the danger of privileging dating and sequence, sorting the evidence according to its place in a presumed linear narrative. In the process, our accounts of the past can appear commonplace and somewhat anonymous. There is nothing wrong with chronologically based narrative, but it is not enough on its own. We have therefore attempted to navigate a different course, tacking between writing about the passage of time, writing about social practice, and interrogating the subtleties of the archaeological record. Additionally, in trying to highlight some of the intricacies of practice that we can witness in what has been deposited and what has survived for us to record, we have drawn out those things that we regard as most telling about what we can glimpse of the concerns of people in their lived experience in the centuries concerned (Fig. 7.4).

The intention has been to produce a different kind of history from one that views the Neolithic remains that have been encountered and investigated as self-explanatory. While we have concentrated on material things, we have not done so in a traditionally empirical way, neither expecting facts to speak for themselves, nor having a grand narrative already in mind, for which we seek correlates in the record that we encounter. Instead, we have tried to enable other kinds of narrative to emerge, in the process of making comparisons and contrasts, rather than seeking exemplars of pre-defined processes.

Along the way, some new reflections on longer-term and wider-scale changes in material practice and society have, we hope, emerged. One such set of changes was, we think, worked through at the scale of the creation of monumentally sized constructions. In reference to the narrative of 'enclosure and meeting places' in the mid to late fourth millennium BCE in Britain, for example, the evident succession from causewayed enclosures to cursus monuments has long been remarked upon. However, our conceptualization of the cursus as a deliberately different kind of enclosure which was built to connect up both physically and conceptually not only a landscape, but previous gathering-places within it, is, we would suggest, an innovative one. Moreover, it is a perspective that acknowledges the probable awareness on the part of the Neolithic people engaged in the activity of creating such structures of a profoundly *historical* connection between places and their unfolding histories of action and meaning. Similarly, we could draw attention to the close spatial relationship between massive conical earthen mounds and both henges and palisaded enclosures that was hinted at in Chapter 5. It could be argued that all of these forms of monumentality were concerned with the deliberate creation of reserved spaces, removed from

Fig. 7.4 Bryn Celli Ddu—a re-enactment of ceremonial deposition

The inner end of the passage and the main chamber of the passage grave at Bryn Celli Ddu have been made the focus for this re-enactment of a simple Neolithic ritual, undertaken by James Dilley, an experimental archaeologist and animateur. *Note the replica Grooved Ware pot in Durrington Walls style.*

Photograph: © Adam Stanford (website: http://www.aerial-cam.co.uk/).

the everyday and the commonplace. While there may have been a certain theatricality to both forms of monument (and henges have for many years been seen to be places where rites or ritual performances took place), it is arguably the fact of removal from the mundane, and the purposeful creation of a locale that was both liminal *and* transcendent, and that represented *the culmination of a history of 'reservation'*, that were the ultimate reasons for the creation of these elaborate edifices.

And so in our respect for the 'lived Neolithic' of the people who inhabited Britain five millennia ago and more, we need to take on board the further realization that was expressed especially in Chapter 6, that not only did people at that time live that history, they also seemingly developed their own historical consciousness of change and continuity down the ages. In other words, they had clear notions of the previous existence of their own communities and the social relations that had brought them into being and had sustained them. But how can we possibly 'know' that this was so? We would argue that this is the implication of the last example that we drew on in that chapter, from our own investigations at Dorstone Hill. One of the patterns that we have dwelt on in this book has been that of the recurrence of activity over long periods at certain locations, often transgressing the conventional 'periods' into which prehistory is divided. We have implied that one of the principal reasons for this is because such places embody a history, which was understood by Neolithic people to have been both a resource and, potentially, a burden. These sites may have been identified as being imbued with ancestral power, which might prove either beneficial or polluting. But we suggest that they may also have been associated with past events or personages, whether these were human or metaphysical, and real or mythic. In any case, they will have been woven into the historical understandings that people will have developed of their communities and their landscapes, and as such they will have required careful management. This management took a number of different forms, whether of adding new layers of events and materials to carry the story forward, or of containment and sealing to mitigate the influence of the place.

At Dorstone, we suggest that the reason why the hilltop retained its significance, and attracted archaeologically visible interventions over a period of many centuries, is because the initial series of events, the construction and conspicuous destruction of a series of timber halls, was one that carried a potent message of *inception*. While the radiocarbon evidence for the site must presently be seen as provisional, the suggestion that these events began in the thirty-ninth or thirty-eighth century BCE gives a hint that this was one of the earliest Neolithic 'places' in what is now the modern border country between England and Wales. As we argued in Chapter 2, the large timber halls of the earliest Neolithic can be identified with the creation of new kinds of community, and the three long mounds on Dorstone Hill amounted to durable memorials to the coalescence of these Neolithic social groups, quite possibly under the direction of new and powerful leaders. The subsequent construction of a causewayed enclosure on the same hilltop, and the digging of pits and a cist into the long mounds, where stone objects and human and animal remains were deposited, demonstrates an imperative to keep connecting back to that moment of beginning. Yet it is the precise and intimate detail of what occurred—the flint knife knapped and placed close beside the location of the original mortuary structure, and the stone-lined pits dug precisely to the level of the burnt house deposit—that demonstrates that this was not a generalized engagement with a place of nebulous potency. Instead, there was a historical understanding of the significance of the hill and the structures that had accumulated there, and of their importance to the enduring identities of specific groups of people. And, with that reflection, we end our account.

Glossary of technical words

Absolute date A date arrived at through independent means, usually from laboratory-based calculation and calibration

aDNA Ancient deoxyribonucleic acid, a molecule that carries genetic information to enable organisms to reproduce

Adze A cutting tool like an axe, but with an asymmetrical blade

Alignment Posts or stones laid out in a row on a particular orientation

Ancestor A deceased relative, often from generations back

Antler The horn growth of a deer, often cut and used to make tools such as an antler-pick, with the tines used to prise out rock

Arc Part of a circuit; a curving line of pits, post-holes, etc.

Ard A hoe-like stone hafted to be used as a hand-plough

Arrowhead A small projectile-point, usually (but not always) in flint

Artefact Any humanly made object

Assemblage A group of artefacts associated by common characteristics (style, context, material, chronology)

Aurochs *Bos primigenius*, post-Pleistocene wild cattle

Avenue A double line of stones; a paved way defined within ditches

Awl A small pointed tool used to pierce holes; similarly a 'borer'

Axehead A (mostly) symmetrically bladed stone or flint tool; in contrast, an 'axe' is such a tool plus its shaft (handle)

Backfilling The deliberate infilling of a ditch or pit after it has been opened

Bank (Earthen): a linear or curving mound

Barrow An earthen raised long mound, often over chambers (q.v.) or (round barrow) over a burial (q.v.)

Bayesian analysis The calculation of probability of selected absolute dates (q.v.) falling in a particular span, depending on site context

Beaker A distinctive kind of beaker-like pot

Beam-slot A slot in the ground that has carried a foundation for a wall

Belt-slider An artefact most often made from Whitby jet (q.v.) with an elongated perforation, assumed to be a belt fitting

Blade A thin (usually flint) flake used as a cutting tool

Bridewealth The money or goods paid or received as marriage-gifts

Burial Usually, the insertion of a body or ashes into the ground

Burnish(ed/ing) The rubbing of pottery with stone to produce a bright sheen

Cairn A pile of stones, often over a barrow (q.v.)

Causation What caused something to happen, and why

Causewayed enclosure A place defined by enclosing arcs or circuits of ditches and banks interrupted by undug causeways

Cavetto (decoration) A concave moulding on a pot, usually at neck or shoulder

Ceremonial Highly structured or ritualized activity; a 'ceremonial monument' would be one designed for staging ceremonies

Chamber An enclosed space lined with timber or stone, and having an entrance (sometimes connected by a passage) and a roof

Chert A flint-like, but opaque, rock

Circuit A linked-together circle or oval of bank, ditch, or posts

Cist A stone-lined and -roofed, sealed, small-scale chamber

Commemoration Lit. 'remembering together'; the celebration of an event with resonances from the past

Conchoidal fracture The smooth, rounded surface resulting from breakage by percussion, in flint and some other stones

Consanguinity Blood relationship; descent from the same ancestor as another person

Context (in archaeology): place. 'In context' = 'in situ'. A discrete stratigraphic entity, often within a sequence such as of pits

Coppicing The pruning of the boles or trunks of trees to multiply their stems to use e.g. as poles

Cordon An incised or applied decorative band around a pot

Cove A boxlike setting of three or four large upright stones

Cremation Act of burning of a dead body, often on a pyre; cremated remains are often (incorrectly) referred to as 'a cremation'

Cultural drift The process whereby cultural practices or traits spread, or are transformed incrementally

Culture, a A set of linked traits thought to represent common ethnicity or shared practices

Culture history A form of archaeology widely practised in the 1920s to 1960s, which identified assemblages of artefacts with (ethnic) groups of people

Cup-mark Ground or pecked cup-shaped recesses in stone

Curation The practice of deliberately retaining items from the past

Cursus (monument) From the Latin for a course, a journey or a procession; a linear monument comprising parallel banks, ditches, pits, or posts

Daub A mix of mud, straw, and often dung: used to create a wall on a post and wattle (woven rod) frame

Debris e.g. 'occupation debris', the detritus from living

Decommission(ed) Take(n) out of use; dismantle(d)

Dedicatory A kind of offering, made in order to inaugurate use of a structure or the placing of offerings in the ground

Dendrochronology Dating by means of matching sampled wood against the growth-ring series ('master chronology') for a region

Deposit The product of deposition: the accumulation, layering, and modification of traces of former activity or soil formation

Deposition The placing of material into or onto the ground, either casually or deliberately (in an orderly or structured way)

Descent The calculation of relatedness of successive generations that (claim to) trace a common ancestry

Diagnostic Typical or characteristic of a particular activity or time

Difference Distinct dissimilarity; the recognition that human groups exhibit contrasts in cultural attitudes and practices

Discoidal (knife) Disc-shaped flint tool made by removal of small flakes from both sides, then grinding/polishing of its edges

Ditch A linear hollow dug and then often deliberately infilled

Dolmen An Early Neolithic stone-built structure comprising two or more upright megaliths supporting a large capstone

Domesticate/s (-d) Species of animal kept for their products; made reliant upon human control, selectively bred for human purposes

Dynamics Forces and processes that drive forward change

Enclosure A contained area, defined either by earthen banks, ditches, walls, or fences, with entrances at one or more points

Enlightenment, The The eighteenth-century period when ideas on rationality, duality of mind and matter, and utility were developed

Entanglement A process whereby human beings become ever more enmeshed in complex interactions with the material world

Excarnation The exposure of corpses to the elements and carrion-feeders to deflesh the bones for further manipulation

Excavation The practice of interrogating physical traces of human activity to understand former sequences of action, involving the removal of deposits of soil and sediment and recording the observed relationships carefully

Expedient technology Tools that require a low investment of effort in their manufacture, and that may be relatively disposable

Fabric A material that comprises a mix of substances, as with a textile or the components that together form pottery

Façade An elaborated frontal feature, for instance for an entrance to a monument (q.v.)

Facet A flat surface forming one side of an object such as a stone axe

Feast (e.g. diacritical) An event where food is consumed, often prodigiously; diacritically: where the feasting reveals social differences

Flint A glassy substance formed under pressure deposited as nodules in layers within chalk during the Cretaceous period of geology (about 146 to 65 million years ago)

Funerary Pertaining to death and burial

Gabbro A rock found chiefly on the Lizard Peninsula in Cornwall and used as a tempering agent in Neolithic pottery

Gallery A side-chamber or tunnel dug or built outwards from a shaft or a passage (q.v.)

Genealogy The tracing of descent and mapping of ancestry; in social science the term can also mean the tracking of a particular phenomenon and its changes through time

Generation Span of time within which population replacement can occur (e.g. 20 years)

Ground and polished The process of grinding and then smoothing the surface of a roughout of an object such as an axehead

Group VI (e.g. axe) One of the 'grouped' rock sources defined by the Implement Petrology Group: this from the English Lake District

Haft The wooden handle or shaft that held (in the Neolithic in Britain) a stone axehead or flint arrowhead in place

Hall An elongated rectangular building, usually timber, larger in size than might be expected of a domestic residence

Hearth A patch of burnt ashy ground representing a fire, assumed to have been used for cooking or an other domestic activity

Henge A circular or oval earthwork with a central level area surrounded successively by a ditch and then a bank

Hermeneutics The originally German tradition of interpreting things and texts, initially applied to scripture and historical documents

Hominin Those forms of primate directly ancestral to humans

House-society Societies organized around the key principle of co-residential kin groups associated with lineage founders

Hunter-forager Hunter-gatherers, hunter-collectors; peoples defined by use of wild food dietary staples rather than farming

Inclusion(s) Organic or inorganic fluxing agents used in pottery-making

Inhumation (interment) The burial of fleshed bodies in graves

Interpretive The practice of interpretation is central to all aspects of this at root inferential discipline: all archaeology is interpretive

Invested lineage A human kin group distinguished by the collective ownership of wealth and resources, and shared investment in facilities

Isotopic analyses; lead, strontium Analyses of human and animal teeth that can determine the likely region in which an organism spent its early life

Jadeitite A form of jade (green translucent stone) quarried from the European Alpine regions

Jet (e.g. belt-slider) A soft, black, rock-like substance from Whitby in Yorkshire, a form of lignite; in Neolithic Britain, used also for beads

Knapping The practice of flaking flint or stone from a nodule or core

Lineage (e.g. invested) Descent-line in human groups; an 'invested lineage' is one with a deliberate corporate holding of shared resources

Linearbandkeramik German(-language) term for a form of Early Neolithic Continental pottery decorated by incised linear bands

Lipids (residue) Organic fats and oils absorbed into (especially) Neolithic pots give insights into what substances were held in them

Macehead A perforated artefact in stone or antler that may be highly decorated or have its exterior faceted

Materiality The manifestation of human culture, materially; the shaping of ideas and social relations through material forms

Matrix (soil) The composition of archaeological contexts (q.v.) in terms of their soil and deposit characteristics

Megalithic Lit. 'large stone' construction

Michelsberg A cultural complex of north-central continental Europe, the later part of which overlapped the British Early Neolithic

Microlith Lit. 'small stone' technology, comprising the use of flint or stone in composite artefacts such as arrows hafted in wood

Midden The accumulation of discarded remains (e.g. of food) forming as heaps of material rotted down as soil

Migration (e.g. chain-) The movement of communities or individuals, often causing displacement of yet others in a chain-like reaction

Mnemonic (device) The creation or use of an object or a monument (q.v.) to facilitate the sustaining of collective memory

Monolith A single upright stone

Monument A created assembly of structures, often of large proportions

Mortuary structure A building created to contain human remains

Motif A repeated decorative device used to embellish artefacts

Mummification The act of preservation of the outward form of a deceased individual, usually bound at point of rigor mortis

Objectivist A belief that the external, phenomenal world has a fixed and unproblematic character, which is decisive in matters of debate

Ossuary A container for storing the bones of the dead

Outwork An earthwork associated with, but built outwards from, a more closely defined monument

Package (cultural) A grouping of material items or traits, regarded as having been habitually in use (and exported) together

Palisade A row of timber posts making a wall or fence

Passage A lined and roofed path linking an entrance and a chamber

Passage tomb (or grave) A megalithic funerary monument in which a chamber beneath a mound or cairn is accessed via a passage

Pavement A deliberately and usually carefully laid surface

Pecked Decorative stone-working involving striking a surface repeatedly to 'peck out' a shape either in negative or relief

Period An artificially defined elapsed length of time, or a particular named span, e.g. 'Neolithic period'

Periodicity The tendency to be periodic, that is, to recur at intervals; often connected to particular subsistence or ritual practices

Peristalith An arrangement of upright stones surrounding or containing a mound or barrow

Phase A further artificial subdivision of a *period* of elapsed time, most often expressed as 'Early', 'Middle', and 'Late'

Pick A flint or stone implement, often with a tranchet (q.v.) edge

Pit A hole dug in the ground and then infilled

Pleistocene The geological epoch lasting from 2.5 million to 11.5 thousand years ago, featuring the most recent glaciations

Polissoir A stone used to grind and polish axeheads or tool edges

Porcellanite A hard, dense, dark siliceous rock, quarried for axeheads in the Neolithic from sources in Antrim and Rathlin Island

Portal A holed entrance-stone into a chambered tomb; a kind of dolmen (q.v.) with an apparent entrance 'door'

Post(-hole) The location of a decayed (or burned, or deliberately withdrawn) timber post

Post-defined Any former timber structure, whose earth-fast components mark out the shape of the monument they formed part of

Practice(s) Way(s) of doing things, often habitually

Pragmatic An approach to investigation that sees itself as straightforward and realistic, based on practical issues and immediate problems rather than theoretical considerations

Prestige-goods Objects prized for the prestige they confer on their owner

Progenitor A person who originated a descent-group or practice

Rampart (Usually) a linear earth and timber bank used defensively

Recut A hole dug into a pre-existing pit or ditch, then filled

Retouch Secondary flaking of a flint or stone object along its edge

Revetment A wooden, stone, or turf wall retaining a bank

Ring-ditch Circular ditched monument with ditch around a central area

Ritual A non-utilitarian practice or ceremony; most practices (however mundane or habitual) involve a degree of ritual

Roughout The shaping out of a material form prior to its refinement

Sapwood The most recent active growth-ring of a plant or tree

Sarsen (stone) Boulders of silicified sandstone, occurring naturally on the chalk downlands of southern England

Scraper (Usually) a flint artefact, used to scrape rather than cut

Secondary products Milk, wool, textiles, and traction: aspects of domesticated animals exploited in a subsidiary way to their meat products

Sedentism The practice of settled occupation of the land

Segmented Of ditches and banks, earthworks dug discontinuously; of society, divided into kin-groups

Shouldered (carinated) Earthen pots or bowls with a sharp change in mid-profile

Silting The gradual natural infilling of a pit or ditch

Skeuomorph(ic) The transformation (or translation) of an object usually made in one material into another, for (social) effect

Social world The shared community environment in which people live, and which enfolds individuals in social obligations

Stable isotopes Lit., isotopes that do not decay; in the archaeological context generally refers to ratios of carbon, nitrogen, and oxygen from human and animal bones, which relate to aspects of an organism's diet during life

Stake(-hole) Similar to a post-hole (q.v.), but of smaller diameter

Strontium isotope Strontium (Sr) is an isotope found in human bone that can (with caveats) be used to infer where individuals originated

Struck flint Artefacts or by-products of knapping from cores or pebbles

Tenon (and mortice) Mutually fitting locating holes and slots, usually in timbers

Terminal (e.g. ditch) The butt-ends of individual lengths of ditch or bank

Thermoluminescence The property of some materials that have accumulated energy over a long period of luminescing when heated, which can be used as a basis for dating ceramics and hearths

Timber/stone circle Uprights arranged in circular or oval formations, sometimes in a concentric manner with more than one circuit

Tor enclosure The stone-built equivalent of a causewayed enclosure, but enclosing the summit of a natural granite outcrop

Trackway A carefully constructed (often timber) causeway

Tradition A set of related practices followed in time-honoured fashion

Tranchet (e.g. axehead) An axehead or arrowhead (usually flint) made by the removal of a flake to create a chisel-shaped cutting edge

Transformation Either rapid or gradual change which nonetheless alters fundamentally a prior state or set of relationships

Transition A process or period of change

Trapezoidal Kite-shaped, with reference to an artefact or monument

Tree-throw (hole) Hollow created by the overturning of the root-plate of a tree

Trilithon An arrangement of two upright stones capped by a third forming a lintel, as exemplified at Stonehenge

Turf-built A mound or revetment created by cutting and laying turf

Upright Stone or timber vertical member of a structure

Variability The variable nature or quality of an entity

Ware Term used to denote significantly different forms of pottery

Worked stone Stone modified to create an artefact

Bibliographical commentary

This book has deliberately featured neither profuse notes nor detailed bibliographical references. What we have provided here is not intended as a direct substitute for either. Rather, our aim is primarily to give the reader what we hope will be an informative introduction to the literature that the preceding chapters have drawn upon. That said, most of the works and key sites mentioned in the text are referenced here, so that it is made easier to consult the sources and interrogate many of the available facts upon which rest the arguments made throughout the book.

INTRODUCTION: NEOLITHIC BRITAIN— ENCOUNTERS AND REFLECTIONS

There are no popular accounts of Neolithic Britain that specifically try to conjure up what it was like to live in those times (although see Edmonds's *Ancestral Geographies* cited below, Ch. 1). Some books provide a vivid popular account of particular Neolithic research projects, and what it was like to be involved at the centre of them. Mike Pitts's *Hengeworld* (Arrow Books, 2000) and Mike Parker Pearson's *Stonehenge: Exploring the Greatest Stone Age Mystery* (Simon & Schuster, 2013) are good examples. More rarely, there are books that convey the flavour of studies focused upon a key class of object, with closely defined questions and an account of a specific research programme designed to discover more about, for instance, their manufacture and distribution. An example is Richard Bradley and Mark Edmonds, *Interpreting the Axe Trade: Production and Exchange in Neolithic Britain* (Cambridge University Press, 1993).

General books on the British Neolithic

David Miles's book *The Tale of the Axe: How the Neolithic Revolution Transformed Britain* (Thames & Hudson, 2016) provides a popular up-to-date introduction to the Neolithic in parallel with our book, but along very different lines (reviewed in detail in reference to the origins of the Neolithic in Britain, discussed in Ch. 2). Its scope extends back to the emergence of a definably Neolithic lifestyle in the Near East and its adoption across Europe. Its characterizations of society and life in the Neolithic are based on the notion that they were 'people like us', which is not necessarily the only, or even the best, way to approach that distant world. Miles's book, however, demonstrates some thoughtful use of ethnography to illuminate aspects of society and social practice, and it includes a number of acute observations arising from the recent development of more precise radiocarbon chronologies.

Vicki Cummings's textbook *Neolithic Britain and Ireland* (Routledge, 2017) has provided a useful up-to-date introduction to the sites and monuments of the Neolithic period right across the British Isles. It mentions most of the key phenomena concerning Neolithic Britain and Ireland, and provides an outline chronological and thematic narrative from the Mesolithic through to the Bronze Age. Its particular strength is in its detailed discussion of long barrows and chambered tombs, and in this regard it supplements, and to a degree supersedes, the similar treatment of many of the same key sites by Chris Scarre in his very much shorter handbook *The Megalithic Monuments of Britain and Ireland* (Thames & Hudson, 2007).

Aubrey Burl's book *Rites of the Gods* (Dent, 1981) includes chapters on Neolithic Britain within a general account of what he termed 'prehistoric religion'. Although by now considerably out of date, as noted in our Introduction Burl's book remains a worthwhile read for its use of site- or artefact-based descriptive vignettes to explore some of the complexity and intricacy of Neolithic cultural practices. Two other substantial, thoughtful, and much-recommended books that give vivid, well-illustrated, and 'user-friendly' accounts of the Neolithic period aimed at an enquiring public have been written by Steve Burrow and published by the National Museum of Wales in recent years. They are: *The Tomb Builders in Wales 4000–3000 BC* (2006) and *Shadowland: Wales 3000–1500 BC* (2011).

Specific sites mentioned in the Introduction (and also elsewhere in the book)

Durrington Walls: In recent years a number of intensive studies of the landscape around Stonehenge and the River Avon to its east have transformed our appreciation of that landscape and Neolithic activity within it. The Stonehenge Riverside Project that re-explored Durrington Walls and other sites has been the subject of various accounts including Parker Pearson's *Stonehenge* (2012, cited above), and *Stonehenge: Making Sense of a Prehistoric Mystery* (Council for British Archaeology, 2015) by Parker Pearson and the other project staff. An interim scientific summary of the 2003–9 investigations was provided in the magazine *Antiquity* in 2012.

Stonehenge: It has become almost obligatory for writers on the Neolithic period (and the Early Bronze Age) to reference from the outset what many people regard as the most remarkable fourth-/third-millennium monument to have survived into the present day in Europe. Certainly to ignore that remarkable structure would be akin to what Americanist archaeologists referred to some while ago when discussing *sampling* in archaeology (see the Conclusion to the present book) as 'the Teotihuacan problem' (Teotihuacan being a pre-Aztec capital north-west of Mexico City). There is the danger, in searching for the 'typical' sites while studying early settlement in a region, that the researcher misses the largest and/or most complex one. So Stonehenge remains not only iconic, but also central, within accounts of the Neolithic in Britain.

1. WRITING NEOLITHIC BRITAIN: AN INTERPRETIVE JOURNEY

The key work that we have referred to as, in a way, initiating the modern study of the Neolithic period in Britain (written, however, before the first 'radiocarbon revolution' of the late 1950s through to the early 1970s), is Stuart Piggott's *The Neolithic Cultures of the British Isles: A Study of the Stone-Using Agricultural Communities of Britain in the Second Millennium B.C.* (Cambridge University Press, 1954). However, this should also be set in context regarding wider writing about the 'revolutionary' advent and spread of the Neolithic, and especially the ideas and writing of Vere Gordon Childe. Particularly influential was his *The Dawn of European Civilisation* (Kegan Paul, 1925), which went through several revised editions into the 1960s.

Colin Renfrew's article entitled 'Monuments, Mobilisation and Social Organisation in Neolithic Wessex', that ushered in a new 'processual' era of study, appeared in a major volume that he edited (*The Explanation of Culture Change: Models in Prehistory* (Duckworth, 1973)). Two of the major sites discussed by Renfrew, the Durrington Walls and Mount Pleasant henges, had been excavated by Geoffrey Wainwright and the results were published by the Society of Antiquaries, in 1971 and 1979 respectively. The former volume featured both a seminal study of the Neolithic pottery by Ian Longworth, and an influential chapter by Longworth and Wainwright reassessing the 'Rinyo-Clacton Culture', as the principal element of the Later Neolithic traditions was then still termed (having been coined first by Childe).

Richard Bradley first wrote of prestige items circulating in the Later Neolithic as 'weapons of exclusion' in his book *The Social Foundations of Prehistoric Britain: Themes and Variations in the Archaeology of Power* (Longman, 1984), Ch. 3. John Barrett expanded upon his own ideas about labour and hierarchy at greatest length in his *Fragments from Antiquity: An Archaeology of Social Life in Britain, 2900–1200 BC* (Blackwell, 1994). Moreover, the results of an important field research collaboration between Barrett, Bradley, and Martin Green that involved a number of seasons' work investigating Neolithic (among other) sites on Cranborne Chase in Dorset (1977–87) were published as *Landscape, Monuments and Society: The Prehistory of Cranborne Chase* (Cambridge University Press, 1991). This dealt with the local implications of a number of their wider themes, and included discussion of sites such as the Dorset Cursus and the Wyke Down henge, mentioned in the present book.

The excavations at Hambledon Hill near Blandford Forum in Dorset (in the 1970s) and at Etton near Peterborough (1980s) were highly influential in the development of current interpretive approaches to causewayed enclosures. Their detailed publication by English Heritage (Etton in 1998 by Francis Pryor; Hambledon Hill in 2008 by Roger Mercer and Frances Healy—see here commentaries for Chapter 2 and Chapter 3) has provided some of the richest site-based data available for any fourth-millennium BCE locations.

The full title of Ian Hodder's wide-ranging book on the European Neolithic, featuring reflections on the concepts of 'domus' and 'agrios', was *The Domestication of Europe: Structure and Contingency in Neolithic Societies* (Blackwell, 1990). At almost the same time, Julian Thomas's book *Rethinking the Neolithic* (Cambridge University

Press, 1991; revised edition issued by Routledge in 1999) introduced to students of the British Neolithic concepts such as 'the genealogy of practices' that he has since elaborated upon and that still feature—more than twenty-five years on—in this volume. The full title of Mark Edmonds's book, also looking at Neolithic cultural and social practices and with a particular focus upon causewayed enclosures, is *Ancestral Geographies of the Neolithic: Landscapes, Monuments and Memory* (Routledge, 1999).

Richard Bradley built upon his early excursions into the interpretation of prestige items, monumentality, and the (especially votive) deposition of objects in innumerable papers, but particularly via a series of influential books. These traced such themes right through from the Neolithic to the Iron Age, and they include *The Passage of Arms: An Archaeological Analysis of Prehistoric Hoards and Votive Deposits* (Cambridge University Press, 1990), *The Significance of Monuments* (Routledge, 1998), and, especially relevant to Chapter 6 of this book, *The Past in Prehistoric Societies* (Routledge, 2002). His *Ritual and Domestic Life in Prehistoric Europe* (Routledge, 2005) underscores, in reference to a much wider range of examples, a number of points made concerning 'the ritual in everyday life' in this book. The full title of Christopher Tilley's ground-breaking (or controversial, depending on your perspective: witness Andrew Fleming's review of the book in *Antiquity*, 1994) book on the careful placing of monuments in the landscape was *A Phenomenology of Landscape: Places, Paths and Monuments* (Berg, 1994).

There are few published reflections upon the extent to which Stonehenge and sites in central southern England ('Wessex') and the Thames Valley on the one hand, and the Orkney archipelago on the other, have dominated and to a large extent skewed our appreciation of what happened in, and what was typical of, Neolithic Britain. However, the starkest critique of the effects of this bias in data and depiction was Gordon Barclay's essay, '"Metropolitan" and "Parochial"/"Core and Periphery": A Historiography of the Neolithic of Scotland', *Proceedings of the Prehistoric Society* 67 (2001), 1–18. Gordon Noble, Kenny Brophy, and others have, since then, shown just how alternative narratives based upon appreciation of the richness and variability of the Neolithic archaeology of mainland and island Scotland can transform our awareness of Britain's Neolithic archaeology (see, especially, Noble's *Neolithic Scotland: Timber, Stone, Earth and Fire* (Edinburgh University Press, 2006); and chapters in K. Brophy, G. MacGregor, and I. Ralston (eds.), *The Neolithic of Mainland Scotland* (Historic Scotland/Edinburgh University Press, 2016)).

The new attention to fine chronologies for the British Neolithic made possible by the adoption of Bayesian statistical analytical methods was ushered in during the early 2000s by a study that was published as a special Supplement of the *Cambridge Archaeological Journal* (17/1) in February 2007. This volume, featuring close redating of construction sequences for five Early Neolithic monuments, was edited by Alex Bayliss and Alasdair Whittle and was entitled *Histories of the Dead: Building Chronologies for Five Southern British Long Barrows*. Following on from this, a much larger research project adopted this approach especially to the dating of (mostly) causewayed enclosures, but also included a review of the dating of the earliest

Neolithic. The publication concerned is Alasdair Whittle, Frances Healy, and Alex Bayliss (eds.), *Gathering Time: Dating the Early Neolithic Enclosures of Southern Britain and Ireland* (Oxbow, 2011). Across two volumes and 992 pages, this publication contained two introductory chapters, nine regional essays, and three chapters of synthesis by a total of forty-three author-collaborators. A companion volume, on the (re)dating of Neolithic sites in northern England, is due to be published in 2018. Work is just beginning on a study of Scottish Neolithic excavations and monuments.

For the debate upon disparities and geographical biases, see again G. Barclay, *Proceedings of the Prehistoric Society* 67 (cited above), 1–16. The problem of regional invisibility and 'alternative Neolithic Britains' was also tackled by the same author in his 'Between Orkney and Wessex: The Search for the Regional Neolithics of Britain', in A. Ritchie (ed.), *Neolithic Orkney in its European Context*, McDonald Institute Monographs (University of Cambridge, 2000), 23–30.

There are, moreover, other ways to write the Neolithic of Britain, not so much from the standpoint of children or women as opposed to men, but rather from an emphasis for example upon the natural world and its influence upon and exploitation by Neolithic people. Just how different such narratives can be is evident in Gordon Noble's exegeses on wood and timber in his *Neolithic Scotland* (2006), but more especially in his recent book *Woodland in the Neolithic of Northern Europe: The Forest as Ancestor* (Cambridge University Press, 2017).

The major contribution to the debate made by Andrew Sherratt in reference to the need for 'grand' (globalizing) narratives alongside more intimate ones was 'Reviving the Grand Narrative: Archaeology and Long-term Change (The Second David L. Clarke Memorial Lecture), *Journal of European Archaeology* 3/1 (1995), 1–32. John Robb's article promoting what might be termed an 'assemblage theory' interpretation of the adoption of farming in Europe is 'Material Culture, Landscapes of Action and Emergent Causation: A New Model for the Origins of the European Neolithic', *Current Anthropology* 54/6 (2013), 657–83.

2. 4000 BCE: A CULTURAL THRESHOLD

Currently the account of the 'Mesolithic–Neolithic' transition that provides the most extensive and detailed evaluation (from data available by 2012) is J. Thomas's *The Birth of Neolithic Britain: An Interpretive Account* (Oxford University Press, 2013). The first 120 or so pages of that book outline what we know of the process of becoming Neolithic in southern and then northern continental Europe. The nature of recent debates, and their empirical and interpretive underpinnings, is then set out in a chapter subtitled 'a critical historiography'. A short chapter then discusses the millennium or so of the final Mesolithic in terms of themes such as 'diet and diversity'. A key chapter considers the timing of the transition, both overall and through discussion of particular places where clues about the nature of, and dates for, the adoption of a Neolithic lifestyle are especially revealing of the complexities involved. There then follow chapters that assess in detail the evidence for contact and seafaring, halls and houses, early timber (and earth and stone) structures, pottery-making and flint extraction, and plants and animals. Though generally well received, the book was criticized for lack of detail on the Mesolithic. To be fair, this data was not as fully marshalled as it might have been: however, relatively few sites had been published by the time of writing, and moreover what is remarkable is the pace of discovery and reporting of 'terminal' Mesolithic sites and features that has characterized the past five years. In the present book we have therefore highlighted some of this new information further.

Arguments for a 'multi-stranded' introduction of the Neolithic 'package' into various parts of Britain by migrant farmers from multiple regions of the European mainland have been expressed with both force and detail by Alison Sheridan in a series of publications. These include 'The Neolithization of Britain and Ireland: The Big Picture', in B. Finlayson and G. Warren (eds.), *Landscapes in Transition* (Oxbow, 2010), 89–105; 'From Picardie to Pickering and Pencraig Hill? New Information on the "Carinated Bowl Neolithic" in Northern Britain', in A. Whittle and V. Cummings (eds.), *Going Over: The Mesolithic–Neolithic Transition in North-West Europe* (British Academy, 2007), 441–92; and 'Ireland's Earliest "Passage" Tombs: A French Connection?', in G. Burenhult (ed.), *Stones and Bones* (British Archaeological Reports, 2003), 9–26.

Among the more general accounts, the transition is treated at length, as one might expect, in Miles, *The Tale of the Axe* (above, Introduction), discussed at some length in Chapters 1 and 2. One should be in no doubt about Miles's perspective. Although he identifies caveats, his is a story primarily about migrating farming pioneers entering a land only sparsely populated by indigenous hunter-gatherers. In some respects the tone is remarkably similar to that of Vere Gordon Childe ninety years previously, his 'axe' a metaphor for the conquest of nature through new technology. But his is ultimately also a moral tale: how farming was a trap that led to a host of problems (social, environmental, epidemiological, economic, and so on) that remain with us until the present day. Meanwhile, one of the best, précis-like chapters (Ch. 3, 'All Change?') of Vicki Cummings's recent textbook, *Neolithic Britain and Ireland* (Routledge, 2017), sketches the European background before outlining current debates concerning the transition in a well-balanced way via a series of 'key questions' concerning its course and consequences.

On the Mesolithic period as a whole, a multi-author thematic overview covering such questions as technology, gender and personhood, subsistence, ritual, landscape, and death is C. Conneller and G. Warren (eds.), *Mesolithic Britain and Ireland: New Approaches* (Tempus, 2006), 139–64. For more detailed studies, including the crucial issue of the 'lost' submerged landscapes of the southern British littoral, see also M. Bell (ed.), *Prehistoric Coastal Communities: The Mesolithic in Western Britain*, CBA Research Report 149 (2007).

The Maerdy oak post discovery is in process of being written up in some detail by its excavator, Richard Scott Jones, in an article entitled 'Late Mesolithic/Early Neolithic Decoratively Carved Timber from Rhondda Valley, Maerdy, Glamorgan'. In the meantime, an interim statement appeared in the Council for British Archaeology's annual publication, *Archaeology in Wales* 53 (2014), 79–82. References to some of the more recently reported Late Mesolithic sites cited in this chapter can either be found online (for example, Langford near Maldon, Essex), or in the pages of the archaeological news magazines *British Archaeology* and *Current Archaeology*. Meanwhile, the sites at Goldcliff by the Severn Estuary and elsewhere in coastal western Britain were fully reported in the monograph by Martin Bell and colleagues in Bell (ed.), *Prehistoric Coastal Communities* (see previous paragraph).

The deposits in the natural shaft at Fir Tree Field are discussed by Martin Green in his book *A Landscape Revealed: 10,000 Years on a Chalkland Farm* (Tempus, 2000), and have more recently been re-evaluated by Frances Healy in 'Timing and Process in the Fifth and Early Fourth Millennium Cal BC', in J. Debert, M. Larsson, and J. Thomas (eds.), *In Dialogue: Tradition and Interaction in the Mesolithic-Neolithic Transition* (British Archaeological Reports, 2016), 69–76. The Perry Oaks site and the Stanwell Cursus are described in J. Lewis et al., *Landscape Evolution in the Middle Thames Valley: Heathrow Terminal 5 Excavations*, i. *Perry Oaks* (Framework Archaeology, 2006).

An interim report on the exploration of deposits located in a low-lying water-logged hollow at Blick Mead adjacent to the Iron Age enclosure known as 'Vespasian's Camp' above the River Avon to the west of Amesbury was published as D. Jacques and T. Phillips, 'Mesolithic Settlement near Stonehenge: Excavations at Blick Mead, Vespasian's Camp, Amesbury', *Wiltshire Archaeological and Natural History Magazine*, 107 (2014) 7–27. The investigations at Carn Menyn and the suggestion of deliberate Mesolithic quarrying of dolerite outcrops in north Pembrokeshire were reported in outline in T. Darvill and G. Wainwright, 'Beyond Stonehenge: Carn Menyn Quarry and the Origin and Date of Bluestone Extraction in the Preseli Hills of South-West Wales', *Antiquity* 88/342 (2014), 1099–114.

The evidence for Mesolithic activity close to (the later monumental complex at) Stonehenge was first fully marshalled in the monograph by R. Montague, R. Cleal, and K. Walker, *Stonehenge in its Landscape: Twentieth-Century Excavations*, English Heritage Archaeological Report 10 (1995). The indications of pre-Neolithic activity at Hambledon Hill above the River Stour near Blandford Forum (including Mesolithic pits and two probable post-holes containing pine charcoal) were published in R. Mercer and F. Healy, *Hambledon Hill, Dorset, England: Excavation and Survey of a Neolithic Monument Complex and its Surrounding Landscape*, 2 vols. (English Heritage Archaeological Reports, 2008).

The important site (in particular for registering likely Late Mesolithic contacts with north-eastern France) at Old Quay, St Martin's, Isles of Scilly, has very recently been fully described in a monograph, D. Garrow and F. Sturt, *Neolithic Stepping Stones: Excavation and Survey within the Western Seaways of Britain, 2008–2014* (Oxbow, 2017). That volume also reports on other fieldwork undertaken as part of the University of Reading's 'Stepping Stones to the Neolithic' project at L'Eree, Guernsey, and at An Diorlinn, South Uist, Outer Hebrides, setting the project results in a wider review of the Neolithic in the archipelagos concerned. Meanwhile, the Warren Field, Crathes, pit alignment and its nearby timber hall located close to the north bank of the River Dee west of Aberdeen has been described in detail in

H. K. Murray, L. C. Murray, and S. M. Fraser, *A Tale of the Unknown Unknowns: A Mesolithic Pit Alignment and a Neolithic Timber Hall at Warren Field, Crathes, Aberdeenshire* (Oxbow, 2009). Discussion of the early pit alignment recorded at Nosterfield Quarry, Yorkshire, was included in J. Harding, *Cult, Religion and Pilgrimage: Archaeological Investigations at the Neolithic and Bronze Age Monument Complex of Thornborough, North Yorkshire*, CBA Research Report 174 (2013).

The Early Neolithic ditch- and post-defined cursus monuments excavated at Hollywood North and Hollywood South, located to the north-west of Dumfries in south-west Scotland, and the post alignment structures at Holm Farm close to Dumfries itself, have been published fully in a monograph edited by Julian Thomas, *Place and Memory: Excavations at The Pict's Knowe, Hollywood and Holm Farm, Dumfries and Galloway, 1994–8* (Oxbow, 2007). The subsequent investigation of the post-defined cursus at Dunragit associated with a Late Neolithic palisaded enclosure nearby has since been published by Julian Thomas as *A Neolithic Ceremonial Complex in Galloway: Excavations at Dunragit and Droughduil, 1999–2002* (Oxbow, 2015).

Middens found underneath (and therefore preceding the construction of) Neolithic long barrows are featured in a number of major monographs on the excavation of these monuments, which include Gwernvale in the Usk valley near Crickhowell (in W. J. Britnell and H. N. Savory, *Gwernvale and Penywyrlod: Two Neolithic Long Cairns in the Black Mountains of Brecknock*, Cambrian Archaeological Monographs 2 (1984); A. Saville, *Hazleton North, Gloucestershire, 1979–82: The Excavation of a Neolithic Long Cairn of the Cotswold-Severn Group*, English Heritage Archaeological Report 13 (1990); and D. Benson and A. Whittle (eds.), *Building Memories: The Neolithic Cotswold Long Barrow at Ascott-Under-Wychwood, Oxfordshire*, Cardiff Studies in Archaeology for English Heritage (Oxbow, 2007)). The last two are featured among the barrows re-studied for *Histories of the Dead* (Bayliss & Whittle, 2007) (above, Introduction), and the middening phenomenon is discussed in some detail in reference to all three barrows in Thomas, *The Birth of Neolithic Britain*, 230–5 and 237–41 (above, this section). Nor were such relationships of Mesolithic middens beneath Neolithic barrows or cairns only known from England, as is evident from the shell midden with Mesolithic flint core found over 100 years ago beneath Glechnabae chambered cairn on the Isle of Bute (Noble, *Neolithic Scotland*, 34) (above, Ch. 1).

The excavation of the complex Burn Ground long barrow in the Cotswolds was reported fully in W. F. Grimes, 'Burn Ground, Hampnett, Gloucestershire'. This was chapter 2 of his *Excavations on Defence Sites, 1939–45, i. Mainly Neolithic—Bronze Age*, Ministry of Works Archaeological Reports 3 (HMSO, 1960). And while the excavation of the Early Neolithic pit at Coneybury was first reported by Julian Richards as part of the Stonehenge Environs Project, an important reassessment of its date and contents has been carried out as part of a comparative regional study of fourth-millennium pottery (see Alistair Barclay, 'Re-dating the Coneybury Anomaly and its Implications for Understanding the Earliest Neolithic Pottery from Southern England', *PAST* 77 (July 2014), 11–13).

Roger Ellaby's comments upon the possible origins of leaf-shaped arrowheads in Britain are to be found in his 'Food for Thought: A Late Mesolithic Site at Charlwood, Surrey', in J. Cotton and D. Field (eds.), *Towards a New Stone Age: Aspects of the Neolithic in South-East England*, Council for British Archaeology Research Report 137 (2004), 12–23. The distinctiveness of the British leaf-shaped arrowhead as an artefact in terms of its mode of manufacture was noted in H. Anderson-Whymark and D. Garrow, 'Seaways and Shared Ways: Imagining and Imaging the Movement of People, Objects and Ideas over the Course of the Mesolithic–Neolithic Transition, c. 5,000–3,500 BC', in H. Anderson-Whymark, D. Garrow, and F. Sturt (eds.), *Continental Connections: Exploring Cross-Channel Relationships from the Lower Palaeolithic to the Iron Age* (Oxbow, 2015), 59–77.

The Yabsley Street burial was described in detail in the article by S. Coles, S. Ford, and A. Taylor, 'An Early Neolithic Grave and Occupation, and an Early Bronze Age Hearth on the Thames Foreshore at Yabsley Street, Blackwall, London', *Proceedings of the Prehistoric Society* 74 (2008), 215–33. The Rough Tor, Bodmin Moor, palynological study was described in detail by Ben Gearey and Dan Charman in their article 'Rough Tor, Bodmin Moor: Testing some Archaeological Hypotheses with Landscape Palaeoecology', in D. J. Charman, R. M. Newman, and D. G. Croot (eds.), *Devon and East Cornwall: Field Guide* (Quaternary Studies Association, 1996), 101–19.

Meanwhile, the White Horse Stone data is available online: C. Hayden and E. Stafford, *The Prehistoric Landscape at White Horse Stone, Aylesford, Kent* (CTRL Integrated Site Report Series, London and Continental Railways, 2006). See also C. Hayden, 'White Horse Stone and the Earliest Neolithic in the South East' (English Heritage: South East Research Framework resource assessment seminar, 2007).

Important discussions of processes of migration in prehistory have been provided by Stefan Burmeister, 'Archaeology and Migration: Approaches to an Archaeological Proof of Migration', *Current Anthropology* 41 (2000), 539–67, and David Anthony, 'Migration in Archaeology: The Baby and the Bathwater', *American Anthropologist* 92 (1990), 895–914. Issues of 'landscape learning', and the difficulties of maritime colonization by agricultural communities are discussed in various papers in the volume *Colonization of Unfamiliar Landscapes: The Archaeology of Adaptation* (Routledge, 2003), edited by Marcy Rockman and James Steele. The report on the DNA analysis of the woman from the Ballynahatty passage tomb is in L. Cassidy et al., 'Neolithic and Bronze Age Migration to Ireland and the Establishment of the Insular Atlantic Genome', *Proceedings of the National Academy of Sciences* 113 (2016), 368–73. DNA results from the Neolithic of the Paris Basin have been published by M. Rivollat et al., 'When the Waves of European Neolithization Met: First Palaeogenetic Evidence from Early Farmers in the Southern Paris Basin', *Plos One* 10:4 (2015), 1–16.

3. NARRATIVES FOR THE FOURTH MILLENNIUM

David Miles's *The Tale of the Axe* is cited fully already (above, Introduction), while *Gathering Time* is also referenced (above, towards the end of Ch. 1). For the Yabsley

Street timber-lined burial, see also above (Ch. 2). Many others among the sites mentioned in Chapter 3 have also been referenced above (Ch. 2).

The mound, pits, and stone settings at Eweford West in East Lothian are described in Thomas, *The Birth of Neolithic Britain*, 243–6 (above, Ch. 2), and were reported in more detail in O. Lelong and G. MacGregor (eds.), *The Lands of Ancient Lothian: Interpreting the Archaeology of the A1* (Society of Antiquaries of Scotland, 2007). Meanwhile, the 'shafts' at Fir Tree Field, Dorset, and Cannon Hill, Berkshire, are also noted at length in Thomas, *The Birth of Neolithic Britain*, 236–7 and 239–40 (above, Ch. 2).

The readily accessible literature concerning carinated bowls (or indeed any of the insular ceramic traditions) is limited in extent. An early exercise in attempting to isolate key features of the earliest ceramics therefore remains important. This is A. Herne, 'A Time and a Place for the Grimston Bowl', in J. Barrett and I. Kinnes (eds.), *The Archaeology of Context in the Neolithic and Bronze Age* (Department of Archaeology and Prehistory, University of Sheffield, 1988), 9–29. A more extensive discussion is found in Alison Sheridan, 'From Picardie to Pickering and Pencraig Hill? New Information on the "Carinated Bowl Neolithic" in Northern Britain', in A. Whittle and V. Cummings (eds.), *Going Over: The Mesolithic-Neolithic Transition in North-West Europe* (British Academy, 2007), 441–92, while new research that addresses the technology as well as the style of vessels has been presented by Hélène Pioffet in 'Societies and Identities During the Early Neolithic of Britain and Ireland in their West European Context: Characterization and Comparative Analysis of Pottery Production between Channel, Irish Sea and North Sea', *PAST* 87 (2017), 5–7. The results of the study of Middle Neolithic period Peterborough Ware and its conservative traditions (cited in the text later in the chapter) are reported in V. Ard and T. Darvill, 'Revisiting Old Friends: The Production, Distribution and Use of Peterborough Ware in Britain', *Oxford Journal of Archaeology* 34/1 (2015), 1–31.

The literature on Early Neolithic halls is now extensive, and much of it is cited in Thomas, *The Birth of Neolithic Britain* (above, Ch. 2). A distinctive perspective on their interpretation has been offered by Kenneth Brophy in his 'From Big House to Cult House: Early Neolithic Timber Halls in Scotland', *Proceedings of the Prehistoric Society* 73 (2007), 75–96.

The important excavations of Cotswolds long barrows at Hazleton North, Ascott-under-Wychwood, and Burn Ground were noted above (Ch. 2). Two of the excavations of Welsh long cairns were reported on by W. Britnell and H. Savory as *Gwernvale and Penywyrlod: Two Neolithic Long Cairns in the Black Mountains of Brecknock*, Cambrian Archaeological Monographs 2 (1984). Meanwhile, A. Whittle, D. Brothwell, R. Cullen, et al. reported on 'Wayland's Smithy, Oxfordshire: Excavations at the Neolithic Tomb in 1962–63 by R. J. C. Atkinson and S. Piggott', *Proceedings of the Prehistoric Society* 57/2 (1991), 61–101. For others of the Cotswold-Severn barrows we are fortunate to have Tim Darvill's book, *Long Barrows of the Cotswolds and Surrounding Areas* (Tempus, 2004), which provides both a comprehensive survey and thematic chapters. As yet, no other regional survey matches this standard, but Audrey Henshall produced major inventories of the Scottish Neolithic cairns, culminating in two volumes produced jointly with James Davidson

(*The Chambered Cairns of Orkney* and *The Chambered Cairns of Caithness* Edinburgh University Press, 1989 and 1991).

An overview of changing subsistence practices through the period under consideration is provided by Rick Schulting, under the title 'Foodways and Social Ecologies from the Early Mesolithic to the Early Bronze Age', in J. Pollard (ed.), *Prehistoric Britain* (Blackwell, 2008), 90–120. The character of garden cultivation of cereals is discussed by A. Bogaard and G. Jones, 'Neolithic Farming in Britain and Central Europe: Contrast or Continuity?', in A. Whittle and V. Cummings (eds.), *Going Over: The Mesolithic-Neolithic Transition in North-west Europe* (British Academy, 2007), 357–75. A more specific argument regarding economic change is offered by C. Stevens and D. Fuller, 'Did Neolithic Farming Fail? The Case for a Bronze Age Agricultural Revolution in the British Isles', *Antiquity* 86 (2012), 707–22. The argument for declining yields following the introduction of cereal cultivation is offered by P. Dark and H. Gent, 'Pests and Diseases of Prehistoric Crops: A Yield "Honeymoon" for Early Grain Crops in Europe?', *Oxford Journal of Archaeology* 20 (2001), 59–78.

Robert Hensey's reflections on the chronology of the Irish passage-tomb tradition are found in *First Light: the Origins of Newgrange* (Oxbow, 2015). The new chronological information on the passage tomb at Baltinglass Hill is found in R. Schulting, M. McClatchie, A. Sheridan, et al., 'Radiocarbon Dating of a Multi-phase Passage Tomb on Baltinglass Hill, Co. Wicklow, Ireland', *Proceedings of the Prehistoric Society* 83 (2017), 305–24.

An important appraisal of the concept of enclosure specific to fourth-millennium sites was Chris Evans's essay 'Acts of Enclosure: A Consideration of Concentrically-Organised Causewayed Enclosures', in J. C. Barrett and I. A. Kinnes (eds.), *Archaeology of Context in the Neolithic and Bronze Age* (University of Sheffield, 1988), 85–96. This essay obviously should now be read and appreciated in reference to the dating programmes concerning the enclosures that are reported in the *Gathering Time* volume (above, Ch. 1). Prior to the latter study, the results of a then-comprehensive survey of such sites had been published as A. Oswald, C. Dyer, and M. Barber, *The Creation of Monuments: Neolithic Causewayed Enclosures in the British Isles* (English Heritage, 2001). The important Etton enclosure was reported in detail in F. Pryor, *Etton: Excavations at a Neolithic Causewayed Enclosure near Maxey, Cambridgeshire, 1982–7*, English Heritage Archaeological Report 18 (1998). Alexander Keiller's excavations at Windmill Hill and a limited re-excavation in 1988 were reported in A. Whittle, J. Pollard, and C. Grigson, *The Harmony of Symbols: The Windmill Hill Causewayed Enclosure* (Oxbow, 1999).

The suggestion that British causewayed enclosures were simply domestic settlements, current in the 1960s and 1970s but not widely accepted since then, has recently been revived in P. Parmenter, E. Johnson, and A. Outram, 'Inventing the Neolithic? Putting Evidence-Based Interpretation Back into the Study of Faunal Remains from Causewayed Enclosures', *World Archaeology* 47 (2015), 819–33. A riposte to this argument has been written by one of the present authors as 'Cattle, Consumption and Causewayed Enclosures: A Response to Parmenter, Johnson and Outram', *World Archaeology* 48 (2016), 729–44.

The most complex among the northern series of large Neolithic round barrows concentrated in the Yorkshire Wolds is at Duggleby Howe, which has been the subject of a recent field study: A. Gibson and A. Bayliss, 'Recent Research at Duggleby Howe, North Yorkshire', *Archaeological Journal* 166 (2009), 39–78, and A. Gibson, 'Report on the Excavation at the Duggleby Howe Causewayed Enclosure, North Yorkshire, May–July 2009', *Archaeological Journal* 168 (2011), 1–63. A full review of the burial and structural sequence was published: A. Gibson, 'Space and Episodic Ritual at the Monumental Neolithic Round Mound of Duggleby Howe, North Yorkshire, England', in G. Robin, A. D'Anna, A. Schmitt, and M. Bailly (eds.), *Fonctions, utilisations et représentations de l'espace dans les sépultures monumentales du Néolithique européen* [*Functions, uses and representations of space in the monumental graves of Neolithic Europe*], Préhistoires de la Méditerranée (Presses Universitaires de Provence, 2014), 117–30.

4. SOCIAL BEING AND CULTURAL PRACTICES

John Robb's article explaining the entanglement of people in the Neolithic was mentioned earlier (above, towards the end of Ch. 1). Overviews of the history and investigative history of the Sussex flint mines have been documented by Miles Russell, *Flint Mines in Neolithic Britain* (Tempus, 2000); and *Rough Quarries, Rock and Hills: John Pull and the Neolithic Flint Mines of Sussex* (Oxbow, 2001). A detailed site-by-site study of the flint mines, including new surveys, appeared as Martyn Barber, David Field, and Peter Topping, *The Neolithic Flint Mines of England* (English Heritage, 1999). Anne Teather has published her (2008) University of Sheffield Ph.D. thesis as *Mining and Materiality: Neolithic Chalk Artefacts and their Depositional Contexts in Southern Britain* (Archaeopress Archaeology, 2016). The 1971–2 excavations at Grimes Graves were reported in R. J. Mercer, *Grimes Graves, Norfolk: Excavations 1971–72* (HMSO, 1981), i. The most recent dating of the phases of activity at the site was reported in A. Bayliss, C. Bronk-Ramsey, G. T. Cook, et al., *Grimes Graves, Weeting-with-Broomhill, Norfolk: Radiocarbon Dating and Chronological Modelling*, English Heritage Research Report 27 (2014).

Among (relatively) recent reviews of the evidence for feasting at particular Neolithic sites is Dale Serjeantson, 'Food or Feast at Neolithic Runnymede?', in D. Serjeantson and D. Field (eds.), *Animals in the Neolithic of Britain and Europe* (Oxbow, 2006), 113–34. The Rudston Wold 'event' was reported in in P. Rowley-Conwy and A. Cohen, 'Grooved Ware Feasting in Yorkshire: Late Neolithic Animal Consumption at Rudston Wold', *Oxford Journal of Archaeology* 30/4 (2011), 325–67. The burial mound at Irthlingborough with evidence of a massive feast was reported in J. Harding and F. Healy, *A Neolithic and Bronze Age Landscape in Northamptonshire*, i. *The Raunds Area Project* (English Heritage, 2008).

Amelia Pannett's discussion of pit clusters in the Towy valley is to be found in 'Pits, Pots and Plant Remains: Trends in Neolithic Deposition in Carmarthenshire, South Wales', in H. Anderson-Whymark and J. Thomas (eds.), *Regional Perspectives on Neolithic Pit Deposition* (Oxbow, 2012), 126–43. This was accompanied in the same volume by overviews of the evidence for pit-digging and depositional practices covering Ireland, Man, western Scotland, lowland Scotland, Northumberland, the Middle Trent valley, the Severn–Wye region, and the Thames Valley. The Kilverstone pit complex in Norfolk was most extensively reported in D. Garrow, M. Beadsmore, and M. Knight, 'Pit Clusters and the Temporality of Occupation: An Earlier Neolithic Site at Kilverstone, Thetford, Norfolk', *Proceedings of the Prehistoric Society* 71 (2005), 139–57.

Joshua Pollard's observation about Grooved Ware pits was made in 'Living With Sacred Spaces: The Henge Monuments of Wessex', in A. Gibson (ed.), *Enclosing the Neolithic: Recent Studies in Britain and Europe*, BAR International Series 2440 (2012), 93–107. Hugo Anderson-Whymark published his Ph.D. as H. Lamdin-Whymark, *The Residue of Ritualized Action: Neolithic Deposition Practices in the Middle Thames Valley*, British Archaeological Reports 466 (2008). And the novel evidence for the use of pottery to store milk products was reported in M. Copley, R. Berston, A. Mukherjee, et al., 'Dairying in Antiquity III: Evidence from Absorbed Lipid Residues Dating to the British Neolithic', *Journal of Archaeological Science* 32 (2005), 523–46.

The Girvan Warehouse 37 site is discussed in an overview report on work across the Girvan Distillery site in I. Banks, P. Duffy, and G. MacGregor, *Archaeology of Landscape Change in South-West Scotland: Excavations at William Grant and Sons Distillery, Girvan*, Scottish Archaeology Internet Report 32 (2009). Also regarding pits and deposition in Scotland and the questions discussed in this chapter, see G. Noble, C. Christie, and E. Philip, 'Life is the Pits! Ritual, Refuse and Mesolithic–Neolithic Settlement Traditions in North-East Scotland', in K. Brophy, G. MacGregor, and I. Ralston (eds.), *The Neolithic of Mainland Scotland* (Edinburgh University Press, 2016), 171–99. In the same book, Kenneth Brophy's 'On Ancient Farms: A Survey of Neolithic Potentially Domestic Locations in Lowland Scotland', 200–35, discusses the whole issue of what is meant by 'dwelling' and 'domestic occupation' in reference to the wide variety of structures that have come to light especially in the last two decades associated with densities of Neolithic deposits. Niall Sharples' observations on the treatment of red deer in the Orcadian Neolithic were published as 'Antlers and Orcadian Rituals: An Ambiguous Role for Red Deer in the Neolithic', in Ritchie (ed.), *Neolithic Orkney in its European Context*, 107–16 (above, Ch. 1).

The questions around warfare in the Neolithic arose in recent decades from the results of excavations at sites such as Hambledon Hill. The relation of arrowheads to warfare was first highlighted in an article by M. Edmonds and J. Thomas, 'The Archers: An Everyday Story of Country Folk', in A. Brown and M. Edmonds (eds.), *Lithic Analysis and Later British Prehistory*, British Archaeological Reports 162 (1987), 187–99. The key article so far concerning 'harm' in terms of the skeletal impact especially of blunt weapons was R. Schulting and M. Wysocki, ' "In this Chambered Tumulus were Found Cleft Skulls . . .": An Assessment of the Evidence for Cranial Trauma in the British Neolithic', *Proceedings of the Prehistoric Society* 71 (2005), 107–38.

The dispersal of human bones across the landscape in the Mesolithic period was discussed in Chantal Conneller's chapter on 'Death' in C. Conneller and G. Warren (eds.), *Mesolithic Britain and Ireland: New Approaches* (Tempus, 2006), 139–64. Jacqueline McKinley's report on the human remains from Hambledon Hill is 'Human Remains and Diet', in R. Mercer and F. Healy, *Hambledon Hill, Dorset, England: Excavation and Survey of a Neolithic Monument Complex and its Surrounding Landscape* (English Heritage 2008), i., 477–535. The remarkable burial pit at Banbury Lane was first reported in M. Holmes, A. Yates, A. Chapman, and Y. Wolframm-Murray, 'A Middle Neolithic Enclosure and Mortuary Deposit at Banbury Lane, Northampton: An Interim Report', *Northamptonshire Archaeology* 37 (2012), 19–28.

5. NARRATIVES FOR THE THIRD MILLENNIUM

The evidence from a number of sites for the development of house architecture and constructed space in Orkney has been gathered together very recently in C. Richards and R. Jones (eds.), *The Development of Neolithic House Societies in Orkney* (Oxbow, 2016). Much of the discussion in the opening pages of this chapter draws upon these and other recent articles. See also papers in Ritchie (ed.), *Neolithic Orkney in its European Context* (above, Ch. 1). The sequence at Barnhouse has been more closely defined recently in C. Richards, A. Jones, A. MacSween, et al., 'Settlement Duration and Materiality: Formal Chronological Models for the Development of Barnhouse, a Grooved Ware Settlement in Orkney', *Proceedings of the Prehistoric Society* 82 (2016), 193–225. An insightful discussion of the organization of space and community at Neolithic Skara Brae is Alexandra Shepherd, 'Skara Brae. Expressing Identity in a Neolithic Community', in Ritchie (ed.), *Neolithic Orkney*, 139–58 (above, Ch. 1). Andrew Meirion Jones's study of the temper in Grooved Ware pottery from the Barnhouse site is to be found in his *Archaeological Theory and Scientific Practice* (Cambridge University Press, 2001). The most recent discussion of the evidence from the Ness of Brodgar is N. Card, I. Mainland, S. Timpany, et al., 'To Cut a Long Story Short: Formal Chronological Modelling for the Late Neolithic Site of Ness of Brodgar, Orkney', *European Journal of Archaeology* (2017), 1–47. The overall chronology of the Orkney sequence has been reassessed by A. Bayliss, P. Marshall, C. Richards, et al., as 'Islands of History: The Late Neolithic Timescape of Orkney', *Antiquity* 91/359 (2017), 1171–88.

Recent re-study of The Sanctuary and new fieldwork in its environs has been reported in M. Pitts, 'Excavating the Sanctuary: New Investigations on Overton Hill, Avebury', *Wiltshire Archaeological and Natural History Magazine* 94 (2001), 1–23.

The relationship between the primary activities at Durrington Walls and the building of Stonehenge has been assessed in O. E. Craig, L.-M. Shillito, U. Albarella, et al., 'Feeding Stonehenge: Cuisine and Consumption at the Late Neolithic Site of Durrington Walls', *Antiquity* 89 (2015), 1096–109.

One of the most extensive discussions of 'henging' (as a practice) is to be found in K. Brophy and G. Noble, 'Henging, Mounding and Blocking: the Forteviot Henge Group', in Gibson (ed.), *Enclosing the Neolithic*, 21–36 (above, Ch. 4).

The question of the sourcing of the bluestones eventually set up at Stonehenge (and in its environs) has been addressed in a series of articles by Mike Parker Pearson and colleagues, one of which reported work at 'Craig Rhos-y-felin: A Welsh Bluestone Megalithic Quarry for Stonehenge', *Antiquity* 89 (2015), 1331–52.

The massive Late Neolithic palisaded enclosure at Hindwell was first reported in A. Gibson, *The Walton Basin Project: Excavation and Survey in a Prehistoric Landscape 1993–7*, Council for British Archaeology Research Report 118 (1999). More recently, the Walton palisaded enclosure has been discovered and test-excavated to the south but in the same area of lowland enfolded in between high hills on the border between England and Wales (Radnorshire and Herefordshire). See N. Jones, *Walton Palisaded Enclosure: Geophysical Survey and Excavation, 2009–10*, Clwyd-Powys Archaeological Trust Report 1026 (2010). A recent investigation of another palisaded site in northern England is found in D. Hale, A. Platell, and A. Millard, 'A Late Neolithic Palisaded Enclosure at Marne Barracks, Catterick, North Yorkshire', *Proceedings of the Prehistoric Society* 75 (2009), 265–304. The Dunragit enclosure, and the nearby Droughduil mound, are described in Thomas, *A Neolithic Ceremonial Complex* (above, Ch. 2).

A discussion of 'monument complexes' (as opposed to individual monuments) is found in Harding, *Cult, Religion and Pilgrimage* (above, Ch. 2), on the Thornborough henge complex and its relationship to the cursus monuments nearby.

The fullest published account of the recently excavated rich Beaker graves in the Stonehenge area is A. Fitzpatrick, *The Amesbury Archer and the Boscombe Bowmen: Bell Beaker Burials at Boscombe Down, Amesbury*, Wessex Archaeological Reports 27 (2011). The dating of Beaker burials to trace a clear developmental sequence for changing styles of beakers has been a major concern of prehistorians in the last two decades, but certainty has remained elusive. As a result, several different historical models have been proposed for how the British evidence fits the European pattern. A traditional perspective on the question of connections between Holland and Britain at the end of the (British) Neolithic was produced by Harry Fokkens, 'Dutchmen on the Move? A Discussion of the Adoption of the Beaker Package', in M. Allen, J. Gardiner, and A. Sheridan, *Is There a British Chalcolithic? People, Place and Polity in the Later 3rd Millennium*, Prehistoric Society Research Paper 4 (2012), 115–25.

One of the most elaborate such interpretive models is Stuart Needham, 'Transforming Beaker Culture in North West Europe; Processes of Fission and Fusion', *Proceedings of the Prehistoric Society* 71 (2005), 171–217, in which he envisaged an initial period, c.2500–2250 cal BCE, in which, as we described in Chapter 5, Beaker burials were 'thinly spread and interstitial' within a Grooved Ware tradition-dominated cultural landscape, followed by a period in which the Beaker emerged as 'instituted culture'. Needham envisaged this as occurring insidiously, through a process in which 'Beaker cultural values, both material and conceptual' overcame existing values and 'the prevailing cultural ethos'. Within the period c.2250–2150 BCE there was, Needham noted, a 'fission horizon' in which pot forms and decorative styles rapidly diversified, signalling the widespread adoption of a Beaker social/cultural lifestyle, reflected in large numbers of standardized burial practices (flexed inhumation in pits or stone-lined cists, in particular), accompanied nonetheless by a huge variety in Beaker pot styles (within a standard overall form) and decorative schemes.

The aDNA study of Beaker-era population movement and population replacement is found in I. Olalde et al., 'The Beaker Phenomenon and the Genomic Transformation of Northwest Europe' (bioRxiv, 2017).

6. KINSHIP, HISTORY, AND DESCENT

The question of the relationship between the extent of forest and woodland and the location of settlement and monuments was one of the themes explored by Mike Allen and Julie Gardiner in 'If You Go Down to the Woods Today: A Re-evaluation of the Chalkland Postglacial Woodland; Implications for Prehistoric Communities', in M. Allen, N. Sharples, and T. O'Connor (eds.), *Land and People: Papers in Memory of John G. Evans*, Prehistoric Society Research Paper 2 (2009), 49–66. The research on pollen cores that indicated the occurrence of large-scale Neolithic clearance around the flank of Rough Tor is documented in B. Gearey and D. Charman, 'Rough Tor, Bodmin Moor: Testing some Archaeological Hypotheses with Large Scale Palynology', in D. Charman, R. Newnham, and D. Croot (eds.), *Devon and East Cornwall Field Guide* (Quaternary Research Association, 1996), 101–19.

The most extensive publication of the Sweet Track and other Neolithic trackways in Somerset has been in the series of *Somerset Levels Papers* produced in the 1970s by John Coles and his collaborators. Copies of these are nonetheless hard to locate, so the most accessible publication remains J. Coles and B. Coles, *Sweet Track to Glastonbury: The Somerset Levels in Prehistory* (Thames & Hudson, 1986), which devotes the whole of ch. 3 to the Sweet Track excavation and finds. Ours is not the only perspective that has stressed the liminal and beyond-simply-functional aspects of the Track: see also C. Bond, 'The Sweet Track, Somerset: A Place Mediating Culture and Spirituality?', in T. Insoll (ed.), *Belief in the Past: The Proceedings of the 2002 Manchester Conference on Archaeology and Religion*, British Archaeological Reports s1212 (2004), 37–50.

The present authors' article on Neolithic cattle and human genealogies is K. Ray and J. Thomas, 'In the Kinship of Cattle: The Social Centrality of Cattle in the Early Neolithic of Southern Britain', in M. Parker Pearson (ed.), *Food, Culture and Identity in the Neolithic and Early Bronze Age*, British Archaeological Reports S1117 (2003), 37–44. A frequently cited article, R. Bollongino and J. Burger, 'Neolithic Cattle Domestication as Seen from Ancient DNA', *Proceedings of the British Academy* 144 (2007), 165–87, asserted strongly that all available evidence pointed towards domesticated cattle in Britain having derived ultimately from Near Eastern populations. However, although no one has apparently yet seriously proposed an indigenous domesticated stock of cattle, there is a view emerging that the history of cattle-breeding in Britain was potentially more complex. One example of this is the article by S. Park et al., 'Gene Sequencing of the Extinct Eurasian Wild Aurochs, *Bos primigenius*, Illuminates the Phylogeography and Evolution of Cattle', *Genome Biology* 16 (2015), https://genomebiology.biomedcentral.com/articles/10.1186/s13059-015-0790-2, accessed 18 January 2018, which identified a 'complex domestic history of cattle, most notably a Northern Eurasian aurochs component to the genetic ancestry of modern British and Irish cattle (specifically, Highland, Dexter, Kerry Welsh Black and White Park breeds) which may have arisen through purposeful restocking with wild aurochs by early herders in Britain'. The analysis of strontium isotopes in cattle teeth from Durrington Walls is documented in S. Viner, J. Evans, U. Albarella, and M. Parker Pearson, 'Cattle Mobility in Prehistoric Britain: Strontium Isotope Analysis of Cattle Teeth from Durrington Walls (Wiltshire, Britain)', *Journal of Archaeological Science* 37 (2010), 2812–20.

The Implement Petrology Group published a series of reports on the analysis of stone axeheads and other prehistoric stone implements from across Britain from the 1950s onwards. The IPG produced a volume edited by T. McK. Clough and W. Cummins entitled *Stone Axe Studies: Archaeological, Petrological, Experimental and Ethnographic,* Council for British Archaeology Research Report 23 (1979). A further, more comprehensive IPG volume also edited by McK. Clough and Cummins was *Stone Axe Studies 2: The Petrology of Prehistoric Stone Implements from the British Isles*, CBA Research Report 67 (1988). This has now been updated (V. Davis and M. Edmonds (eds.), *Stone-Axe Studies III* (Oxbow, 2011), comprises a series of disconnected essays on stone axe researches internationally, with a handful of British studies of particular and mostly newly explored source-locations in Britain).

A nonetheless similarly comprehensive study of axes, but focusing exclusively on those thought to have been imported into Britain, was undertaken by Katherine Walker in the past few years and was produced as a Southampton University Ph.D. thesis in 2015. Entitled 'Axe-heads and Identity: An Investigation into the Roles of Imported Axe-heads in Identity Formation in Neolithic Britain', it examined the jade and jadeitite examples made subject to recent sourcing and contextual study in the international 'Projet JADE', along with the highly polished marbled flint axes and the robust triangular-sectioned flint axes whose bona fide Neolithic Continental origins have, in the past, been questioned.

The incised chalk-block from The Trundle is discussed in Anne Teather's book *Mining and Materiality: Neolithic Chalk Artefacts and their Depositional Contexts in Southern Britain* (Archaeopress Archaeology, 2016), 54–5. In reference to Stoney Littleton, it may be worth noting the relative proximity of the rare Mesolithic cemetery discovered in Aveline's Hole in the nearby Mendip Hills. The undated, but presumed late Upper Palaeolithic, ochre-accompanied double burial found in the cave has recently been reassessed as more likely of Mesolithic date by Chantal Conneller in her chapter on 'Death' in C. Conneller and G. Warren (eds.), *Mesolithic Britain and Ireland: New Approaches* (Tempus, 2006), 139–64. It may be simply coincidental, but it is of interest to note that buried close to the head of one of these two skeletons was a pile of seven fragments of ammonites (148–54);

see also R. Schulting and M. Wysocki, 'The Mesolithic Human Skeletal Collection from Aveline's Hole: A Preliminary Note', *Proceedings of the University of Bristol Speleological Society* 22 (2001), 255–68.

The principal published discussion of the meaning of the contrasts observable between the Kingsborough 1 and 2 causewayed enclosures is M. Leivers and M. Allen, 'Landscape, Enclosure and Ceremony', in M. Allen, M. Leivers, and S. Ellis, 'Neolithic Causewayed Enclosures and Later Prehistoric Farming: Duality, Imposition and the Role of Predecessors at Kingsborough, Isle of Sheppey, Kent, UK', *Proceedings of the Prehistoric Society* 74 (2008), 235–322.

The Malagasy 'take' on the purpose of the Stonehenge stones was published as M. Parker Pearson and Ramilsonina, 'Stonehenge for the Ancestors: The Stones Pass on the Message', *Antiquity* 72 (1998), 308–26. Colin Richards has discussed the individuation of stones in stone circles, and the significance of their places of origin, in his book, *Building the Great Stone Circles of the North* (Windgather, 2013).

The description of axe-smashing in north-west Wales is contained in J. Llewellyn Williams and J. Kenney, 'Graig Lwyd (Group VII) Lithic Assemblages from the Excavations at Parc Bryn Cegin, Llandygai, Gwynedd, Wales—Analysis and Interpretation', *Internet Archaeology* 26 (2009), https://doi.org/10.11141/ia.26.30, accessed 18 January 2018. Mark Edmonds's account of the fragmented and whole axeheads from Etton causewayed enclosure is to be found in his contribution to the report 'Polished Stone Axes and Associated Artefacts', in F. Pryor, *Etton: Excavations at a Neolithic Causewayed Enclosure near Maxey, Cambridgeshire, 1982–7*, English Heritage Archaeological Report 18 (1998), 260–8. The definition of the Neolithic practice of 'cultural reclamation' is owing to a personal comment by Anne Teather, and her forthcoming article, 'Revealing a Prehistoric Past: Evidence for the Deliberate Construction of a Historic Narrative in the British Neolithic', which she kindly gave us sight of prior to its publication.

The Neolithic settlement of the Links of Noltland on Westray is described by D. Clarke and N. Sharples in their chapter on 'Settlements and Subsistence in the Third Millennium BC', in C. Renfrew (ed.), *The Prehistory of Orkney* (Edinburgh University Press, 1985), 54–82.

CONCLUSION: A LIVED NEOLITHIC

A discussion of the issues surrounding the Orkney vole can be found in A. Bayliss, P. Marshall, C. Richards, et al., 'Islands of History: The Late Neolithic Timescape of Orkney', *Antiquity* 91 (2017), 1171–88. The analysis of red deer DNA in relation to their arrival in the northern and western isles is found in D. Stanton, J. Mulville, and M. Bruford, 'Colonization of the Scottish Islands via Long-Distance Transport of Red Deer', *Proceedings of the Royal Society B* (2016).

Andrew Sherratt's reflections on the distinctive character of the Neolithic in Britain, Ireland, and north-west France are to be found in the chapter 'Changing Perspectives on European Prehistory', in an invaluable collection of his papers, *Economy and Society in Prehistoric Europe: Changing Perspectives* (Edinburgh University Press, 1997), 1–34.

An outline of chronologies

This outline is intended as a brief guide to how the passage of time is compre-
hended in archaeological studies and also how accounts of Neolithic history are
created by archaeologists from the remains, including structures, deposits, artefacts,
and, for example, palaeo-environmental and laboratory analytical data, that they
investigate. The outline discusses how chronologies (reckonings of the passage of
time and dated sequences) are established and what they mean, historically and in
terms of lived lives. It also provides a summary *timeline* that correlates developments
in different parts of Britain across the centuries concerned.

This account of time as it affects our understanding of Neolithic life and history
does not set out to survey all the different scientific dating methods used by archaeologists, nor does it explain in any detail the science behind them. Rather, it first
provides some basic information about radiocarbon dating and its calibration, and
about dendrochronology, since these are the techniques most commonly used, particularly in relation to the Neolithic period (other methodologies are more useful
in addressing more ancient, or more recent, eras). It then discusses in general terms
how archaeologists set about creating chronologies (meaning, in this context, interpretations of past sequences of activity) both within and between individual 'sites'.
It goes on to set out how historical narratives are derived from these chronologies,
and how this relates to and compares with the temporalities (the varied scales and
unfolding of time as they relate to lived experience in the past or the present) of
individual and social existence. Finally, a chart is provided that maps (in simple
terms) the elapsing of time against cultural development as set out especially in the
narrative chapters of this book.

HOW CHRONOLOGIES ARE BUILT: BACKGROUND AND BRIEF SUMMARY

Radiocarbon dating (also termed 'carbon-14 dating') has been around now for
many years, starting in the late 1940s when the American chemist Willard Libby
originated a means of establishing how long ago a once-living organism expired
and no longer absorbed carbon from the atmosphere. Most carbon comprises two
isotopes, carbon 12 and carbon 13, and these are inherently stable. A very small percentage of carbon, however, comprises radiocarbon (carbon 14), and this is unstable,
meaning that it decays. A living organism continues to absorb carbon 14 along with

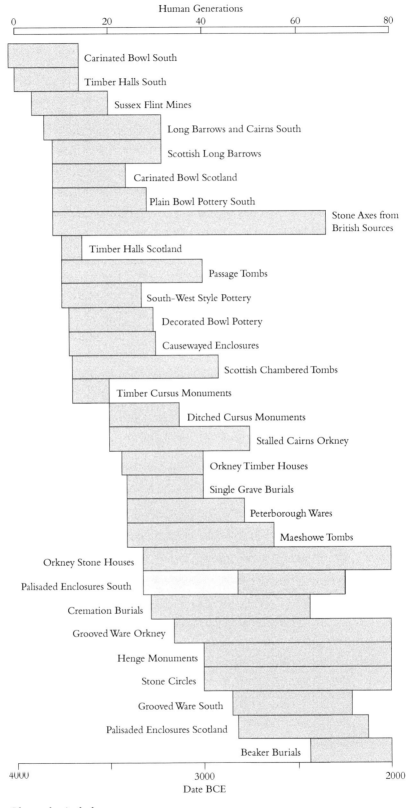

Human Generations

0   20   40   60   80

Carinated Bowl South
Timber Halls South
Sussex Flint Mines
Long Barrows and Cairns South
Scottish Long Barrows
Carinated Bowl Scotland
Plain Bowl Pottery South
Stone Axes from British Sources
Timber Halls Scotland
Passage Tombs
South-West Style Pottery
Decorated Bowl Pottery
Causewayed Enclosures
Scottish Chambered Tombs
Timber Cursus Monuments
Ditched Cursus Monuments
Stalled Cairns Orkney
Orkney Timber Houses
Single Grave Burials
Peterborough Wares
Maeshowe Tombs
Orkney Stone Houses
Palisaded Enclosures South
Cremation Burials
Grooved Ware Orkney
Henge Monuments
Stone Circles
Grooved Ware South
Palisaded Enclosures Scotland
Beaker Burials

4000   3000   2000
Date BCE

Chronological chart

the other isotopes, so the lost amount is replenished. When the organism dies, how-ever, the radiocarbon that it has absorbed when living reduces on its decay path logarithmically, and the rate of decrease is by one-half of the quantity at death every 5,730 years. It was Libby's discovery that this decay is measurable against the elaps-ing of time since the organism's death calculated against the constant of the amount of carbon in the Earth's atmosphere that enabled 'absolute' dates to be cal-culated. As noted in Chapter 1, this revolutionized prehistoric chronology.

A complication was soon noted, however, in that objects in the Near East that were closely dated historically were found to have anomalous returns when dated by the radiocarbon method. This confirmed the suspicion that the ratio of carbon 14 to carbon 12 has varied through time, due to different quantities of carbon in the atmosphere through time (so causing variable rates of absorption). It was realized therefore, that to approximate 'true dates', the measurements in 'radiocarbon years' would need to be calibrated against the ring-counting of long-lived ancient trees, starting with California's bristlecone pines. This produces a 'dating curve' that indicates the degree of variation from a standard mean through time. When linked to a calculation of probability for individual dates falling within the parameters of the curve at different points, this can provide a close estimate (through programmes such as INTCAL and OxCal) of the likelihood of the date from an individual sample falling within a span of as little as ten years in many cases. A refinement of the processing of carbon 14 samples, involving the application of Accelerator Mass Spectrometry (AMS), has meanwhile enabled much smaller entities, such as seeds, to return radiocarbon dates.

A north-west European tree-ring chronology has been built up by linking the ring-counts and patterns of growth-width from living trees back through an oak-based master chronology derived from archaeological or bog-oak samples. This enables dendrochronology to provide closely reliable radiocarbon calibration for the past 7,429 years in Ireland and 6,939 years in England. In detailed scientific reporting of the dating of radiocarbon samples from wood, bone, seeds, and other organic materials, the standard deviation is normally quoted at different probabilities. However, in books such as this a particular quoted date is stated only as 'cal BCE' to indicate that this is a calibrated date. Dendrochronology not only depends upon the survival of wood that can be appropriately sampled, but also upon long enough series of growth-rings in trees to enable matching against the master-chronologies. The growth-ring pattern of oaks in western Britain has been highly susceptible to climatic variation through time, so producing more easily matched series. Dendrochronological dates are usually rendered as time before present (BP). Other techniques of dating applicable to the Neolithic period have been developed in recent decades that enable sequences of activity to be 'bracketed'. An example is Optically Stimulated Luminescence (OSL) dating, which measures the last occasion when particular deposits were exposed to sunlight. See Mike Walker, *Quaternary Dating Methods* (Wiley, 2005) for details of radiocarbon, dendrochronology, OSL, and other methods.

BUILDING CHRONOLOGIES FOR INDIVIDUAL SITES

Paradoxically, an archaeological 'site' is regarded by archaeologists as two different things. A site is both any locus of past activity (complex and apparently confined and coherent examples of which are routinely referred to as 'monuments'), and any location that happens to be a focus for archaeological investigation (referred to in inventories of sites as an 'archaeological event' affecting the site concerned). So an archaeological 'site' can be either a place that witnessed activity that happened in the past, or a place of archaeological labours in the present (or recent past).

The chronology of a 'site' that existed in the past is created by archaeologists in both relative and absolute terms. The first is independent of any dating of the spans of time represented by the sequence of activity on that site, while the capacity to achieve the second depends upon the survival of organic or other material that can be sampled and that is therefore capable of returning a date. However, it is not just survival that matters in producing reliable determination of dates. First, the material to be sampled must relate to a particular event, such as, for example, the digging of a pit or an episode in its infilling; or the digging of a post-hole, the raising of a post within it, the withdrawal or the decay of that post *in situ*, or the burning of that post. And this context must have been *sealed*, that is, not affected by later disturbance or contaminating effects from soil processes, up until the point when archaeological excavation and the retrieval of the sample takes place. Moreover, the sample itself must be protected from modern contamination between the archaeological site and the laboratory.

In recent years the crucial importance of dating short-lived organisms, and bones that have entered the ground articulated together (and therefore discarded at a single point in time, rather than having derived from earlier deposits), has come to be fully appreciated. Further, it has been realized that the obtaining of a multiple series of samples taken from different contexts within the span of activity represented by the stratigraphic sequence within a site are vital to the creation of a reliable site chronology. It is this, combined with Bayesian statistical analyses, that identifies and hopefully removes 'anomalous' dates from the series, that has enabled the close estimates of the likely beginnings and endings of episodes of construction and abandonment of structures (components of monuments or major phases of activity) to be defined for sites like the long barrows or causewayed enclosures mentioned especially in Chapter 3 of this book.

CROSS-DATING BETWEEN SITES AND BUILDING REGIONAL CHRONOLOGIES

How, then, do we correlate activity that has taken place, or patterns of change or development, between sites in different locations, to build up regional or supra-regional narratives? This is, of course, dependent in the first instance upon the availability of master-chronologies, and the increasing numbers of reliable radiocarbon determinations in different areas. So it continues to improve as more samples are retrieved and date-series and sequences are developed. To tighten the correlations and relate them to cultural sequences, it is helpful to be able to match these absolute dates recording closely similar practices and structures (for example) from different areas, and it is also helpful to be able to link artefacts with dated events and sequences. This is one reason why one of the most exciting developments of recent years has involved the dating of organic residues that have survived actually adhering to the surface of pots.

MAKING HISTORY: DEVELOPMENTAL STORIES

Historical narratives, as will have been evident from the main text of this book, can relate either to broad trends and the unfolding of cultural change across substantial spans of time and space, or to the intricacies of the trajectories of particular practices or cultural phenomena. For the former, what correlations between sequences of actions between sites, within regions, and across Britain as a whole enable is the identification of significant historical developments that otherwise might not be so evident. What this does *not* automatically imply, as we have been at pains to point out at various points in our account, is that change proceeds either very slowly or rapidly as a 'wave of advance'. Rather, change occurs at different rates in different places, tending towards the stochastic (random, unpredictable), and with movements and moments that may be syncopated (with weaker or stronger pulses, abbreviated or extended durations) and/or staccato (with abrupt disconnections). The reasons for these discontinuities are human and social, and concern also the inheritance of cultural practices within descent groups. As a result a change that may be registered at one geographical location may be expressed simultaneously some distance away, while much of the cultural 'landscape' in between may be devoid of such indication. The reason for this 'leap-frogging' is best sought in the patterns of connectivity created and sustained through kinship ties and the time-honoured exchange of marriage partners between affines spread out across the landscape in the interstices of the settlements of other, non-related kin-groups.

For the latter, the correlations made between sites and sequences, aided by refined individual site chronologies and their comparison and summation, enable a more sophisticated understanding of pattern in changing practices. This, for example, makes it possible for archaeologists to move beyond the idea of 'fashions' (for instance for building particular kinds of tomb) to the correlation of trends in changing *practices* such as the beginning of the building, and the ceasing of the building, of trough-like chambers contained within large timber uprights in the first half of the fourth millennium.

THE TIMES OF THEIR LIVES

Time as lived is complex. At its simplest, the elapsing of time is experienced within one's own life-experience at its briefest as the time spent in performing an individual task, or engaging in a particular social intercourse (a conversation, for example).

The lifespan of a *transaction*, however (such as the barter-exchange of a sheep for some timber, for example), can take place elastically—either completed within the span of a conversation or protracted over months or years. In this case, the passage of time is not that of time calibrated mechanically or digitally, but in terms of the understanding of change as lived, or more especially as reflected upon as time passes. Traditional societies, therefore, have a variety of mechanisms such as initiation (including coming-of-age ceremonies or entry into secret societies), age-grades (the identification of age-based cohorts), and extended mortuary ceremony (such as the practice of second-burial in which corpses are reprocessed and reburied at intervals of certain durations following decease) by which they reckon time's passing. And they have developed social and historical devices through which 'history' has been both reckoned and expressed. Such devices include genealogy used for the reckoning of descent, and oral literature reflective of times past that have been used to register both significant events (such as volcanic eruptions or visitations of plague) and mythic individuals and histories.

TIMELINES: CHARTING CONTEMPORANEITY AND CHANGE

Archaeological deposits and the artefacts retrieved from them 'capture' or embody these various contrasting temporalities. This means that although we may be limited in our means of representation of time either in narrative, or graphically, we are constantly dealing with the biographies not only of people (aided nowadays by the studies of dentition and DNA that we have mentioned at various points in the main text of this book) but of the objects they have created, used, and discarded.

It is extremely difficult, in the light of these complexities, to create simple graphic illustrations of the passage of time and the advent (let alone experiencing) of cultural changes. We do think, however, that it may be useful, especially for those readers less familiar with archaeological chronologies in general, and the British Neolithic in particular, to have a 'ready-reckoner' tabulation of change as registered in the currency (duration) of many of the individual cultural phenomena discussed in the book (see the chart on page 366).

At the top of this chart is a bar that gives an approximation of the elapsing of time reckonable via individual lifespans. In these terms, and using a standardized single generational turnover of twenty-five years, the period of 'scientifically calibrated' time from 4000 BCE to 3500 BCE would have witnessed twenty human generations (or approximated lifespans). This is the equivalent in modern British historical terms of the span between the dawning of the 'Age of the Tudors (monarchy)', and the mid twentieth-century ending of the Second World War. The elapsing of 'absolute' time is shown in the bar at the bottom of the chart. In totality, the period of approaching 2,000 years within which the Neolithic occurred witnessed the passing of eighty generations of people, approximating to the breadth of history from the birth of Christ (as registered in Christian calendars) and the present day.

Index

Page references in italics indicate illustrations.